Hoover Institution Publications

The Myth of "Mau Mau": Nationalism in Kenya

The Myth of "Mau Mau":
Nationalism in Kenya

By

CARL G. ROSBERG, JR.

and

JOHN NOTTINGHAM

Published for
The Hoover Institution
on War, Revolution, and Peace
Stanford University, Stanford, California
by

Frederick A. Praeger, Publishers
NEW YORK • WASHINGTON
Pall Mall Press
LONDON

FREDERICK A. PRAEGER, PUBLISHERS
111 Fourth Avenue, New York, New York 10003, U.S.A.
77–79 Charlotte Street, London W.1, England

Published in the United States of America in 1966
by Frederick A. Praeger, Inc., Publishers

For ELIZABETH *and* MUTHONI

Acknowledgments

We first met in Nyeri in December 1960. Each of us had for many years been deeply concerned with Kenya, one as a political scientist and the other as an administrator. We at once found a common interest in attempting to understand the development of politics in a country just emerging from a critical traumatic experience. Our inquiry into the phenomenon of "Mau Mau" led us to make a more extensive study of the development of African politics in Kenya.

Any non-African faces immense difficulties in recording, analyzing, and interpreting the response by Africans to the European intrusion. This study of a controversial subject on which men have strong views, sincerely held, and which has only recently aroused deep emotions, will inevitably offends some. This has, however, not been our intention; rather we have sought to reconsider these events from a new perspective.

Without the willing cooperation and understanding of hundreds of people in Kenya this book would not have been possible. To all these we owe a debt of gratitude that we can never repay. We must also thank the Ministers and officials of the Republic of Kenya who gave us most generously of their time when it was difficult for them to do so. In a project that has occupied many years, there have also been numerous people—politicians, administrators, missionaries, settlers, and others—who have made available data or given us insights into different facets of Kenya's history.

The problem of acknowledging those who have been of most specific assistance to us is immense. We owe much to Mugo Muratha, our field research assistant. Not only did he give us essential guidance and help, but also his dedication and enthusiasm were instrumental in turning an idea into reality. We need also to express our indebtedness to David Koff for his many stimulating comments and suggestions, which have made an important contribution to this book. A particular debt is owed to Roger Leys and Richard Stren for their constructive criticisms, unfailing assistance, and encouragement. In addition, we should like to thank Clyde Sanger, Colin Leys, George Bennett, Donald Rothchild, Michael Lofchie, David Apter, and James S. Coleman, who have each in their own way made a distinctive contribution to scholarship in East Africa. This is not to imply that they bear any responsibility for our interpretation but to say that their constant counsel and advice have been invaluable.

We would also like to thank Mr. Nathan Fedha and Mr. Derek Charman, Kenya Government Archivists, and Mr. Gordon Hazeldine of the Macmillan Library in Nairobi, for their unfailing kindness and cooperation. We have also received every courtesy and help from officials at the headquarters of the Presbyterian Church of East Africa and the Church Missionary Society in Nairobi.

We are more than grateful for the generous grants we have received: Mr. Rosberg would like to acknowledge the support of the Carnegie Corporation of New York, the Rockefeller Foundation of New York, the African Studies Center, U.C.L.A., and the Institute of International Studies, University of California, Berkeley; Mr. Nottingham the patience and forbearance of the Department of Political Science, Makerere University College and the University College, Nairobi. We would both like to thank the Hoover Institution at Stanford University, California. None of these institutions, however, bears any responsibility for the text of this book.

Mrs. Linda Brownrigg has been invaluable as our editor. We would also like to thank the Principal and staff of the

College of Social Studies, Kikuyu, and the Panafric Hotel, Nairobi, for their hospitality.

Finally, we also make grateful acknowledgment to the following authors and publishers for permission to quote from copyrighted works in this volume:

Elspeth Huxley and Chatto and Windus, Ltd., for permission to quote from *White Man's Country* (1935) by Elspeth Huxley.

Jomo Kenyatta and Martin Secker and Warburg Limited, for permission to quote from *Facing Mount Kenya* (1953) by Jomo Kenyatta.

George Allen and Unwin Limited, for permission to quote from *Kenya From Within* (1927) by W. McGregor Ross.

The East African Literature Bureau, for permission to quote from *The Story of Kenya's Progress* (1953) by Tom Askwith.

The Earl of Lytton and Macdonald and Company Ltd., for permission to quote from *The Desert and the Green* (1957) by The Earl of Lytton.

Lucy Mair and Penguin Books Ltd., for permission to quote from *Primitive Government* (1962) by Lucy Mair.

Sir Michael Blundell and Weidenfeld & Nicolson Ltd., for permission to quote from *So Rough a Wind* (1964) by Sir Michael Blundell.

The Hogarth Press, Ltd., for permission to quote from *Kenya* (1924) by Norman Leys.

Sir Philip Mitchell and the Hutchinson Publishing Group, Ltd., for permission to quote from *African Afterthoughts* (1954) by Sir Philip Mitchell.

Her Majesty's Stationery Office, for permission to quote from *History of the Great War—Military Operations, East Africa, Vol. I* (1941), Lt. Col. Charles Hordern, Compiler.

The Highway Press, for permission to quote from *Kikuyu Conflict* (1953) by T. F. C. Bewes, and from *Kikuyu Martyrs* (1958) by E. M. Wiseman.

Victor Gollancz, Ltd., for permission to quote from *Jomo Kenyatta* (1961) by George Delf.

Doubleday and Company, Inc., for permission to quote from *Jomo Kenyatta* by George Delf. Copyright © 1961 by George Delf.

Victor Gollancz and Fenner Brockway, for permission to quote from *African Journeys* (1955) by Fenner Brockway.

Berkeley, California
and Nairobi, Kenya

February 1966

Table of Contents

List of Illustrations and Maps

Introduction

On December 12, 1963, Kenya* became an independent African state after seventy-five years of British colonial rule. As a new state, Kenya faces most of the problems of nation-building that lie ahead for other African countries; yet her difficulties are compounded by the nature of her legacy. During the years of British occupation, the fundamental problem of the country—the relationship between the indigenous peoples—was obscured by the struggle arising out of a clash of interests between the small European élite and the subordinate African population. Even this conflict was partly obscured for some years by the assertions of a second immigrant group, the Indians, who claimed equality with the Europeans. However, following the declaration of the principle of the paramountcy of African interests in 1923, the largely middle-class oriented and religiously fragmented Indian population played only a marginal role in the expanding conflict between the white power élite and the dominated African population.

At first Africans sought to obtain redress for their griev-

---

* Kenya is one of the most beautiful and varied countries in Africa. Placed squarely on the Equator, it is a compact area of land of some 224,900 square miles. On the north, it is bounded by the ancient Coptic Empire of Ethiopia and the torrid Sudan. Its western neighbor is Uganda and to the south is Tanzania. It contains vast, underpopulated, arid regions as well as some of the most fertile, densely populated areas in the continent. The most dramatic geographical feature of Kenya is the great crack of the Rift Valley which divides the western half of the country, including the fertile plateau and highlands of the southwestern quadrant, where some four-fifths of the population are concentrated. Much of the rest of the country is relatively inaccessible semi-desert bush, capable of supporting only a sparse and hardy nomadic population. Along the coast, however, there is a narrow agricultural belt and a modern deep-water port at Mombasa, one of several historic Arab settlements in the region.

ances within the framework of the settler-oriented colonial state; following the Second World War, however, many came to challenge its very legitimacy. A nationalism of petition and constitutional protest ultimately gave way to a militant nationalism employing direct action in seeking a new political and social order. Political violence led to the Declaration of an Emergency in October 1952. At first violence and later reform characterized the seven-year ordeal of the Emergency, culminating in dramatic changes in British policy in early 1960. The day of white rule was over. Kenya was to become an African state and it was but a question of time before the country reached independence.

"Mau Mau" is identified with the militant nationalism and the violence that characterized the politics of central Kenya before and during the early years of the Emergency. Few mass movements in Africa have attracted more controversial comment than what has been called "Mau Mau." The Kenya colonial administration, missionary church leaders, settlers, and many others have regarded "Mau Mau" as the apotheosis of unreason. It was seen primarily as a barbarous, atavistic, and anti-European tribal cult whose leaders planned to turn Kenya into a land of "darkness and death." "Mau Mau" was looked upon as a dangerous hypnotic obsession based not on intellect but on primitive emotions. It could not be eradicated simply by military measures to stamp out militant resistance or by political and economic reform. A return to a normal state of mind among those "infected" demanded the extensive and exhaustive "rehabilitation" of tens of thousands of Africans. "Rehabilitation" required the confession of individual guilt, hard work, and the reestablishment of Christian values and respect for constituted colonial authority.

Critical to this interpretation has been the widely held view that "Mau Mau" was mainly the product of the Kikuyu people's failure to adapt fully to the demands of rapid modernization. Moreover, the exploitation over the years of real and imagined grievances by "unprincipled" African leaders, as well as the "perversion" of traditional institutions and values for the achievement of a new, backward-looking tribal unity, were seen by these observers as major contributory factors to this failure. Such a view regards "Mau Mau" as an atavistic escape from modernity; it therefore attempts to argue that the phenomenon needs to be analyzed or seen in religious and psychological terms.

This book presents an alternative interpretation of "Mau Mau," in which we will be concerned with the modern origins of African politics and their pattern of development, with particular emphasis on the politicization and mobilization of the Kikuyu people. It is our contention that the history of Kikuyu protests against aspects of the colonial state may be more clearly understood as the history of a developing nationalist movement. In our view, the outbreak of open violence in Kenya in 1952 occurred primarily because of a European failure rather than an African one; it was not so much a failure of the Kikuyu people to adapt to a modern institutional setting as it was a failure of the European policy-makers to recognize the need for significant social and political reform. In suggesting that the European conception of "Mau Mau" constituted a myth, we maintain that "Mau Mau" was indeed an integral part of an ongoing, rationally conceived nationalist movement.

There are certain distinctive features of Kenya nationalism that will merit close attention. The crucible of Kenyan nationalism in the pre-Emergency period was that area of central Kenya comprising the city of Nairobi, the Kikuyu Reserves, and the areas of European settlement in the Highlands and the Rift Valley. In these areas there developed a protest movement against the colonial settler system that had certain significant attributes. First, the mass membership of these organizations was largely, but not solely, confined to the Kikuyu tribe. Second, very few of the élite of these movements ever received a higher education and many had only an elementary schooling. Continuity in leadership was remarkable, and many that were active in the protest politics of the 1920s and 1930s retained leadership positions in postwar period when a younger and more zealous leadership became important, particularly in Nairobi. Third, political organizations did not grow only from the towns but depended on a close and reciprocal relationship between Nairobi and the rural areas. Partly because of this unique rural-urban political blend, the organizational character of African politics showed an interesting combination of "modern" and "traditional" structures. Finally, the alienation of land to European settlers was a dominant and unifying theme in the polity. It is to the setting and first stirrings of modern African politics that we now turn our attention.

The Myth of "Mau Mau": Nationalism in Kenya

CHAPTER 1

The Background of Modern Politics: 1888–1920

The interaction between Africans and Europeans, together with new forces of social change introduced by the colonial state, provide a general setting for the development of politics in early Kenya. During the colonial period (1888–1963), Africans sought, often within their traditional way of life, to meet the varied demands of the Europeans in Kenya —administrators, missionaries, settlers, soldiers, and employers. At the same time, the Europeans' demands introduced changes in African social organization that greatly affected the form and location of conflicts between Africans and Europeans.

Against the background of intertribal relations before the arrival of European power, we shall examine in this Chapter six important spheres of African-European contact and social change in the period 1888–1920: primary African resistance to "pacification"; missionary activity; European settlement and the beginning of land alienation; the growth of Nairobi as an urban center; the mobilization of Africans in the First World War; and the establishment of settler-dominated political institutions. The growth of African nationalism after the war was an outcome of the extensive changes that each of these areas of encounter independently and cumulatively worked on African social and economic life.

Patterns of Intertribal Relations Before Colonization

There is no reliable means of judging the size of the various tribal groups in Kenya at the beginning of British occupation in 1888. The first definitive census of Africans was not taken until 1962, when it recorded a population of 8,365,942 or 97 per cent of Kenya's total population.[1] Each of four tribal groups—the Kikuyu, the Luo, the Luhya, and the Kamba—had a population of nearly a million or more, while a further ten had a population of at least 100,000 or more. Despite the fact that there are only some twenty-seven main tribal groupings, the population of Kenya is remarkably varied. They have commonly been separated into the following major divisions: the Hamitic and Nilo-Hamitic peoples, who tend to be pastoralists, and the Nilotic and Bantu peoples, who in Kenya have largely become settled agriculturalists.

This diversity is in part due to Kenya's centrality in eastern Africa and the special geographical features of the country, such as the Rift Valley and the fertile regions clustered round Mt. Kenya (17,058 feet) and Mt. Elgon (14,178 feet). People migrated into this area for centuries from nearly every direction. Pastoralists and nomadic peoples came from the north and northwest down the funnel of the spacious uplands in search of water and grazing. Others who were, or became, agriculturalists came from the west, south, and east to settle more permanently in areas they could relatively easily defend. Most of the country was occupied by the minority of pastoralists, while the vast numbers of agriculturalists held comparatively small but strategically important islands of fertile land. Territorial power in the precolonial era was the prerogative of the pastoralists, whose social organization became a superb military tool. But the advances of the twentieth century were to transfer the means of power to the agriculturalists.

Apart from the coastal areas and the Pokomo-Bantu settlements along the Tana River, the pastoral and nomadic Hamitic peoples occupy most of the eastern half of Kenya. With a population of some 300,000, there are not more than three persons to the square mile in this hot, low-lying, and semi-desert region. There are three main divisions of peoples—the Somali, the Galla, and some minority groups. The Somali, who make up over half the population, today dominate the North Eastern Province, which runs north from the Tana River to Ethiopia and shares Kenya's eastern border with Somalia. This Somali dominance was achieved quite recently; Somali immigration only became a real threat about the time British rule was established. Until 1925 the province of Jubaland extended Kenya's frontier some 100 miles further eastward, but in an effort to control Somali penetration the British created the Somali-Galla line, which roughly coincides with the western boundary of today's North Eastern Province. Attempts were also made to stabilize the nomadic Galla (Boran and Orma) and the Rendille by establishing formal tribal grazing areas. During the colonial period the whole northeastern area was placed under semi-military rule and legally declared a closed district. This action may have prevented Somali and Galla impingement upon the productive south, but it also isolated these peoples from sources of rapid social change. The first major strain on the stability of independent Kenya arose from Somali secessionists.

The Nilo-Hamitic pastoral peoples have historically occupied a band of territory running from north to south in western Kenya, broadly following the Rift Valley but spilling over on to its adjacent plateau. They comprise three groups of people, the Turkana, the Kalenjin, and the Masai, but it is the last two who have been most politically significant. The Turkana (pop. 181,387) live in a hot, low, and uninviting area to the northwest of Lake Rudolf and have remained relatively isolated from the rest of the country. In the latter part of the nineteenth century they were moving south toward the Highlands, but with the establishment of British rule at the turn of the century this threat was contained.

Immediately to their south are the Kalenjin, comprising more than 800,000 people in eleven separate groupings. These groups vary greatly in size, but all retain many elements of a common culture. The two largest groups are the Kipsigis (341,771) and the Nandi (170,085) *; the latter rose to military pre-eminence in western Kenya toward the end of the nineteenth century. Apart from the increasing impact of modern education, the most radical change among the Kipsigis and Nandi has been the adoption of settled farming, a process greatly facilitated by the fertility of the land they occupied.

The Masai (154,079) undoubtedly played the most important role in shaping the political geography of Kenya before the British occupation. At the peak of their power during the first half of the nineteenth century they controlled an area about 500 miles long and 150 miles wide, stretching from Lake Rudolf in the north to the southern end of the Masai steppe deep in what is now Tanzania. Commanding the heart of the Rift Valley and ranging far beyond in their constant raids for cattle, they were the critical factor in regulating the movements of other peoples both within Kenya and from outside.[2] However, a disastrous civil war in the middle of the nineteenth century, followed by a great cattle plague (pleuro-pneumonia or rinderpest), further inter-sectional strife in the 1880s, and an epidemic of smallpox in 1892, brought a dramatic decline in their fortunes. The British incursion thus came at a seminal moment in Kenya's history, when a new balance of forces was undoubtedly in the offing. The British moved European settlers into much of Kenya Masailand, consolidating the Masai them-

---

* Among the others are the Elgeyo, the Pokot (or Suk), the Marakwet, and the Tugen (or Kamasia).

selves by 1911 into a single large Reserve south of the railway extending to the Tanzanian border. Here they were permitted to continue their nomadic, pastoral life and encouraged in their resistance to social and technological change. They played little part in the politics of the colonial interlude.

The peoples living in Kenya's narrow, fertile coastal belt and those in the immediate hinterland comprise a remarkably heterogeneous population. The Bantu peoples—the Pokomo (30,350), the Taita-Taveta (88,468), and the Mijikenda (414,887)—make up the overwhelming majority. But more than 50 per cent of the Mombasa labor force today comes from people of the upcountry areas, mainly the Kikuyu, the Luo, and the Luhya. The coastal Bantu have lived in this region since they migrated south, perhaps five hundred years ago, from the legendary city of Shungwaga under pressure from first the Galla and later the Somali. The Pokomo live along the banks of the lower Tana River; the Taita and Taveta inhabit the Taita hills and upland areas some 100 miles inland from Mombasa; and the Mijikenda—Digo, Duruma, Giriama, and other tribes—have come to occupy an area more or less parallel with the coast both to the north and to the south of Mombasa.

The dominant influence at the coast has been that of the Arabs, although Persians, Indians, Chinese, and Europeans have all played a part. Centuries of intermarriage and association between Arabs, Africans, Persians, and others resulted in the formation of the Swahili people and contributed to the development of the Swahili language. Though the Arabs have never been numerous (they numbered 34,048 in 1962), their ancient ports at Mombasa, Malindi, and Lamu controlled the coast and for centuries were important points in the network of Indian Ocean commerce. Their influence upon the hinterland of Kenya, however, was negligible.

Kenya had two main areas in which most people were concentrated and modernization occurred most rapidly—the Lake Victoria basin and the central region. The cluster of agricultural Nilotic and Bantu peoples bordering Lake Victoria accounts for nearly 32 per cent of Kenya's population, or some 2,750,000 people. The Nilotic Luo (1,148,335), dominating the lands surrounding the Kavirondo Gulf, are related to the Acholi and Alur in Uganda and to other Nilotes in the southern Sudan whence they originally migrated. Forming about 13 per cent of the population, they are the second largest tribe in the country. The main Bantu group, the Luhya (1,086,409), live to the north, while a smaller group, the Gusii (538,343), inhabit the hills to the south and east of the Luo. Both the Luo and Luhya are divided into various subtribal entities. The Luo recognize nineteen and the Luhya sixteen. Both groups have found tribal unity and cohesion difficult to maintain.

Not only does the Kikuyu-Kamba complex in central Kenya account for about 36 per cent of the country's population, but their lands border on the country's strategic center, the Nairobi area. The Kikuyu (1,642,065) live directly north of Nairobi on the densely populated lower slopes of the Nyandarua (Aberdare) range. Northeast of them on the foothills of Mt. Kenya live many peoples closely related to them, the most prominent of whom are the Embu and the Meru. To the southeast the Highlands gradually fall away toward the coast, and in this area, generally less fertile but with some productive hill areas, are the lands of the Kamba (933,219).

The Kikuyu then are Kenya's largest single group of people, accounting for nearly 20 per cent of the African population; they also have been in the forefront of the country's political development since the British arrived. European settlement replaced Masai domination on their frontiers and immediately posed a far greater threat to their institutions and social organization. Unlike nearly all the other tribal groups, who had enough land to cushion the impact of a foreign civilization, the Kikuyu from the outset had little surplus or marginal land to bring into use in adjusting to the new order.

In brief, then, the period immediately before the British arrival in Kenya was marked by a significant decline in the power of the Masai, a rise in Nandi influence, and an increased assertiveness on the part of the Kikuyu. In the north the Somali, pushing the Galla before them, were thrusting ever deeper toward Meru, the Laikipia Masai, and the peoples of Mt. Kenya. Clusters of agricultural groups were surrounded by vast areas under the control of pastoralists, some of whom were becoming agriculturalists. As these groups collided in the competition for limited resources, the history of the region acquired a restless quality. It was into this environment that European interests first extended themselves.

Primary Resistance to "Pacification"

The resistance by many African peoples to the intrusion of British power at the end of the nineteenth century was the earliest expression, in history and myth, of nationalism in Kenya. The resistance intensified as British agents, first of the Imperial British East Africa Company (IBEAC) and later of the Foreign Office, sought to consolidate their influence beyond the immediate neighborhood of a handful of forts spread across the country. These first attempts by African societies to preserve their integrity, and the nature of the European penetration, had significant consequences for the later development of African nationalism in Kenya. African opposition to colonization was widespread; there were few sections of the country that did not experience some violent confrontation with European-led expeditions against them. Moreover, since many of the most severe encounters took place in the early years of this century, they fell within the memory of some participants in the later era of militant nationalism. Whether exploited in myth or simply recalled in conversation, these events had a powerful effect; they marked a distinct turning point in the lives of individuals and in the history of tribes throughout Kenya.

The nature and the consequences of early African-European contact depended to some extent on the internal organization and strength of the African tribes themselves. Moreover, the established power positions of the various peoples relative to each other strongly affected their response to the European incursion. Elements among the Masai, for example, sought by collaborating with the new forces to arrest the decline in their fortunes. But other pastoral and nomadic tribes strongly opposed British rule. In the north there was vigorous resistance by the Somali for several years and in the northeast the Turkana proved to be formidable fighters. Military patrols were conducted during the First World War and military administration continued until 1926. To control the frontier with Ethiopia, forts or posts were established and were maintained by the King's African Rifles until 1942, when the Kenya Police assumed the responsibility during the War.

The Kalenjin group proved among the most difficult for the British to deal with.[3] The Nandi in particular were incensed at the new railway that thrust through their traditional grazing grounds in the Nyando Valley. In spite of their small numbers, their military reputation was such that the original caravan route (pioneered by Arab and Swahili traders and slavers from Mombasa to Buganda) had been greatly lengthened to avoid contact with them. Between 1895 and 1905 five military expeditions were sent to deal with them. Their resistance lasted until 1905, when the Nandi Field Force, the largest "punitive expedition" ever assembled in Kenya, was mounted against them. At a meeting arranged for negotiations their politico-religious leader (*or-*

koiyot), Koitalel, was shot by an Army officer.[4] Though
the Nandi generally accepted the decision to be confined to a
Reserve a few miles north of the railway, the temptation to
plunder remained, and Koitalel's death was always regarded
by the tribe as a dishonorable breach of a truce. In 1907 the
Government still found it necessary to deport some of
Koitalel's closest associates.†

In 1902 and 1905 expeditions were also sent against the
Kipsigis.* In 1911 another was dispatched against the Elgeyo
and Marakwet, following a series of clashes over cattle and
land with the Boer settlers in the Uasin Gishu plateau, which
had culminated in the murder of one settler.[5] As late as 1919
another expedition was sent against the Elgeyo,[6] while in
1923 there were reports of grave unrest among the Nandi,
led by Parserion, Koitalel's successor as senior *orkoiyot*.

The more settled and much larger agricultural groups also
refused to submit passively to the alien authority, although
they found mobilization more difficult than the pastoralists.
For twenty years in the east of the country sporadic and
uncoordinated opposition was shown by sections of the
Kamba, who had once controlled the main trade routes from
the coast to the Highlands.

In the far west of the country Mumia, a master of clan
politics, was expanding Wanga hegemony in association with
armed Swahili slavers, such as Abdullah bin Hamid of
Mombasa and "fat" Sudi from Pangani,[7] and also by making
effective use of the Uasin Gishu Masai as mercenaries. His
stronghold (known as Mumia's), opposite a strategic ford on
the Nzoia River, was located on the vital caravan route
between Baringo and Buganda and at the threshold of a

---

† The power and influence of the *orkoiyot*, however, remained and on
three further occasions in the colonial period (in 1923, 1938 and 1957) there
was considerable unrest on the occasion of the political ceremony when power
is traditionally handed over from one age group to the next.

* Also known as the Lumbwa.

major ivory-producing area. By the 1890s it had become an important base for the British. Mumia himself found many advantages in a loose alliance with them as he advanced his influence and power over wider areas. Mumia's remained the headquarters of the British presence in western Kenya until, with the coming of the railway, this was transferred to Kisumu in July 1899. Mumia's authority was to be significant for the next two decades.

Early contact with the Luo was indirect and sporadic; it increased only when the completion of the railway had confirmed British intentions and largely removed the need for alliances.[8] In 1896 a punitive expedition was mounted in support of Mumia in Ugonya against the Kager clan led by Gero and 200 were quickly killed with a maxim gun.[9] In 1899 C. W. Hobley led an expedition against Sakwa, Seme, and Uyoma Locations in which 2,500 cattle and some 10,000 sheep and goats were captured.[10] By late 1900 Odera was providing 1,500 porters for an expedition against the Nandi. But others in Nyanza became restive as the Europeans with their Wanga agents slowly extended their administrative control. Large military expeditions, reinforced by auxiliaries from Mumia and other client chiefs, were sent out against the Vugusu (Kitosh) on the slopes of Mt. Elgon in 1895, 1907, and 1908,[11] while there were also five campaigns against various other Luhya people in Nyanza between 1895 and 1907. Two battles fought at Lumboga and Chetambe in 1895 in which C. W. Hobley initially subdued the Vugusu have played a significant role in the traditions of Vugusu nationalism and the *Dini ya Msambua.*

In the southwestern highlands of Kenya there were sizeable expeditions against the Gusii in 1904–5 and 1908. In 1905, according to a British police officer who was there, several hundred Gusii warriors were killed by machine guns in a "massacre."[12] In 1908 a King's African Rifles column entered Kisii, burning huts, destroying standing crops, and capturing all livestock within their reach.[13] Over 100 Gusii were killed, and 5,636 cattle and 3,281 sheep and goats were seized.

On and near the coast there was a similar pattern of violent resistance. In 1890 in Taita there was a fierce action between a punitive expedition under a Captain Nelson and the local inhabitants in which Mangeka, Chief of Mwanda, and many of his followers were killed,[14] and in 1898 there was further resistance in the Mgangi and Irisi areas of the district owing to the "constant and exigent" demand for porters for the Uganda road.[15]

In 1914 on the coast the Giriama, a small group occupying a land of desolate scrub behind the hills between Mombasa and the Sabaki River, plunged into full-scale revolt. The Government had made little effort to penetrate the area until 1912, when it first tried to collect tax there in the hope that in order to pay, the Giriama would have to enter the labor market. In late 1913 administrators, intending to open up 100,000 acres of land for European plantations, tried forcibly to remove all the Giriama from the north bank of the Sabaki River, where they had cultivated extensive *shambas* (small farms). The Giriama "bound themselves by oath to live or die there."[16] An armed patrol was sent to the area, a £100 fine levied, and two of the leaders, Me Katilili, a woman, and Wanji Madori, an old man, were deported to Kisii.[17] But the effect was only temporary. A year later the Government tried to conscript 1,000 porters for military purposes.[18] On August 17, 1914, the Giriama attacked the Assistant District Commissioner and his party, killing a policeman. Within a few days resistance was widespread throughout the District, both the northern and southern groups combining in a "concerted act of the whole tribe"[19] whose "popular doctrine was clearly 'Giriama for the Wa Giriama.' "[20] An administrator noted that "a state of passive resistance is likely to continue indefinitely."[21]

This situation was complicated by the outbreak of war with Germany and attempts by agents of the exiled Mazrui family to involve the dissident Giriama in a grander anti-British design.* Strong measures were called for and carried out. In September 1914 an expedition ruthlessly crushed the revolt, and the District was placed under martial law. In the ensuing operation some 400 Giriama were killed, hundreds of homesteads burnt, and thousands of goats captured. The Government's peace terms demanded the handing over of the Giriama leaders, the complete evacuation of the area north of the Sabaki River, the provision of 1,000 recruits for the Government's Carrier Corps (see below), and a fine of some £7,500.[22] This fine was recovered in full within a year by seizing goats, crops, and ivory.

In central Kenya contact with the large Kikuyu cluster was made as the agents of the IBEAC moved inland after 1888, followed by British governmental administration in 1895. The Kikuyu, in the centuries since their arrival in the southern foothills of Mt. Kenya, had gradually multiplied and extended the area under their control. The fertility of the forest soil had encouraged them to become settled agriculturalists. Their functionally diffuse social and political institutions were readily adaptable to an era of prosperous expansion. A belt of dense forest, the formidable military reputation of the Masai and Kamba control of the trade routes,[23] shielded them from the depredations of the growing coastal traffic and the corrupting guns of the Arab ivory and slave caravans, although John Boyes, an early visitor to Kikuyu, noted that Wangombe, the foremost

---

* A short-lived rebellion led by Mbarak bin Rashid—the Mazrui leader—in 1895 had ended in the spring of 1896 after the arrival of an Indian infantry regiment, a naval brigade and Zanzibar soldiers. The Mazrui and their followers fled to German East Africa. See D. A. Low, "British East Africa: The Establishment of British Rule 1895–1912," in Vincent Harlow and E. M. Chilver, *History of East Africa*, vol. II (Oxford: 1965), for a fuller treatment of the rebellion.

leader of the northern Kikuyu, had several firearms in his possession when Boyes first met him in 1898.[24]

Before the British intrusion outstanding local leaders, such as Wangombe and Kakeri in Nyeri, Karuri in Murang'a (later Fort Hall), or Waiyaki and Gathirimu in Kiambu, would on occasion lead combined forces from several ridges, or even of Masai and Kikuyu or Kamba and Kikuyu,[25] in limited operations against neighboring ridges. But there was no tradition of large-scale mobilization. The lack of central-ized tribal authority or military unity among the Kikuyu people, already a disadvantage in their frontier skirmishes with the Masai, both handicapped concerted tribal resist-ance and helped the British to play off one section against another. The colonial power thus extended its rule over the Kikuyu piecemeal.

In 1890 Captain Frederick Lugard (later Lord) of IBEAC established a fortified depot at Dagoretti in southern Ki-kuyu, but before the buildings were complete he had to leave for Uganda. He left behind a civilian, George Wilson, with a weakened garrison. For reasons that even then were not wholly clear, the Kikuyu turned against Wilson and began a virtual siege of his post. Wilson soon abandoned the site and fought his way through the forest to Machakos. The following year Captain Eric Smith established a new post at Fort Smith, a few miles away. Thus began a process that was to alter fundamentally Kikuyu history. Although there had been a brief period of neighborliness, the agents of the undercapitalized Company, then extended to the financial breaking point by involvements in Buganda and Bunyoro, had for some time been under pressure to make the new depot self-sufficient. This had disastrous effects on the cooper-ative relationship developed by Lugard[26] with the southern Kikuyu in the early days of contact. Within a few months the local leader, Waiyaki, who might have consolidated an alliance as mutually advantageous as that of Mumia in Nyanza, was deported to the coast. On the morning after the return of a major punitive expedition against the "Waguru-guru" section of the Kikuyu, Waiyaki had visited Fort Smith, possibly to remonstrate against the action. While there he allegedly tried to assassinate a Company official, one Purkiss, in his room.[27] Waiyaki died, it is said by his own hand, at Kibwezi, on the way to his exile. He became the first Kikuyu martyr, and this incident is still a turning point in Kikuyu nationalist mythology. Following Waiyaki's death, Purkiss was "besieged for 6 days."[28]

After the Protectorate was established and the IBEAC had handed over its responsibilities to the Foreign Office, in June 1895, further "punitive" expeditions, made up of regular troops of the King's African Rifles and Masai levies, were sent out with the administrators as they penetrated the areas which became the districts of Kiambu, Fort Hall,* Nyeri (first called South Nyeri), Embu, and Meru. Francis Hall, one of these administrators, has vividly described part of this "pacification" of Kikuyu country. In one expedition in 1894, four men from his column (which included 100 Swahilis with Snider rifles, 120 Masai, and 65 friendly Kikuyu) had died of cold on the approach march to the disaffected area. Despite this setback, Hall decided to carry out the original plan to punish the area. "We soon set to work, lit up a kraal and got the men warm again. . . . we made a mess of all their villages and, as the other column was working along about two miles off, the natives had a warm time, but they wouldn't stand, so I had no chance of trying my war-rockets. The Major [Smith] with his one arm carried a shot gun and bagged a brace in the first kraal but I had no fun for a long

---

* In June 1901, Mbirri military station was renamed Fort Hall after Francis Hall. The first administrator to be stationed there, Hall died in March 1901. In June 1904, it ceased to be a military station. Moyse-Bartlett, *The King's African Rifles*, pp. 204–5.

time. . . . We brought in 1,100 goats and loads of grain
. . . but we didn't manage to do much execution as the
brutes wouldn't stand."[29]

These years saw a series of more or less serious clashes occur in Hall's area, with casualties reaching 90 dead in one
encounter,[30] and with heavy confiscations of goats and cattle.
Though the Kikuyu at no time suffered more than local de-
feats, some of these were shattering. Hall's account of a
later "pacification" episode in southern Fort Hall District
in January and February 1899 will illustrate this. His
column this time had 150 rifles and 500 "friendly natives."
They approached the selected area through the bamboo
forest.

> As usual the natives had deserted their village and bolted with
> all their livestock. However we scoured the forest and collected
> a good deal and then proceeded to march quietly through the
> country, sending columns out to burn the villages and collect
> goats etc. We rarely saw any of the people; when we did, they
> were at very long ranges, so we did not have much fun, but we
> destroyed a tremendous number of villages and, after fourteen
> days, emerged on the plains to the eastward, having gone
> straight from one end to the other of the disaffected districts.
> We captured altogether some 10,000 goats and a few cattle, and
> this on top of the previous expedition, must have been a pretty
> severe blow to them.

The number of villages destroyed, in reality individual
homesteads, was in the hundreds.[31]

Five years later, further north, Col. R. Meinertzhagen
notes that in ten days in February and March 1904 his
column, one of three in the Iriaini (Nyeri-Embu border
country) expedition, killed 796 Kikuyu and captured 782
cattle and 2,150 sheep and goats.[32] There was another expedition to quell a "revolt" of the Embu in 1906.[33] However,
despite these locally crippling episodes, the tribe as a whole
avoided the overall, crushing disasters inflicted in other

parts of Africa on people who either were smaller in number or whose social and political organization permitted substantial tribal mobilization against the intruder. The absence of any decisive early confrontation between the Kikuyu and the British also meant that, in contrast with some major tribes in South Africa and Rhodesia, there was no symbolic moment of surrender to the new authority. While acquiescing to British rule—a station was established at Mbirri (later Fort Hall) in 1901 and another at Nyeri in 1902—the resilient Kikuyu seldom behaved with the timidity, apathy, or obsequiousness that might have been displayed by a more decisively conquered people.

Missions and Settlement

During the early period of half-military and half-civil administration, other major events were determining the future social, political, and economic pattern of Kenya: the building of a railway, the transfer in 1902 of the Eastern Province of Uganda to the East Africa Protectorate (this diminished the influence of Buganda on policies pursued in western Kenya), the coming of the first European settlers, and the arrival inland of the first missionaries.

On December 20, 1901, the Uganda Railway, begun in 1895 from Mombasa, reached Port Florence on Lake Victoria near Kisumu. The religious missions, which had confined most of their activities to the coast (including Taita) and to Buganda, engaged in a fresh scramble for the newly accessible areas. In central Kenya the Rev. Thomas Watson reached Kikuyu country from Kibwezi in 1898 and established a mission that was taken over in 1900 by the Church of Scotland (CSM). In 1899, the Roman Catholic Mgr. Allgeyer of the Holy Ghost Fathers (already established at Teita and on the slopes of Kilimanjaro) arrived, and in October 1900 the Rev. A. W. McGregor of the Church Missionary Society (CMS) came up from Taveta. In 1902 the Rev. and

Mrs. Harry Leakey arrived to take over from McGregor, who moved up to Fort Hall. The Africa Inland Mission (AIM), an American-British interdenominational organization, first opened stations at Nzawi (1895) and Kangundo (1896) in Machakos District. In 1901 it set up its headquarters at Kijabe on the southern Kikuyu Escarpment just below Lari, and in 1902 the Rev. C. F. Johnston opened another station at Machakos. Italian and French Roman Catholic Societies in a joint missionary endeavor opened a mission near Nairobi in 1901, following this with further stations at Kiambu and Tuso in 1902, Limuru and Nyeri in 1903, Mangu (near Thika) in 1906, and Meru in 1911.[34]

In Nyanza, the Church Missionary Society from Uganda resumed work in the Maragoli Hills in 1905,[35] opening a station at Maseno, on the border between the Luo and the Luhya, in January 1906. The AIM opened a station at Nyakach in 1911. The Roman Catholic Mill Hill Fathers, also operating from Uganda, established themselves at Kisumu in 1904 and at Mumia's in 1905. The Friends Africa Mission, an American Quaker group, arrived in 1902 to work among the Luhya from Kaimosi. The Church of God (originally the South African Compounds and Interior Mission), an American fundamentalist group, operated from Kima in Bunyore after 1906. In South Nyanza the Seventh Day Adventists, from Canada, first opened a station at Gendia in Karachuonyo in the same year, and were closely followed by the Nilotic Independent Mission and the Apostolic Faith Mission of Iowa.

In the rural areas the missions created African Churches whose leaders were inevitably young people; the missions' gift of literacy brought them the possibility of great power. These young men, in both central and western Kenya, were to become an alternative focus for political organization beyond the traditional influence of the elders. The establishment of missions not only disturbed the social balance between young and old, but also created tensions that were not always easily contained and that the Administration was often shrewdly to manipulate in its own interests. In the years just before the First World War, the limited form of elementary education introduced by the missionaries had already reached a small group of young men, encouraging in them a common wish to "progress" and enter fully into the new social order. Among them was Jomo Kenyatta, born Kamau Ngengi, who was baptized August 1914 at the Church of Scotland Mission, Kikuyu, where he also received his first five years of education.[36] For the moment, this group accepted European power almost without question, perhaps not yet comprehending the full consequences of its permanence.

Although missionary activity influenced both the growth of new leadership and the choice of some of the issues on which nationalism later focused, white settlement was to be the single most decisive factor in shaping the character of that nationalism. The new railway made possible a European settler economy based on the export of cash crops from the fertile temperate land of the Kenya Highlands. The need to make the railway pay certainly strengthened the case for white settlement, and a new policy of encouraging settlement soon received the official blessing of the Foreign Office. Subsequently, under Colonial Office supervision, European settlement rapidly became the cardinal influence in the social, economic, and political development of the new country.

In the decade before the First World War European settlement swept resolutely forward on a wave of vigor and enthusiasm. One of the largest early applications for land (500 square miles) was made in April 1902 by the East Africa Syndicate, a company with a strong South African interest. After some questioning, the British Government granted it. With only a dozen settlers established at the beginning of 1903, in August the Commissioner, Sir Charles Eliot, sent his Collector of Customs, A. Marsden, to South Africa to encourage settlers to migrate to the country.[37] By the end of 1905 over a million acres of land had been leased or sold by the Protectorate authorities. In 1906 a large party of Boer "Irreconcilables" trekked overland from the Transvaal to the Uasin Gishu plateau; others poured in by boat from Britain and South Africa. Already the urge to create a new "white man's country" had taken root, and the search for this political kingdom was to be a central theme in Kenya's colonial history.

These developments had a profound effect on the lives of Kenya's African peoples—most momentously perhaps on the Kikuyu. Between 1903 and 1906 most of the areas of Kikuyu land that were to become the focus of major dispute in the future were alienated in the rich Chura and Limuru areas.[38] Some 8,000 shillings was paid in compensation to 8,000 Kikuyu, but more than 3,000 received nothing at all. The alienation was openly undertaken; it was Eliot's public policy. After his resignation in 1904, he wrote that "no one can doubt that the rich and exceptionally fertile district of Kikuyu is destined to be one of the chief centres of European cultivation, and the process of settlement is facilitated by the fact that there are gaps where there is no native population."[39] Interpenetration, one ridge European, the next Kikuyu, and no Reserves, was Eliot's method. But his views were not supported by all administrators. Indeed, as early as December 1903 John Ainsworth, the Chief Native Commissioner, asked Eliot for permission to "bunch up" the Kikuyu into Reserves at intervals along the railway; however, it was several years before the Reserve boundaries were first tentatively delimited.[40]

By the time the war began in 1914 the framework of the exclusive "White Highlands" system had already been constructed, and the Europeans were demanding the conventional right of British colonists to elect their own representatives to the Protectorate's Legislative Council. In 1905 the Colonial Office assumed responsibility for the Protectorate from the Foreign Office. Not until 1920 did the Protectorate become a Colony, but in 1906 a new constitution was created and the Commissioner became a Governor with Executive and Legislative Councils. The all-European Legislative Council, which first met in 1907, consisted of six Government officials and two non-officials, the European settlers, A. A. Baillie and Hugh Cholmondeley, Baron Delamere;[41] the latter was the recognized political leader of the Europeans and a militant advocate of further large-scale land alienation. It was not until 1909 that the first Indian, A. M. Jeevanjee, an influential trader and property owner,* was appointed to the Council as an experiment. Jeevanjee attended only one session, and his appointment expired in 1911. For the next decade there was no direct Indian representation on the Council. Moreover, during this period the European non-official members increased their strength in the Legislative Council, and participated increasingly on various Boards and Committees that were recommending policy over a wide range of social and economic subjects, including land, education, and labor. In short, a colonial state was being established in which the interests of European settlers were paramount.[42]

The increasing preponderance of settler influence in shaping administrative policy is clearly illustrated by the problems of obtaining African labor in order to foster modern

---

* Alibhoy Mulla Jeevanjee was born in India; he made a fortune as a railway contractor, shipping in and then feeding the 25,000 workers who constructed and built all the stations and hospitals between Mombasa and Port Florence. He presented a marble statue of Queen Victoria to Nairobi and became the capital's leading builder.

economic development. After giving some consideration to the encouragement of Indian peasant immigration, the Government rapidly came to regard the growth of a profitably based white settlement as a primary goal, and the role of Africans in this economy as principally that of wage earners. Underlying this orientation toward economic development was the assumption that Africans would be more productive working for European settlers than working in their own areas. There was, in addition, the belief that Africans would more rapidly become "civilized" by coming into direct contact with Europeans. Whatever basic conflict arose between Government and settler interests concerned how much land should be alienated for settlement and what concrete methods should be employed to obtain African labor to work the land; the postulate that the Africans' role in the economy should be confined to wage earning was not in itself an issue.

One early and constant source of labor for European farms was the African squatter, who either was made landless as a result of alienation, or was unable to meet his needs in crowded African rural areas. These people were encouraged to settle on European farms, cultivate crops and pasture cattle, in return for varying periods of service each year. Squatters were always inadequate to the labor needs of Europeans, and from the beginning of settlement the creation of an expanding African labor force was a central feature of the economic history of the country. Among the direct and indirect means that were employed to create a labor force was an African taxation program with the avowed purpose of securing revenue, but had the effect of compelling Africans to seek employment from Europeans. Settlers at various times advocated more extreme measures, such as cutting down the size of the African Reserves. The general attitude of the Administration and settlers was that Africans lived a lazy and shiftless life in the Reserves. Settlers acted as well to discourage the development of cash crop production by Africans since they believed it might restrict the flow of labor.[43] The settlers constantly argued that the advancement of European production was essential to the well-being of the country and should be the guide line in shaping "native" policy.

In 1908, under instructions from the Secretary of State for the Colonies, the Kenya Government had abandoned direct assistance in recruiting labor for settlers, and now merely "encouraged" Africans, by means of suggestions and instructions, to seek work. During the critical labor shortage immediately following the First World War, however, methods approaching compulsion were employed. Norman Leys in his incisive study calculated that by 1920 more than 50 per cent of the able-bodied men in the country from the agricultural tribes were employed in European agriculture at one time.[44] This figure may well be too high, as it now appears that the African population was at that time underestimated. Nevertheless, the entry of Africans into the labor market was extensive.

At the same time as these thousands of Africans from central and western Kenya were leaving their homes to find employment on the European estates, their horizons were being widened through new social settings and intertribal contact. Similarly, as the railway and administrative centers developed into townships, Africans who sought work and new opportunities not available under tribal social and economic systems were attracted to them. Indeed, the new pattern of law and order across the country and the steady improvement of communications greatly facilitated this movement.

Urban Growth in Nairobi

Unlike some other large towns in West Africa, Nairobi was not a traditional trading center or an urban cluster around some tribal capital. But its role in the development of African nationalism was to be as significant as that attributed to urban centers throughout the continent.[45] Initially established in 1896 by the Uganda Government as a transport depot near the safari camp just above the Nairobi River, Nairobi's importance as an administrative center began in July 1899 when the Uganda Railway transferred its headquarters there from Mombasa.[46] Later in the same year the Administration of Ukamba Province was transferred there from Machakos. By December 1901 the first Municipal Committee had been created.[47]

Six years later the tented-railhead camp described by Francis Hall in 1900 as "a tin-pot mushroom township" and "the most lawless dangerous spot in Africa"[48] replaced Mombasa as the capital of the East Africa Protectorate. This 300-mile transfer inevitably diminished the influence on Kenya's development of the coastal Swahili culture that became so important in Tanganyika's history. In Kenya the Swahili language, instead of becoming the language of unification, was for long to be despised as the language of colonial domination. But perhaps more significant in the development of African nationalism was the location of the new town on the very edge of Kikuyu country and the gradual swamping of its original Muslim African majority by increasing numbers of Kikuyu. At the same time, the new capital's rapid expansion and the added attraction to European settlers of land near it perpetually reminded the Kikuyu in Kiambu that the tenure of their own lands under the colonial system was highly insecure.

From the start Nairobi was laid out to accommodate a European and Indian population, not an African one. The new town soon became the headquarters of an array of expatriate soldiers, hunters, settlers, and traders that made up the original colonial community. But its African population was always greater than the European or Indian population. Apart from the African railway workers, who lived in dormitory barracks, the town also contained hundreds of Sudanese and Somali soldiers, Somali and Swahili traders, Nyamwezi and Digo porters, and Ganda, Nandi, and Masai camp followers. Their existence might not be officially recognized but they were nevertheless there.[49] Accordingly, some distance away from the neat railway quarters various unplanned villages grew up to house the different groups, for example Kibera for the Sudanese and two Somali settlements. Some of the first African settlements were soon evacuated or destroyed; others flourished awhile and then decayed. But by 1921 eight had become well established and accommodated most of Nairobi's African population, then estimated to be 12,088.[50] These included Mombasa (whose inhabitants had originally been moved from some huts in Hospital Road) and Masikini, both near Forest Road; Kaburini;[51] Kariokor; Kileleshwa, to the west, where in 1925 a thousand Africans from various tribes were living on 728 acres of Crown Land;[52] and Kibera. The two most important were Pumwani and Pangani.

Pumwani, planned in 1911 as the first stage in the resettlement and control of Nairobi's African population, was not actually declared open until January 1921.[53] It was to be the official "native location," and the site was then thought large enough to accommodate all the Africans who might migrate to Nairobi in the foreseeable future. But its growth was inordinately slow; ten years later (1931) Pumwani contained only 317 houses and a population of 3,996.[54]

By contrast, Pangani grew rapidly. First used by porters in 1890 even before the railhead reached Nairobi, it soon absorbed a nearby hamlet known as Unguja (Zanzibar).[55] Numerically the Kikuyu and the Kamba soon dominated Pangani's expansion. While few Kikuyu owned houses there, even by 1913 many must have been renting lodging rooms.

Pangani had a Swahili ambiance, and remained a stronghold of the Muslim faith until its final demolition in 1938.[56] By the end of the First World War, if not before, Pangani had become a convenient asylum for African, and especially Kikuyu, Muslims. Its inhabitants thrived on providing lodgings for Africans employed by shooting safaris and by the small Indian industries gradually becoming established across the Nairobi River, and by supplying other urban amenities such as home-brewed beer, brothels, and hotels. It had three mosques, for the Kikuyu, Luo, and Kamba Muslims respectively.

As Nairobi was the locus of Kenya African politics, so Pangani was the focal point within the city. After the war, the Pangani *hotelis* (tea-shops) became the nerve-center of African political discussion and the meeting place for town and country. Every Sunday afternoon, cooks and servants employed in the expanding European and Indian residential areas on the other side of the river went across to the mass meetings on the sports-ground there, Nairobi's and Kenya's Hyde Park Corner. A contemporary newspaper report says: "Out Pangani Village way the natives are very busy these days holding meetings of the mass kind. Every Sunday thousands of Jeroges and Kamaus may be seen listening raptly to others of their kind holding forth on, presumably, the question of the hour. It is fairly apparent that these meetings have a savour of politics about them and that the natives are discussing matters connected with, say, registration, taxation and so on. For the most part, of course, the addresses are in Swahili."[57] As we have seen, Pumwani was established by the Administration in the hopes of centralizing the African population, but Pangani refused to die; in 1931 it contained some 312 houses with a population of 3,177. Finally, in 1934, the compulsory removal of its houses, with limited compensation, was decided on, but the problems of executing this decision were still troubling the authorities in 1938.[58]

It was in Pangani that many of Kenya's early political

leaders served their apprenticeship, among them Harry Thuku, Jesse Kariuki, James Njoroge, and Job Muchuchu. In the vanguard were two of Nairobi's first Kikuyu converts to Islam—Mwalimu Hamisi, the first Kikuyu to teach the Koran, and Abdullah Tairara, who was conspicuous in the political activity of Nairobi for the next two decades. It was in Pangani soon after the war that the *Kururo*, a famous Kikuyu political song, was first sung and danced, and it was in Pangani sometime during 1919 that the organization which became the East African Association was born. Thus, from the first, Nairobi, through Pangani, established its position as the fount and focus of African politics in Kenya. Although Nairobi's influence on the development of nationalism was to waver from time to time, its role in the final confrontation before the 1952 Emergency was to be of crucial importance.

The First World War

The First World War played its part, too, in forcing the pace of change among the African peoples of Kenya. It kindled the growing consciousness that the world was larger than tribe and clan, and that Africans were now part of a social system no longer under their own control. Indeed, East Africa was one of the few active theaters of war outside Europe. Nairobi became a major base, and the country, threatened by invasion, reverted to virtual military administration. Despite some talk of a "live and let live" agreement between British East Africa (Kenya and Uganda) and German East Africa (Tanganyika), a long, costly, and frustrating campaign was undertaken by the British to conquer German East Africa. Somewhere in the Kenya Africans' collective experience in the war, whether from participating in small numbers with regular military units or in large numbers as porters in the Carrier Corps, lies the source of their first experiments in organized political activity. After the war nationalism would begin to fashion effective alternatives to the spear.

The official historian has narrated the origins of the Corps:

> Among the African population an ardent loyalty and alacrity to serve were equally striking. On all sides offers of help and generous gifts of cattle and food-stuffs came in from the native chiefs. At this time, when it was still hoped that the war would be short, and when it was taken for granted that any additional troops would come from India, no expansion of the KAR [King's African Rifles] was contemplated; but it was at once apparent that for a campaign in country widely infested by tsetse fly large numbers of carriers would be required, and steps were soon taken to raise them.
>
> On the 13th of August [1914] Messrs. O. F. Watkins and J. M. Pearson, of the Civil Service in British East Africa, were selected for this duty and instituted what was soon to become the extensive and indispensable organization known as the Carrier Corps. The organizers' difficulties were many; nevertheless with the aid of local officials, estate-owners and influential native chiefs, large contingents of carriers enrolled in all parts of the country reached Nairobi to be equipped and distributed. By the 11th of September the Carrier Corps consisted of five units each 1,000 strong, in companies of 100 under native head-men. It had been intended that the organization should be a civil department; but various difficulties made it necessary to give Army rank to the two officers in charge, and the force was put on a military basis.[59]

By March 1915 the need arose for a corps of machine gun carriers requiring specially trained men of exceptional physique for carrying machine guns and ammunition into the firing line. Joseph Kang'ethe, later president of the Kikuyu Central Association for nearly twenty years, became a sergeant in this force, which by November 1918 had recruited 12,129 men.[60]

Lt. Col. O. F. Watkins, commander of the Carrier Corps and later Deputy Chief Native Commissioner, has summed up in a personal narrative something of the deep impact of this experience.

> From Somaliland in the north, from Portuguese East Africa in the south, from Nigeria, Gambia and Sierra Leone in the west, from the Seychelle Islands, Zanzibar and Comoro in the East, from the central kingdom of Uganda, from the great lakes and headwaters of the Congo and the Nile, from the great snow-clad peaks of Kilimanjaro and Kenya, came contingents to the Corps. Men who a few years ago had never seen a white man, to whom the mechanism of a tap or a doorhandle is still an inscrutable mystery, have been trained to carry into action on their heads the field wireless or the latest quick-firing gun. Men of tribes which had never advanced so far in civilization as to use wheeled transport, who a few years ago would have run shrieking from the sight of a train, have been steadied till they learn to pull great motor lorries out of the mud, to plod patiently along hardly stepping to one side while convoy after convoy of ox-carts, mule carts and motor vehicles grazed by them, till they hardly turned their heads at the whirr of passing aircraft.[61]

The social effects of this experience must have been almost as shattering among those who were left behind as among those who were taken. The main areas for recruitment were Kikuyu, Kamba, and Luo country, the chief recruiting depots Nairobi, Kisumu, and Mombasa. In March 1917, at a point of supreme crisis in the East African campaign, John Ainsworth, the Chief Native Commissioner, was placed at the disposal of the military to improve recruitment. By the end of that year about 160,000 men, including thousands of Kikuyu, had been enlisted, many of them compulsorily.[62] One administrator estimated that 77 per cent of the able-bodied population of Machakos District were recruited, and 75 per cent in Kitui.[63] In Nyanza 92,906 military porters had been registered by 1919.[64]

The methods of enlistment became increasingly harsh as the need became more desperate. C. W. R. Lane, an administrator, has described a press-gang raid for recruits in Kiambu District:

> A raid was made on the natives living on the Bacon Factory Lands, Uplands, on April 16th, 1917 in order to obtain recruits for the Carrier Corps. It was arranged by D.C. [District Commissioner], Kyambu that Muturi's Capiteni and T.R.'s[65] from Kyambu should guard paths leading from Uplands to Muturi's and that Dagoretti Spearmen should actually raid the huts. Owing to an error, a section of the former entered Uplands Estate towards sundown, before the Dagoretti Spearmen had arrived. A serious fight occurred during the night and several persons were injured. In the morning the natives resident on the Estate set upon the Government Spearmen opposite the Factory and secured the escape of about 100 recruits for the Carrier Corps. In this they were not hindered by Mr. Strange, the Manager of the Factory. Whereupon another fight took place and several more persons were injured. The A.D.C. [Assistant District Commissioner], Dagoretti was at Limuru and proceeded to Uplands by train; the D.C., Kyambu arrived the following day April 18th and held an enquiry into the matter. Further raids were made on the African Inland Mission Estate at Kijabe, Mr. Caine's Estate and all farms in the Limuru area. Later raids were held on farms in the Kedong while several raids were made on the Lari and Escarpment Forest Reserves.[66]

It is hardly surprising that such methods stimulated a Kikuyu exodus to Masailand, where they became an increasing embarrassment to the Administration, always sensitive to outside influences on this pastoral tribe.

Between September 1916 and March 1917 the Corps faced its greatest crisis. Watkins wrote that by

> September 1916, when they were suddenly called upon for a supreme effort on short-rations, the men were already debilitated and overworked. As a final torture the rains broke early,

and converted large areas into swamp, throwing still more work on the Carrier, who in one stretch on the Dodoma-Iringa road had to carry nine miles mostly waist-deep in water, much of it on raised duck-walks made of undressed poles laid side by side, while the Mikesse line was little better. The European staff also had a very high degree of morbidity, with a corresponding effect on the natives in their charge. The sufferings and casualties of this period . . . will never be fully known.[67]

Norman Leys, who served as a medical officer in the Protectorate and was to become an important critic of white settlement,* noted in 1924 that it was

sad to read, in the earlier reports, of how great a boon we bestowed by stopping intertribal war. Since then, our own War has destroyed more life than a generation of intertribal wars. Mr. G. L. Beer, the American representative at the Paris Peace Conference, states that we recruited over 350,000 unarmed porters in the campaign against the Germans in East Africa, of whom 150,000 were raised in Kenya. (About 14,000 natives of Kenya were included in the armed forces engaged.) The officially recorded deaths among these men are:

	Killed	Died of Disease	Total
Armed Forces	1,377	2,923	4,300
Unarmed Porters	366	41,952	42,318
	1,743	44,875	46,618

Of these 46,618 dead men, the relations of 40,645 are still untraced.[68]

Casualties in the Carrier Corps were indeed little short of disastrous, and as the statistics show, enemy bullets did far less damage than deplorable quartermastering, inadequate

---

* In his opinion the Government in 1911 broke faith and the 1904 Agreement with the Masai when it moved them from Laikipia south of the railway to make room for more European farms. Some Masai leaders took this affair to the Courts where it was held that the Courts had no jurisdiction as the Treaties were "acts of State." See G. R. Sandford, *An Administrative and Political History of the Masai Reserve* (London, 1919) , pp. 186–222.

diet, and poor medical services. One commentator later noted that "the Carriers were not being fed but starved."[69]

The official Carrier Corps casualties figure was 23,869 killed, but "there was much sardonic comment, some of it angry, at the Government's conservative and precise estimate of 23,869 as the African death-roll in our war."[70] In Kenya alone £50,000 due in arrears of pay to the relatives of those who officially died or were reported as missing was not paid out because the relatives were never satisfactorily traced. Ironically, sixteen years after the Armistice, the Kenya Land Commissioners advised that this "debt of honour" should be used to finance the implementing of their decisions, including the payment of compensation, on African land claims. The Secretary of State agreed.[71]

The war was followed by extensive famine in most African areas; the famine in turn by severe influenza epidemics. Dr. John S. Arthur, in charge of the Church of Scotland Mission Station at Kikuyu and in command of the Mission Carrier Corps, reckoned the combined Kikuyu death roll from the war and from the Spanish influenza epidemic of 1918 at 120,000 in a population of less than one million.[72] Dr. Philp of Tumutumu in Nyeri estimated that between November 1918 and January 1919 there were 17,000 deaths from influenza in Nyeri District alone.[73]

Several future Kikuyu political leaders served in the Kikuyu Missions Volunteer Carrier Corps, 2,000 strong, which was raised during the 1917 crisis from among adherents of the Church Missionary Society, the Church of Scotland Mission, the African Inland Mission, and the Gospel Missionary Society.[74] Philip James Karanja, later a chief and secretary of the Kikuyu Association, who was said to be the first Kikuyu with a working knowledge of English, became the headman in charge of a battalion of 500 under Dr. Arthur. Johanna Karanja, later chairman and leader of the Kikuyu Karing'a Educational Association, was also among those who served in the Church of Scotland Mission contingent, as was Ng'ang'a Ngoro, later chairman of the Kikuyu Land Board Association. Marius Ng'ang'a Karatu, later prominent in the Kikuyu Central Association and leader of the struggle for the recovery of the Tigoni lands in Kiambu District, joined the Catholic Labour Corps in 1914.[75] Jonathan Okwirri, later first President of the Young Kavirondo Association, became a headman in the Carrier Corps and was stationed at Tanga.[76]

In the Carrier Corps limited intertribal contacts were not the only important new experiences. There was also the sight of Europeans shooting each other, of Indian troops fighting for Europeans, and the great leveling effect of hardship and death endured together. In Kenya twice within a generation African and European were to face the same enemies, on many occasions each trusting the other with his life. But R. W. Hemsted, a pioneer administrator who was appointed one of the Kenya Land Commissioners in 1933, commenting on the return of the ex-soldiers, brings out another aspect:

"Chiefly, perhaps, they brought back the knowledge that there were different kinds of white men than those they had hitherto known; but they also brought back some idea of the power of organization. Combined with other causes it is probable that the growth of native political associations and of native independence of thought, really dates from the War years."[77]

Consolidation of Settler Power

In 1916, partly in recognition of the enthusiastic support of the European community in the East African campaign during the First World War, the privilege of elected representation was granted in principle to the settlers.[78] In 1917 a committee of the Legislative Council recommended that ten Europeans be elected, that two Indians be nominated, that Arab interests be represented by the Resident Magistrate at Mombasa, and African interests by the Chief Native Commissioner.[79] In 1920 eleven members were elected by the European community out of a Council of thirty-one. The change in Kenya's status from a "Protectorate" to a "Colony" in the same year subtly reinforced the concessions to settler pressure that both these moves implied. Before the war the issue of representation or the difference between the status of a "Colony" and a "Protectorate" had little significance to Africans, but with the changed level of awareness following the signing of the Armistice, this major shift in the composition of the Legislative Council was an important factor contributing to the rapid development of African politics.

In July 1918 Major-General Sir Edward Northey was appointed Governor of the East Africa Protectorate and High Commissioner for Zanzibar. Said to have been chosen in response to pressure from the settlers' organization for a military governor, he arrived fresh from commanding the Nyasa-Rhodesia Field Force in the campaign against the elusive German commander, Von Lettow-Vorbeck, in Malawi (then Nyasaland). Sir Edward, a direct, decisive, and successful man of action, entertained no doubts about his duty to extend the paramountcy of European interests in Kenya. He personally encouraged many of his former soldiers to take part in the government's postwar soldier settlement scheme.

Originally devised in 1915 by the "War Council"[80] to counter the disturbing effect it was thought the war would have on the Africans, the scheme planned to double the European population by close settlement. In the event, a further 4,560 square miles were alienated in the Highlands.[81] This included a special project for the British East Africa Disabled Officers Colony (BEADOC) on 25,000 acres at Kericho. BEADOC "was organized on strictly military lines and bugle calls were even sounded to regulate the day's work or play."[82] The settlement schemes, badly planned and ineptly implemented, became a lottery and all too often ended in economic disaster and personal tragedy for many of the thousand ex-servicemen involved. BEADOC itself was closed down in 1924, and the land was turned over to tea estates.[83]

In February 1919, within a fortnight of assuming office, Northey announced that two Europeans would be on his Executive Council, whom he would consider as "members of the Government." For two years he promoted a system that Lord Delamere, the settler leader, later christened "government by agreement." Both Government and settlers bound themselves by certain conventions. Any important Government measure was, by agreement, submitted to the elected members for their comments before being placed before the Legislative Council. At the same time the elected members, on their side, undertook to support any measure once it had been passed and to urge their constituents to do likewise.[84]

This system introduced an era of increasing cooperation between the settlers and the colonial government. Though there were often areas of conflict, a community of interests between the Administration and the settlers was to grow steadily during the next two decades. There was to develop a conception that the relationship between the Kenya settlers and the representatives of the British Government was something special and that the ties that linked Kenya and Britain represented a unique colonial pattern.

But while settler power and influence consolidated in the immediate postwar years, a new African leadership was slowly coming into being. A product of the new social and political forces and the war, this leadership began to question the "paramountcy" of European interests. At first the Africans' activities were particularly centered on finding ways to obtain redress for specific grievances. Their methods were experimental, even fumbling; they were often unsure how best to proceed. In the process, however, they formed their first political organizations, and in so doing, took the first step in the long march toward independence.

CHAPTER 2

The Beginnings of Modern Politics

The first formal political associations among Africans in Kenya reflected the new pattern of interests precipitated by the social changes we have discussed. In urban areas, problems of wages and the political ferment of the ongoing European-Indian conflict directly influenced the growth of transtribal politics among Africans. At the same time, rural interests began to project themselves in a more complex manner, especially in central Kenya. Underlying all rural politics was the land issue, in its initial stages not so much a question of recovering lost property as of ensuring the security of tenure on that which remained. Superimposed on this issue were others involving the poll tax, labor recruitment, and local administration. Furthermore, the association of Africans with the Government as chiefs and headmen in the rural areas introduced a new social order and a new basis of loyalty on political questions.

But perhaps the most significant aspect of early political organization concerns the relationship between Nairobi and the rural areas. In central Kenya each of the three Kikuyu districts—Kiambu, Fort Hall, and Nyeri—stood in a different relationship to Nairobi and to each other, and each developed politically in a different way.* At the coast and in

* For further discussion of the political geography of these areas see pp. 73–80.

the west, additional impetus to political organization came from some individuals trained in the emerging urban politics of Nairobi. In this Chapter we shall look at the beginnings of urban and rural politics and at the process by which they often inspired and conflicted with each other, especially in Nairobi and Kiambu. Many of the divergences in objectives and tactics that appeared later in Kikuyu politics had their origin in developments during the early postwar period.

Urban Politics

There are conflicting stories of the exact origin of Nairobi's first political organization, the East African Association, and some confusion has arisen over the names of its first leaders. The activists of Pangani—Thuku, Kariuki, Njoroge, Muchuchu, Hamisi, and Tairara—were certainly among its founders. But as elsewhere in Africa, nationals of other countries were also prominent. Jesse Kariuki maintains that the original secretary was Z. K. Ssentongo,[1] a Ganda, and that the first treasurer was a Nyasa[2] who worked on the railways but was deported to Nyasaland shortly after the Association was closed down in 1922. Both assertions are likely. By 1921 the Ganda in Nairobi had established a "Union of Buganda natives working in Nairobi," and there was a branch of the Young Buganda Association.[3] They also had their own newspaper, *Sekanyolya,* with a circulation of over 2,000 copies.[4] As for Nyasa participation, several employees for the expanding railway had been brought from Nyasaland, where a long start in missionary education was reflected in a lively political consciousness.

The East African Association was certainly transtribal, its name probably reflecting the name of the territory, the East Africa Protectorate. But its membership was predominantly Kikuyu, primarily because two sides of Nairobi jutted deep into the Kiambu District: indeed, even today many suburbs in the city are still claimed by Kikuyu families as their land, including Muthaiga, Westlands, Parklands, and other residential areas.[5]

The East African Association was given direction and life by Harry Thuku, a young clerk working in the Treasury. Though he was to become a pillar of the colonial and missionary establishment, the beginnings of African political protest owe much to his leadership, and he was the first undisputed hero of the politically conscious Kikuyu. Thuku was born in 1895; he traces his descent from one of the most influential families in Kikuyuland. "My grandfather Gathirimu was a great Kikuyu landowner and noble.[6] He had eight wives. My father Kairianja, who died in 1899, was the son of his third wife. My father himself had four wives, and I was the last born of his third wife. When I was twelve, I spent four years at the Kambui Gospel Mission." In 1911 Thuku was sent to prison for two years for forging a check. On his release he was employed as a compositor by the *Leader,* a settlers' newspaper. "I was one of the first Kikuyu to read and write English. I stayed on the *Leader* until December 1917, when I left and rested for two months at home. In January 1918 I was engaged as a clerk-telephone operator in the Treasury."[7] His vantage point on a telephone exchange in a major Government department in Nairobi was an important factor in the events that followed.

In mid-1921 in the face of an economic depression, the European District Associations of the parent Convention of Associations organized a campaign to cut African wages by one-third. Their success in uniting the Europeans all over Kenya dramatically demonstrated the advantages of organization. Nairobi Africans reacted vigorously. Almost overnight the East African Association, heretofore a loosely linked group of like-thinking young men, precipitated itself into an active political body. The wage cut affected all tribes and all kinds of workers.[8] Many of the African civil servants had been "Sunday" members of the Association, and among them Harry Thuku soon became a dominant figure, partly because of his listening post in the Treasury, partly from the prestige gained from his comparatively advanced education, and partly because of his real courage, fire, and outspokenness in challenging European authority.

He had also become acquainted with M. A. Desai, editor of the *East African Chronicle,* a radical Indian newspaper.* As a leader of Kenya's Indians, Desai was engaged at this time in a bitter, racialist struggle with the Europeans for equality of opportunity and rights. The Indians argued that they had as much right as the Europeans to unrestricted immigration, to the purchase of land in the Highlands, to equal representation with Europeans on the Legislative Council (with elections conducted by means of a common European-Indian electoral roll); and they demanded the ending of racial segregation in the towns. In 1919 the Indians brought their grievances to the attention of the British Government, and sent representations to the Government of India in order to gain the support of the Secretary of State for India in the British Cabinet.

The Europeans of Kenya based their opposition on an argument whose main premises were to be heard repeatedly during the 1952 Emergency. They had come to Kenya not merely as farmers, traders, or administrators, but as the proud guardians of a superior civilization possessing certain standards of conduct that they intended gradually to transmit to the Africans, who might be expected, in the fullness of time, to absorb most of them. The Europeans had no doubts

---

* Desai came to Kenya as a Solicitor's clerk in 1915. He was elected President of the East African Indian National Congress in 1922 and was a member of the Indian deputation to the British Colonial Office in 1923. He died suddenly in 1926.

The *East African Chronicle* closed down in April 1922, after having £2,000 damages awarded against it in an action with a European settler. *LBEA,* April 8, 1922, p. 25.

at all that the values usually associated with the Anglo-Saxon Christian civilization were the highest yet achieved by man and would spread throughout the world. In concert with European missionaries, they deplored many aspects of Indian society and customs, and argued that to allow unrestricted Indian immigration could lead to the Indians' swamping East Africa numerically and culturally. They maintained that this would be a betrayal of a sacred responsibility for which the British race had prepared itself "by centuries of evolution."[9]

The European position was unambiguously set out in 1919 in the final report of an Economic Commission appointed by Northey's predecessor, Sir Henry Belfield. Its members, who included such influential settlers as Lord Delamere, Edward Powys Cobb, E. S. Grogan, and W. C. Hunter, "hoped that the frank discussion of this subject will not cause offence, but it is one which calls for plain speaking." They did not shrink from this self-imposed burden. "Physically, the Indian is not a wholesome influence because of his incurable repugnance to sanitation and hygiene. In this respect the African is more civilised than the Indian being naturally clean in his ways; but he is prone to follow the example of those around him."[10] In addition, the "moral depravity of the Indian is equally damaging to the African, who in his natural state is at least innocent of the worst vices of the East. The Indian is the inciter to crime as well as vice, since it is the opportunity offered by the ever-ready Indian receivers which makes thieving easy." This section of the report concludes: "It is our firm conviction that the justification of our occupation of this country lies in our ability to adapt the native to our own civilisation. If we further complicate this task by continuing to expose the African to the antagonistic influence of Asiatic, as distinct from European, philosophy, we shall be guilty of a breach of trust."[11] Lord Delamere, the energetic, eccentric, and paternal settler leader, put the same point slightly differently: "If it is determined that unchecked immigration from India is to be allowed, then the British Government must understand that it really does mean the swamping of the European leader and creator of civilisation, and of the African who is trying to attain to a standard of competence where he can compete with the Indian."[12]

While Europeans and Indians both argued their case in terms of African welfare, Desai and Jeevanjee (the first Indian member of the Legislative Council) made friends with Thuku and the other leaders of the East African Association. Desai, who had a printing press, money, and considerable political expertise, allowed Thuku to use his office for a headquarters.[13] He personally was genuinely in sympathy with African grievances; moreover, his community needed allies so badly at this time that they were willing to assist anyone who might, in turn, help their cause.

There are other instances of African-Indian cooperation. In mid-1921 a tea-party was held in Parklands, an Indian suburb of Nairobi, for about thirty Africans representing a number of different tribes. An Indian drove Thuku in a car to political meetings in the Kikuyu rural areas. The *East African Chronicle* printed broadsheets in Swahili for Thuku, and Desai gave him help with the wording and addressing of cables and petitions to the Colonial Secretary in London. The *Chronicle* also published articles concerning Kikuyu grievances.[14] It should be remembered that while at this time Gandhi was openly fighting for *Swaraj* (self-determination) in India, neither the Indians nor the Africans in Kenya were demanding self-government. They were both fighting for the removal of certain specific grievances.

Rural Politics

Among the rural Kikuyu the critical problem in the immediate postwar period was to secure their rights to the land they still possessed. It is not surprising that the location of the earliest political organization directed toward this goal was southern Kiambu, where the Kikuyu had lost the most land to the settlers. Called the Kikuyu Association, its formation may actually have preceded that of the urban East African Association. The first documentary evidence of the Kikuyu Association is a letter that appeared in the *East African Standard* in November 1920, signed by Matthew Njoroge as Secretary.* Njoroge was to spend much of his life translating the Bible into Kikuyu, working first with Canon Harry Leakey and then with the Leakey's daughter, Gladys.†

In describing the formation of the Kikuyu Association, Njoroge explained that it arose from an attempt by the Government to alienate some of his family's land. [Kikuyu-*mbari*].[15] He said that

> there was always trouble at Kabete about our *mbari* land which bordered on the Mission station. In 1908 there was a Director of Agriculture called Macdonald who took some of the land from our *mbari*. In 1919 Captain W. H. Wood, Superintendent of the Reformatory at Kabete, told the Government he needed more land and, to our horror, they started to mark it out from the 67 acres we still had left. Stephen Kinuthia,‡ my brother and one of the first Africans to read English, was working with Canon Leakey at this time translating the Bible, and so he asked Canon Leakey to write a letter from us to the Government saying that 240 acres of our land

---

* *EAS*, November 15, 1920. In an interview, Njoroge said he could not remember writing this particular letter, adding that other officials of the Association would sometimes write under his name and tell him about it afterward.

† See the article by Gladys Beecher in *EAS*, April 15, 1949 and June 16, 1966. Leonard Beecher, her husband, was the first Archbishop of the Kenya Province of the Anglican Church and in 1943 was appointed a Member of the Legislative Council to represent African interests. He was also chairman of a Committee that published a controversial report in 1949 on African education.

‡ Stephen Kinuthia went with Canon Harry Leakey to England in 1905 and later became Chief Interpreter in the Supreme Court, Nairobi. See Leakey, *White African*, pp. 14–15.

had been taken in 1908 and now the Government was taking some more and we had nowhere to go. The letter was written, Stephen and I signed it on behalf of our *mbari* and it was sent to the Government. They listened and the land was not taken and we all thought the power of this letter a most wonderful thing.

Then Leakey suggested that we should call Paramount Chief Kinyanjui and explain our success to him, and suggest that if Kinyanjui, and the other chiefs and all the ordinary people unite and write a letter to the Government about the other lands that had been taken, the Government might listen. And so late in 1919 all the headmen from round Kabete—people like Kimani Wanyaga, Chege Muthemba, Kariuki Muti, Karanja Chege, and others—met with Kinyanjui, and he agreed to start the association. Later we were all called to Kinyanjui's *boma* at Riruta, just outside Nairobi, and people came from all over southern Kiambu, including Philip James Karanja, Josiah Njonjo, and the great patriot Koinange. I became the first Secretary [of the Kikuyu Association]. But because I was working in Nairobi I got out of touch and could not attend many of the meetings, and Philip James Karanja from the Church of Scotland Mission over at Kikuyu, and later a chief, took my place. Kinyanjui became a kind of patron and Koinange became Chairman.[16]

Stimulated by the missionaries, this rural group, many of whose members held administrative posts as chiefs and headmen in Kiambu District, was claimed by the Government to be more representative of African, and particularly Kikuyu, opinion than Thuku's East African Association. Sooner or later a clash between the two groups was inevitable, for they represented what were later to be recognized as two different approaches to politics. The leaders of the rural Kikuyu Association accepted the colony's basic political structure, under which they had achieved great power and status as the new élite in the tribe. They sought only its modification and reform. On the other hand, the leaders of the East African Association tended to reject the fundamental premises of white rule, adopting a more militant and uncompromising approach to political change.

Both associations articulated a number of grievances that arose from the Administration's policies of land alienation and labor recruitment, and each fiercely regarded itself as the only legitimate channel for the expression of such grievances. Each sought, for example, to secure tenure of the land that remained to the Africans and to effect the return of the land that had been taken. Both based their stand on the "definite promise" made to the Kikuyu in August 1914 by the Governor, Sir Henry Belfield, that "their Reserves should not be interfered with," a promise about which G.A.S. Northcote, District Commissioner of Kiambu, vainly reminded the Government's Land Settlement Commission in 1919. "Such promises," he warned, "are not lightly to be disregarded."[17] That further alienation of Kikuyu land was envisaged by some at this time can be seen in the 1919 Economic Commission's recommendations for the Reserves. They should no longer "be regarded as sacrosanct"; rather, a scheme should be devised "for concentrating the natives in a number of areas distributed as widely as possible throughout the Reserves, sufficient, but not more than sufficient, for their requirements, leaving the interspersed tracts not needed for native occupation as available for white settlement."[18]

The trial of strength between the two African associations came very early and was unexpectedly violent. It left its mark on two generations of African politics. Early in 1921 the Kikuyu Association, with the help of A. R. Barlow, a Church of Scotland missionary, drafted a petition to the Government outlining various grievances. There were no Local Native Councils reflecting a broad range of opinion at this time, and

the nominated advisory councils that did exist were embryonic and ineffectual; so the colonial government still had
only one way of dealing with African grievances—calling a
baraza or public meeting.* It called for a *baraza* to be held
on June 24 at Dagoretti, just outside Nairobi, to discuss the
petition. On June 10, Harry Thuku called a meeting in
Pangani to form a Young Kikuyu Association; presumably
he had heard of the *baraza*. He may have realized that he
could not use the intertribal East African Association on
specifically Kikuyu questions, and it seems possible that he
founded the Young Kikuyu Association solely for this occasion. Certainly there is no evidence of further meetings by it
and ample evidence of meetings of the East African Association. The Kikuyu Association apparently already had a
Nairobi branch.[19]

Together with the senior European officers, including
Watkins, then the Acting Chief Native Commissioner, the
Senior Commissioner from Nyeri, and the District Commissioner, Kiambu, most of the recognized Kikuyu leaders
attended the Dagoretti meeting: Kinyanjui and Thuku,
Koinange and Joseph Kang'ethe, Philip James Karanja and
George Mugekenyi. Barlow and other missionaries were also
present. A number of resolutions were passed following the
general lines of the petition, condemning "forced" labor
(especially of young women) , the alienation of Kikuyu land,

---

* Some of the early administrators had not been concerned with the
problem of consulting tribal opinion; others had set up various types of
transitory councils at different levels, whose composition was often changed
by their immediate successors; still others merely consulted the Court
Tribunals. Usually they resolved important issues by calling general *barazas*
at district headquarters. "It was a natural development, to avoid unnecessary
expense and useless travelling, that general *barazas* should be confined to big
occasions when some important order or decision had to be announced while
only chiefs, leading elders and a few prominent natives of the younger
generation would be called together at more frequent intervals for purposes
of discussion." See S. H. Fazan, *Report on the Relations between Government
and Local Native Councils* (Nairobi, 1938) , p. 5. Copy in Kenya Government
Library.

the increase in the hut tax and the poll tax,* and the *kipande* system, as the regulations for registration were called. The *kipandes* were registration certificates placed in a small, solid metal container, which usually hung from the neck of the owner on a piece of string. To Africans they were a perpetual reminder of a subordinate status, and, as such, they remained a political issue up to and through the Emergency. Underlying the protest on the *kipande* at this time was the Africans' rejection of the settler view that the African was a second-class human being. The presence of a large contingent of South African settlers undoubtedly played its part in reinforcing this view. M. W. H. Beech, the Assistant District Commissioner at Dagoretti, had said in 1912 that there was an "unfortunate" class of settler in the country "whose sole idea was that the native was especially created to perform the manual labour, which they, in any other country but Africa, themselves would be doing." One such settler was "in the habit of harnessing his natives to a plough and, when remonstrated with, excused himself on the ground that it was only a 'light cultivator.' "[20]

The Government's policy on labor problems, embodied in the *kipande* system, was influenced by attitudes that already prevailed in the southern part of the continent. The Native Labour Commission of 1912–13, composed of administrators, missionaries, and settlers, recognized that more must be done to provide labor for European farms. To bring more Africans into the labor market they recommended that the size of the Reserves be limited and that taxes "be based upon the number of wives and be progressive," and they argued it was "absolutely essential" in tackling the problem of desertion for there to be a system of identification by registration, based upon the Southern

---

* In 1920–21 the hut and poll taxes were each increased from six to eight rupees (twelve to sixteen shillings). The currency change from rupees to shillings occurred in 1922.

Rhodesia Native Pass Consolidation Ordinance. The Commission also suggested ominously that if registration proved inadequate, then a Pass Law,[21] on the lines of the one in force in Southern Rhodesia, should be introduced. An Ordinance to this effect, requiring the registration of all African males over 16 years of age, was passed in 1915, though its provisions were not implemented until after the war, in 1919. The *kipande* system was expensive to administer, for by 1921 it was costing the Government £20,000 a year. Thuku suggested, in his speeches out in the districts, that the metal containers should be collected, loaded into lorries, and dumped outside Government House.

Philip James Karanja was made secretary of the Dagoretti meeting, but Thuku, and the shadow of Nairobi, dominated the proceedings. The Kikuyu Association leaders never intended that the resolutions should be sent to anyone without further discussion by the chiefs. Kinyanjui, Koinange, and the other chiefs and headmen were sufficiently experienced to realize that any resolutions that were passed were conventionally sent to the Governor, not directly to England. Thuku, however, advised by Indian leaders who had despaired of Sir Edward Northey's Administration and were themselves appealing over his head both to India and to the British Government, decided upon returning to Nairobi to send a copy of the resolutions directly to the Colonial Secretary in Britain under his own name. He sent it and gave the Treasury post-box number as his address. In July a mass meeting of the East African Association was held in Nairobi. Thuku's actions were unanimously supported. The Government, particularly angered by his use of the Treasury address, told him to choose between his job and politics. He chose politics, and in July he sent a cable to England condemning the attitude of certain missionaries on the Indian Question.

Thuku's *fait accompli* put the Kikuyu Association chiefs

in an embarrassing position with the District Commissioner, and probably contributed greatly to the intensity of their subsequent vendetta against him. It is said that at a meeting of the Association held on July 25, 1921,[22] at Thika to discuss Thuku's activities, he would have been sentenced to death had it not been for the intervention of Chief Njegga Gioke of Embu. The meeting was attended by sixteen chiefs and headmen from Fort Hall, Embu, and Nyeri. "The object of the meeting was to ascertain the cable and resolution sent to the Prime Minister by the name of the Kikuyu Association signed by (Harry Thuku) of Nairobi African Association and various matters effected in the Kikuyu country."[23] Thuku and his Indian friends were strongly condemned. Kinyanjui seems to have regarded Thuku's activities as an impertinent challenge to him personally, and he felt that Thuku's effrontery called for violent measures. Kinyanjui and other chiefs gave support to the Government's eventual decision to deport Thuku.

The "Thuku Troubles"

In the rural areas of central Kenya, Thuku boldly precipitated a crisis between the East African Association and the Kikuyu Association. After the Thika meeting, he went north to Fort Hall and Nyeri seeking support and holding mass meetings. Together with Abdullah Tairara and one "Mohamed Sheika," he even visited Machakos District in an attempt to win Kamba support. He convened a meeting of local Swahilis and headman Mathendu and his council. Thuku asked the Kamba to combine with the Kikuyu, since "though natives had rendered Government great assistance in the past, Government had done little or nothing for the native. Papers were presented by Thuku for signature." The Kamba response was apparently lukewarm and no papers were signed.[24]

In his tour of Kikuyu country he was followed by a group

of Kikuyu Association leaders condemning his speeches and opinions. Someone even organized a "mass" meeting of "Nakuru natives" to condemn Thuku.[25] The Kikuyu Association effectively controlled at least the southern half of the Kiambu District, and Thuku made little headway there. But in the Church of Scotland Mission (CSM) at Tumutumu near Karatina, Thuku made several converts, and "there was some open insubordination which resulted in the cancelling of more than 20 apprenticeship contracts,"[26] including those of Hezekiah Mundia and Johanna Kunyiha.* In Nairobi itself Thuku probably inspired the presentation of an address in October 1921 to the Rev. C. F. Andrews, a missionary friend of Gandhi from India, who was strongly pressing the Indian case.[27]

By the end of the year, Thuku was obviously gaining ground. On November 29, he held his own mass meeting at Thika; the resolutions passed were listed in a press release of the East African Association:

That the Government is respectfully requested to repeal the Native Registration Ordinance or to suspend its operation for a period of five years. That the Government is requested to issue instructions to district officers to treat native chiefs with due respect and dignity and not compel them to carry loads like porters. That the Government is requested to repeal the Hut Tax and to charge only Poll Tax as is done in the case of Europeans and Asiatics. That the Government is requested to allow natives to purchase land throughout their country. That if no satisfaction is obtained from the Local Government the Chairman is authorized to make further representations to the Secretary of State for the Colonies.[28]

---

* Mundia was later the Kikuyu Central Association's leader in Nyeri; Kunyiha was for fifteen years the president of the Kikuyu Independent Schools' Association. These two men organized a group at Nyeri to be the first Kikuyu to greet Thuku in January 1931 on his journey back from restriction at Marsabit.

The Government could not afford to ignore Thuku much longer. At Weithaga and Kahuhia CMS stations in Fort Hall District, Thuku had lit a flame that never expired in the storms to come. The District Commissioner, Fort Hall, and the Reverend A. W. McGregor, the Weithaga CMS missionary, busily organized the swearing of affidavits (necessary under the Removal of Natives Ordinance, 1909) "to justify the Governor in ordering the arrest of the leader and leading members of his inner council at Nairobi."[29] In Fort Hall the split between the chiefs and the young educated group was complete. The District Commissioner reported on March 4, 1922, to the Senior Commissioner, Nyeri, that "the Chiefs here are thoroughly upset and ask that immediate steps be taken to deport him,"[30] while Dr. Arthur noted that in Fort Hall District "practically the whole of the younger generation of native Christians were solid for the agitator."[31] Events moved swiftly. Jesse Kariuki, vice-president of the Kikuyu Central Association in the early 1930s, says he was with a group which on March 9, 1922, hired a car for 1,300 rupees [about £100]. He adds, "We all went, Thuku, Waiganjo Ndotono, Njoroge Kangacha, Harun Mutondu, Abdullah Tairara, George Mugekenyi and myself to hold meetings to undo the damage the last round of chiefs' *barazas* might have done. On the 9th of March we had a meeting at Kiguoya, on Friday the 10th of March at Kahuhia in Fort Hall (even the Roman Catholic priest came), on Saturday the 11th of March at Gakindu in Nyeri and then back to Nairobi. On Tuesday the 14th of March we held a meeting of the East African Association committee at Tairara's house in Pangani and Thuku was arrested there.[32] On the next day we collected money to hire [F. H.] Dracott to be his lawyer."[33] Kariuki's story is confirmed elsewhere, where it is reported that Chief Inspector Sat Bachan Singh found Thuku addressing a meeting in Pangani and induced him to ride pillion on his motorcycle to the Police Lines.[34]

Employing the Removal of Natives Ordinance of 1909, the Governor directed that the African leader "one Harry Thuku, a Kikuyu native, be deported from Nairobi to Kismayu. In pursuance of this order the Acting Commissioner of Police on the 14th of March 1922, arrested the said Harry Thuku and confined him in the quarter guard of the Police Lines, Nairobi, preparatory to his being deported as directed by His Excellency."[35] As this event was taking place the *East African Chronicle* offices were cordoned and searched.[36] It is interesting to note that on this same day, Indians were holding a mass meeting in Nairobi's Jeevanjee Gardens, protesting against the arrest on March 11 in India of Mahatma Gandhi, and Sir Edward Northey went off to Mombasa on Kenya's coast to unveil a memorial to one of the defenders of the British Empire.[37]

The morning after Thuku's arrest, the leaders of the East African Association decided to call what amounted to a general strike in Nairobi.[38] Following two mass meetings, held during the day behind the Metropole Hotel, pickets, some on bicycles, patrolled the town. The striking workers marched in the afternoon to the Police Station (then located on the site of the present University College opposite the Norfolk Hotel) to secure Thuku's immediate release. The original crowd numbered about 1,000, many of them armed with heavy sticks. The crowd turned several Europeans out of rickshaws, and ordered the rickshaw-drivers to join them. At this point it was said to number 2,000.[39]

That evening a letter was delivered "by certain Kikuyu" to Sir Charles Bowring, the Governor's Deputy, inquiring as to the cause of Thuku's arrest; meanwhile, at the request of the leaders and after some fifteen minutes of prayers for Thuku's safety, most of the strikers returned home for the night. Somewhere between 500 and 600, however, kept a vigil at the Police Station until morning, when the assembly rapidly grew again to an estimated 3,000, and, by mid-day, to between 7,000 and 8,000.[40] "The crowd there was mostly seated in groups and very orderly," stated the Rev. W. J. Wright, Vicar of All Saints, the English Church in Nairobi. "He [Wright] walked through most of the groups and was struck by their apparent peacefulness. It reminded him more of a Sunday School treat . . . several times they had prayers . . . there were fully 200 women collected together there. The women made a great noise . . . very slowly the women made towards the corrugated fence. They came to within a yard of the bayonets. The askaris in front of the actual gate knelt down and appeared to raise their rifles, probably at what was termed the 'engage.' "[41]

Job Muchuchu, who was to be a dominant figure in Fort Hall politics for forty years, was also present. In 1964, although seventy-eight years old, he could still vividly recall the scene. "I went to the Police Lines with Harun Mikono. We had been there the previous evening, the fifteenth of March, thousands of us, and we were determined to get Harry Thuku out. We heard later that he had been secretly removed during the night,* although some of our men had been vigilantly keeping guard. During the morning of the sixteenth we sent a delegation of six to the Secretariat[42]— Abdullah John Tairara, David Njuguna, Douglas Mwangi, Lawi Mwangi, Ndimgoe and I believe, one person from Kisumu way."[43] When they returned at mid-day, they spoke to the crowd, telling them that the Government had promised to give Thuku a fair trial and that they should now disperse. But the temper of the crowd was by now too high. They accused the delegation of having been bribed, and the women in particular became very excited. Muchuchu continues:

Mary Muthoni Nyanjiru (from Weithaga in Location 10 of Fort Hall District) leapt to her feet, pulled her dress right up

---

* He had not and was still there.

over her shoulders and shouted to the men: "You take my dress and give me your trousers. You men are cowards. What are you waiting for? Our leader is in there. Let's get him." The hundreds of women trilled their *ngemi** in approbation and from that moment on trouble was probably inevitable. Mary and the others pushed on until the bayonets of the rifles were pricking at their throats, and then the firing started.† Mary was one of the first to die. My companion, Harun Mikono, was badly wounded in the right leg.

On the other side of the lines the European settlers sitting drinking on the verandah of the Norfolk Hotel joined in the shooting, and it is said that they were responsible for most of the deaths over there. One of our people employed at the mortuary told us that 56 bodies were brought in, although the Government said only 21 were killed. No Africans in Nairobi were working those two days. We had pickets out to make sure people did not break the strike.[44]

The newspaper files contain a somewhat more prosaic account of the events that precipitated this tragedy. Captain Cary seized a person, threw him backwards, but fell in so doing. "The crowd shouted, threw stones, and rushed towards the corrugated iron fence at the south gate, and on this onrush by the crowd a rifle went off and it was followed immediately by a fusillade by the askaris guarding the gate into the oncoming crowd, and the firing was taken up by the askaris at Government Road side. This firing by the askaris lasted between one and two minutes."[45] So B. A. Crean, the Nairobi Resident Magistrate, described the so-called riot after the inquest in his courtroom on 21 Africans, among them 4 women and one 15-year-old boy, killed by the Police on March 16, 1922. Officially 28 were also wounded.

But although police bullets had effectively broken up the

---

* Kikuyu ululation.

† According to *Native Disturbances in Kenya*, Cmd. 1691, p. 7, at 12:40 p.m. Abdullah Tairara returned to the Secretariat to report their failure with the crowd, and the firing started while he was still with the Governor's Deputy.

crowd of Thuku's would-be liberators, there were others
working on his behalf. The *ad hoc* committee formed on
March 15 to handle the crisis sought to raise funds to hire a
lawyer for Thuku, and to organize collections of money.
This latter need was the more pressing when it became
known that some fifty persons[46] had been arrested for unlawful assembly, and that Thuku's chief lieutenant, Daudi
Waiganjo Ndotono, was also being held by the police.
(Ndotono, who had been dismissed from his job as a Tribal
Retainer in 1921 after allegations of extortion,[47] was soon
deported to Lamu, an ancient and remote Arab settlement on
the Kenya coast.) George Mugekenyi, one of Thuku's half-
brothers, used some of the money that was collected to enlist
the services of F. H. Dracott, a lawyer. Together they went to
the Secretariat in Nairobi, only to be told they should see
the District Commissioner at Kiambu. They traveled out
there together, but Dracott returned to Nairobi alone and
told the other committee members that Mugekenyi had
been detained on arrival at the D.C.'s office. This proved but
the first step to his eventual restriction at Vanga in Kwale
District at the coast.[48]

From March to May 1922 money for legal expenses
remained a crucial consideration, and the organization to
collect it stayed in existence. Abdullah Tairara, a prominent
member of the East African Association's delegation to Sir
Charles Bowring on March 16, successfully appealed against
a sentence of two years' imprisonment "in connection with
the native riots."[49] Mr. Justice Pickering reduced the sentence to a fine of 100 shillings or six weeks' imprisonment.
Dracott, who also defended Tairara, was apparently told by
the Government after the trial that his presence in Kenya
was no longer desirable.[50] He then left for Bukoba in
Tanganyika.

Reporting on the events of March 16, Northey reassured
the Secretary of State: "By next morning everything was

again normal and has so continued—further proof, if any is needed, that the large majority of the crowd attended out of curiosity or owing to compulsion, and not from any conviction of grievance or other deeper-seated sentiment."[51] In the Government's view the East African Association represented nothing. It was made very clear that its activities had to end. The Association may still, however, have been in some kind of existence as late as August 1923, when a certain Henry Kariuki sent a report to the *East African Standard* that "a mass meeting of Africans consisting of Kikuyus, Mkambas, Kavirondos and other native tribes numbering about 800 had been held under the auspices of the East African Association near the race course, Nairobi."[52] Kariuki signed the report as secretary of the Association and himself presided at the meeting. Resolutions were passed requesting the Government to state the reasons for deporting Harry Thuku, asking that the country should revert to its former status of a "British Protectorate," and deploring an alleged intention by the Government to interfere with certain existing marriage customs.[53] The *East African Standard* commented that "the Association, though it may represent Town natives, is repudiated on behalf of the country Natives by responsible chiefs."[54]

The violent end to the Thuku demonstration in 1922 and the rapid decline thereafter of the East African Association were to serve as a dramatic illustration of the limits within which the new politics could be conducted. The events lingered long in the general political consciousness, and the African version of what happened became part of the political education of new generations. The *Kanyegenuri*, for example, a famous political song, commemorates the deeds of the Nairobi women on this day and in particular the bravery of Mary Muthoni Nyanjiru, who had taunted the men present with cowardice. Certainly many of the witnesses at the inquest had been greatly impressed by the women's courage and unity. While waiting for fifty soldiers of the King's African Rifles to arrive as reinforcements, the Town Magistrate said he "heard the women of the Wakikuyu making their peculiar cry, which is very distinctive and has an exciting effect upon the menfolk."[55] Over the next few decades many other Europeans were to hear this noise and from time to time have evidence of the power and strength of the Kikuyu women when politically aroused.

Politics in the West

During the latter half of 1921, at the time Thuku's new movement was rapidly spreading out from Nairobi into the furthest part of Kikuyu country, African discontent with Administration policies was also being expressed in Nyanza Province. Even during the war, the Administration had foreseen the significance of frustrating transtribal political links and movements there. In October 1917 the Provincial Commissioner, Kisumu, sent to the District Commissioner, Kisumu, a confidential minute from the Acting Governor's Private Secretary on "The Influence of Mohammedanism on the Future Administration of British East Africa." The minute noted with foreboding that the "participation of natives in British East Africa in the campaign in German East Africa, whether as soldiers or as porters has given them unprecedented opportunities of enlarging their ideas by contact with natives of other African dependencies. Certain of the men who return will have become acquainted with the Pan-African ideal of the Ethiopian Church, with Native politics from Abyssinia, and, for the first time in the history of this Protectorate, a conception may have arisen in the native mind of the possibilities of a black Africa." After remarking that "German East Africa is common ground for Pan-Islam and Pan-Africa . . . and the German administrators have confessed to a feeling of apprehension respecting an African Jehad, i.e. a conjunction of an African political

Islam [*sic*] against Europeans," the Provincial Commissioner noted the comment in the minute that a "definite policy of encouraging strong and isolated tribal nationalism may be one of the most effectual barriers against a Pan-African upheaval" and asked his District Commissioners' views on "the best method of arriving at this condition."[56] In these circumstances then, it was hardly to be expected that the Nyanza Administration would welcome the growing evidence of political activity transcending tribal institutions both within and without the Province.

James Beauttah, later vice-president of the Central Province regional organization of the Kenya African Union, had seen the new politics developing in Nairobi; he was now to play a part in fostering the early political movement in Nyanza.* Born Mbutu Ruhara at Gatande in Lower Muhito in the Nyeri District, he later altered part of his name to Beauttah.

> I left my Kikuyu country for Mombasa . . . and I found people there had European names as they had originally been slaves and I thought that my children would be unhappy to use the name Mbutu and might just use my baptismal name of James and so I decided to modify it as it is now.
>
> When I left home to work in Nairobi in 1903 my father was already very old, nearly eighty. My mother, Wanjiru, was killed by a Government military expedition. This was in Dr. Hinde's time at Fort Hall. Soon after she died I started work as servant of one of the soldiers. In Nairobi I worked in hotels and with a European employed in the railways.

Beauttah agreed to go with him to Europe, but when he reached Mombasa and saw the sea he was frightened and refused to leave Kilindini Pier. He decided to stay with an auctioneer called Hilton until his employer returned. "One day I went for a walk with Hilton's son, Willy, who later

---

* Harry Thuku denies he ever visited Nyanza before his arrest, although McGregor-Ross, *Kenya from Within*, p. 228, and others who have followed him maintain that he did.

came to farm at Kamiti, in the Mackinnon Gardens where we met Daudi Gakure, son of old Chief Karuri of Fort Hall. We started talking and he told me he was in Mombasa for education. He was living with a missionary called Rev. H. K. Binns[57] near Mombasa Cathedral." This meeting led to Beauttah's going to stay with the Rev. Binns "for education," and he was baptized at Kisauni. Enabled to attend Buxton High School in Mombasa, he says, "I used to study in the morning and at 2:00 p.m. go to teach the newcomers. I was given the job of monitor to teach Jaluos Christianity. I used to study English very hard, even at night times."[58]

In 1910 he attended the Post Office Training School at Rabai, and after completing the course, he was assigned to Kampala. For a brief period in 1913 he was an interpreter in the Kenya Supreme Court, but he soon rejoined the Post Office service, where he spent the rest of his official career. Despite strong objections from all his family, he married a Christian girl at Mombasa in 1914. During the war, Beauttah served in Rabai (1914), Eldoret (1915), and Mombasa (1917 and 1918). "In early 1919 I was transferred to Nairobi to learn touch typing. I struggled with this until in September I was tested by the Governor himself, that was General Sir Edward Northey. When I passed I was given 41 rupees and promotion. I was also made to type a large sheet of paper to be sent to the Colonial Office to prove Africans could type. I was doing 35 words per minute." In 1919 Beauttah was transferred to Kisumu, but not before he had witnessed the first political stirrings in Nairobi among the eventual members of the East African Association.

He was soon moved from Kisumu Township to take charge of the Telegraphy School at the nearby CMS station at Maseno, replacing a Ganda named Daudi Basudde.[59] Basudde, a Roman Catholic and an editor of *Sekanyolya*, had earlier begun to interest the educated group at Maseno in a politics broader than their clan affairs, explaining to them some of the possible implications of the change in Kenya's status from Protectorate to Colony in October 1920, especially the new legal status of their land.* When the Maseno school, comprising some 100 students—three-quarters Luo and one-quarter Luhya—went on strike over these issues, he was suspected of fomenting the stoppage. His removal from the staff signaled the gradual ending of a long tradition of direct Ganda influence in Nyanza. This had begun with the British use of Ganda agents and workers† when the Province was still part of the Uganda Protectorate, and had been sustained by their employment as hut counters and teachers and by continuing control of Nyanza CMS missionary activity from Uganda. Kavirondo remained part of the Diocese of Uganda until 1921; in contrast to the Diocese of Mombasa, the CMS authorities pursued from the earliest days a liberal policy of Africanization of the Church.

Beauttah, fresh from the atmosphere of postwar Nairobi where Africans were openly questioning various aspects of the new social order, actively encouraged the developing Nyanza political consciousness. At Maseno, on the border between Luo and Luhya country, he was in direct touch with some of the young educated group in both tribes and acted as a link between them and the East African Association in Nairobi. Their discussions, which Beauttah attended, culminated on December 23, 1921, in a mass protest meeting at Lundha in North Gem. The crowd numbered several thousand, mainly Luo but with some Luhya present. An anonymous newspaper correspondent, who estimated the

---

* In 1921 he was a founder and first secretary of the National (Buganda) Federation of Bataka; as such, he was keenly involved in the controversy over *mailo* land in Buganda. *Mailo* land is the 9,003 square miles of land distributed under the 1900 Agreement to leading Ganda in private freehold. See Welbourn, *East African Rebels*, pp. 19–20.

† In 1904 there were 500 Ganda at Kisumu, working on the railway and at the docks. See J. J. Willis, "Christianity or Mohammedanism in the Uganda Diocese," *Church Missionary Intelligencer*, vol. XXIX (1904).

attendance at 8,000, described the scene as follows: "When one of the newly arrived [from England] officials heard of this meeting he sent out an ADC [Assistant District Commissioner] with some police. The sight of the police infuriated the natives and bloodshed might have resulted had not an older District Commissioner from another district turned up and by his widsom prevented anything in the way of an exhibition of force."[60] Three officers, one from North Nyanza District and two from Central Nyanza District, "were turned away" from the meeting-place, and the Administration realized it had all the makings of a serious outburst on its hands.[61]

Beauttah notes subsequently that "in January 1922 Ishmael Thongo [a Court interpreter] came to Kisumu with the Assizes. He was, by this time, no longer a member of the East African Association. He had been warned that he would be sacked if he did not leave it. So I arranged for him to visit Maseno. By that time I wanted to bring unity of the Luo and the Kikuyu for the liberation of our country and I wanted Ishmael to meet my Luo friends. They slaughtered a sheep for him at Maseno and we had a wonderful time together that day." Beauttah here hints at an early realization that whoever united the Luo and Kikuyu heartlands would unite a major portion of the country.

"On the seventh of February, 1922, they[62] called a meeting at Nyahera. When the [Provincial] Commissioner, H. R. Tate, asked them why they were meeting, they answered, 'We are *Piny Owacho*,' which means 'We, the People say.'* The Leaders at that time were Rev. Simeon Nyende, Reuben Omolo, Jonathan Okwirri, Mathayo Otieno, Benjamin Owuor, who was acting as secretary, and Joel Omino, who was clerk for Mr. Britton, the headmaster of the Industrial

---

* This was meant as a pointed rejoinder to the District Commissioner's baraza, which usually started off with "The Government says . . ." or "The D. C. says . . ."

Training School, at Maseno."* This group was known as the Young Kavirondo Association, and at this meeting they presented Tate with a memorandum of their grievances similar to those enunciated a few months earlier by the East African Association and the Kikuyu Association. Some 4,000 people were present at Nyahera, and the Nyanza Provincial Report notes: "Although both the demeanour and senti- ments of the speakers were at times disrespectful and at times defiant, the Chiefs, Headmen, Elders and young men—both Mission adherents and pagans—who spoke were so palpably acting under strong emotion that it would have been both impolitic and inadvisable to have silenced them."[63] Like the Kikuyu groups, the Young Kavirondo Association sought the abolition of the *kipande* system, protested against the high tax rate, demanded security of their land, and wished to have a clear explanation of the meaning of the new "Colony" status.

These widely separated upheavals of African political activity highlighted in part that Sir Edward Northey had indeed proved to be the answer to the European settlers' prayers. His governorship, from 1919 to 1922, saw the introduction of a series of measures designed to meet Euro- pean needs and demands. It may be argued, of course, that once the decision to bring European settlers into the country was taken during Eliot's administration, there was a logic about what followed in the growing dominance of European interests and development. Sir Edward, a military man, did

---

* Nyende was an evangelist from Gem, ordained a priest in 1933. Okwirri was later chairman of the Kavirondo Taxpayers Welfare Association and, later still, a chief. Owuor was later secretary of the Kavirondo Taxpayers Welfare Association and a dresser at the Maseno Hospital. Mr. Britton was the Rev. J. Britton. B.A. Joel Omino later became Secretary of the Central Nyanza Local Native Council.

Beauttah has omitted from this list the Rev. Ezekiel Apindi, another teacher, who represented the Kavirondo Taxpayers Welfare Association before the Joint Select Committee of the British Parliament in 1931. Apindi was the pioneer of CMS work in South Nyanza.

not long debate the pros and cons of policy issues. To meet the acute needs of settlers for labor, he signed in October 1919, the strongest of a series of labor circulars, drafted by John Ainsworth, one of Kenya's pioneer administrators and then Chief Native Commissioner. It instructed government officials to exercise "every possible lawful influence to induce" Africans to go out to work. M. W. H. Beech, the A.D.C. at Dagoretti, had wryly commented in 1913 that it "was a difficult matter for a Chief to understand the difference between influencing natives to go out to work and forcing them to do so."[64]

Northey's labor policy and the close identification of the colonial government with settler interests was challenged by liberal forces in Britain and Kenya. At first the Secretary of State for the Colonies supported the Governor in arguing that only encouragement and not compulsion was intended; after further pressure by British humanitarian elements, however, instructions were sent to Kenya in 1921 to the effect that no administrative official in the future should take part in recruiting African workers for private employment.

The needs of white settlement for labor continued to exceed the supply of African workers at least until the depression in the early 1930s, and new pressures were brought by settlers on the Government to encourage Africans to work on European estates. After the late 1920s, however, there was less need for the Administration to be concerned with influencing Africans to enter the labor market. A number of factors—such as the declining capacity of African agricultural areas to support adequately a growing population, the taxation program, new habits and values generated by education, the development of a money economy, and urbanization—all contributed to stimulate Africans to become wage earners.

While labor issues and a demand for the reduction of the twin hut and poll taxes became part of common grievances shared by many Africans, at the meeting in February 1922, the Young Kavirondǫ Association also asked for increases in the pay of the chiefs, the establishment of a Government school in Central Nyanza, and the appointment of a Paramount Chief. As early as November 1920, the District Commissioner, Central Nyanza, gave his opinion that "the real crux" of their demands was the request for a Paramount Chief, who would be "the nominee of the Maseno mission natives." Under his wing "mission natives will have a secular prestige and authority which they have not got under the present regime." Responsible for these demands were Ezekiel Apindi of Maseno and Jacobo Ochola of Gem, and behind them was Onduso, until recently chief of Gem, who aspired to the position of Paramount Chief.[65]

Two of the Nyanza Africans' demands, however, spotlighted most dramatically their unity with the Kikuyu political movement in a growing awareness that crucial decisions affecting not only their own future, but that of their children, were being taken without their knowledge. The first demand protested against the substitution of the status of "Colony" for that of "Protectorate." While there were certain significant legal implications in this change of status, Africans seemed to see it primarily as a strengthening of the local European position at the expense of the Crown's former obligation to protect African interests. The second demand was for individual title deeds for African lands as a safeguard against further losses to European settlement.

In 1921 a Supreme Court decision made it clear that the combined effect of the Crown Lands Ordinance (1915) and the Annexation Order (1920) was to prevent Africans from owning land on the same basis as Europeans.[66] Africans were now tenants-at-will of the Crown, tenants who could theoretically be removed *en masse* or individually on the order of the Government of Kenya with the permission of the Secretary of State for the Colonies. The legal facts were not as important as the growing African awareness of them and the grave sense of insecurity over land that this knowledge induced. These feelings were most intense among the Kikuyu, for unlike other tribes they had little or no spare land. Before the advent of the European, land had meant no more to the Kikuyu than to other predominantly agricultural peoples; but by the 1920s, confined as they were by European settlement, it was rapidly becoming the only source of opportunity and self-betterment in an economy increasingly built around European-controlled agriculture.

The meeting of the Nyanza Provincial Commissioner with the Young Kavirondo Association on February 7, 1922, had little immediate effect; it was followed on May 25 by a further public meeting at Nyahera, addressed by the Chief Native Commissioner. This again was inconclusive, but on July 8, General Sir Edward Northey himself appeared at Nyahera and announced the abolition of labor camps and a reduction of the hut tax and poll tax from sixteen shillings to twelve shillings. He further stated that the boundary of the Luo Reserve would be demarcated and published in the Official Gazette and that the tribe would not henceforth be disturbed. However, he sidestepped the crucial issue of land by saying merely that the change of name from "Protectorate" to "Colony" had nothing to do with the introduction of the registration system or the rise in taxation. To people concerned with fundamental changes in the status of their land this seemed an irrelevant reply.

There was one other consequence of the first Nyahera meeting. Shortly afterward the Administration transferred James Beauttah to Eldoret, the main town in the settler district of Uasin Gishu, and henceforth he became a marked man. Talking about the Young Kavirondo Association, he said, "I collected 91 rupees from them in early 1922 which I sent to Norman Mboya Wagura, who worked in the railways.

He was very active and I knew that he would hand it over to the East African Association. It was a contribution to show that people in Nyanza were interested. I was transferred to Eldoret in March 1922, and on the fourteenth of March 1922 I heard Nairobi offering a message saying that Thuku had been arrested. I thought I might be arrested too: indeed, before leaving Maseno I dreamt I had been arrested but the Government's plan was to get rid of me by transferring me to Voi."[67]

Hence for the first time the two great cradles of population in Kenya, Nyanza Province and the Central Province, were linked in a community of grievances, in part through the activities of Beauttah. The sudden postwar spurt in politics in both centers may be explained by the growing political consciousness of Africans, the example of European and Indian political activities that had helped to accelerate African efforts at organization, and grievances arising from the one-sided and European-oriented policies of Sir Edward Northey's Administration. But communication difficulties and a different social environment enabled the Government to deal with Nyanza as a separate problem. It was in central Kenya and Nairobi that they found themselves faced with the more difficult and explosive situation.

European "Rebellion"

By mid-1922, following Thuku's arrest and deportation, African politics had received a temporary setback. However, the leaders who remained were soon able to contrast the Government's treatment of the European settler leaders, who were engaged in an all-out campaign to defeat Indian demands for greater participation in the oligarchy. In 1919 the settler members on the Economic Commission had argued that official members of the Legislative Council be allowed to vote according to their own judgment and that a Cabinet selected from the Legislative Council should replace the Executive Council.[68] Denied this, in 1921 the inner caucus of the settlers' political body, the Convention of Associations, established its own embryo cabinet, "the Vigilance committee, to advise the Convention." Its members met in secret. "Their task was a difficult one. They had to map out a plan which would enable a handful of settlers, unrepresented in England and scattered in Kenya, to defeat the avowed intentions of the Government of India and to persuade the Colonial Office to reverse its policy."[69] The Government of India, with a voice through the Secretary of State for India in the British Cabinet, supported the Indian case in Kenya. They had enough worries on their hands with resurgent Indian nationalism at this time without further explosive material from Kenya.

Lord Delamere and a soldier settler from New Zealand, Lt. Col. Griffiths, went to London via South Africa. They did not see General Smuts, then Prime Minister of South Africa, but at the East African dinner held in London on January 27, 1922, Winston Churchill* made three promises concerning the "White Highlands," the control of Indian immigration, and equal rights for all *civilized* men. He stated: "We do not contemplate any settlement or system which will prevent British East Africa—Kenya as it is now known— from becoming a characteristically and distinctively British colony, looking forward in the full fruition of time to responsible self-government."[70] Delamere returned well satisfied.

On August 15, 1922, Sir Edward Northey was abruptly recalled to England, and Sir Robert Coryndon arrived from Uganda to replace him. The "Vigilance committee," anticipating trouble, re-established itself on a crisis footing. On September 5 the substance of a new settlement of the so-called Indian Question, hammered out between the Colonial

---

* Then Secretary of State for the Colonies.

and India Offices, and known as the Wood-Winterton agreement, was cabled out from London. It opposed segregation, rejected restriction of immigration, and turned down Indian representation by mere nomination. European and Indian representatives should be elected from a common roll based on educational and property criteria designed to ensure that 10 per cent of the electorate will be Indian. Four seats should be reserved for them.[71]

This was the sharpest possible slap in the face for the Vigilance committee. In growing resentment they redoubled their preparations for direct action, while continuing negotiations with the new Governor, Sir Robert Coryndon. When pressed for a declaration of where he stood, he reminded the settlers that he had been born in South Africa. But he could only represent his and their opinions in London, he could not ultimately lay down policy. The colonists, disappointed at his temporising, set about plotting a coup d'état. For the latter part of 1922 and the first part of 1923 the atmosphere of the country reeked of open conspiracy. The settlers in their clubs and their hotels and on their polo fields had only one real topic of conversation. It was to be an original kind of rebellion, paralleled only by the situation in Ulster in 1914:—"a rebellion which aimed, not at breaking away from the Empire, but at remaining in it."[72]

Elspeth Huxley, long a protagonist of the settler point of view, has provided an interesting account of its organization.[73] "The Vigilance committee had, for some time past, been quietly organising an emergency military and political machine. The country was divided up into districts and in each area a 'connecting link' was selected to act as liaison with the Vigilance committee. Plans were explained verbally to the 'links' so that few incriminating documents would be found if the leaders were arrested. In each district a census of rifles, ammunition, cars, petrol supplies and horses was taken. Plans of mobilisation were worked out to the last detail." The secret organization included a set of alternative sub-committees, so that if any group of leaders was arrested another batch would be ready to step into their places immediately.

"The colonists, though ludicrously small in numbers, were strong in military experience." Elspeth Huxley described a meeting at the Norfolk Hotel with some former senior officers one Sunday morning soon after the Wood-Winterton proposals became known. After an all-day discussion, "the most senior of the officers brought his fist down on the table and exclaimed: 'I feel we ought to do it!' " A remarkable feature of the proposed rebellion was its deep sentiment of loyalty to the Crown of England. The settlers held that they were only preparing to rebel against meddling Ministers who were betraying the true interests of the King and the British Empire. Their motto was "For King and Kenya"; their rebel councils of war always ended with enthusiastic renderings of the British National anthem.[74] Honestly and earnestly they prepared to defend western civilization in Africa by means which entailed for most of them breaking some of their most cherished principles of conduct.

The Governor was to be kidnapped and isolated in a lonely farm, where the trout-fishing was good, some sixty miles from Nairobi. Powys Cobb, later a member of the Legislative Council for the Rift Valley in Delamere's absence and the original developer of Mau Narok, or Powys Land as it was called, became the Hon. Secretary of the "Vigilance committee." Brigadier General Philip Wheatley, a settler from Nanyuki was regarded as likely to be appointed General Officer Commanding in the event of revolutionary forces having to take the field. Wheatley's cousin, the Earl of Lytton, then an officer in the King's African Rifles in Nairobi, has described a conversation with the rebel army leader: " 'We are not disloyal,' he said. 'We are for King and Kenya, but we are not going to submit to this injustice. We shall take over the Administration here and pull up the railway between here and Mombasa, and make it as difficult as possible to get water on the 300-mile journey to Nairobi. It will take three months before troops from England can reach us, and by then the British public will have chucked out the Government, and others will see that we have justice done to us! I cannot say what we intend to do with you [the King's African Rifles], but we suppose that no one will be so foolish as to use coloured troops against us.' " Lytton's own calculations on the strength of the rebel forces were "that a few settlers with a smoking pistol in one hand and a brandy and ginger ale in the other would not be a formidable military force."[75] But the British Government was taking no chances, and during the height of the crisis three cruisers, H.M.S. *Southampton,* H.M.S. *Cairo,* and H.M.S. *Colombo* called at Zanzibar harbor, less than seven hours steaming from Mombasa.

The missionaries refused to have anything to do with this settler activity and even reprimanded the Convention for setting such a bad example to the Africans. The reluctant rebellion collapsed, without a shot being fired, but not before Delamere, to calm his followers, had claimed from London a victory on the Indian Question. But it was a pyrrhic victory and both sides were to reap some bitter fruits from their appeal to African interests. The 1923 Devonshire White Paper contained as part of its general settlement of the European-Indian conflict, the famous declaration on the paramountcy of African interests, a declaration whose real father was J. H. Oldham, secretary of the International Missionary Council.[76] The statement in theory subtly protected Kenya from being surrendered either to those oriental influences which the Church deplored or to the exclusive feudal and racial oligarchy the Europeans wished to entrench.

"Primarily, Kenya is an African territory, and His Majesty's Government think it necessary definitely to record their considered opinion that the interests of the African natives must be paramount, and that if, and when, those interests and the interests of the immigrant races should conflict the former should prevail. Obviously, the interests of other communities, European, Indian or Arab, must be severally safeguarded. Whatever the circumstances in which members of these communities have entered Kenya, there will be no drastic action or reversal of measures already introduced, such as may have been contemplated in some quarters, the result of which might be to destroy or impair the existing interests of those who have already settled in Kenya. But in the administration of Kenya His Majesty's Government regard themselves as exercising a trust on behalf of the African population, and they are unable to delegate or share this trust, the object of which may be defined as the protection and advancement of the native races."[77]

For twenty years European interests in the colony had in fact been paramount and Northey only did with less finesse what others had been doing before him. But the settler leaders did not rest content with these results; they felt they must publicize them and then ask for more. In 1922, as in 1952, they pushed too hard and at both times helped to bring a new perspective and vision to British policy. To win their struggle with the Indians they brought in the issue of African rights, and this led to the establishment of the moral principle of the paramountcy of African interests from which, however hard they pulled, they could never shake loose any future British Government. By 1926 the Kenya Government was proceeding to define and gazette the African tribal lands, whereas before 1923 both settlers and

Government were tacitly agreed that more land could be excised from them if it were fundamentally in European interests. Indeed, the official 1919 Land Settlement Commission, whose Chairman was the Attorney General (J. W. Barth), had recommended for soldier settlement schemes, in addition to 83,000 acres of Kikuyu land already surveyed, "land in the Kikuyu Reserve between Nairobi and Limuru, extending for a distance of 10 miles on each side of the Uganda Railway."[78]

By itself the Devonshire declaration meant little. It had to be implemented, and just so long as the settler voice was dominant in Kenya Government counsels, this implementation could always be diluted or even wholly thwarted. In 1923 the Africans had no institutions, no organizations by which they could force its implementation either at the local or at the national level. For the next two decades the Europeans from their position of strength sought to increase their influence to the utmost, while the Africans in their weakness struggled to build up the institutions they needed to make their presence felt and gain greater consideration of their interests.

CHAPTER 3

Patterns of Protest
in the Twenties

With the virtual demise of the East African Association, African politics in the interwar years evolved primarily within a rural, tribal setting. The thrust of administrative policy—limiting African participation in representative institutions to local councils, developing the Tribal Reserve system which restricted land rights to local areas, and emphasizing the distinctiveness of each tribal grouping—contributed to the parochial and fragmented character of African politics. In addition, uneven patterns of social change led to a differential African political response to European domination. Not until after the Second World War would African leaders be able to begin the process of building country-wide political organizations capable of challenging the effective authority of the colonial state.

Northey reinforced the framework within which African politics were to take place by further separating European and African administration at the local level. The decision to segregate the country for administrative purposes had been accepted as early as 1913; in 1920 he announced the approval of the Secretary of State for the Colonies to implement this policy. And in 1924 Sir Robert Coryndon initiated a Bill under which Local Native Councils could be established in each district of the Reserves, with limited powers of taxation

and self-government.* Sir Edward Grigg, Coryndon's successor, completed Northey's design. He brought up from South
Africa Mr. Justice Feetham, a former associate, to advise on
the development of local government and introduce a system
of municipal and district councils for the European areas.
The judicial and administrative segregation of the country
into racial compartments was crystallizing; indeed, European
dominance at the local government level in the White
Highlands was retained almost until independence was
achieved in 1963.

The new rural-based politics inevitably reflected differential African experience of the forces of social change within
an economic and social framework dominated by European
settlers, missionaries, and administrators. Thus, while the
Masai and the Kalenjin peoples had yet to enter the modern
political arena, the more intense impact of social change
among the Luo and the Luhya had led to the emergence of
modern politics in Nyanza. Here the protest politics of
1921–22 rapidly gave way to the activities of tribal welfare
associations and attempts to achieve intratribal unity.
Within the numerous tribes making up the Nyanza complex
of peoples, politics remained essentially locally oriented and
fragmented. As land became less plentiful and boundaries
more important, traditional antagonisms and problems between and within the Luo and the Luhya tribes tended to
consume an increasing proportion of their political energies.

Kikuyu politics, closer to the heart of African-European
contentions, were of a different character. Although among
the Kikuyu, too, the traditional social system and geographical factors powerfully obstructed the growth of pan-Kikuyu
unity, social change was rapid and abrupt, and economic
grievances induced a deeper level of anxiety about the future

---

* The Chief Native Commissioner, G. W. Maxwell, appears to have based
the new system of Local Native Councils on similar institutions developed in
Fiji.

development of the country. As the Kikuyu leaders attempted to develop a wider polity, there emerged within the tribe two different approaches to political change and development, the first moderate, the second more militant. In this Chapter we shall look more closely at the geographic and social factors that contributed to these different approaches and at the political organizations associated with each, particularly the Kikuyu Association and the Kikuyu Central Association.

*Political Geography of the Traditional Kikuyu Areas**

Among the rural Kikuyu the impact of land alienation, European settlement, and increased mobility between ur-

---

* The administrative boundaries of the traditional Kikuyu areas have been changed a number of times since the country was divided in 1909 into the 6 provinces of Nyanza, Naivasha, Tanaland, Seyidie, Ukamba, and "Kenia." Not until 1924 were the three "traditional" Kikuyu districts grouped together in one province. Kiambu, called the Kikuyu District until 1924, was then part of Ukamba Province, while Fort Hall and Nyeri, as well as Embu and Meru were in "Kenia" (after 1918 spelled Kenya) Province. In 1920 Nyeri was split into North and South Nyeri Districts, the former being regarded as a settler area.

Kenya Province was renamed Kikuyu Province in 1924, and its boundaries were made to conform to the traditional frontiers of the Kikuyu, Embu, and Meru peoples. By 1929 the administrative boundaries of the Province were extended to embrace North Nyeri District. A more significant alteration was made in 1933 when Ukamba and Kikuyu Provinces were combined to form the Central Province. Nyeri District was known as the South Nyeri District before the Second World War, and included Ndia and Gichugu Divisions, which became at this time part of Embu District. In this book we have referred to the District throughout its history as Nyeri District, as we have with regard to Kiambu (which was first spelled Kyambu). During the Emergency in 1953 the two Kamba districts of Machakos and Kitui were separated from the Central Province and joined with the two Masai districts of Narok and Kajiado to form a new Southern Province. In 1963 the provincial boundaries were radically altered, and six regions conforming to political and ethnic factors were created. The Central Region included only the "traditional" and new Kikuyu areas of the Rift Valley. By 1965 these new regions were redesignated as provinces. See *Kenya: Report of the Regional Boundaries Commission,* Cmnd. 1899 (1962), p. 4, and the maps in the Appendix for a more complete statement of changes in administrative divisions. For a map of the present provinces, see *Kenya: Report of the Constituencies Delimitation Commission,* Cmnd. 1921 (1963), Appendix IV.

ban and traditional societies varied to some degree, according to the district. The densely populated Kiambu District partly surrounded Nairobi, and during the interwar years became a dormitory area. It was here that the policy of land alienation had its deepest political and economic effects. By mid-1904 large numbers of settlers had been allocated land in the area, and by 1905 some 11,000 Kiambu Kikuyu had lost 60,000 acres.[1] Many of these people were taken on as "squatter" laborers on land which they regarded as their own. Some families lost much more than others, the greatest incursions being made in the Limuru, Chura, and Kikuyu areas. White settlement in Kiambu in effect denied the possibility of further expansion to the Kikuyu and closed the southern frontier. The closing of the frontier was to assume greater importance in the 1930s, when population pressures, restricted resources, and limited opportunities led to a growing desperation among the people. In turn, new demands were stimulated, both for what had been taken and what might have been available had the development of Kenya been regarded primarily in the interest of Africans.

In 1950 ex-Senior Chief Koinange, who had retired in 1949, explained something of what land had come to mean to the people of Kiambu: "When someone steals your ox, it is killed and roasted and eaten. One can forget. When someone steals your land, especially if nearby, one can never forget. It is always there, its trees which were dear friends, its little streams. It is a bitter presence."[2] Such feelings could only have been exacerbated when the Europeans who had settled on the land industriously developed some of the finest and most productive coffee estates in the world, and at the same time acted to prevent any parallel planting of coffee by Africans. Owing to the haphazard nature of much of the original settlement in Kiambu, a pattern of interpenetration existed that made it impossible for Europeans to ban

African plantations on the grounds of the climatic unsuitability of the district. The settlers, therefore, alleged their fears of theft and the transmission of disease. As late as July 1950 the Director of Agriculture maintained that a "barrier between African and European coffee growing is advisable for some time to come."[3] This attitude was hardly acceptable to the Kiambu Kikuyu, who realized that the settlers were dependent on the thousands of low paid coffee-pickers supplied during the season by action of the district chiefs. They compared their own relative poverty and minimal social services with the visibly growing affluence of their settler neighbors, epitomized by their private hospital, their segregated golf club, and their luxurious way of life. Not until 1951 were Kiambu Africans allowed to plant coffee.

In no part of the district were these contrasts more marked than in Chura Division in the south, and it was here, as might be expected, that there occurred the most intense and sustained political activity and acculturation. In the years immediately following the collapse of the Thuku movement, the Kikuyu Association consolidated its political hold on this part of the district. Strongly influenced and supported by the directors of both major Protestant missionary societies,[4] the leadership retained their control until the late twenties. However, their pre-eminence declined with the advent of the circumcision crisis in 1929, and during the next decade, owing also to the upsurgence of the land issue, Kiambu politics increasingly became dominated by the Kikuyu Central Association.

The district, strategically located at the crossroads of the country, was also the site of the Alliance High School, the most important secondary boarding school for Africans in Kenya. Here specially selected Africans drawn from every district in Kenya received a vigorous education modeled on

British Public School lines. Many of Kenya's future political leaders first met at Alliance.*

The Kikuyu living in Fort Hall District (now Murang'a) further to the north developed a different relationship with Nairobi. While most Kiambu Kikuyu can commute daily to the capital, the Fort Hall Kikuyu who decides to work there for any length of time has to take up local residence. Though he may retain every possible link with his home, he rapidly becomes more committed to the urban way of life. A large number of African businesses in Nairobi today were started by Fort Hall Kikuyu, and many of the early African political influences in the city originated in that district. Both Mwalimu Hamisi and Abdullah Tairara in Pangani originally came from Fort Hall.

Fort Hall District as a whole occupies a central geographical position in Kikuyuland and holds the traditional spiritual home of the tribe, *Mukurwe wa Gathanga*. In contrast with Kiambu, it is a hard country, a land of wide and deep valleys where communication, and hence development, is difficult. There is a long tradition of emigration to the northern and southern frontier areas. Further expansion to

---

* The importance of the Alliance High School as a common training ground for the African élite is demonstrated in the continuing dominance of political and administrative roles by former Alliance students. For example, 8 of the first 14 African elected members of Parliament in 1958 had attended Alliance, as had 15 of the 33 Africans elected in 1961, and in the first Republican Cabinet, 10 of the 17 Ministers were Alliance alumni. In the civil service, the significance of the school was evident as early as 1960, even before a full-scale program of Africanization had been established; 4 of the 5 African District Officers, 18 of 54 District Assistants, 8 of 11 Education Officers, 12 of 31 assistant Agricultural Officers, 8 of 9 assistant Veterinary Officers, and 12 of 15 Medical Officers had passed through Alliance, many as classmates; in addition, the first Africans to hold the posts of Assistant Secretary, Crown Counsel, and Agricultural Officer were products of Alliance. By 1965, 18 of the 26 Africans in the highest administrative grade (permanent secretary or departmental head) and 4 of Kenya's 6 Ambassadors, had at one time attended the Alliance High School. (From a forthcoming study of Kenya's African Élite by David Koff.)

the west was inhibited by the high bracken-covered ridges of the cold and misty Nyandarua range (named the "Aber-dares" by the Europeans), while to the east lay a dry, inhospitable, and relatively infertile lower zone where a frontier was shared with the Embu. Young people could find few opportunities inside the district, and this was a spur to leave it. Even today most district leaders have only a nominal residence there.

As in Kiambu, the CMS missionaries were initially sympa-thetic and helpful, and for many years politics in Fort Hall revolved about the struggle of the new educated élite against the uneducated chiefs with their conservative attitudes. Land was not such an important issue; European settlers took over only some of the most marginally exploitable land to the east of the district. But there were persistent demands for an elected, educated Paramount Chief. Many of the politically inclined, finding no way to exploit their potential within the district, moved to the capital. In time they fed back a valuable urban experience to the young movement that developed, led by such men as the Rev. Petro Kigondu and John Mbuthia, at the CMS stations at Weithaga and Kahuhia. After the Second World War, when Nairobi's attraction had turned into a bitter frustration, Fort Hall political activity became extremely militant, while during the Emergency her forest forces were known for a tenacious bravery and a degree of open military action without parallel elsewhere in Kikuyuland.

The headquarters of the third Kikuyu District, Nyeri, is situated a hundred miles from Nairobi in the fertile rain-swept cradle between Mt. Kenya and the Aberdares. In general, the gorges are neither as deep nor as wide as those in Fort Hall. Easier lateral communications have given the area a greater compactness and homogeneity. Its first inhabitants represented the northern arm of nineteenth-century Kikuyu expansion. Like the Kikuyu settlers in southern Kiambu, they reflected the vigor and individualism of the frontier. By the time the Europeans arrived they had transformed the virgin forest lands of Tetu and Mathira into richly productive gardens, and had achieved a coexistence with their pastoral Masai neighbors that on occasions extended into sectional political alliances.

The Nyeri Kikuyu clung tenaciously to their independence. In November 1902, Col. Meinertzhagen led a company of the East African Rifles with Masai levies against the people of Tetu, who had killed some Indian traders in the bamboo slopes of the Aberdare mountains. "The Tetu country being occupied and the chief suing for peace [Kakeri, the Principal Chief, was deported to the coast], work was started on the new station in December."[5] In February 1904 action was taken against the Konyu and Iriaini in Mathira Division.[6] For a time all seemed quiet, but trouble soon flared up again in Iriaini, and in June "a column"[7] returned to deal with their "troublesome behaviour." Until August 1906, when the troops were finally withdrawn from the district, the new Administration was barely effective even within a mile or two of the Nyeri Fort.

In 1904 the first European settlers took up land.[8] Most of the early land alienations in Nyeri were in areas where Kikuyu influence was still secondary to that of the Masai, and the feeling on land issues was never as intense as in southern Kiambu. Yet there was a blunt rawness in political reactions in the district that was to be dramatically illustrated both at the time of the controversy over female circumcision and during (and just before) the Emergency.

After the First World War the district became a pivot for several major European farming enterprises. While the Kikuyu from the South Tetu areas of the district generally worked in Nairobi, those in Othaya traveled over the Aberdares to the Kinangop farms, those in Karatina and

Mathira to the Nanyuki European farms, and those in North Tetu to the Kinangop and Mweiga areas. Nyeri people going to Nairobi, particularly before the completion of the rail link between Nairobi and Nyeri Station in 1927, cut themselves off more from their home areas than did people from Fort Hall.

As the country's future became more assured toward the end of the world depression, Nyeri began to rival Kitale as a small corner of England in Africa; the influx of civil servants and Army officers from India after Britain's withdrawal in 1947 further emphasized this character. The town's main hotel, vast and comfortable, includes a Minstrel Gallery, and the churchyard contains Baden-Powell's grave. Water from a carefully built furrow ran down between Kikuyu-owned farms to irrigate the beautiful gardens of the Provincial and District Commissioners and other colonial officials, but any up-furrow Kikuyu farmer who helped himself was liable to punishment. The hub of European life and politics in the town was the Nyeri Club, reconstructed late in the Emergency a few yards from the site of the public gallows erected in 1953 to hang Kikuyu convicted of Emergency capital offences. Touching the boundaries of this quiet and pleasant town and the rich European coffee farms on the ridges nearby was the Kikuyu Reserve, a conveniently close reservoir of coffee-pickers, milkers, and herders. During the Emergency, Nyeri became the center of the massive military and administrative effort against Kikuyu resistance in the forests, the headquarters of two brigades and thousands of Police and Home Guards.

Kiambu, Fort Hall, and Nyeri were the heartland of Kikuyu politics. On the periphery, but increasingly affected by Kikuyu attitudes, were two other districts to the north and east, each inhabited by people closely related to the Kikuyu. Embu District and Meru District, isolated from the

main arteries of communication, were to remain largely on
the fringes of the new political developments. Neither had
urgent land problems; in each there was enough land to
absorb an expanding population. Missionary penetration
came rather later,* as did effective administration. In both
districts it was administrative policy to build up the traditional authority structures, particularly the *Njuri Ncheke* in
Meru. Though the female circumcision controversy in
1929–31 revealed latent dissatisfactions with European rule
in both districts, only improved communications and education could provide the base to support sustained political
action in areas so bereft of the basic requirements of social
mobilization.

Chiefs and Status

The early administrators were faced with a number of basic
problems. They had to have reliable agents, or chiefs, whom
they could trust to carry out their orders even against public
opinion; but they also wished to have some contact with the
existing authority structure within the tribes, of whose
organization they usually had little knowledge. Indeed,
disputes were being settled and criminals punished long
before Europeans ever set foot in East Africa. And throughout the period of colonial administration many matters
continued to be settled outside the new framework the
British slowly introduced.

John Ainsworth, Frederick Jackson, Captain Frederick
Lugard, and other Europeans in the latter part of the
nineteenth century had found in Kenya no centralized or
hierarchical political system such as in southern Uganda.
There were few clear local authorities on whom the new
Administration could lean and whose roles they could de-

---

* The Church Missionary Society opened the Kabare and Kigari Stations in
Embu in 1910; the Catholics opened Kieni, Baricho, and Kianyage in 1923.
D. N. Michuki, *Bururi wa Embu* (Nairobi, 1962), pp. 104, 109.

velop; moreover, most of these traditional leaders had only local influence.

With the beginning of British Administration by the Foreign Office in 1895, headmen or chiefs were appointed as local territorial agents by the Administration. They owed their authority to the Government and few could claim that their role was sanctioned by customary authority. The Native Authority Ordinance of 1902 regularized the appointment of chiefs as the executive head of locations—a territorial and administrative unit of a district. Following the transfer of the control of the Protectorate to the Colonial Office, a phase of more intensive of Administrative control began, and some 100 new chiefs were appointed in 1908.[9]

In some tribes, the tenuous position and credentials of many of the early appointed chiefs and headmen were recognized by administrators. The Hon. K. R. Dundas, writing in 1911 about administration among the Kamba, said "in almost every case it will be found that these petty headmen owed their position solely to their success in imposing upon our ignorance. In the great majority of cases the basis of their authority rested upon some trifling 'chit' given them by some white men far back in the dark ages; such 'chit' might take the following form: 'received from so-and-so one sheep.' Insignificant as these 'chits' might be in themselves, the authority with which they invested the possessor would be enormous."[10]

In Nyanza, governed initially from Uganda, where administrative ideology stressed rule through traditional authorities, there was a recognition of Wanga hegemony over much of the area occupied by the tribes making up the Luhya people. Wanga agents became chiefs of the new administrative locations, but demands in the twenties by the various tribes and clans for their own chiefs brought to an end Wanga paramountcy. Among the Luo people, clan heads were usually appointed chiefs of locations, but since a location often embraced more than one clan, there existed a basis for continued conflict in the selection of chiefs and the boundaries of locations.

In Kikuyu country British rule made far less use of traditional authorities, in part because different sets of elders had different responsibilities. Local leaders were one source of recruitment for headmen or chiefs. Sometimes these local leaders were useful; at other times they inhibited effective administration. In southern Kikuyu country for example, the most prominent leader at the time the Europeans arrived was Waiyaki, to whom the great Kikuyu prophet Mugo Kibiru had handed over his powers and responsibilities in a manner prescribed by tradition. As we have seen, the British mistrusted, arrested, and exiled Waiyaki; they chose as his successor a former hunter[11] of no tribal standing at all. H. R. Tate described him in the Kiambu District early records: "Kinyanjui (whose real name was wa Nugu)[12] lived near Fort Smith and was a youth absolutely without property. He acted as guide and intelligence agent to successive officers at Fort Smith and adopted the more honourable name of wa Gathirimu. He is said to have snared wild animals for food before Govt. took him up. Subsequently he was made Chief of the southern part of Kikuyu having risen to this position by continuous hard work on transport duty, punitive expeditions and general Govt. service. He was rewarded for his services by presents of livestock. He thus became very wealthy."[13] As one who owed so much to the British Administration, he served loyally. Kinyanjui was made Paramount Chief soon after the First World War, although his paramountcy appears to have extended only to Kiambu and meant little in Fort Hall and Nyeri districts. He died on March 1, 1929.

The early Kiambu Political Record Books, with their recurrent theme of chiefs being deposed and locations being added to or subtracted from, bear vivid witness to the experimental character of the first period of British rule in Kikuyuland. As administration developed, these Government-appointed African chiefs were not necessarily considered by the population to be mere administrative puppets. The more exceptional and gifted were able to play both the administrative and representative roles. A man like Kinyanjui, who had emerged from the masses and achieved great personal success in the colonial state, commanded admiration and respect. In years to come, however, the growing legacy of bitterness and conflict made it increasingly difficult for the chief to walk this tightrope between nationalism and collaboration.*

The four great pillars of the Kikuyu Association in southern Kiambu were chiefs Philip James Karanja, Josiah Njonjo, Waruhiu Kungu, and Koinange Mbiu. All four were stalwart supporters of their local mission churches. They were also tenacious defenders of Kikuyu land rights. They dominated affairs in Kiambu for a generation and their descendants were to play an influential role in shaping independent Kenya. District Commissioners almost invariably sought their advice, for few projects could succeed without their sanction. Waruhiu was eventually killed in 1952 by an assassin's bullet; his murder touched off the declaration of an Emergency. Koinange ultimately rejected negotiation and became a moving spirit in the pre-Emergency nationalist build-up. Although acquitted of involvement in Waruhiu's murder, he was detained throughout the Emergency. He eventually came home to die on the farm he loved so much. His funeral was attended by perhaps the

---

* In Nyeri, for example, Chief Muhoya, once a member of the Kikuyu Central Association, became its implacable opponent after 1928. He continued for many years to take an active part in moderate-oriented local Nyeri political associations, and during the Emergency became a prime target for the groups fighting in the forests. But even he became suspect to the Administration. He protested strongly at some of the coercive measures being used and in 1956 he was ordered to remain in Mombasa for several months.

biggest crowd ever assembled in Kenya for such an occasion.

Koinange, first appointed a headman in 1905,[14] had begun the fight for his land before the First World War and continued it up to his death. Gentle and courteous, he was also a great Kikuyu patriot. During the interwar years he was convinced that cooperation with the colonial Administration and British Government was the means to the betterment of his people. In 1937 the District Commissioner, Kiambu, wrote that "without doubt [Koinange] is the outstanding personality in the Kiambu District. His influence is paramount. He has a good brain, is progressive and his opinion is always worth listening to. I cannot stress too strongly the great help he has been to me in helping to implement the terms of the Land Commission Report, in exerting a sober and moderating influence over the Kikuyu in times of potential trouble and generally backing Government in any scheme which he is satisfied is for the good of his tribe. Koinange is in my opinion quite the most remarkable African I have worked with in over 20 years in the Administration."[15] By the 1940s, however, he had been disillusioned by the treatment of his land claims and the uprooting of his coffee trees because coffee planting in Kiambu was confined to the European estates.[16] Increasingly he came to believe that only the strongest political action could save his people.

Moderates and Militants

Throughout Kikuyuland during these years there was widespread support for a policy of reform through cooperation. The basic principle of the developing moderate approach to politics emphasized the responsibility of the colonial government to effect reform. Since the government was all powerful, the best way to advance African interests was to cooperate fully with "constituted authority." By and large, this "moderate" and "constitutional" wing of African politics was composed of the new élite, who as we have seen owed their rise to power to the colonial state, and their privileged positions largely to the colonial Administration. The Kikuyu Association, whose leaders were the chiefs and headmen dominating the affairs of southern Kiambu, remained the strongest organized framework for this viewpoint. The leaders prepared detailed petitions for the procession of investigating commissions that probed Kenya's affairs during the twenties and early thirties. Yet despite the Government's general support, their activities were often treated by it with reserve and even suspicion. In 1923 they petitioned the King on the land problem.[17] Later in the same year they were refused permission "to send a Kikuyu deputation to London in connection with the Indian question and on the subject of native land tenure."[18]

In the Administration's view, the need for an organization like the Kikuyu Association was removed by the establishment of Local Native Councils in 1925 throughout Kikuyuland and elsewhere; these provided for the representation of chiefs and elected members and were specifically designed in part to give the "younger and more educated natives" a "definite avenue along which to develop."[19] For some time the Government seemed to be of two minds as to whether or not to allow the Kikuyu Association to continue. By 1928 its influence was on the wane, and R. W. Hemsted, then Senior Commissioner of the Province, could write that the Association "cannot claim the right to represent the Kikuyu people or even any considerable proportion of them."[20] About 1932 the Association changed its name to the Kikuyu Loyal Patriots to avoid confusion with the Kikuyu Central Association and to indicate its loyalty to the Government.[21]

We have mentioned two approaches to Kikuyu politics. The second not only was concerned with preparing petitions of grievances and presenting them to the Government, but also emphasized alternative ways of achieving reform. These other leaders were ready to adopt a wider range of political action to achieve their objectives. They soon found that the predominantly rural organizations they built to express their beliefs had to be adapted to meet the needs of the tribal situation. As a result, they found it expedient to declare their views over a broad range of issues covering not merely political and economic grievances, but cultural matters as well. They faced a formidable task in overcoming general apathy, the entrenched position of the appointed chiefs, and the opposition of many missionaries and administrators. Finally, this group had to contend with the apparent impossibility of any immediate change in the political structure of the colonial-settler state. The Kikuyu Central Association, which first emerged in 1924 and also called the "Central Kikuyu Association," at this time was the most important embodiment of this second kind of approach.

The two Kikuyu groups differed in their ideology as well as in their strategy. The leaders of the Kikuyu Association in southern Kiambu, and of its Nyeri counterpart, the Progressive Kikuyu Party,[22] and the chiefs in general tended to accept the values of the British administrators and missionaries, and therefore they implicitly condemned those facets of their own culture, such as female circumcision, that conflicted with these values. They adopted many of the élitist, paternalist, and authoritarian attitudes that permeated the ideas and actions of their District Officers and some missionaries. In short, they accepted in practice their subordinate role in the colonial state.

The Kikuyu Central Association (KCA), on the other hand, represented the elements within the tribe that psychologically did not fully accept European dominance. They were from the start incipient nationalists with a more militant approach to political change, and their attitudes reflected more the influence of a leveling egalitarianism, expressed in part through the new western values and in part through the traditional values of the Kikuyu. Membership in the KCA by itself became a personal symbol of dissent. The KCA leaders felt they had a right to reject those aspects of the new cultural patterns which did not suit them. They were groping for an ideology that would bring the Kikuyu into the modern world without abandoning their dignity and independence, both politically and also in social and cultural terms. Apart from directly and persistently questioning the policies and actions, and sometimes the motives, of the District Commissioners, the KCA tried as well to express its nationalism through the Local Native Councils, only to find itself often opposed there, too, by the District Commissioners, who were always *ex officio* chairmen of these bodies.

The KCA leaders were never able to articulate these objectives very precisely, and their opponents found it easier to condemn their administrative weaknesses and frequent failures of organization than to explain their persistent sources of support. Moreover the strain of developing a protest association within a colonial system that precluded any dramatic political successes entailed much frustration; as a result there always existed opportunities for a dissipating politics of personality, faction, and violence.

From the beginning the KCA represented, however inefficiently (and a lack of education was responsible for much of this), a solid nucleus of the tribe in their rejection of the racial and authoritarian scaffolding erected over them. Ultimately, after the Second World War, they were to persuade the majority to their way of thinking. But even at this early period of political development, there were indications that the incipient conflict might end in violence unless the Administration, who always held the final responsibility for government, fashioned ways of channeling this nationalism into constitutional patterns of change and development.

In a very real sense, African politicians spent much of the 1920s and 1930s simply drawing attention to their existence. While the British genuinely acknowledged the importance of African interests, there was little recognition of the people's ability to express these for themselves. Though their interests were indeed at the very center of the Kenya debate as the settlers strove to achieve self-government, it was not a debate that Africans could attend, much less one in which they could participate. Missionary statesmen acted as their spokesmen, and men such as J. H. Oldham in London and Canon G. Burns, Rev. Harry Leakey, and Rev. John Arthur in Nairobi tirelessly rallied the humanitarian stream in British politics in their defense. But whereas these European spokesmen accepted the Kikuyu Association and the Kavirondo Taxpayers Welfare Association, they were hostile to the KCA; and a large part of the growing antagonism on the part of Europeans was due to the KCA's increasing rejection of non-African advocacy and the degree of independence of thought that this rejection showed.

Petition and Protest

Something of the approach and attitudes not only of the two Kikuyu bodies—the Kikuyu Association and the Kikuyu Central Association—but also of the Kavirondo Taxpayers Welfare Association, which claimed to represent the Luhya and Luo peoples in Nyanza, may be illustrated from evidence they gave before two Parliamentary Commissions to East Africa, the 1924 Ormsby-Gore Commission and the 1928 Hilton Young Commission.

The first of these, the East Africa Commission of 1924, came to Kenya as a result of a motion by Sir Sydney Henn in the House of Commons in April 1924. Henn was Chairman of the Joint East Africa Board, an organization of businessmen with interests in East Africa which had considerable influence for two decades on British Government policy in the region. Henn asked for a commission to examine the practical issue of coordinating policy and services in East Africa and to advise on future economic development.[23] W. G. A. Ormsby-Gore,[24] a Conservative M.P. and seconder of the motion, was made chairman. The Commission[25] heralded the re-emergence of the issue of federation, or "closer union" of the East African territories. The idea had its roots in the early days of British administration, and had revived with the postwar entrusting of German East Africa to Britain as a mandated territory.

The Commissioners found little support for federation at this time from any of the racial groups in Kenya, but they also concerned themselves with the general problems of economic development that were central themes of the African memoranda. In a petition to the Commission, the Kikuyu Association maintained that "the matter that above all else continues to give us grave concern is the question of the security of our tenure of our tribal lands, now known as the Kikuyu Reserve. Deprived of our land, we Kikuyu should be dispossessed wanderers, dependent upon the Whiteman for home and livelihood. We feel we have reason, as we hope to show, still to feel insecure about this matter, despite the many appeals we have made and the answers we have received." Recognizing the significant role of the Legislative Council in the Colony's decision-making process, they expressed their gratitude that "provision is now made for the formation of Local Native Councils. . . . At the same time we look forward to the time when we may have direct representation on the Legislative Council."[26]

The Kikuyu Association said that it was confident it expressed the feelings and desires of all the Kikuyu people, not just those in Kiambu, and described its credentials as follows:

The Kikuyu Association was formed, with the consent of the Administration, in the year 1919. Its meetings take the shape of open gatherings of Headmen and people of all classes, land-holders and non-landholders, educated and uneducated, Christian and non-Christian. The Association meets from time to time to discuss matters affecting the interests of the Kikuyu people, and on various occasions has made representations to Government in relation to matters which have arisen. Its ordinary membership embraces the section of the tribe included in the Kyambu Administrative District. The Association welcomes the presence and advice of the Administration officers at its meetings, as also of certain Missionaries of long residence in the Kikuyu country and close acquaintance with its people.[27]

Both this memorandum and that of the Kavirondo Tax-payers Welfare Association (KTWA) showed clear signs of missionary guidance and influence. Indeed, there had already been indications the two groups might be linked. In June 1923 the Kikuyu Association leaders published in the settler newspaper a letter they had written to the Young Kavirondo Association asking their views on the Indian Question.[28] Archdeacon W. E. Owen of the CMS replied on behalf of the KTWA, saying they had already sent a memorandum to the Secretary of State and welcomed further Kikuyu-Kavirondo collaboration, especially on "welfare lines" and the problem of "uplift."[29] Owen, upon returning from England in 1922, had skillfully put into action a plan to convert the Young Kavirondo Association (YKA) into an educational welfare organization for social and economic development, the renamed KTWA. Prior to this the Administration had been thinking seriously of banning the Association.

The KTWA now aimed at the closest cooperation between Government officials, chiefs, and the Christian community. All the chiefs, the District Commissioners, and the Senior Commissioner of the Province were to be ex-officio vice-presidents of the Association. The Governor was even invited to be their patron, but he temporarily declined. By 1924 there were seventy branches in the locations and 5,000 people "in touch with it."[30] Each full member promised "to plant 200 trees and to replace those that die; to build proper latrines and to prevent flies from breeding in them; to kill off rats as far as possible and to report any rats found dead; not to foul the water in rivers, springs or wells; not to aid or abet the marriage of girls under 16 years of age; not to mix cow's urine with milk; to supply beds for my household and to supply bedclothes; to clothe myself properly and to keep my clothes clean; I promise not to get drunk." The 1924 Phelps-Stokes Educational Commission to East Africa considered the KTWA "a great experience in mass education."[31]

What had been a nascent protest movement was thus transformed into a tribal welfare association. Owen sought to extend its coverage over the whole of Nyanza Province, but his efforts were doomed to failure, if only because in the struggle for souls the Catholics would inevitably suspect his religious motives. He never succeeded either in overcoming the innate hostility over boundaries between the Luo and the Luhya, or in offsetting the inherent and persisting parochialism of Nyanza politics, bereft of any deep, unifying grievances to compare in intensity with the growing economic and social problems of the Kikuyu. Almost immediately, a split developed in the Association between its Luo and Luhya members, which was formalized in 1925 by the establishment of separate "Luo" and "Bantu" sections. In October 1924 the formation of the Native Catholic Union (NCU), with the Reverend Father J. A. Wall of the Mill Hill Mission as "Director," challenged the KTWA's authority and representative character still further.[32] The NCU continued until at least the Second World War, with branches in the major Catholic mission stations in the Province.[33]

In the memorandum to the 1924 Commission the KTWA members expressed their loyalty to the King of England, asked for the demarcation of the Reserves, their vestment in a Central African Land Trust Board, and the establishment of local land boards to decide intertribal boundaries. They also pleaded for maximum agricultural development within the Reserves, and made suggestions about road and rail transport, social development, education, and the publication of Colony laws in Swahili. The petition was signed by Benjamin Odour Gumba (Secretary), Jonathan Okwirri (Chairman), and W. E. Owen (President),[34] the first two having been leaders of the YKA when James Beauttah was at Maseno.

At the time of the 1924 Commission the KCA (then called as well, the Central Kikuyu Association) was organized in little more than name, and its petition only just reached the Commissioners in time. Beauttah, who had returned to central Kenya, describes the adventures of this petition to Ormsby-Gore:

> I wrote the petition to the Ormsby-Gore Commission myself.* People wanted me to meet the Commissioners and so I asked for a sick sheet† from the Post Office in Nairobi where I then was, so that I could write and deliver it. But when we went the petition was torn by Petro Kigondu at Fort Hall so we had to type another somehow. Gideon suggested we go to the CMS Mission at Kahuhia to borrow Henry Hooper's‡ machine. So we went and asked him to help us. He gave us a typewriter and I began banging away at it near his kitchen. He was greatly surprised to see the speed with which I typed. I finished it and we all delivered it to the Commissioners at Fort Hall in the name of the Kikuyu Central Association. We were John Mbuthia, James Njoroge, Ishmael Mungai, Henry Kiiru, James Kabarariri, Gideon Mugo, and Lawi Mwangi. Lawi had

---

* There is a reference to this petition, which also asked for the release of Thuku and the other deportees, in a letter written to Sir Edward Grigg on December 31, 1925, by the "Members of the Committee of the Kikuyu Central Association." KNA: PC/CP 8/5/2.

† A government medical form that had to be signed by a departmental head before a civil servant could take sick leave.

‡ Rev. Henry Hooper, CMS missionary at Kahuhia, Fort Hall.

been one of the delegation to Sir Charles Bowring during the Thuku incident.[35]

By 1928, however, the KCA as well as the Kikuyu Association was able to present formal memoranda to the Hilton Young Commission, which had been appointed to investigate means of achieving closer union or federation in Eastern Africa. Both associations rejected any form of federation, as they had in 1924, since they feared it would mean an expansion of settler power. Settler support for some form of closer union was linked to their demand for a majority of European non-official members in the Kenya Legislative Council.

Recognizing the importance of representation on the Legislative Council as an index of a "community's" political significance, the Kikuyu Association and the KCA both held that there should be twelve representatives of African interests. The KCA desired that these should be "native representatives" of the different tribes but including at least three Kikuyu, while the Kikuyu Association sought only four African members, the other eight to be administrators and missionaries. Besides calling the attention of the Commissioners to the need to safeguard African land from further alienation, and requesting the abolition of the *kipande*, both associations also felt that the Government should allocate more of the hut and poll tax funds to the advancement of African education. The KCA memorandum pointed out that Government policy tended to foster separation among the tribes. Holding that the Kikuyu form a "compact solid tribe," they renewed their request for an elected educated Paramount Chief, "who could rule over them in accordance with tribal customs,"[36] and asked for the establishment of a "Central Native Council" for the whole country.

In addition to the formal printed memorandum, a group of KCA leaders also gave oral evidence before the Commission at Nairobi on February 14, 1928.[37] The delegation comprised Joseph Kang'ethe (the President), Jomo (then known as Johnstone) Kenyatta, Henry Mwangi Gichuiri, Parmenas Githendu Mukeri (who went to London with Kenyatta in 1931), Petro Kigondu,* Hezekiah Mundia (leader of the KCA in Nyeri), and Ishmael Mungai (leader of the KCA in Kiambu after the Second World War). Asked what was the central objective of their organization, they immediately referred to land. "We have tried for many years to make the government give us title deeds for our land but we have not got them and we cannot know whether it is our land or whether it is Crown land."[38]

Next they raised the issue of a Paramount Chief for the tribe. The Chairman asked them if there had ever been one, and they replied, "Yes, Wangombe of Nyeri." Behind this agitation was a desire to have their interests more adequately protected and represented in the councils of government. The attraction of a Paramount Chief lay in the difficulty of denying the right of such a man, symbol of a united tribe, to be heard. Beauttah, who had been once again transferred, this time to Uganda, had been highly impressed with the development of the Ganda political system through the Kabaka and Lukiiko, and felt that some chiefs and other Kikuyu leaders might come and see how the Baganda are "running their country."[39]

During the twenties there had been much anxious debate on this issue in Kikuyu country, where the KCA found itself on common ground with the Kikuyu Association. This helps to explain the recurring emphasis on Wangombe,[40] who had died in 1902. Fifty years later his son, Senior Chief Nderi of Nyeri, was killed just after the Emergency was declared, when he tried to break up a mass-oathing ceremony on the banks of the Gura River in his location. There had been no

---

* He was later detained and present at the detention camp at Hola where on March 3, 1959, eleven detainees died as a result of a "rehabilitation" operation. See below, Chapter 9.

obvious successor to Wangombe, and the KCA and the Kikuyu Association differed fundamentally on the method of selecting one. The KCA demanded an *elected* Paramount Chief, while the Kikuyu Association sought an enlargement of the powers of Kinyanjui, their patron, and, on his death, the appointment of an existing chief to succeed him. Had this procedure been accepted, Koinange would probably have been the most obvious choice.

The KTWA also prepared a memorandum for the Hilton Young Commission. They "rejoiced" that the British Government wished "to discover how the Dual Policy can be applied Politically as well as Economically," but like the Kikuyu leaders they rejected federation as a "disaster" if it meant that "Africans would have no representation on a Federal Council, if European commercial or planting interests should be paramount." Claiming that the Local Native Councils were "a first step in the training of our people in civilized methods of Local Government," they asked that Provincial Councils and "a Central Consultative Council (African) for the whole of the Colony" should be established. Their demands were in general pitched in a lower key than those of the KCA. They supported a communal franchise, absolutely opposed "a settler majority in the Legislative Council over all other parties," and asked for nine representatives of African interests in the Legislative Council, to comprise one senior official, one senior missionary, and "one English-speaking African" from each of the three "great areas"—the Coast, the Highlands, and the Lake. They also asked that there should be three representatives of African interests on the Executive Council, a senior official, a missionary, and an African. They concluded with an appeal for national political organization. "That no machinery has yet been devised which would enable Africans of Kenya from the Coast to the Great Lake, to meet by their representatives, and interpret African opinion and sentiment to such a body

as your Commission, seems to us one of the strongest
arguments for the application of the Dual Policy to the
Political Sphere. No rulers can be as just as they might be
who do not consult those over whom they rule."[41]

The Nyanza Administration had become increasingly
disillusioned with Owen and the KTWA; the Chief Native
Commissioner had written in 1927 that "its activities appear
to be chiefly political and of a nature likely to damage the
reputation of the Association, for natives use the meetings
for airing grievances, often imaginary, instead of going to
their Administrative Officers. This is especially unfortunate
in an Association which is directly connected with a missionary society." The Local Native Council was the "proper
place" where the "proper representatives" should discuss
political questions.[42] Owen was further attacked on the
grounds that while he had been on leave in England
mid-1920s, the KTWA had nearly become defunct, and a
proposal had been put forward to absorb their funds in the
Local Native Council budget. The KTWA "only functions
when driven by the Ven'ble Archdeacon Owen, and most of
the suggestions, grievances alleged or otherwise emanate
from that gentleman."[43]

Early Kikuyu Nationalism and the KCA

The trauma and violence of the Thuku affair temporarily
discouraged political activity in Nairobi, though political
discussions had continued in somewhat desultory fashion,
mainly among African leaders from Fort Hall. An important
center for small meetings was the first African-owned hotel in
River Road, started by James Njoroge, Josiah Macharia
Gichigo, and Job Muchuchu. It was not until mid-1924, however, that the Kikuyu Central Association was formed, at a
meeting in James Njoroge's house in Pumwani. As James
Beauttah recalls, "by this time everyone had deserted us,
even our brothers of Kiambu and Nyeri. We members from

Murang'a [Fort Hall] kept the banner flying. We created that name of KCA which meant the Central District of Murang'a and we made its house at Kihumbu in Kahuhia where members used to meet and KCA was accepted by the Government."[44] It was said that Joseph Kang'ethe was chosen as first president because of his imposing presence and chest full of war medals, which would be bound to impress the Ormsby-Gore Commission. Harry Thuku, however, even in his absence, was looked upon as the real father of the new association. Its members wrote several letters to him in restriction telling him of their activities.

In 1925 two KCA founder-members, Joseph Kang'ethe and John Mbuthia, were elected to the first Fort Hall Local Native Council. Both of them were impressed with the ceremonial involved, especially the oath of allegiance to the Crown, and it was shortly after this, in 1926, that a simple oath of loyalty to the Kikuyu people was first introduced within the KCA. While a Bible was held up in the left hand, a handful of earth in the right was pressed to the navel, and the member swore to serve his people faithfully and to look after their money should he be entrusted with it.[45] Arthur Champion, a pioneer administrator, commenting on the development of the KCA in Nyeri, noted that "it is curious but an undoubted fact that the institution of District Councils and the elective principle gave their Society (KCA) considerable encouragement."[46]

When the new Governor, Sir Edward Grigg, visited Fort Hall at the end of 1925, the KCA presented him with a list of their grievances. They protested against the 1915 Crown Lands Ordinance and asked for the release of Harry Thuku, George Mugekenyi, and Daudi Waiganjo Ndotono, describing them as "absolutely innocent and constitutional patriots."[47] Permission was sought to hold meetings as in Nyanza without interference by the "Resident Commissioner or any other officer. . . . The Association is also desirous to see that Your Excellency appoints one paramount learned chief for our Kikuyu country with judicial powers for trying our cases, one who should be well educated and to be elected by majority of our own peoples."[48]

Compulsory rebuilding of unsanitary huts to prevent plague, hospital training facilities, a high school, a school for girls, permission to plant coffee and cotton, and the translation of the Colony's laws into Kikuyu were also requested. Finally the Association "beg to inform Your Excellency that we bought a casket for Your Excellency on the day of your arrival in Kenya and were forbidden by our Chief Native Commissioner not to present it to your Excellency in the Court compound, but to keep the same till Your Excellency's arrival at Fort Hall and that it is waiting Your Excellency's arrival together with the address."[49] The "casket" lay undelivered for four years; the Administration had no wish to encourage the "pretentions" of the KCA, nor indeed did the Governor. At a general *baraza* in Nyeri on January 4, 1927, he told Hezekiah Mundia, the local KCA leader, that the question of Harry Thuku's return home was "not one with which young men of the tribe should concern themselves."[50]

Yet despite the Administration's general disapproval of the KCA, the District Commissioner of Fort Hall could write in 1927 that "there is little doubt that the Association, however irresponsible a body it may be, and however unmethodical its methods, nevertheless includes in its ranks some of the most progressive and educated young men in the District. Its cooperation with Government is valuable enough to be encouraged by conciliation rather than alienated by antagonism and some progress has been made in this regard. One of its leaders, John Mbuthia, was recently chosen as sub-headman and is doing loyal and useful work."[51] Again in 1928 the Fort Hall District Commissioner wrote: "It can no longer be said that the Kikuyu Central Association is unrepresentative of the Kikuyu people. It includes in its ranks a vast proportion of the more enlightened and progressive youth, and wields an increasing influence on the counsel of the elders."[52] The term "youth" was somewhat misleading, members had to be married and heads of households.

The KCA members soon found that a Nairobi office was essential, and in effect they moved the headquarters there in 1927, although their notepaper continued to describe Fort Hall as the "Head Office" and Nairobi as the "Correspondence Office." "We had to bring the main office to Nairobi because that is where the Chief Native Commissioner was and where we could keep in touch with newspapers and events."[53] This had the immediate effect of bringing the young Association into close contact again with Kiambu politicians, although Kiambu for all its surface calm had not been wholly quiescent since the days of the East African Association. Marius Ng'ang'a Karatu notes that "at Limuru we had a secret group formed in 1926 called Kimuri—The Torch—to fight for land and collect money for political purposes. . . . I was its secretary and Bernedette Kamuhea its chairman."[54] However, the move to Nairobi enabled the KCA to act as an effective channel for Kiambu as well as Fort Hall grievances.

Jomo Kenyatta, after completing his early education at the Church of Scotland Mission headquarters near Nairobi, and after a short period as an interpreter in the Supreme court had been working for some time in the Water Department of the Nairobi Town Council, measuring pipelines, reading meters, and supervising employees.[55] Like Beauttah, he was not able to engage openly in politics without giving up his job. According to Kang'ethe, the KCA was having such great difficulties with problems of English translation that he was sent to persuade Kenyatta to join them. Kang'ethe states that in 1927 at a full meeting at Kahuhia it was decided to ask him to become General Secretary,[56] and he took up the post early in 1928.

Kenyatta's appointment, and the revival of the old links between the Kiambu and Fort Hall politicians, immediately gave a new dimension to the organization. From this time onward it was only called the Kikuyu Central Association and was no longer as well referred to as the Central Kikuyu Association. As the KCA's General Secretary, Kenyatta concentrated on fostering pan-Kikuyu political consciousness and the development of a broad base of political support, traveling to meetings throughout Kikuyuland, the largest conceivable political unit at this period.

As part of a growing emphasis on cultural nationalism, the KCA decided in 1928 to start a monthly journal, published in the Kikuyu language and called *Muigwithania* ("He who brings together" or "The reconciler"). Kenyatta was the first editor, and he continued to direct this lively publication for its first nine issues; he was succeeded in March 1929 by Henry Mwangi Gichuiri, also to be Acting Secretary of the KCA during Kenyatta's first absence in England. Gichuiri carried on for three months until June 1929, when Crispin I. K. Keiru took over, to be succeeded in 1931 by Josphat M. Kamau.

The contents were an interesting mixture of advice, proverbs, and news items, including long accounts of various meetings. One early issue[57] (September 1928) started with an article by Gidion Kagika on the word "association," in which he says to his readers, "As from now I request you not to say that you do not belong to that Association. You are members of the Association since you are all *Kikuyu Karing'a* (real Kikuyu)." This is followed by a long article by Kenyatta on the importance of making land productive now that the boundaries of the African Reserves have been gazetted. He called on his readers to plant African fruit trees as well as European ones, to follow Agricultural Department instructions, to keep their houses clean, to try to attend higher schools, "say in Europe." In another piece Kenyatta advised Christians who were members of the Association "to try and follow Church rules . . . since our Association is not here to show people that churches are useless or divide their followers." Another article described "how the British prepared an Empire. The first thing is that all people are governed justly, big or small—equally. The second thing is that nobody is regarded as a slave, everyone is free to do what he or she likes without being hindered."

There was also a long account of a meeting held on September 12 with the P. C., Nyeri, the D. C., Kiambu, and the A. D. C., Dagoretti, together with chiefs Kinyanjui, Koinange, Josiah Njonjo, Philip James Karanja, Waruhiu, and Waweru, and the KCA officials, Kang'ethe and Kenyatta, with each group appealing for cooperation. Another article had a description of the Prince of Wales' visit and itinerary and an extract from the Government Swahili newspaper, *Habari,* on how to bring up children.

The monthly KCA meeting was also described; it had been held at Kahuhia on August 25, and resolutions were passed and forwarded to the District Commissioner. These included inquiries about the KCA casket for Sir Edward Grigg, a gift to be presented to the Prince of Wales, a road that had been closed, and unnecessary arrests in Thika. Parmenas Mukeri contributed a letter appealing to all Kikuyu to become educated. Kenyatta described a lengthy tour he had made in August of Fort Hall, Nyeri, Nanyuki, and Meru, where there was now a flourishing branch of the Association under Meru leadership. He had talked to many chiefs on the way and he concluded by calling on the people to obey the District Commissioners and chiefs.

Muigwithania seems to have been the first newspaper produced by Kenya Africans, and its monthly appearance was eagerly awaited throughout Kikuyu country. It did much to help unite the attitude of progressive elements in the tribe while at the same time its riddles, proverbs, and stories encouraged its readers to think of themselves still as Kikuyu. The impression left from reading copies today is of its responsibility and dedication and its determination to encourage and educate its readers.[58] There is a strong reflection in its pages of an attempt to restore pride in being a Kikuyu and an African.*

Kenyatta in London

By 1928 the KCA leaders had decided to send a representative to London to present their grievances directly to the British Government. James Beauttah, with his command of English, was an obvious candidate, but he felt unable to go because of his responsibilities to his growing family. Instead, he wrote to Kang'ethe suggesting the names of five other possible English-speaking Kikuyu candidates: Paul Kahuhia, Jomo (then Johnstone) Kenyatta, Ishmael Thongo, Parmenas Mukeri, and Thomas Bell Mwathi (a Dorobo). The KCA committee decided that Kenyatta should go, and the KCA members held a farewell ceremony for him at the Pumwani CMS church in December 1928, at which Petro Kigondu made him swear before a packed congregation to abide by his people and their land.

On February 4, 1929, Kenyatta had an interview with the Acting Governor concerning his forthcoming trip. A. de V. Wade, the Acting Chief Native Commissioner, and Canon Leakey were also present. Kenyatta said that the KCA membership was now 3,800. The Governor argued, as others had before about similar associations, that "it was quite clear from these admissions that Johnsone Kinyatta [sic] could only claim to represent the 3,800 members of his association as opposed to the Kikuyu tribe which numbered approximately 250,000 males." He felt that it was therefore unlikely

---

* Publication of the newspaper lapsed in the early thirties, but it was revived in June 1935 and continued to appear intermittently up till the outbreak of the Second World War.

that Kenyatta would be granted an interview by the Secretary of State in England. While not wishing to prevent Kenyatta going there, he urged him to reconsider "if it were worthwhile wasting money on an expedition that seemed likely to be fruitless." Kenyatta replied that his mind was fully made up and that he proposed to sail on February 17 in a French boat.[59]

Accompanied by Isher Dass,* Kenyatta traveled to England to represent the problems of the Kikuyu. He never had his interview with the Secretary of State, though he did meet the Under-Secretary, Dr. Drummond Shiels, to whom he presented a special petition calling for the release of "our popular and respected Harry Thuku," chairman of the KCA.

In another petition, in addition to a detailed list of grievances arising from the land and labor issues, requests were made for educational advancement, and also for direct African representation on the Legislative Council. Altering the number of African members they had sought in their petition to the Hilton Young Commission, the KCA now requested that there should be three elected Africans and two Europeans to represent their interests, and "that ultimately the number of African representatives in the Legislative Council should predominate."[60] African political advance should also take place in the representation of their interests on the new Nairobi Municipal Council.

In England Kenyatta was helped by the Rev. C. F. Andrews, who had visited Kenya in 1921–22 at the height of the Indian controversy, and William McGregor Ross, for-

---

* Isher Dass was born on August 20, 1901 at Multan, India. In 1923 he went to England for further study. He came to Kenya in December 1927 as clerk to A. M. Jeevanjee and was General Secretary of the East African Indian National Congress for four years. In 1934 he was elected a member of the Legislative Council and was re-elected in 1938. He supported the KCA on many occasions, both in Kenya and in England, and was especially prominent during the Kamba de-stocking crisis in 1938 (see below, pp. 164–177). He was shot dead in 1942 while Director of Indian Manpower.

merly Director of Public Works and an outspoken critic of
European settlement in Kenya. The League against Imperialism, an organization formed in 1927 and with which Isher
Dass had connections, gave him some financial aid and also
arranged for him to address meetings. He traveled to Moscow
in August 1929 and returned in October; soon thereafter he
attended the International Negro Workers Conference in
Hamburg, later meeting in Berlin some Communist leaders.[61]
Returning to Britain, Kenyatta continued to seek ways to
represent the views of the KCA.

By October 1930 Kenyatta had returned to Kenya as a
more experienced leader. For some months he had had
financial difficulties, since the KCA had only been able to
send him money in dribbles. A special edition of *Muigwithania* had been issued in July to help raise money to facilitate
his return.[62] He was welcomed back at Mombasa by Beauttah and the members of his Kikuyu *Kiama gia Kunyamara*
(Society for the Destitute).[63] At this time there was no
formal branch of the KCA in Mombasa; Beauttah, still a
civil servant and therefore not permitted to take part in
politics, had instead founded this new Kikuyu social association. He described it as an "indirect" branch of KCA, and
became its chairman.

Kenyatta returned to find a major crisis among his people.

CHAPTER 4

Cultural Nationalism

The crisis over the circumcision of women that gripped Kikuyuland from 1928 to 1931 brought about a bitter and enduring division between the forces of Kikuyu nationalism and the Protestant missions. The roots of the conflict are located in the Kikuyu challenge to the total cultural transformation demanded of them by the missionary church. The missions excluded any possibility of selective change, by which the Kikuyu might absorb some elements of Western culture while rejecting others as unacceptable to their values or social institutions. Rather, Western culture and Christianity were identified together as an integral corpus of belief and practice; the rejection of one element in the whole was defined as a total rejection and hence as "cultural atavism." As we shall see, this theme, strongly developed in the female circumcision controversy, was to return even more clearly in the interpretation of "Mau Mau" and in the philosophy of "rehabilitation" during the Emergency.

For the Kikuyu, however, the problem was one of finding an independent social and religious framework that did not conflict with the colonial state. Given the entrenched belief at this time in the legitimacy of European administration, settlement, and missionary activity, complete autonomy even within the colonial state was unachievable; yet both the conflict that arose over female circumcision and its resolution weakened the authority of an important element in the colonial structure. The conflict precipitated the independent school movements and was among the inspirations for Jomo Kenyatta's *Facing Mount Kenya,* itself a text in cultural nationalism. In addition, and in part because it involved the missions and the Government, the conflict also hardened the differences between the new African élite associated with these institutions and the more militant adherents of the KCA.

The Missions and Female Circumcision

Four Protestant societies—one from the United States and three from Britain—originally divided the Kikuyu missionary field. Each brought different Christian traditions and beliefs, different levels of commitment, different techniques of proselytization, and different attitudes to education. Moreover, each found itself dealing with geographical areas that varied considerably in their accessibility to the new forces of social change whose principal agents the missionaries had rapidly become. It is scarcely surprising that strong differences of opinion should emerge.

Apart from Kiambu, the first Kikuyu district to be reached, which was especially attractive because of its proximity to Nairobi and the center of government, Kikuyuland was divided up into "spheres of influence" among the societies "in order to reach the largest number of people; and to avoid overlapping and reduplication of work."[1] The Church Missionary Society (CMS) of the Church of England, long linked with the British Establishment and its traditions of compromise and gradualism, took over Fort Hall District north of the Maragua River and also spread across the Tana River into Embu. Fort Hall District south of the Maragua River was allocated to the Africa Inland Mission (AIM), interdenominational but primarily Baptist and Adventist, who under American leadership operated from their station at Githumu.* The CMS's policy was to open a considerable number of small stations in order to maintain close personal touch with a large number of people. In northern Fort Hall they established Weithaga in 1903, Kahuhia in 1906, and Kathekeini in 1913. In Embu District, Kabare and Embu were started in 1910 and Mukira in 1911.

The Church of Scotland (CSM), puritan and rigid in attitude and belief, were allocated Nyeri, the district on the northern Kikuyu frontier, and established a mission station there at Tumutumu in 1909, also reviving an abandoned CMS outpost at Mahiga. Their method was to establish large comprehensive mission stations in the manner of those set up in South Africa. Each of their establishments was planned to include a hospital and schools as well as the mission buildings. When the Chuka-Mwimbi salient, which had been closed by the Administration to all but its own officials, was opened up after the First World War, it was allotted to the CSM, who opened another station at Chogoria in 1922 between the Embu and the Meru peoples. The main Meru mission, among a large tribe occupying a huge area to the northeast of Mt. Kenya, was undertaken by the United Methodist Mission (UMM), doctrinally less rigid than the CSM and more in sympathy with the approach of the CMS, with whom they had been closely associated in Mombasa since Krapf first brought Christianity to the coast in 1844. All the mission stations had minor medical facilities, but only the Church of Scotland, which had in Kenya a higher proportion of medical missionaries than the other societies, established major mission hospitals in Kikuyuland, at Tumutumu, Kikuyu, and Chogoria.

Kiambu, the prize, was carved up among three of the

---

* The AIM had tried two other sites nearby, at Kinyona and Matara, before finally settling on Githumu.

societies. Southern Kiambu was informally divided by representatives of the first two groups to arrive, the CMS (Canon
Harry Leakey at Kabete) and the CSM (Dr. Ruffelle Scott
at Kikuyu). Northern Kiambu was allocated to the AIM. In
1902 a fundamentalist group within the AIM, whose missionaries came from New England, formed itself into the Gospel
Missionary Society (GMS). The GMS soon founded stations
at Kambui (1902)[2] in Kiambu and at Kihumbuini in
southern Fort Hall. It continued, however, to retain close
connections with the AIM.

Missionary development in Kikuyuland thus presented a
confusing and uneven pattern. In the early days this mat-
tered little. Each missionary within his "sphere" was confident of his own objectives. The strong-willed early pioneers,
men such as Rev. Harry Leakey, Rev. A. W. McGregor, and
Rev. H. D. Hooper of the CMS, Dr. Ruffelle Scott, A. R.
Barlow, and Rev. J. W. Arthur of the CSM, W. P. Knapp
and Dr. J. E. Henderson of the GMS and C. E. Hurlburt and
L. H. Downing of the AIM, built up their stations with their
own hands and very little money. They made their converts as
much by the strength of their personalities as by the power
of their faith. In the first few years, African response to the
missionary effort was limited; indeed it took the CSM six
years to make its first convert.[3] Allegiances remained very local
and personal. But even before the First World War it was
apparent that religion could not so easily be confined within
geographical "spheres of influence." There was the problem
of the towns: the CMS had a virtual monopoly there, but
adherents of other missions from the rural areas were con-
verging in growing numbers; some were converted to the
Church of England, posing a further problem when they
returned to their homes eager to establish CMS churches.
There were difficulties of church discipline—a teacher dismissed by one mission for disobeying church laws would
apply for a post with another mission whose rules were less

strict. Increasingly, the need grew for some coordinating body.

Bishop Willis of Uganda initiated preliminary discussions as early as 1907, which culminated in a conference at Kikuyu in June 1913.[4] Willis had long seen the advantages of coordination; in his own diocese the AIM worked in the West Nile directly under his control. He naturally wished to extend the system to Nyanza, which was then still in the Uganda Diocese, though part of the East Africa Protectorate.

In attempting to achieve unity, the Kenya missionary societies suddenly found themselves in the vanguard of a worldwide Christian movement, and "Kikuyu" overnight became an international Christian symbol for Church unity. Significantly, the members of the conference of 1913 did not discuss uniting the separate European and African churches that were evolving in Kenya. In their debates, at which no Africans were present, they were merely considering a loose confederation of the missionary societies dealing with Africans or, as the highest ideal, a possible "United Native Church." Not until after the Second World War were there any moves to unite the separate European and African churches that had grown up in the country.

Even this small degree of unity involved doctrinal concessions by the Anglicans to the Presbyterians and Methodists that aroused bitter opposition from the "High Church" Anglo-Catholics. Representing their views, Frank Weston, Bishop of Zanzibar, formally charged the Bishops of Uganda and Mombasa before the Archbishop of Canterbury "with propagating heresy and committing schism."[5] The outbreak of war gave time for such passions to cool. The drive for unity was given extra impetus in an emotional situation by the need for common forms of worship in the Mission Volunteer Carrier Corps. In July 1918, shortly after the Corps' disbandment, over a hundred delegates again assembled at Kikuyu for a second conference. This time the leaders of four societies (AIM, CMS, CSM, UMM) formally established the Alliance of Protestant Missions, with a senior executive body called the Representative Council. A leading figure in these negotiations, and first secretary of the Alliance, was the Rev. Dr. Arthur of CSM, Kikuyu. In the future he was to set much store by the preservation of this new body, through which his own station at Kikuyu had won international fame.

The Alliance soon faced a severe test. Ever since the Bishop of Zanzibar's charge (which had led to a major controversy in 1914), the AIM had suspected that the Anglican CMS, strongly divided within itself between those who took an uncompromisingly fundamentalist view of the Bible and those who accepted the results of Biblical scholarship, would sabotage the Alliance by introducing to Kenya missionaries who were not in sympathy with the fundamentalist views. In September 1922, on a threat of breaking up the organization, they forced through a resolution that henceforth all member societies of the Alliance would send out as missionaries to Kenya only those "who hold the conservative Evangelical position."[6] Thus they hoped that the CMS stations would be manned by men sympathetic to the uncompromisingly strict attitude they maintained on matters of church discipline and to the developing campaign against various "pagan" customs. This policy meant that most of the CMS missionaries found the company and theology of the AIM missionaries far more congenial than that of the more High Church group within their own Missionary Society.

The Alliance, as a representative missionary body, also saw itself playing an important role as a political pressure group representing the "best" interests of Africans. In defending and protecting these interests, Dr. J. W. Arthur projected himself forcefully into two intense controversies of the early postwar period. In the 1919–20 crisis on "forced" labor, Arthur joined with the East African Anglican bishops in a public memorandum strongly criticizing the Northey circular, on the grounds that the "encouragement" envisaged would really be compulsion, for the benefit of the settlers. In the exigencies of the Kenya situation compulsory labor was not in itself wrong; it would be acceptable if properly organized and used for legitimate national purposes. The Representative Council expressed approval of this principle of legalized compulsory labor for Africans.[7] Though the memorandum was to play a significant part in amending the manifest intent of the Northey circular, the home authorities of the Church of Scotland refused to sanction any legalized compulsion and told their Kenya representatives to withdraw support for the statement.

In 1923, the same year the colonial government refused permission to send a Kikuyu deputation to London in connection with land tenure and the Indian question, Arthur was appointed, with the approval of the Alliance, to go to London with the Governor, Sir Robert Coryndon, to advise on the African aspects of the European-Indian controversy. The assumption that European missionaries could adequately articulate *African* interests was questioned by Archdeacon Owen, who held that "any missionary chosen represents European Missionary opinion, and has no mandate whatever from the Natives."[8] Arthur, on the other hand, stood for the view of the Alliance that "the responsibility for education and development of the backward native races in East Africa must be borne by Europeans alone, with the background of Christian civilisation, and not shared with Asians."[9]

By the mid-twenties, Arthur was the dominant missionary figure in Kikuyu country. A likeable and affectionate man, with a great fondness for rugby football and mountaineering, he was an imperious and autocratic leader of his mission. His strong personality thrived on the opposition he invariably stirred up. Coming to East Africa in December

1906, at a time when the position and values of the European were unquestioned, he lived through a period of intense social change. He had rapidly become the foremost missionary adviser to the Government, and had already served on several advisory committees, including the important Native Labour Commission in 1912–13 and the Education Commission in 1919.

As a medical man he had early reacted strongly against the manner in which the Kikuyu women carried out the "entirely unnecessary" operation of female circumcision.[10] Yet in Kikuyu culture only a circumcized girl could be considered fully a woman. It was widely believed that uncircumcized girls would not physically be able to bear children. Not to be circumcized was to be debarred from developing the personality and attributes of womanhood and to be condemned to remain psychologically a little girl (*kirigo*) forever. In Kikuyu eyes an uncircumcized girl of marriageable age was an object of derision, indeed almost of disgust. Far from being unnecessary, the operation symbolized the most important moment in a girl's life, and her bearing during the pain that accompanied it was a matter of great pride or shame to her family.

Until 1923 there had been little overt African opposition to the teaching of the missionary churches that female circumcision, non-burial of the dead, and *ngomas* (dances) were indecent and barbaric practices. The CSM had first started systematic instruction against these practices in 1906, and by the 1920s it could look back on considerable success. Specifically, motions had been passed by the African elders of the CMS, the CSM, the AIM, and the GMS condemning the practice of female circumcision by Christian Kikuyu. The authority of the missionary churches seemed unimpeachable as they continued to expand their influence.

From 1923 onward, however, the Kikuyu increasingly began to question missionary motives and objectives, no longer taking this authority for granted. The need to abandon Kikuyu customs, in particular the circumcision of girls, in order to become or remain a true Christian, began to be challenged. The KCA stood as a champion of Kikuyu cultural nationalism; its members did not seek the rejection of Christianity, but the preservation of selected aspects of Kikuyu culture. Indeed, it seemed to them that it was not Christianity which was in danger, but Kikuyu culture, as the processes of modernization deepened and spread across their country. There was a growing demand by the Kikuyu for a more selective approach to social change. But such a demand implied a direct challenge to the cultural assumptions of the colonial state, which had always proclaimed as its mission the imposition of western Christian civilization in Kenya.

From the earliest days, the Protestant missions had made constant appeals for Government support and encouragement in stamping out the custom of female circumcision. The response, while not wholly negative, was tempered. In September 1925 a confidential Circular of the Native Affairs Department, though pointing out that premature action might unite "native authorities against the Government in defence of old customs," nonetheless held that the time was ripe for a declaration of policy to "the effect that Government unhesitatingly and emphatically condemns the practice. District Officers, in districts in which it is prevalent in its more aggravated form, will explain its dangers to Local Native Councils, and endeavour to secure their opposition to it. In all districts attempts by individual natives to put down the practice will be supported in so far as the law allows."[11] Model by-laws regulating the custom were passed in many Local Native Councils almost immediately after their establishment in 1925.[12] These made it an offense to remove more than the clitoris and allowed the operation to be performed only by skilled operators licensed by the Councils. In 1926 the East African Governors decided at their first joint conference that the "practice of female circumcision, which was of very ancient origin, should not be interfered with, but that the respective Governments concerned should endeavour to persuade such tribes as practised the more brutal forms of it to return to the more ancient and less brutal form."[13]

The crisis came to a head in Nyeri District in 1928. The CSM and the KCA had a history of conflict in that district; in 1925 the use of land by the mission outschools for agricultural demonstration plots was challenged by the KCA. But the circumcision controversy introduced a new level of bitterness into the relationship of the missions with the Association. A leader of the opposition was Dr. Philp of the Tumutumu Mission; he describes how in 1915, "owing to great pressure from two lady members of his staff," he reluctantly allowed three of the girls being taught at the station to have the operation carried out at the mission by a Kikuyu practitioner. "But the cruelty shown by the old woman was so great that he vowed he *never* would allow anything of the kind again."[14] In 1924, Philp published a pamphlet condemning the custom, and also wrote articles on its medical consequences, especially in maternity cases.[15]

In March 1928, the question was brought up at a *baraza* called by the Government at Nyeri to discuss various problems affecting the tribe. The meeting was attended by both Paramount Chief Kinyanjui and Jomo Kenyatta, in his new position as General Secretary of the KCA. The KCA representatives announced their intention of contesting the forthcoming Local Native Council election on a platform of preserving tribal customs, including the circumcision of girls. This public declaration brought the KCA into open conflict with the CSM in Nyeri and later throughout the province.

Following this *baraza,* Church of Scotland missionaries

held a meeting in April 1928, in Nyeri, with their church elders, who included Willy Jimmy Wambugu Maina from Mahiga (later to become the Nyeri District Chairman of the Nyeri Kenya Independent School Association). They announced a campaign against female circumcision in the district, whose Local Native Council, alone among those in Kikuyu country, had refused to pass the by-law regulating the custom. Seven of the church elders[16] disagreed with any attempt to force the issue at that time and shortly afterward left the church.

The Nyeri CSM, from its headquarters at Tumutumu, now demanded assurances from those KCA leaders and members who were also baptized members of the Tumutumu church that they would continue loyally to accept all the laws of the church, including the one prohibiting female circumcision.[17] In default they would be automatically suspended. The initial response was wholesale defection, but the church retrieved the situation somewhat, and at the end of a two-year period of grace only 200 names (or 7 per cent of the total Tumutumu baptismal roll as it stood in December 1930) had been removed from the Communion roll.

In opposition to the KCA, the CSM at Tumutumu sponsored a political association of "really educated, sane men."[18] Called the Progressive Kikuyu Party (PKP), it stood for the complete abolition of the custom, and it intended to put up candidates to fight the Local Native Council election on this platform. It also affirmed "its desire for active cooperation with men of *all races* (white, brown, black) in progress for the Kikuyu country in particular, and for Kenya Colony."[19]

Arthur quotes with approval a Government condemnation of the KCA for not being content with representation in the Local Native Councils and preferring "less constitutional methods, such as mass meetings, letters to the Press and direct petitions to Government." He contrasts such activities with the moderate behavior of Tumutumu's Progressive Kikuyu Party: "According to its constitution, it can only hold meetings in the day time; it also asks Government's permission to do so and invites local Government officials to attend. It stands for the fullest progress of the Kikuyu people, educationally and otherwise. It affirms its desire for active co-operation with men of all races in promoting the progress of Kenya Colony in general and the Kikuyu country in particular. It wishes to abolish all harmful customs such as the sexual mutilation of girls and to retain only such customs as are decent. . . . It thus resembles in its loyalty to Church and State, and in its aims the Kikuyu Association of Kiambu. A few meetings have been held between the leaders of both, but the areas of the two Associations are so far separated that little effective co-operation has taken place."[20]

In May 1928, at the Nyeri Local Native Council elections, each party had some success. Among the party candidates returned was Muhoya Kagumba, later appointed Senior Chief of the district during the Emergency, who carried Tetu on the PKP ticket. Muhoya, then about 30 and an adherent of the CSM, had joined the KCA in 1925, being admitted to its inner circles "because of his social position and ability. While in the KCA he invested money with them in the purchase of a motor bus, but received no dividends nor share of the money received for the bus when sold." He left the KCA in 1927 and strongly attacked the leaders at the March 1928 *baraza* at Nyeri. Stanley Kiama, a young man educated at Tumutumu, also later to become a chief, stood as a PKP Candidate and carried the area round Tumutumu.[21] But Mahiga (Willy Jimmy Wambugu Maina's stronghold) and Nyeri Township (where Hezakiah Mundia's coffee shop was the KCA headquarters) returned two KCA candidates.

The Assistant District Commissioner noted in his report that though "the elected members include Kikuyu Central

Association representatives, none of the prominent paid political agitators of this body stood as candidates."[22] In the five Nyeri divisions, which then included Ndia and Gichugu in Embu, 6,667 votes were polled, out of an estimated voters' roll of 62,282, for 37 candidates for the ten seats.[23] Elsewhere in the province, KCA-sponsored candidates had greater success in winning seats: nine were returned in Fort Hall and six in Kiambu.[24]

Uneasy calm prevailed for the rest of the year in Nyeri as the crisis in the district slowly worked itself out. But early in 1929 the issue dramatically spread to affect much of central Kenya. A conference of forty Kikuyu church elders, representing the Alliance mission stations in the province, met at Tumutumu from the eighth to the twelfth of March. Observing the proceedings were nine of the most prominent European missionaries in the country. The conference dutifully resolved (with one dissentient) that female circumcision was an "evil" custom "and should be abandoned by all Christians." A large majority agreed "that all submitting to the rite, or requiring their children to submit to it, be suspended by the churches everywhere." A minority of nine "declared that they could not agree to this at present, as their people would not consent and advised the churches to go more slowly."[25] After the conference had dispersed, the crisis flared up in Kiambu.

Dr. Arthur, Mr. Knapp of the GMS at Kambui, and Canon Harry Leakey of the CMS at Kabete, led the new Kiambu campaign against the custom and the KCA. In April 1929, a case was brought against two women for circumcising a GMS convert, aged 15, without her consent.[26] Although fined for committing a technical offense against the Local Native Council by-laws by performing the major rather than the minor operation, neither the Magistrate nor the Supreme Court, to whom he was compelled, after pressure from Arthur or the Attorney General, to state a case, would convict them for causing "grievous hurt." Arthur was furious, especially at the "frivolous" comments made by Mr. Justice Thomas in the Supreme Court. Thomas, newly arrived from England, compared what happened to the girl with the mishaps of surgery or the barber's shop. On August 10, 1929, Arthur took the step which he himself later realized was critical. He carried the battle into the newspapers, writing a forthright letter to the *East African Standard* to explain his point of view. The newspaper published an editorial backing his stand.

One week later the KCA retaliated. The President, Joseph Kang'ethe, signed a circular letter to each of the 74 chiefs in the province, asking them to approve a mass meeting of the Kikuyu people "so that we may know where this ruling has come from, and who are responsible for the passing of this law which is to cover all Akikuyu."* On August 29, Kang'ethe wrote another letter to Arthur and Knapp demanding an explanation and also sent a letter to the Senior Commissioner, with a copy to the press. The last sentence summed up the KCA position: "Missionaries have tried on many occasions to interfere with the tribal customs, and the question is asked whether circumcision being the custom of the Kikuyu Christian, he is to be a heathen simply because he is a Kikuyu."[27]

The missionaries redoubled their efforts to gain influential outside support. The East African Women's League (the settler women's organization) and the Convention of Associations itself, alarmed at what they termed the "seditious

---

* Senior Chief Koinange Mbiu's copy of this letter in the original can be found in the File on Female Mutilation (PCEA, Nairobi). See CSM, *Memorandum*, p. 40, where it is stated "that this letter misrepresented the position taken up in Dr. Arthur's article. It told the Chiefs that a law had been passed abolishing 'female circumcision' among the Kikuyu, and that Dr. Arthur and Mr. Knapp had been responsible for its being passed. The letter, undoubtedly, caused a ferment within the tribe, and gave the K.C.A. the temporary support of the majority of the older pagan members."

tendencies among a section of the natives,"[28] both passed vigorously worded resolutions. Arthur could hardly have thought this would have influenced the KCA leaders; he undoubtedly hoped it would stir a vacillating Government into supporting him more firmly. Under the extreme pressure the Government had already temporized with a further circular that was issued in September 1929. This immediately drew a sharp rejoinder from the Senior Commissioner, Ukamba: "I do not in fact favour any legislation in this matter. It is all very well for Dr. Arthur, living outside the native reserve, to suggest the rather drastic measures he does, but the position of Government and the natives must be considered as well. I happen to know that the Wakikuyu do very much resent our activities and those of the Missions in this matter." Later he added: "After all the feelings in the reserves as regards this question are rather parallel to those held by quite a number of people in England towards vaccination, and certainly conscientious objectors to vaccination do not render themselves liable to 6 months hard labour and a fine of £10.0.0"[29]

The Progressive Kikuyu Party and the leading chiefs of the Kikuyu Association supported Arthur's view. As a final broadside the elders of the CSM station at Kikuyu were encouraged to prepare a petition to the Government, asking that it should introduce the necessary legislation to ban the custom. On September 19 the last draft of the petition was approved, and they began the business of collecting signatures. It was at a meeting of the CSM church members at Kikuyu to consider this petition that Johanna Karanja finally broke with the mission. Ng'ang'a Ngoro, later Chairman of the Kikuyu Land Board Association also left. "I was a Christian," Ngoro says; however, "if the choice lay between God and circumcision, we choose circumcision. But it is a false European choice."[30] The KCA leaders argued that nowhere in the Bible was there any reference to this matter.

Indeed, the term used in the Kikuyu translation of the New Testament for the Virgin Mary was *Muiritu*,[31] the Kikuyu word for a circumcized girl. This then must be Dr. Arthur's Eleventh Commandment, they said, and since they had joined God's church and not Dr. Arthur's, they would leave him to his own devices. A further Commandment was said, with some truth, to be: "Thou shalt not join the KCA."

At this point Arthur made a curious decision: to undertake a crusade through Kikuyu country, rallying support for the CSM position. The safari lasted from September 24 to October 2, and he has left a manuscript account of his journey that reveals a lot about missionary attitudes to the KCA at this time.[32] After a mild meeting at the CMS station at Weithaga, he received a hostile reception in Kahuhia. "When I finished, matters at once became aggressive, several rather Bolshevist looking individuals trying to take the lead and fighting for the floor. Why was it I wanted to add to the 10 Commandments and who had given me the authority to do so." The meeting broke up in disorder, and Arthur commented that the "spirit of indiscipline and absolute devilment must be exorcised somehow. I see no alternative to the strong ruthless hand." At Kabare, in Embu, Arthur found that the missionary, the Rev. Comely, "would allow no agent or elder to have anything to do with the KCA, and consequently it had no hold in his church," which then had some 2,000 adherents. Nevertheless, Comely asked Arthur not to mention the female circumcision issue, for "the time was not ripe." At Chogoria Arthur stated the issue in plain terms. "I gave the reasons why both circumcision and the KCA must go. There could be no discussion: it was an order. The Church has made its laws: it would not go back. The KCA had made the law the test of the allegiance of its followers: it had joined issue with the Church and therefore they must now choose the church or the KCA." The church membership fell from 120 to 14 overnight, but Arthur was almost overcome with joy. "Chogoria's pentecost and revival had come. . . . The spirit of the Scottish Covenanters was with us." So possessed was he by the spirit of his crusade that he could even write in anger that "Joseph Kang'ethe and Johnstone Kenyatta deserve to be hanged. Kikuyu Church is the next for testing and Kahuhia and Weithaga, to say nothing of Embu and Kabete, will never be right till they too are made to face their Church members with the choice of two masters."

While the CSM at Kikuyu and the American missions, the AIM at Kijabe and the Gospel Missionary Society at Kambui, were adamant and uncompromising on the issue, neither the Roman Catholics nor the CMS were disposed to support such an inflexible attitude. Indeed, the cautious CMS elders at Kabete were disinclined to publicize, let alone sign, the petition prepared at Kikuyu. But in September at Kihumbuini, in Fort Hall, a Communion service broke up in confusion because Knapp refused Communion to all those who had not signed the declaration of loyalty to the church. Four people were charged and convicted.[33] The country was in a ferment. Many rumors were spreading, including one that the Europeans, whether missionaries, settlers, or administrators, opposed the circumcision of girls only so that they might marry them and obtain control of the land of the Kikuyu. People were divided into *"Karing'a"* (pure Kikuyu) and *"Kirori"* (thumbprint or sign), and those who had signed were subject to abuse. *Muthirigu,* a Kikuyu adaptation of a coastal song with a rousing chorus and an unlimited number of improvised verses, was first heard during October 1929. The apprentices from the Kabete Native Industrial Training Depot (NITD), a trade school that had been started at Lord Delamere's urging, brought the tune back with them after completing a construction job in Mombasa. It spread rapidly across Kikuyu country and into the "White Highlands." The song comi-

cally and tragically recreates the frustrations and emotions of
the Kikuyu people. Among the many stanzas current in the
1930s were:[34]

> "Little knives
> In their sheaths,
> That they may fight with the Church
> The time has come."

> "I'm going to break all friendships,
> The only friendship I shall retain
> Is between me and Jehovah!"

As well as stanzas in opposition to church teaching, there
were those about land:

> "The D. C. ———
> Is bribed with uncircumcized girls,
> So that the land may go."

And there were verses about KCA leaders and chiefs. Philip
James Karanja and Koinange, Secretary and Chairman respectively of the Kikuyu Association, were at this time
outstanding in their support of the Government and missions. Hence:

> "When Johnstone [Kenyatta in England] shall return
> With the King of the Kikuyu [Thuku in restriction]
> Philip and Koinange
> Will don women's robes."

In November 1929 at the NITD, 2,000 young men and
women sang the song in the school compound. The ex-Naval
Officer in charge was furious "that they had the brazen
impudence to gather on his compound. That crowd dispersed in double quick time. Forty NITD boys were
flogged on the Monday, and fifteen were given a month in

detention camp, and amongst these were most of the leaders of this whole business, caught at last."[35]

A powerful and emotive political ballad, the *Muthirigu* was banned in early January 1930. Heavy penalties were imposed on the singers by the Courts, but it continued to circulate underground as an anthem of resistance. Although banned, it never wholly disappeared, and in May 1964, it was danced by the Prime Minister, Jomo Kenyatta, and Malcolm Macdonald, the Scots Governor-General, at Kenyatta's home at Gatundu in Kiambu.

Inspired by his emotional experience at Chogoria, Arthur returned to clean up his own headquarters at Kikuyu. In October 1929, every paid "agent" of the CSM there had to sign a declaration of support of the mission's position on female circumcision and of their non-membership of KCA. Thirty-six signed, five agreed to make a verbal declaration, but twelve teachers refused and left CSM employment. The church elders of CSM were also asked to make a declaration of loyalty to the church law on female circumcision. Unlike the African mission teachers, they could still retain their membership in KCA. Of the fifty involved, sixteen declined.[36] The AIM and CMS followed Arthur's lead. On November 9, 1929, under pressure from the Government, Arthur resigned the seat that he had held on the Governor's Executive Council since 1928. His uncompromising stand on the issue had acutely embarrassed the Government, who believed that many Kikuyu were coming to look upon him as an official Government spokesman. After all, since the 1926 Governors' Conference, official policy on the subject had clearly been to temporize and stress the role of education in the custom's eradication.

In one striking passage in his voluminous writings on the issue, Arthur shows some consciousness of the real nature of the dilemma he was in. Commenting on a discussion with one of the three Alliance teachers who had refused to sign, Arthur notes that the teacher "tried to explain it to us; would it not be a betrayal of his nation if he took a vow, not against the circumcision, but against the KCA? In some way, in spite of its very evil leadership it stands in a peculiar way for Kikuyu nationality."[37]

In November and December 1929 and January 1930, there were several reports of illegal meetings and dances throughout Kiambu District. Thirty more Kikuyu were charged with "holding the Muthirigu song and dance," and there were disturbances at AIM and CMS outschools; and then on January 2, Miss Hulda Stumpf of the AIM was murdered.* But strong Government counter action eventually restored the situation.

In the short run, the dispute cost the CSM at Kikuyu 90 per cent of its communicants within the first month, while the AIM at Kijabe lost all but 50 of its 600 adherents.[38] Arthur's attitude had also rocked the foundations of the Alliance he had struggled so hard to create and greatly strained relations between the Government and the missions. Slowly the counsellors of moderation prevailed. In August 1931 there was a conference of African church leaders in Kikuyu country. Following this, on October 12, 1931, the Anglican Bishop of Mombasa issued a circular letter defining future policy on the subject. This left the door open for those who "believed that the ultimate aim and object of us all could better be brought about by less drastic methods for the present."[39] The issue would be more easily solved by being blurred than by being brought sharply into focus.

---

* Considering the fundamental issues the dispute raised, surprisingly little violence took place, although rumors "were in circulation among both Europeans and Africans in regard to expected conflict between the races;" see CSM, *Memorandum*, p. 62. Miss Hulda Stumpf of the African Inland Mission, Kijabe, died on January 3, 1930, after some men broke into her house at night and forcibly circumcized her. Those involved were never found. See T. F. C. Bewes, *Kikuyu Conflict* (London. 1953) , p. 45.

Indeed, in a joint memorandum to the Kenya Land Commission the European leaders of the AIM, the CMS, the CSM, and the GMS could pass the blame for the episode to the African church elders. For "the insistence of the African church on the abandonment of certain native customs as a condition of Church membership had led to secessions among Church and mission adherents."[40]

The Independent Schools

By the end of 1931 church attendance had substantially recovered, but neither mission nor governmental authority could any longer command the veneration it once possessed. "Individuals no longer [accepted] as a matter of course decisions of Administrative Officers or judgments of Magistrates but [were] only too ready to appeal against either."[41] The missions were increasingly regarded by the KCA as the spiritual edge of the imperialist sword. In particular, the dominant mission role in education was no longer considered sacrosanct. Out of the controversy there developed a positive drive to establish a comprehensive educational system independent of missionary control. Some of those who seceded from the church and who owned the land on which schools had been built reclaimed possession, in two instances taking their cases up to the Supreme Court. Others who had subscribed money for buildings demanded its return. In some instances they organized boycotts of the school.[42] On the other side, the withdrawal of church support from teachers who refused to sign the circumcision pledge led to the closing down of other schools. By early 1931 there was a major educational crisis in central Kenya. Two groups emerged to meet it—the Kikuyu Karing'a Schools and the Kikuyu Independent Schools Association. The former was to become associated with the African Orthodox Church, while the latter was to establish the African Independent Pentecostal Church.

The Karing'a movement was most closely associated with those who had broken with the CSM at Kikuyu. There, as we have seen, the female circumcision controversy had been the most bitter and intense, and the rupture with the mission church had been sharp and final, reflecting an attitude not of mere rebellion but of incipient revolt. According to Johanna Karanja, who became the movement's president in 1932, they called themselves Karing'a (which appeared in one of the verses of *Muthirigu*—"I am a Kikuyu Karing'a," or "pure" Kikuyu) to emphasize their complete break with the Kenya missions. Karanja added, however: "We never said we would have nothing to do with God. We were anti-mission, not anti-God."[43] During the next twenty years, the Karing'a movement fostered small schools in different parts of Kikuyu country and in the various colonies of the Kikuyu dispersion (most of whose members came from southern Kiambu), in Forest Department villages, on the Rift Valley farms, in Kisii and Kipsigis in the west, in Moshi and Arusha in northern Tanganyika, and at the Olenguruone Settlement in Masailand. Its spiritual center, however, remained the southern and western part of Kiambu District.

The second movement that grew out of the female circumcision controversy was the Kenya Independent Schools Association (KISA). In its development it was able to build on two embryonic independent schools that had been founded shortly after the First World War. These two schools, Githunguri, founded by Musa Ndirangu in 1922 in northern Kiambu, and Gakarara, founded by Daudi Maina Kiragu in the same year in southern Fort Hall, could hardly be considered effective educational instruments. The very fact of their existence, however, formed a beginning on which the movement was able rapidly to build a network of small schools across Kikuyuland. As the movement grew, so did the need for a pan-Kikuyu organization that could contain and express the interests of the independent schools in each district, and speak to the Government and the missions with the strength of a united body.

By the end of 1934 the movement was formalized into KISA, a kind of federal organization uniting the separate district committees, whose objectives were "to further the interests of the Kikuyus and its members and to safeguard the homogeneity of such interests in matters relating to their spiritual, economic, social and educational upliftment."[44] As a venture in self-help, its interest was educational within a Christian environment yet outside white control. Having asserted its independence, the movement was prepared to seek the help of a sympathetic mission church; chiefly, the need was for an ordained ministry that could baptize converts and perform the other sacramental rites.

After a long discussion with the District Commissioner and the Inspector of Schools in the Fort Hall area, the Independent Schools Committee in southern Fort Hall, under the leadership of Daudi Maina Kiragu, wrote in July 1933 to the Bishop of Mombasa, asking him to allow two of their men to undergo theological training "to be taught how to baptize in our schools."* A special conference of all missions in the Fort Hall area took place at Kahuhia from October 13 to October 16, 1933, when a deputation of the Independent Schools Committee was interviewed. At the Committee's request, Jesse Kariuki of the KCA attended as an observer.[45] Faced with the imminent danger of the group forming an independent African church, the Conference broke the Alliance's rule of spheres and recommended that the CMS should appoint an African minister for the Fort Hall area and should also consider Independent candidates

---

* "Kahuhia Conference, 1933," CMS Office, Nairobi. There were seven KISA schools in Fort Hall at this time and four other Independent Schools—possibly "Karing'a." Five were receiving grants-in-aid from the Local Native Council.

for theological training. These recommendations were subject to the Fort Hall Independent Schools Committee's assurance that they would not form an independent church, and that their men, when ordained, would be subject to the Bishop's authority and would obey all the rules of the Church of England. The proposals were meant to apply only to the limited area of southern Fort Hall, since the Conference members were drawn from missions in that area.

The Standing Committee of the Alliance approved these proposals on October 24, and the Bishop wrote to the Fort Hall Committee on December 27 in this vein. However, the negotiations that followed in early 1934 were beclouded by a misunderstanding. The CMS representatives were under the impression that the agreement applied to all KISA schools anywhere in Kikuyuland, whereas the CSM thought that southern Fort Hall was the only area under discussion. In fact Barlow of the CSM mission at Tumutumu had already advised the Bishop to reject an application written on September 23 by the Nyeri Independent Schools Committee.

By May the misunderstanding had come to the surface and the original Fort Hall Committee request had been engulfed by the problem of "spheres" in Nyeri and Kiambu. Thus the Independent Schools movement had triggered off another crisis in the Alliance. The movement was held at bay while the missions tried to sort themselves out. The African churches met in Nairobi on September 21, 1934, but agreement was hardly likely as long as the CSM members held that "the 'Independents' desire a temporary association with the Church Missionary Society in order to secure legitimate orders for an Ethiopian Church under their sole control, which would sanction polygamy and other evils of heathenism, as well as Female Circumcision in its traditional form."[46] The CSM offered the CMS a straight choice between helping the Independents or continuing the Alliance.

The negotiations finally came to a head at two meetings on December 5 and 28, 1934, when the African members of the CMS Highland District Church Council met a large deputation at Kahuhia from the newly formed provincial KISA body. This had been established at a preparatory conference at Gakarara.[47] During the year of frustrated waiting, the Independent Schools' position had hardened and now included propositions that a church connected to the schools must be called the Kikuyu Independent Church and that no laws regarding circumcision could be laid down by the CMS.[48] Although the meetings resulted in some softening of this attitude, it was becoming increasingly probable that the negotiations would fade out, and they did, although there were further desultory attempts to reach agreement in both 1935 and 1936.

The independent schools forming KISA had become less interested in resuming links with the missionary churches since another way of meeting the problem of baptism, which by the mid-thirties was becoming critical for both Karing'a and the Independents, seemed to be in the offing. In late 1932 James Beauttah, who was at that time working in Mombasa, chanced to meet Archbishop Daniel Alexander of the African Orthodox Church, recently arrived from Uganda where he had ordained Reuben Spartas[49] as a priest. Alexander was on his way back to South Africa, but he agreed to return soon to Kenya in order to train and ordain an African clergy for KISA. After some three years, during which he had intermittent contact with Kikuyu leaders and even welcomed (with a band) Parmenas Githendu Mukeri in South Africa on his journey back from London, Alexander finally reached Mombasa again on November 8, 1935. He was met by Beauttah and KISA's reception committee, headed by their president, Johanna Kunyiha of Nyeri.[50] He held his first baptism in Beauttah's house. A week later Alexander went to Nairobi and Kikuyu country, where he remained for nearly eighteen months, baptizing, teaching new converts, and training a priesthood.

Alexander's arrival initiated a period of cooperation between KISA and the Karing'a Schools of southern Kiambu. Arthur Gatungu became the Karing'a candidate at the small seminary run by Alexander; others were sent by KISA. On June 27, 1937, the Archbishop ordained four students— Philip Kiande, Arthur Gatungu, Harrison Gacokia, and Daudi Maina Kiragu. While Kiande and Gatungu now gave their first loyalty to Alexander and the African Orthodox Church, Gacokia and Maina remained with KISA. The split is dated by Maina from a meeting at Ngangariithi (Nyeri) on September 3, 1937.[51] Though the members of KISA regarded Alexander as their spiritual father, they established their own church, the African Independent Pentecostal Church (AIPC), with Harrison Gacokia (of Kiambu) and Maina as its ministers. Kiande, dismissed from KISA, founded one branch of the African Orthodox Church and associated schools in Nyeri.* This became increasingly isolated and independent. Gatungu formed another in Kiambu which became closely associated with the Karing'a schools and the other Orthodox churches in Kenya and Uganda. When Alexander sailed from Kenya on July 7, 1937, he left behind him an ordained African clergy functioning outside the auspices of any Kenya mission.

Although no overall unity existed among the various African independent groups, KISA and AIPC were now established and expanding their influence in Kiambu, Fort Hall, Nyeri, and Embu districts and in the eastern part of the Rift Valley Settled Areas. Concerned primarily with educational and religious matters, KISA sought to provide an African answer to problems of social development and

---

* The Nyeri AOC itself split, four schools with the same name being led by Timothy Githori, originally Kiande's right-hand man. Welbourne, *East African Rebels,* p. 150.

spiritual needs. It represented a genuine effort in institution-building by providing a focus and means of fostering social integration. In the intense political conflicts of the late 1940s and early 1950s, KISA was to become a divided movement, with the majority ultimately supporting militant national-ism.

Karing'a, by contrast, could never boast the quantitative achievements of KISA, but from the beginning it repre-sented a more politically oriented approach to the solution of its problems. The degree of disillusion and dissent seems to have been greater within Karing'a than within KISA, in part reflecting the differences in the rate of social change between southern Kiambu, the center of Karing'a, on the one hand, and north Kiambu, Fort Hall, and Nyeri, the heartland of KISA, on the other. In contrast with the other Kikuyu areas, the impact of social change in southern Kiambu had been far more abrupt and intense; moreover, anxiety arising out of the loss of land and increasing population pressures was more widespread. Members of Karing'a were more closely touched by land issues whose only solution was increasingly seen to be in political action. The Karing'a movement flourished among those who lived on the rough edge of Kenya's racial frontiers.

A Text in Cultural Nationalism

Jomo Kenyatta's book, *Facing Mount Kenya,** provides an underlying explanation of the cultural nationalism that was expressed at different levels of intensity in both Karing'a and KISA, as well as in the circumcision crisis. First published in 1938, it developed out of three papers given in 1936 to a seminar at the London School of Economics, where Kenyatta was taking a postgraduate diploma in anthropology[52] under Professor B. Malinowski. A wide-ranging study of Kikuyu culture, it was the first major work devoted to the tribe since

---

* When praying the traditional Kikuyu faced Mount Kenya.

the Routledges' ethnographic volume *With a Prehistoric People,* published in 1910, and Cagnolo's more discursive book *The Agikuyu,* published in 1933.

In his preface Kenyatta attacks the idea that Africans cannot speak for themselves but must always have their opinions interpreted by a well-meaning missionary or an anthropologist who has learned their language. Kenyatta took a diploma course in anthropology that would enable him to fight these "pretenders to philanthropy" on their own ground. "I am well aware that I could not do justice to the subject without offending those 'professional friends of the African' who are prepared to maintain their friendship for eternity as a sacred duty, provided only that the African will continue to play the part of an ignorant savage so that they can monopolize the office of interpreting his mind and speaking for him. To such people, an African who writes a study of this kind is encroaching on their preserves. He is a rabbit turned poacher."[53]

But the matter was more intricate even than this. There was also a feeling that it was wrong for an educated African so much as to talk about, much less to write about, his culture, because he should only be concerned with modernity. An interest in his people's past was unhealthy, any praise of the past was a betrayal of the civilization to which he attached himself when he was educated and baptized a Christian. The act of becoming a Christian entailed the uncritical adoption at the same time of the totality of western civilization. Kenyatta not only asserts with pride that there is value in the traditional unlettered Kikuyu educational system, but he also challenges the missionary attitude at its most sensitive point—on female circumcision. "The missionaries who attack the *irua* [circumcision] of girls are more to be pitied than condemned, for most of their information is derived from Gikuyu converts who have been taught by these same Christians to regard the custom of female circumcision as something savage and barbaric, worthy only of heathens who live in perpetual sin under the influence of the Devil."[54]

Kenyatta was also able to articulate the basic Kikuyu argument for the retention of the specific practice of female circumcision. He claimed that the missionaries failed to see the connection between clitoridectomy and initiation; between the admittedly painful operation of *irua* and the whole Kikuyu culture. Circumcision, Kenyatta argued, is an institution which marks the boundary between childhood and adulthood and is hence of great social and educational significance. Kenyatta also showed how, in the battle for selective modernization, anthropology becomes an important tool:

> The real argument lies not in the defence of the surgical operation or its details, but in the understanding of a very important fact in the tribal psychology of the Gikuyu— namely, that this operation is still regarded as the very essence of an institution which has enormous educational, social, moral and religious implications, quite apart from the operation itself. For the present it is impossible for a member of the tribe to imagine an initiation without clitoridectomy. Therefore the abolition of the surgical element in this custom means to the Gikuyu the abolition of the whole institution.
>
> The real anthropological study, therefore, is to show that clitoridectomy, like Jewish circumcision, is a mere bodily mutilation which, however, is regarded as the *conditio sine qua non* of the whole teaching of tribal law, religion, and morality.[55]

It was probably Kenyatta's appeal for a more scientific approach to such phenomena as female circumcision and the "Watu wa Mungu" (Kikuyu *arathi* or "prophets"), who suddenly appeared in Kiambu and Fort Hall districts in the aftermath of the circumcision crisis and whose relations with the Government were punctuated by violence, which convinced some that the book was a blueprint for atavistic revolt and "Kikuyuism." It was on the contrary an appeal for selectivity and moderation to those in the van of the battle against his people's culture. But Europeans had been conditioned to regard Africa as a *tabula rasa*, as the greatest field for missionary endeavor since St. Paul's journeys, as a continent populated by heathen whose barbaric culture could not conceivably contain anything worth holding on to. The Africans of Kenya had been regarded as among the more primitive, lacking even the pale replica of the monarchial bureaucracy that had evolved among the Baganda. To Kenya Europeans who read it, Kenyatta's book was both a shock and a presumption. He challenged their frontal assault on the absence of any worthwhile Kikuyu culture with an academic dissertation showing what that culture was and a fierce assertion that it also had valuable aspects.

It is not surprising that the book had its critics, and that Dr. H. R. A. Philp (after describing how Kenyatta once cooked for him a substantial and appetizing rice pudding) should note how he "has been immersed in politics, to the annoyance even of many of his own countrymen, has visited Moscow, and lived in London for long." And now, "he is an anthropologist and writes a book." Attacking the book, Philp continued: "The author glories in shame and parades that which is indecent, and this in the name of science. How contrary to the Spirit of true Christianity (Eph. v.12). Further, we detect the most obvious inaccuracies in the supposed technical parts of the book." He concludes, "here surely is an aspect of the conflict with the 'unfruitful works of darkness' that the young Kikuyu Church is engaged in."[56]

The independent churches and schools were to face many setbacks during the next twenty years, and the process of their growth was often haphazard. But the long-term effects of the circumcision crisis went far beyond any question of the successful establishment of an Orthodox or Pentecostal Church or an independent educational system.

In the midst of the crisis, in 1930, the District Commissioner, Kiambu, said: "I have no longer any doubt but that the movement is primarily and consciously nationalist . . . 'Africa for the African' and elimination of the European is probably the star to which the young Kikuyu hitch their wagon."[57] During the crisis many Kikuyu began to query the direction of social change and its effect on their indigenous culture. Henceforth they demanded the right of selective modernization and the history and legend of the crisis gave a great impetus to the nationalist ideology of the Kikuyu political movement.

The KCA had seen the attack on female circumcision as extraneous to the doctrines of Christianity. The issue itself was not one that was central to the preservation of the colonial state. The missionaries themselves were not even united on it, let alone able to command wide support outside the church. KCA politics remained essentially one of protest. Hardly, however, had the situation calmed down when the appointment of the Kenya Land Commission precipitated a further crisis, this time on an issue where the economic interests of the settler and the Kikuyu were fundamentally opposed and apparently irreconcilable.

CHAPTER 5

Racial Entrenchment and Dissent in the Thirties

Issues associated with land have dominated Kenya politics. Indeed, it is convenient, if superficial, to treat the development of Kenya nationalism in the 1930s by concentrating on the politics of land, for it was the center of much, though by no means all, of the political activity during this decade. This followed inevitably from the recommendation of the Joint Select Committee of the British Parliament in 1931 that a Kenya Land Commission should be set up, followed by its appointment in 1932, the hearing of evidence in 1932 and 1933, the publication of its Report in May 1934, the debate in the Kenya Legislative Council in October of the same year, and the constant pressure for or against the implementation of its recommendations right up to the outbreak of the Second World War. While the struggle over land intensified the growth of political consciousness among the Kikuyu during this period, this consciousness was by no means restricted to them. Associations among the Luo and Luhya in Nyanza, the Kamba in central Kenya, and the Taita near the coast, protested Government policies and actions and demanded redress of economic and land grievances. Major urban protest was expressed in a strike at Mombasa in 1939.

Thus by the end of the decade a sense of nationally shared problems and a nascent national consciousness was emerging, although no recognized transtribal leadership group or country-wide African political organization existed. Nonetheless, as a prelude to the territorial nationalism of the postwar period, new educated leaders began to participate in politics, and the KCA sought to encourage and support all African protest. The banning of the KCA, the Taita Hills Association, and the Ukamba Members Association, and the detention of some of their leaders in 1940, disrupted African political institution building. But the momentum was resumed near the end of the war when the Kenya African Union was formed and began to seek a territorial-wide African constituency.

Thuku and the KCA

By 1930 the KCA was an established political association with branches in all districts in central Kenya and in many parts of the Rift Valley. While it could not yet be described as a mass movement, its leadership was beginning to adopt modern organizational techniques. Men such as Jesse Kariuki, Job Muchuchu, Gideon Mugo, Kirori Motoku, and Ishmael Mungai enthusiastically followed the lead of Jomo Kenyatta and George Ndegwa in building up the party's network of branches. The KCA journal, *Muigwithania,* was sent out "even into Chagga country"[1] (Tanganyika), and the KCA tried to initiate transtribal conferences. Having grown rapidly during the female circumcision controversy, its membership numbered several thousand; and its prestige had been considerably enhanced in the eyes of many Africans by Kenyatta's mission to England.

Chiefs were increasingly dismayed by the growing support for the KCA and sought additional powers from the Government to control its activities. To the Government, the KCA was anathema and a subversive influence undermining constituted tribal authority, that is, the Government-appointed chiefs and headmen. At a *baraza* held at Kiambu on February 26, 1930, the Governor, Sir Edward Grigg, announced that he had strengthened the Native Authority Ordinance. Unauthorized collecting of money would be prohibited as well as the "formation of associations" that encouraged "the dancing of lawless dances." The latter were the occasion for the singing of the *Muthirigu* in which the government, missionaries, and chiefs were "held up to ridicule."[2]

Meanwhile, in London Kenyatta vigorously denied that the KCA was a subversive organization; rather, its object was "to help the Kikuyu to improve himself as a Mu-Kikuyu— not to 'ape' the foreigner."[3] He summarized the KCA's aims as being the security of the tribal lands; increased educational facilities of a practical nature; the abolition of the hut tax for women; and elected representatives in the Legislative Council; as well as "to be permitted to retain our many good tribal customs, and by means of education to elevate the minds of our people to the willing rejection of the bad customs." He asked "if any fair-minded Briton considers the above outlined policy of the KCA to savour in any way of sedition? The repression of native views, on subjects of such vital interest to my people, by means of legislative measures, can only be described as a short-sighted tightening up of the safety valve of free speech, which must inevitably result in a dangerous explosion—the one thing all sane men wish to avoid."[4]

In early January 1931, four months after Kenyatta's return to Kenya, Thuku was released, having been restricted in various remote district headquarters for nearly nine years. Shortly after he came back to Kiambu, the Provincial Commissioner "warned him that he must settle down to a quiet life, and give up politics: that work on behalf of his people either in the Local Native Council or as a paid

servant of Government was open to him."[5] Though Thuku
took no major role in the KCA for a year, he had returned as
its acknowledged leader and the uncrowned "King of the
Kikuyu." In 1932 he became President of the KCA, with
Jesse Kariuki as his Vice-President and George Ndegwa as
the Assistant General Secretary.

Within a short time a leadership crisis emerged inside the
party. The specific quarrels and disagreements remain confused, but criticism of Thuku's leadership, and efforts by
other KCA leaders to usurp his role, led to a lawsuit between
Thuku and Jesse Kariuki.[6] In 1933 the organization split,
and after a year in which there were two KCA's in existence,
Thuku left his to form a new group, the Kikuyu Provincial
Association (KPA). This event represented a major setback
for the KCA. Thuku's high standing in Kikuyu country
would be difficult to overcome, and the KPA was potentially
a far more effective alternative to the KCA than any of the
previous "loyal" Kikuyu bodies (such as the KA and the
Progressive Kikuyu Party). Moreover, the KCA was left
without a dominant leader able to give coherence and
meaning to the movement, which became prey to district and
personal rivalries. But Kenyatta, as ambassador at large of
the Kikuyu in London, was safely isolated from the factional
strife of Nairobi and Kikuyu politics. His strength and
stature in the tribe were rising rapidly.

The KPA was officially founded in April 1935. By early
1940 it claimed about 4,000 paid-up members, including
women.[7] It required every member to pledge his or her
loyalty "to His Majesty the King of Great Britain and the
established Government," to be bound to act in a constitutional manner according to British traditions, and to refrain
from doing "anything which [was] calculated to disturb the
peace, good order and Government."[8] To the KCA leaders
this pledge merely confirmed their belief that Thuku had
given an undertaking to Government in order to obtain his

release in 1931. Aside from this issue, however, Thuku had clearly abandoned the "nationalist" approach in favor of moderation.

The KPA had little strength in southern Kiambu, being "almost entirely confined to the Gatundu Division,"[9] but was stronger in Fort Hall and had several clusters of members in Nyeri, especially in Othaya Division, where KPA members later formed the nucleus of several Home Guard groups during the Emergency. In 1941 Thuku was urging his followers to "co-operate with Government . . . especially in anti-erosion measures."[10] Later in the same year the District Commissioner, Nairobi, officially opened the new KPA offices in Eastleigh.[11] By 1943, the D.C., Kiambu, could write that Thuku "was considered a whole-hearted supporter of Government."[12]

Koinange in London

After Kenyatta's return to Kenya in the Fall of 1930, the KCA met to choose two representatives to go to London to present its views to the Parliamentary Joint Committee on Closer Union in East Africa. The committee's investigation was to embrace the whole issue of closer union of the East African territories including critical questions of European settler-African relations. Kenya's Colonial Administration had already sent an official African delegation comprising Chief Koinange, president of the Kikuyu Association, James Mutua, a Kamba sub-headman from Muputi Location in Machakos, and Ezekiel Apindi, president of the Kavirondo Taxpayers Welfare Association. The KCA was slow in deciding on its delegation, but Kenyatta was an obvious choice as one representative. For the second, the KCA finally decided to appoint Parmenas Githendu Mukeri, a teacher trained at Makerere College, Uganda, although there had been some discussion that Thuku might be sent.[13] Kenyatta and Mukeri swore before the elders at Pumwani that they would take the grievances of the Kikuyu to a far country and while on their way would not reveal their message to anyone, while the elders on their part swore not to let them go hungry. The two representatives left Nairobi on April 28, 1931, a thousand people coming to see them off at the railway station, on the very day the Government's official African delegation was giving evidence in London.[14]

Though the KCA delegation arrived in London too late to be invited to give evidence, Koinange and his colleagues had forcefully and impressively argued the African case before the Parliamentary Committee. Their demands and complaints differed from those of the KCA only in degree, a demonstration that there was a considerable community of grievances even if African political organization was fragmented. Chief Koinange, in particular, spoke out fearlessly for his people, and clearly felt that his position as a civil servant did not require him to support the Government's position.

Cataloguing African problems and needs, he drew attention to the plight of the landless squatters on European farms, the alienation of Kikuyu lands, the search for means to accelerate development, and such issues as the education of girls, since "it is women who look after the children, and who make the race."[15] All three African witnesses were dissatisfied with the level of African participation in government. The Local Native Councils served a limited and useful purpose, but since it was the Legislative Council that made the decisions most vitally affecting their well-being, it was imperative that their interests should be adequately represented on it, and this could only be accomplished by Africans themselves.

The settler thrust for a European unofficial majority on the Legislative Council had dramatically demonstrated the central role of that Council in constitutional and political development. "Closer union" of the East African territories

with another level of administrative hierarchy imposed between Kenya and Britain seemed likely to confuse, if not
actively to hinder opportunities for African social and political development. What was needed for East Africa was not
the High Commissioner that had been suggested, argued
Koinange, but for the Governors to carry out established
British policy. Though Koinange opposed the KCA at this
time, his implied criticism of Sir Edward Grigg as another
"settler's governor" was as strong as anything the KCA delegates might have said.[16] Koinange, hardly a rebel in the early
thirties, was to become a nationalist after the Second World
War and to spend the closing years of his life in detention. In
May Koinange cabled the D.C., Kiambu, from the ship on
which he was returning to Kenya to ask that Chiefs Njonjo,
Waruhiu, and Philip Karanja be sent down to Mombasa to
meet him. The District Commissioner refused this on the
grounds that they were already going to Nairobi for the
King's Birthday ceremony, and La Fontaine, the Acting
Provincial Commissioner, Nyeri, commented, "I hope Koinange does not suffer too much from swelled head. His cable
from midocean suggests the beginning of inflammation."[17]

The Report of the Committee in late 1931 effectively
brought to an end for the moment the debate over the
creation of an East African Federation. African leaders were
later, in the 1960s, to revive the concept, but in 1931
economic depression and fear on the part of the various
racially organized groups in East Africa caused its abandonment. The Committee accepted the African argument for
improvement in African representation. While the development of Local Native Councils "should be actively fostered,"
African representation in the Kenya Legislative Council
needed to be augmented. Some of the Committee thought
that three African members should be nominated, but the
Report itself recommended only in general terms an increase
in nominated representation for African interests.[18]

Responding to the Report in February 1932, Brigadier-

General Sir Joseph Byrne, who had become Kenya's Governor in 1931, recommended that the number of representatives should be increased from one to two, and that the restriction limiting the selection to a Christian missionary be removed. Representation of African interest by Africans themselves was premature, he continued, but might be considered in the future. Few, if any, could be found who would be able to understand and contribute to the work of the Legislative Council. It was doubtful, even if a qualified person were available, that he would command any significant degree of confidence from his people. Moreover, there existed no need to provide representation for the small numbers of "detribalized" Africans; indeed, "detribalization" itself should be discouraged and avoided.[19] Gradualism thus continued to dominate official thinking on African political development.

The Secretary of State accepted the recommendation for an increase in representation and the desirability of African interests being represented by other than missionaries.[20] In 1934, following constitutional changes incorporating these principles, R. W. Hemsted joined Archdeacon G. Burns in the Legislative Council to hold a second brief for African interests. Both men had lived in East Africa some 35 years and were now retired. Hemsted was a former administrator, while Burns had been a missionary. Some missionary representation of African interests was to continue until 1938; then for the next five years both seats were occupied by paternalistic ex-civil servants, whose conservative predispositions led them to ignore aspiring African leaders. The appointment of the Rev. L. J. Beecher, in August 1943, brought a new realism into the Legislative Council, for he vigorously defended and sought to advance African interests. In favor of direct African representation, Beecher not only welcomed the appointment of the first African in 1944, but soon pressed for more.[21]

The Joint Select Committee in 1931 also urged the Kenya

Government to give sympathetic consideration to a number of long-standing African grievances, including the *kipande* system, the hut and poll taxes, prohibitions against the cultivation of coffee and "cash" crops, and other issues of social and economic development in the African Reserves. But the most significant of its conclusions was the immediate need for a "full and authoritative" examination of Kenya's *African* land problems. When, however, in April 1932 the Kenya Land Commission was appointed, the emphasis had been subtly changed. An official summary of its terms of reference states that it was charged with the "giving of a sense of security to the African population by the settlement of their claims to land and by the assurance of sufficient land for their future needs, and to the European by defining the area in which he was to enjoy a privileged position."[22] These terms of reference were to circumscribe critically the concerns and recommendations of the Commission.

The Commission's chairman was Sir Morris Carter, a former Chief Justice of Uganda and Tanganyika and chairman of the Land Commission appointed in 1925 in Southern Rhodesia shortly after the achievement of European self-government there. The task of that Commission had been to determine whether the country should be divided into European and African areas with the rights to hold land in each area being confined to the respective racial groups. The Southern Rhodesian Commissioners stated that separation of the races was both expedient and practicable. They held that "however desirable it may be that members of the two races should live together side by side with equal rights as regards the holding of land, we are convinced that in practice, probably for generations to come such a policy is not practicable nor in the best interests of the two races, and that until the native has advanced much further on the paths of civilisation it is better that points of contact between the two races should be reduced."[23] The other Commissioners were

R. W. Hemsted and F. O'B. Wilson, a large landowner in
Machakos District. The secretary was S. H. Fazan, an administrator who had been one of a group appointed in 1929
to produce the Report on Kikuyu Land Tenure. Both
Hemsted and Fazan, who had also retired in Kenya, had intimate personal knowledge of the Kikuyu case.

The news of a special commission on land led to feverish
activity among Africans throughout Kenya, especially among
the Kikuyu in Kiambu, where most of the alienation of
Kikuyu land had taken place. Political organization was
stimulated by the creation at this time of a direct link
between the *mbari* (the Kikuyu sub-clan, lineage, or extended family), and the KCA through the Kikuyu Land
Board Association (KLBA),[24] led by Ng'ang'a Ngoro, which
was established as a subcommittee of the KCA. Its task was
to help organize the claims of the various *mbari* so that the
KCA could present a comprehensive case to the Commission.
In describing the activities of the KLBA, Ngoro says that
there was a "committee of about thirty people which used to
meet every Saturday morning to hear the latest news of our
preparations for the Commission."[25] The immense problems
that faced the *mbari* committee arose because the Kikuyu
had evolved a system of land tenure somewhat akin to
individual ownership. Most of the land alienated to European settlers south of the Chania River in Kiambu was
subject to claims, however tenuous, by Kikuyu families. At
this point we must look more closely at the central question
of Kikuyu land and social organization.

Kikuyu Land and Social Organization

The Kikuyu were traditionally made up of some nine clans,
each having become widely dispersed geographically. The
clans were relatively unimportant in the daily life of an
individual, but their dispersion probably broadened iden-
fication with the Kikuyu people as a whole. The important

kinship group was the *mbari* (pl: *mbari*), which, depending on the state of its growth, could be called a sub-clan, sub-sub-clan, lineage, or joint family. Each *mbari* had rights over a particular piece of land, or *githaka* (pl: *ithaka*), which at one time had been claimed by one man. In most cases the original *githaka* covered much more territory than could be used by the polygamous family of the founder.

In the southern part of Kikuyuland, the Kiambu area, land rights were in a significant way more absolute than in the central and northern areas, for land in the south was purchased from members of the residing tribe, the Dorobo. In the central and northern areas—to become Fort Hall and Nyeri districts—no other tribes were present when the Kikuyu arrived; *githaka* rights in these areas spontaneously developed wherever a kinship group decided to settle.

Upon the death of its founder, absolute rights in the *githaka* were established in the *mbari*.[26] Those rights were passed on to the eldest son, who became the *muramati* (pl: *aramati*) or titular head of the *mbari*. His authority within the *mbari* was limited to ceremonial functions and to questions concerning the reallocation of land. And circumscribing his authority over brothers and the admittance of tenants were the rights of every son to some land. Each received a share of land which he took over when he married. These sons in turn became the heads of families, passing their authority of reallocation on to their eldest sons—who became the *aramati* of their respective family groups—while passing their rights of ownership on to all of their sons. Each *mbari*, then, had one principal head—usually the eldest son of the eldest family—who was a *muramati*. Further, each distinct segment within the *githaka* had its own *muramati* who usually recognized the principal *muramati* as the family's head.

There is some evidence to suggest that the authority of the principal *muramati* was not always maintained, even over contiguous *mbari*. In Nyeri and Fort Hall, for instance, there was a tendency over time for the authority of the principal *muramati* to lapse and for emerging segments to subdivide the traditional *githaka* and to "treat its part of the original *Githaka* as a new and separate *Githaka*."[27] When a *githaka* became crowded, this budding off process and consequent greater independence became even more pronounced, since, as we shall see, it accelerated the tendency to segment into non-contiguous *mbari*.

Because of various interdependent needs, however, complete autonomy among *mbari* would have been suicidal. Large-scale units were required for warfare and defense, and for deciding disputes between members of different *mbari*. These organizational problems were partially solved by the age-grade system. A complete solution was limited by the fact that the most inclusive institutional forms of the system were on the district level, and there was no common body that had authority over all of Kikuyuland.[28] But age-grade rituals, such as the initiation or the handing-over ceremonies, were carried out in similar fashion throughout the country, thereby giving rise to common cultural patterns beyond the local area.

Age-grades and age-sets (the latter being the specific groups in which individuals of roughly the same age would continue throughout their lives) cut across the various *mbari* kinship groupings and organized the population on the basis of age. Three broad divisions existed. At the lowest level were those too young to be warriors; next were the warriors; and finally came the elders—those too old to fight, and men of great esteem, and elders. Within these broad categories various levels existed which could be attained by a combination of age and achievement. Especially within the elder grades the latter criterion became all important. It is significant here to note the different requirements needed to enter the warrior grade as compared to those needed to enter the lowest elder grade. Once a youth reached the proper age, the only other requirement for his entrance into the junior warrior grade was the payment of one goat to the senior warriors.[29] This was not a high price to pay, and only rarely did it prevent a boy from being initiated with his peers. On the other hand, for a senior warrior to become an elder, not only did he have to pay a goat but further he had to be married and had to have established his own homestead. Because of the livestock needed for a bride price and as a minimum for establishing a farm, such contingent factors certainly did not fall equally on everybody.

Over time almost every son married, but these contingent factors and others—such as ritual knowledge—in the higher elder groups resulted in some age-mates moving up swiftly to higher councils while others, unable to gain these status requisites, were retarded. Within the elder grade factors other than age controlled status allocation. These factors depended only to a limited degree upon the advantages of birth; initiative and achievement were of greater importance.[30]

Thus at both major levels of Kikuyu social organization, roles were allocated on the basis of an important mixture of both achievement and ascription. So, for example, even though the distribution of land within an *mbari* took place essentially along an ascriptive axis, the superordinate role within the *mbari* itself was often an achieved one. For the age-grade too, as we have seen, achievement—whether by owning land and goats or by founding an independent household—was a prerequisite for many prestige-bearing roles, although age was a basic criterion for initial entry. Kikuyu society was a relatively open one, in which individuals could often make significant choices between roles on the basis of ability and good fortune.

These mutually reinforcing factors of achievement orientation and a relatively wide range of choice in major role recruitment in Kikuyu society may be illustrated by the traditional child-rearing practices. These are important for our understanding of Kikuyu social and political organization in that they were congruent at many points with patterns in the *mbari* and the age-set. For instance, strong and intense hierarchical relationships between parents and their children were not a Kikuyu norm. The authority structure of the family was loose, and when a child was punished, which occurred only rarely, he could usually run and hide at a relative's home, especially that of a grandparent. The implicit moral was that in many circumstances his security lay in the entire village group, rather than in one particular mother or father. Within the lineage structure there was always somebody who would be his father or mother even if his own biological parents died. At the same time, peer groups were a major focus of the child's life. In playing with others, he learned adult roles by imitating elders and warriors.

The child was treated in a manner which could be termed indulgent. He was given food whenever he was hungry, his hygienic training was late, and he was allowed considerable freedom. Furthermore, he was rarely punished. When he was, the type of sanctions used were not usually physical. Underlining this point is Kenyatta's remembrance of the punishment meted out to a young boy who made a mistake of observation during his training as a goat herd. "No harsh remark is made, but quietly he is asked to go through again and point out such-and-such a sheep or goat which has been purposely hidden."[31]

Although arbitrary authority was by no means totally absent in Kikuyu socialization practices, important areas of permissiveness and peer-group-oriented behavior tended to reinforce the inculcation of values of achievement. Related also to achievement values was a tendency toward equalitarianism, which was in turn strengthened by patterns of adult learning. A youth was admitted to the warrior category after completing the initiation rites, the key ceremony being circumcision. All men and women had to be circumcised before they were ritually fit to be tribal members. An age-set comprised those circumcised at the same time and, as Kenyatta notes, the members of this group "stand in the very closest relationship to each other. When a man of the same age-group injures another it is a serious magico-religious offence. They are like blood brothers; they must not do any wrong to each other. It ranks with an injury done to a member of one's own family."[32] What occurs here is that the initiation ritual formally establishes a pseudo-kinship among age-mates. Upon meeting one another, the expression of salutation is *wanyua-wa-kiine,* my tribal equal.[33] Within various districts these sets carry out almost all social functions as a corporate group. For instance, pre-marital love making (*ngweko*) with circumcised girls occurred in a common hut where switching partners was an accepted practice. A. H. J. Prins and Kenyatta both relate that this practice not only prepares the participants for polygamy but also establishes a normative pattern which allows age-brothers to have intercourse with each other's wives without breaking the customary law or arousing paternal jealousy.[34] In general, the relationship between men of the same age grade tended to stress their shared and equal attributes.

Equalitarian values were further reflected in the authority patterns within the elder councils themselves. Each unit, or geographic ridge, within a district was administered by a council of nine elders. The leading figure within each of those bodies, the *muthamaki,* was a chairman of the council. His authority was never absolute, for he was merely first among equals. Whether or not he would be an effective leader depended upon his personality in relation to others on the council and the extent to which his policies were accepted as the best course of action.[35] The equalitarianism of the council thus seems to have acted to prevent undue intra-group conflict in a situation where achievement values were a major leadership criterion.

Our discussion thus far has concentrated on the modal value orientations implicit in the Kikuyu traditional system; we have tried to suggest how the central value of achievement has been reinforced by other values—such as peer-group orientation, permissiveness, and equalitarianism—both in early socialization and in adult group life. Of course, as we have noted, emphasis upon achievement and universalistic values did not preclude some aspects of social organization where somewhat incompatible principles obtained. While roles within the adult age-grade system were allocated so significantly on the basis of wealth and ability, roles within the *mbari,* which determined initial entry into the elder age-grade, were allocated by ascriptive criteria. It is our contention that the conflict between these contradictory principles of role allocation became most acute among younger sons. Starting a new homestead on unclaimed land was the major means of resolving this conflict. Some of the important factors conditioning this process may now briefly be described.

A major index of wealth and achievement in Kikuyu society was to be at the head of an *mbari.* The prestige of this role was emphasized by the fact that the key criterion for entrance into the *ukuru,* the highest grade of elders, was genealogical status, although their duties were primarily ritual.[36] The chief *muramati* of an *mbari* lineage group frequently served as an ukuru elder. This procedure of selecting ritual elders, Lucy Mair points out, should not be difficult to understand "in a society where the spirits of the ancestors bulk so large in religious belief, since such spirits are always believed to be concerned only with their own descendants and approachable only by them."[37] Since there could be only one chief *muramati* to an *mbari,* the pattern was established for younger sons, desirous of reaching high status within the elder grade, to set up separate *mbari*. Another factor that might easily have led to pressure to leave one's own *mbari* was the possible incongruence between high status within the wider age-grade unit and lower status in the lineage.[38] In a society where there were such intense commitments both to the lineage and to the age-grade, status incongruence undoubtedly played an important part in the dynamics of agricultural expansion.

While the more prosperous members of an *mbari* could establish their own unit forthwith, those who had initiative but little wealth usually became tenants (*ahoi;* sing. *muhoi*) on newly founded *mbari*. Here their chances of accumulating wealth and in turn setting up their own *mbari* were much greater than on their already crowded home *githaka*. Agricultural expansion at the margins of Kikuyuland thus reaffirmed the principles of role allocation within the age-grade and the *mbari,* while at the same time relieving population pressure. Although different ways of resolving the strains within Kikuyu society might hypothetically have developed, the important point to note for our purposes is the particular way in which they seem to have been resolved. In the absence of dramatic changes in cultural patterns, social structure and agricultural productivity, the removal of the possibilities for acquiring extensive new land was to have critical consequences for the Kikuyu.

There is ample evidence that at the time of the first wave of European settlement in 1903–4, Kikuyu occupation of southern Kiambu was considerably less extensive than it had been before the famine and the outbreak of smallpox in the disastrous years of 1898 and 1899.[39] A resident at Kikuyu Mission in 1898–99 estimated that between one-half and two-thirds of the nearby population died in these years.[40] If Europeans had not come, or if they had come only as missionaries, traders, and administrators, those areas that later became European coffee estates and dairy farms in Kiambu District would have been Kikuyu settlement and expansion areas. Fort Hall to the north was not so vitally affected by European settlement, although much of the low-lying Maragwa area to the east would have been an important expansion zone. In 1900 Nyeri was a comparatively recent area of settlement for the Kikuyu, and it was not until after the Second World War that population increases became a pressing issue there.

Prior to European settlement, African lands were secured by the Protectorate Regulations of 1897, which provided that no alienation could occur with respect to land regularly utilized by Africans. It could take place only if the Administration was satisfied that the land was no longer regularly used and that Africans would not be adversely affected. Within five years the situation was radically altered as a result of Orders-in-Council, in 1901 and 1902, and the Crown Lands Ordinance, 1902, which gave the Protectorate Government jurisdiction over all lands subject to the right of occupation by Africans. No conception of African ownership of land was recognized; only the occupation and use of land. While land "in actual occupation" could not be sold or leased to settlers, the Crown Lands Ordinance, 1902, did not clearly define the meaning of actual occupation. The decision as to whether or not land was occupied was left to the Administration, and we have seen that time and again large tracts were alienated despite the fact that Africans often were in occupancy and claimed rights to the land. Many Kikuyu on the Kiambu frontier who lost land became squatters on the new European farms; in some cases, on land they regarded as their own. At the most, they received a token payment of compensation for "occupier's rights."

While African rights and claims to lands were frequently overridden in the rush of colonization, not until the Crown

Lands Ordinance, 1915, was it formally recognized that Africans had no inherent or legal rights to land. In addition, few administrators accepted the Kikuyu argument that their system of land tenure approximated a western type.[41] The established official position that "the theory of individual *ownership* of land as understood in English is absolutely foreign to the mind of any African until he has begun to absorb the ideas of an alien civilization" was upheld in the courts.[42] In effect, the provisions in the 1897 Regulations protecting African holdings against land grabbing had disappeared, and any part could be alienated, if the Governor together with the Secretary of State for the Colonies was convinced that the land was not being "beneficially occupied." Not only did the Ordinance of 1915 radically increase African anxiety and insecurity, but also further alienation and encroachment by the Administration on African land, threats of alienation by Administration officers, adverse court decisions regarding African land claims, and the expansionist attitude of the European toward land, all acted to produce widespread discontent and lack of faith in the Administration.

There was, however, accompanying Government's policies of land alienation, a belief that African lands should not be encroached upon to the extent that the people's immediate needs were unable to be fulfilled. In short, Africans should have some security in their own distinct areas despite the continued demands of settlers for more land. This belief developed into a policy that had as its primary aim the fostering of African security by establishing a system of tribal Reserves. Initially the method of reserving land to Africans was to declare their areas to be under the authority of the Outlying Districts Ordinance, which had the effect of regulating non-African entry into the area. The Crown Land Ordinance, 1915, gave statutory recognition to "native" Reserves, but it was not until 1926, after years of African agitation and the recommendation of the East Africa Commission of 1924, that the boundaries of the Reserves were gazetted. This action gave Africans little sense of security since they were still only tenants-at-will living on Crown lands which could be alienated. By 1932, in Kiambu especially, the growing pressure on the land and the insecurity of squatters was expressing itself in an increasing wave of emotion for the return of the "stolen lands." With land as the only real form of security in Kenya's European-dominated, low-wage economy, the cry for the return of "our lands" was from this time forth to prove a most effective theme for nationalist politics.

The Kenya Land Commission

It is hard to exaggerate the ferment caused in Kikuyu country (particularly Kiambu) by the Land Commission. Each *mbari* had to meet and decide what its land claims were to be. It was a time of great expectation and hope. The list of witnesses contained all those with any claim to eminence in Kikuyuland, ranging from senior chiefs through members of Local Native Councils to leaders of the KCA and heads of large and small *mbari*. The demands were much the same, whether they came from representatives of moderate organizations, such as the Loyal Kikuyu Patriots of the Southern District of Kiambu (formerly the Kikuyu Association) and the Progressive Kikuyu Party in South Nyeri, or in the memoranda of the KCA branches or in the verbal testimony of the Kikuyu Land Board Association. There was general support for the same things: the repeal of the 1915 Crown Lands Ordinance, compensation for *githaka* lands that had been alienated for European settlement, control of land to be placed in the hands of Kikuyu Councils, and the provision of more land for the greatly increased population.

The Land Commissioners pursued their difficult task most conscientiously. They heard 736 witnesses, including 487

Africans and 94 European administrators, past and present; read 507 memoranda, 212 recorded statements, and some 400 letters and other documents received from Kikuyu claimants. The Commission's answer to the Kikuyu took up one-third of their Report. They clearly doubted whether any Kikuyu had actually purchased land from the Dorobo, and they rejected the *githaka* concept, scrupulously avoiding awarding any compensation to individuals. They found the Kikuyu evidence conflicting and exaggerated, and estimated that only some 60,000 acres of their land had been alienated by the Government for white settlement. As a result of expansion since 1895, the Kikuyu had already been allocated additional land by the Government, and so the Commission recommended an addition of only 21,000 acres in compensation for all claims, exchanges, and disturbances. For future requirements some 350–400 square miles of poor agricultural land, largely waterless, in the Yattas were made available. These recommendations seemed to hark back to John Ainsworth's testimony before the Land Committee of 1904–5, when he stated that "all we require to do is to see that the native has what is necessary for his existence, and what is necessary for any reasonable increase in numbers of a tribe."[43]

The general effect of the Commission's recommendations was to institutionalize the tribally and racially organized land system that had gradually developed in Kenya since the turn of the century. The closing of the frontier had now been legalized. Africans and Europeans were both to have the maximum possible security in their own separate tribal and racially defined land units. Moreover, in considering African grievances and future needs, the viewpoint was not that of the African population as a whole, but that of each separate tribal group. Tribal boundaries were meticulously designated, even though the Commission at the same time recognized the need to move away from tribalism. The

Commission upheld the privileged position that Europeans had held in the White Highlands from Kiu in Machakos to Fort Ternan in Nyanza since 1903, and which had been confirmed by the Governor, Sir James Hayes Sadler, to the "Colonists Association" in 1906.[44] Two years later Sadler's promise was in turn confirmed by the so-called Elgin Pledge, in which Lord Elgin wrote that "It is not consonant with the view of His Majesty's Government to impose *legal* restriction on any particular section of the community, but as a matter of administrative convenience grants in the upland area should not be made to Indians."[45] Early African attempts to buy land in the Highland areas had quickly been discouraged, Kinyanjui being among those rebuffed.

All claims and rights that Africans had to land in the White Highlands were extinguished with a small payment of compensation to the Local Native Councils. An exclusive "reserve" for Europeans, comprising some 16,700 square miles, was defined. Africans now joined Asians in being denied any rights in the White Highlands, and an agrarian color bar was rigidly drawn around the heartland of the country. Land, always the crucial index of economic enterprise in Kenya, was now used to minimize contact and competition between the races and to differentiate the economic opportunities open to each group. The Report of the Kenya Land Commission was accepted by the British and Colonial Governments, and between 1938 and 1944 various orders-in-council and local ordinances, affecting both land and labor issues, were enacted to implement its recommendations.[46]

Another important consequence was a subtle change in the whole basis of the economy evolved by the Kikuyu in the first decade of the century to meet the problems posed by the redefinition of their frontier situation. The Commission induced the Europeans to reconsider the development of their land unit. Its defense depended on a growth in their relative power, and this depended in turn on a rapid increase in European immigration. This in its turn postulated an intensive form of development to replace the extensive system in vogue up to this time. An intensive system might well require a large labor force, as in the past, but it would be of a different character. In place of the African family sharing the European farm as a permanent fixture in an extension of the tribal way of life, the need was for a temporary laborer without livestock and without roots who would serve out his time and then retire to his Reserve. What the implementation of the Kenya Land Commission Report portended for the Kikuyu people, then, was not merely the closing but also the contraction of their frontiers and a further massive increase in economic problems already intractable enough.

After the Report the White Highlands became a rigid legal term no longer susceptible to the individual pressure and protest that had previously eased its working. As Sir Robert Shaw, the European Member for Ukamba, put it in the Debate on the Report: "The settlement of the Colony is no longer a haphazard, hand-to-mouth system. We are now a definitely settled community, rooted in this land, and the time has quite definitely come when our rights having been established our power to protect these rights should now be vested in our own accredited representatives."[47] The White Highlands had become central to the concept of Kenya as a "white man's country." The very name came to represent a way of life. Increasingly, Europeans became uncompromising in the definition and defense of their White Highlands.

While Government regarded the Commission's recommendations as a "final solution" to the land problem, many Africans, and particularly the Kikuyu, refused to accept it as such. In June 1934, within a month of the publication of the Report, the KCA wrote to the *East African Standard* asking the Kenya Government to defer any final decision on its recommendations until "the Kikuyu people" had a chance to digest its contents.[48] On October 13, 1934, the conflicting Kikuyu political groups, representing the two streams of political thought in the tribe, united together in frank and outspoken condemnation of the Commission's proposals. The KCA, the Loyal Kikuyu Patriots, and the Progressive Kikuyu Party sent a joint memorandum to the Secretary of State for the Colonies in which they said they were appealing the commission's recommendations and that the King should not approve the Report until they had had a chance to send delegates to him.[49]

Land, and all it had come to stand for, remained an emotional force capable of creating a degree of unity among the otherwise divided Kikuyu. They continued year after year to petition the Government, despite the latter's repeated refusal ever again to review Kikuyu claims and grievances. The Land Commission's settlement became a communal charter defining on a racial and tribal basis the amount of land each group possessed. Designed theoretically to encourage feelings of security for both Africans and Europeans, it acted rather to increase African bitterness and frustration without really providing for any additional European security. It prevented any rational allocation and development of land on a national basis, and helped to perpetuate narrowly based tribal economies that were unable to meet the rising aspiration of the growing number of Africans who rejected the economic values of the subsistence society.

Until 1934 "land" was merely one among many grievances on which nationalism could have fed. Others in their effects could have been of equal or more importance—restrictions on the growing of coffee, the absence of good roads or railways in the Reserves, the low level of the agricultural extension services, discriminatory taxes, discrimination in education, marketing, and employment. But "land" was the most visi-

ble, and it had the most immediate effect on the Kikuyu way
of life. The Kenya Land Commission finally assured "land"
of its place as a key political issue. As a barrier to national
integration, the communal charter created by the Commission endured until 1959, while the attitudes to land that it
created remained a persistent theme in Kenya politics up to
the moment of independence.

Developments in the West

Although the land problems of central Kenya played the
dominant role in the unfolding pattern of African nationalism, protest and organization elsewhere in the country were
also making an important contribution during the thirties to
the growth of political consciousness. In the west the Luo
and the Luhya peoples of Nyanza remained in the forefront
of political development. Nyanza politics, however, continued to reflect a different environment and historical experience. Among the array of factors involved was a marked
parochialism stemming from endemic tribal and clan rivalries, and the integration of new leadership elements into
subordinate roles within the colonial state. Social change was
less abrupt in Nyanza than in central Kenya, and tended to
be channeled into new institutions fostering integration and
minimizing conflict. Though land was limited, there was no
critical shortage that could be attributed to alienation for
European settlement. Unlike Kikuyuland there was no major cultural clash with the missions that could form a basis
for agitation. Moreover, the intense anxieties and frustrations felt by many Kikuyu had no counterpart in the west.
Nevertheless, in spite of these factors, two new points of
protest developed in the west during the thirties. The first of
these was among the traders based on Kisumu, whose
interests were beginning to conflict with the Asian domination of commerce in the area.

Founded in 1927 by John-Paul Olola from Alego Location, the Kisumu Native Chamber of Commerce (KNCC) submitted a memorandum to the Kenya Land Commission in which they attacked the KTWA as being a tool of Archdeacon Owen of the CMS, Maseno. In oral evidence they said that the KTWA "recognize the ability and weight of his right arm; we don't know his left."[50] The KNCC rejected the KTWA's request for a Land Register, and attacked the Asians (and the chiefs as their agents) for their monopoly in the marketing of agricultural produce. The issue was free of the emotional haze that surrounded the land question among the Kikuyu; they picked out other factors that were preventing the maximum economic return from land in Nyanza, particularly the prohibition on coffee growing and the discouragement of cotton planting.[51] The KNCC inspired the creation in North Nyanza of a similar body— the North Kavirondo Chamber of Commerce.[52] However, both Olola and the Secretary of the KNCC, Zablon Isaac Nyandoje, were also members of the KTWA, and when Owen gave up the presidency of the KTWA in the mid-thirties, these two men increasingly played prominent roles in the organization, sustaining much of the protest it displayed in the years immediately before the Second World War, when it cooperated with the KCA.

But the most significant protest in Nyanza in the thirties emerged in North Nyanza. It was centered on Kakamega, to which the district headquarters had been transferred from Mumias. The discovery of gold in the district in March 1931 and the subsequent miniature gold rush stimulated the formation of the North Kavirondo Central Association (NKCA), also known as the Abaluhyia Central Association or, more rarely, the Nyanza Central Association. The manner in which an amendment to the 1930 Native Lands Trust Ordinance was rushed through the Legislative Council just before Christmas in 1932 had aroused African suspicions. Under the new law compensation could be paid in money rather than land. The NKCA sought to capitalize on this issue as well as on a projected visit to Kakamega of Sir Philip Cunliffe-Lister, Secretary of State for the Colonies in 1934.

From its inception the NKCA was faced with immense problems of unity and organization in an area of separately defined tribal units with no cross-cutting social institutions. Its first President was Andrea Jumba, a Maragoli schoolmaster living in Tiriki Location, and its first Secretary Erasto Ligalaba from South Maragoli. Ligalaba had been a compositor in Nairobi on the Government Swahili newspaper, *Habari*. Ligalaba was soon replaced by John Adala, from Bunyore Location, who was a master at the Government African School, Kakamega.

Poor communications and the lack of a community of grievances confined sustained political activity to the densely populated southern locations of the district, Maragoli and Bunyore. Even within these southern locations land pressures could be reduced in part by successful emigration within the district into the Tiriki and Nyangori locations and outside it to South Nyanza. It was no coincidence that the militant NKCA thrived in the sphere of influence of the Friends African Mission (FAM). The FAM had not welcomed Archdeacon Owen's activities with the KTWA, the strength of whose Luhya branch largely lay in the CMS sphere of influence in North Nyanza, to the west of the road from Kisumu to Mumias. What missionary help the NKCA did get came from Dr. Bond of the FAM.[53]

As part of an attempt to broaden the basis of support and add legitimacy to the new concept of a united Abaluhya nation, the NKCA soon demanded the recognition of a Paramount Chief as had been exemplified in the career of Mumia (the *Nabongo* of Wanga). For several years they supported the claims of his half-brother, Chief Joseph Mulama, for this position. Like Koinange, Mulama had long been considered by the Administration to be the most able and outstanding man in the district. In 1935 the NKCA proclaimed Mulama the Paramount. He was immediately suspended by the Government, but in pursuit of his goal he visited the Kabaka in Buganda and was also hoping to visit England.[54]

The continuing difficulties, however, in the way of uniting the different groups in the district were reflected in their long search for a satisfactory name to express the new concept they sought. The Luhya branch of the KTWA had discussed this in 1929 and rejected the suggestion of *Abalimi*—"the cultivators." Eventually the NKCA published a pamphlet titled *Avaluhya*—"kinship,"—to publicize and explain their chosen name.[55]

Despite its grave organizational problems, the NKCA remained a factor in the politics of North Nyanza during the thirties and carried on some of the traditions of the KTWA by doing "some useful work in improving water-supplies, including the building of cement wells."[56] In August 1934 they attacked the Kenya Land Commission Report and began developing links with the KCA. In September 1938 Jesse Kariuki, Vice-President of the KCA, accompanied by Isher Dass, visited Mulama. In November 1938, together with the KCA and the KTWA, the NKCA made a joint protest to the Secretary of State against compulsory destocking. This was reprinted in *Muigwithania*. In 1939 there was a further joint KTWA-KCA memorandum to the Secretary of State protesting against the Highlands Order-in-Council, which was read out by Isher Dass in a Legislative Council Debate.[57] In February a joint telegram had been sent to the Secretary of State describing the Government's land policy as "disastrous both to Government and people alike."[58] In March 1940 there was a joint meeting of representatives of the NKCA, the KTWA, and the KCA in Nairobi. Following the example of the KCA, the NKCA also mounted a campaign against soil conservation measures, alleging that the marking-off of areas for conservation was but the prelude to their alienation.

The Kamba "Protest Camp"

Just as the NKCA represented a new protest in the west that in part reflected the issue of the security of African land, so too among the Kamba in central Kenya and the Taita in the hills of the Coast Province issues of agrarian protest became prominent during this period. Agitation against Government policy threw up new leaders and organizations that allied themselves with the KCA.

Kamba protest was by far the more important. The Kamba are closely related to the Kikuyu, and there has been considerable interpenetration of the two tribes in the northern part of the Machakos District of Ukambani, as their country is called. Thuku and Tairara had visited Machakos in the heyday of the East African Association. In 1930 it was reported that KCA leaders had approached the Kamba to get "subscriptions to the political funds" and to suggest that Kamba "representatives should visit other parts of the country to indicate their support of the movement."[59] But according to the Chief Native Commissioner, the Kamba "had refused to receive the agitators and had sent them away."[60]

That the Kamba, the tribe from which so many members of the King's African Rifles and Police recruits had been drawn, and which was renowned for its cheerfulness and loyalty, should become a center of resistance is an ironic commentary on the side effects of the Kikuyu-European land dispute that had in large part led to the appointment of the Kenya Land Commission. The Commissioners, failing to recognize the paradox in reducing the cattle stock in supposedly economic and self-sufficient Reserves, recommended in Machakos the introduction of a policy of active destocking combined with a scheme for reconditioning areas that had been destroyed by erosion.[61] In late 1937 the Government confidently introduced a policy of compulsory destocking.

As we shall see, the action was vigorously opposed, the protest culminating in the following summer, when some 2,000 Kamba, including women and children,[62] trekked forty miles to Nairobi, where they demanded an audience with the Governor, Sir Robert Brooke-Popham, dramatically challenging the "final solution" of Kenya's land problems at the very moment that some of the new legislation it necessitated was under debate in the Colony's Legislative Council. When the Governor refused to see them, they patiently camped near the Nairobi Racecourse for more than three weeks,[63] deaf to the threats of the Nairobi sanitary officials and the appeals of senior Government officers. The extreme care with which the Government treated this outburst of passive resistance in the capital was a tribute to the high esteem in which the Kamba people were held.

The huge ranches alienated to the Europeans along the railway line between Nairobi and Kibwezi, originally planned as a buffer area between the Masai and the Kamba, border the Kamba Reserve. From the increasingly eroded land on his side of the fence the Kamba herdsman cast covetous eyes on the lush grazing land on the other, especially on certain unoccupied ranches. Before the Europeans had been given their frontier lands, the Kamba had developed a mixed economy, primarily based on cattle and admirably suited to the geography and ecology of their country. The greater portion of this was dry grazing land studded with massive hill lumps, usually well watered, on which sustained agriculture was possible. Traditionally, if there was not sufficient grass for the herds the Kamba would take their chance and march over their borders into the various no-man's lands with which they were surrounded. Sometimes they would be successful, sometimes not. But European settlement and closer administration gradually removed even this outlet from them at the same time as modern veterinary skills were preserving their herds from diseases that had previously carried out some natural destocking. The zeal for eradicating stock disease also meant that "most of the native reserves having been kept in perpetual quarantine,"[64] and therefore the sale of cattle outside the Reserve was drastically restricted.

No Kamba would willingly take his cows onto eroded land if there were good grass available. But as modern medicines increased the numbers of both his people and his herds, and British rule confined him within a Reserve, he was forced to; and red hillsides, deeply scarred by erosion, became prominent features of the landscape of Ukambani. An unsigned article in *The East African Agricultural Journal* in July 1935 argued that "as the overstocking problem is the direct result of British rule, there is an obligation upon Government to devise adequate remedies." The author commented that the "optimum carrying capacity of the native reserves was probably reached in 1920, since then the cattle population has doubled."[65]

The local European farmers quickly realized that the contrast in conditions between their land and that of the Reserve might have dangerous consequences, and as early as 1924 the Ulu Settlers Association had demanded immediate action on the problem from the Government. The Government claimed that it had tried as early as 1919 to establish a meat factory.[66] In 1928 the Governor appointed a Committee to enquire into overstocking.[67] Sir Daniel Hall, Chief Scientific Advisor to the British Ministry of Agriculture, visited the district, saw people "beginning to starve by reason of erosion,"[68] and prescribed compulsory limitation of stock and the building of a meat factory for its disposal.[69] In 1930, in a debate on overstocking in the Legislative Council, Lord Francis Scott (who was to succeed Lord Delamere as the settlers' leader) called for 70 per cent of the stock in the district to be culled.⁷⁰ In 1934 the Kenya Land Commission recommended that a special committee be set up to deal with the problem and that compulsion be used to reduce herds "in areas in which the land is being devastated by over-stocking."⁷¹

Another unsigned article in *The East African Agricultural Journal,* in January 1936, pleaded for the use of "compulsory measures" in the interests of "the generations to follow."⁷² In 1937 Colin Maher, the dynamic officer in charge of the Kenya Soil Conservation Service, considered the moment had come for an all-out assault on Machakos, whose increasing population and dearth of overspill areas, even in tsetse regions, made the problem far more serious than in the other Kamba district of Kitui. Maher commented that "every phase of misuse of land is vividly and poignantly displayed in this reserve, the inhabitants of which are rapidly drifting to a state of hopeless and miserable poverty and their land to a parching desert of rock, stones and sand." The "end result of forty years of British administration is that the Reserve stands as a cruelly self-evident indictment of the Kenya policy of modified indirect rule." Maher stated that "the only way out of the vicious circle of overstocking and decreased carrying capacity" was "systematic culling and destruction of the unwanted animals by Government, with or without compensation to the owners," at a rate of 100,000 within four years. He also recommended the extermination of all goats (estimated at 269,000 in Machakos in 1928) within three years, and the closing of 100,000 acres a year to human beings and animals so that the vegetation could regenerate. The population would be resettled in uninhabited parts of the district then dominated by the tsetse fly. These would be cleared and fly-belts established.⁷³ His views were generally supported by Sir Frank Stockdale, Agricultural Advisor to the Colonial Office, in a further report made on a visit to East Africa early in 1937.⁷⁴

The Kenya Land Commission had recommended that

what was called the B2 section of the Yatta Plateau, an area of some 300 square miles between the Athi and Mwita Syano rivers to the east of Machakos, should be added to the Kamba Reserve on condition that its use was tied into a general reconditioning scheme for the Reserve.[75] One aspect of the scheme was the use of machines to recondition the hillsides; the other was to find some outlet for the surplus stock. In August 1936, therefore, negotiations were begun with Liebig's, a commercial meat-canning firm that as early as 1922 had sent two representatives to Kenya.[76] The negotiations resulted in their building a factory, which was opened by the Governor in March 1938, at Athi River on the edge of the Kamba Reserve. It would be unlikely that they would have committed themselves this deeply without some indication from the Government that they could expect a steady flow of cattle. In fact, they were promised 100,000 annually, and an immediate supply of 30,000 head at the prices they mentioned.[77] Such a factory would undoubtedly also have the effect of enhancing the value of the Machakos European ranches.

On July 14, 1937, at a *baraza* at Machakos the Governor announced that action was imminent and that Government would be "prepared to meet resistance."[78] At the beginning of 1938, with a £23,000 loan to the Machakos Local Native Council from the Colonial Development Fund,[79] new staff was drafted in "to destock the reserve by compulsory sales."[80] A free grant of £10,000 was also made "for the comprehensive treatment of 100,000 acres . . . to ascertain what can be done to save these Reserves in Kenya from absolute destruction."[81] A. N. Bailward, the Machakos District Commissioner, estimated that he had 250,000 cows in his District, and that at least 100,000 would have to be removed to bring the numbers down to the carrying capacity of the land.[82] He decided on the following plan to accomplish this within two years. Each sub-location would have an estimated quota, and six elected elders would decide how that quota would be divided among individuals. This would form the basis of "a kind of Doomsday book." All stock would then be brought to a central point, and those over the quota would be disposed of, while those within it would be given a special local brand.

In early 1938 the plan was put into operation. Many former administrators had tried to carry out a destocking program among the Kamba, but none had been very successful. Bailward, however, meant business. Machakos was to be a pilot scheme for other disaster areas in the country, and there were considerable funds invested in it. But opposition kept pace with the program. Soon after the campaign began, some of the Kamba leaders made contact with the KCA in Nairobi, and on March 1 they sent a telegram to the Governor. By April they were sufficiently organized to draft and send a petition to the Secretary of State,[83] a copy of which Jomo Kenyatta also received in London. He wrote the first of five letters on the subject that he was to send to the *Manchester Guardian* within the next four months.[84]

The petition was dated May 2, 1938, and signed by Isaac Mwalonzi, Elijah Kavulu, and Samuel Muindi. It read: "Recently a European firm and Company has erected a factory for the canning of beef and other meat products, on lands adjoining the Athi River Station. It seems that, as a result, efforts are being made by the administration to ensure a steady supply of cattle for slaughter at the factory. The said factory adjoins European owned farms where cattle are stocked. Whether because there are no, or not enough European owned cattle to keep the factory going, pressure is being brought to bear on our tribe to dispose of our stock."[85] The signatories represented a new phenomenon in Kamba politics—the rise of an educated nontraditional leadership. All three had primary education and all three had lived and worked in Nairobi. Mwalonzi had been a teacher, Kavulu a clerk in government service, and Samuel Muindi (also known as Muindi Mbingu) a policeman. It was Muindi who was to prove the most forceful and resilient leader in the tense months that lay ahead. He used the columns of *Muigwithania* and the *East African Standard* to state the Kamba case.

By mid-August Bailward had disposed of 20,000 head at prices that he accepted were "below the value placed by the natives on their stock and less than they have been getting."[86] In fact, some animals went for as little as five shillings, while calves were fetching one shilling or two. Bailward admitted that it was not possible in an auction dealing with 3,000 head of cattle to sell each one individually. The animals were roughly graded in three or four pools, and the average price in each pool was paid to the owners.[87]

In many ways, what land is to the Kikuyu, cattle are to the Kamba. "They are a means of livelihood and the traditional symbol of wealth and honour and are of the utmost importance in almost every transaction in tribal affairs."[88] In May and June in part of sub-headman Nzau's sub-location (Ngelani) of Iveti, the opposition to the Government grew and the people decided not to cooperate. Ngelani is the area nearest to the fertile Mua Hills whence Kamba families had been evicted to make room for European settlers in the early years of the century. Bailward called in police reinforcements from Thika and Nairobi.[89] On July 7, 2,500 head of cattle were seized (from an area of 11,000 acres estimated to have a carrying capacity of 500 head) by a force of some 116 Kenya and Tribal Police armed with rifles. "This action was taken because the natives concerned had adopted an attitude of passive resistance."[90]

The three leaders decided to create an organization called the Ukamba Members Association (UMA). From the start the UMA had close links with the KCA[91] and was also greatly helped and supported by Isher Dass, then a Member of the Legislative Council.[92] Vigorously and vociferously they protested to their headmen, chiefs, and the District Commissioner, none of whom took much notice. Money was collected and meetings were held in Nairobi among the Kamba in the KAR and the Police. Other collections were made in Mombasa, from among the Kikuyu, the Kamba, and other tribes. Protest continued, and the Kamba involved took a general oath of unity, swearing "to refuse any form of co-operation with the administration."[93] There was a "formal cursing"[94] of certain individuals prepared to cooperate with the government.

Then on July 28, about 2,000 Kamba men, women, and children marched to Nairobi to see the Governor. Within the first week, two babies were born in the "Protest Camp," as their bivouac near the Racecourse was christened. "Every night they shivered in their tents, every day vainly sought an audience with the Governor."[95] Isher Dass and the KCA leaders strengthened their resolve and helped them with supplies. Isher Dass himself acted as liaison between the "Protest Camp" and the Chief Native Commissioner.[96] The Governor persisted in his refusal to see them, while they refused to move out of Nairobi until he did. However, Brooke-Popham must have caught a glimpse as "hundreds of Wakamba stood to attention and greeted His Excellency the Governor as his car passed their 'camp' near the Native market on Racecourse Road on Saturday afternoon. He was on his way to the races."[97] On August 3 a letter appeared from Samuel Muindi in the *East African Standard*: "For centuries, we have regarded cattle as the most valuable form of wealth, and now it is a little difficult for us to agree with the sudden and unexpected policy of the Government that destocking sales are in our own interests. More so, when we remember that the best part of our land has landed in the laps of foreigners who have their farms adjoining the reserves." During August protest meetings and demonstrations against Government officials occurred at several places in the Machakos Reserve.

Eventually a compromise was reached. On August 17 the Chief Native Commissioner announced in a Legislative Council Debate in which Dass strongly pleaded the Kamba case that the Governor would hold a *baraza* at Machakos on August 25, when on his way to Kitui and the coast. The Chief Native Commissioner added that no other country had dared to strike at the root of the evil (overstocking), and that the Government was determined to carry it through.[98] The news of the Governor's *baraza* was conveyed to the "Protest Camp," which closed down on Friday, August 19,[99] concluding the campaign of passive resistance.

At the *baraza* 10,000 Kamba listened to a sermon in which the Governor delivered a paternal rebuke.[100] Describing the Kamba as the children of their officers, he attacked their new leaders as agitators who "came in without their head-men; they never put up any complaint or petition through their officers." The leaders of the UMA then presented a memorandum in which they said that they were not opposed to the principle of destocking but protested that the pace was too fast for the ordinary man to comprehend. People with only one cow had been deprived even of it. With respect to the Local Native Councils, they were "a farce as far as effective representation by the people is concerned."[101] The Governor, in announcing the end of the forced sale of cattle by auction and the reintroduction of voluntary sales, had already conceded the victory to the "Protest Camp," although on September 29, Samuel Muindi was arrested under the Deportation Ordinance and on October 4 he was sent to Lamu.

By late November the Governor had reconsidered the policy of forcible destocking, and he wrote that "the whole work is being carried out for the benefit of the Akamba and their children. We shall not have achieved this object if we have to enforce orders with bayonets and machine guns, nor will it be possible to carry out a programme of soil restoration without the full cooperation of those concerned."[102] On December 1, the Governor decided to call off the compulsory culling campaign and return unconditionally to their owners the 2,500 cattle from Ngelani still held by the Government.[103] The adoption of an alternative proposal for "encouraging enclosure of individual holdings,"[104] shut the door on this particular episode of Government policy.

The epilogue came softly, in the Report of a Committee set up by the Government in 1939 to study methods of destocking. Two of its settler members resigned as soon as the Committee rejected compulsion. The Committee, its problems eased by large-scale war-time buying of slaughter livestock for the Army, suggested that improved marketing would be the most practicable solution.

In the areas of low rainfall and poor soil in much of Ukambani, cattle played an essential economic role. But the intense emotion with which the Kamba have always viewed destocking proposals can only be understood in terms of the additional importance of cattle as a social asset and as an integral part of Kamba culture. The 1938 controversy brought forth a group of politicians among the Kamba, much as the female circumcision crisis had among the Kikuyu. Muindi had also clearly seen the artificial nature of the problem, created in part by the land alienation policies of the Government. The Mua Hills, a fertile area from which Kamba families had early been moved to make room for Europeans, remained as much a bone of contention as the grazing in the Yatta plateau. Both were natural expansion areas for the tribe, the Mua Hills being especially coveted by the people from the locations whose inhabitants were most involved in the "Protest Camp." In its destocking proposals the Government exceeded the limits of interference with the ideas and values that cemented the Kamba social structure. The problem of the Kamba cattle could not be handled in isolation as a purely economic question.

In the months before the war the Government anxiously watched the growing liaison between the Kikuyu and the Kamba politicians.* The Administration felt that this alliance had been assisted because administratively the two tribes were in the same Province. After the war, as the bonds grew closer, the Government became sufficiently worried to excise the two Kamba districts from the Central Province. This occurred on August 1, 1953;[105] the Kamba now joined their ancient rivals for grazing lands, the Masai, to form a new Southern Province. In many ways the Kamba episode in 1938 was a precursor of the development of nationalist politics in Central Province after the war, when in so many districts the movement initially took the form of local incidents of passive resistance to Government policies aimed at agricultural betterment. This resistance, though often against the economic interests of the people, was justified in terms of the national struggle.

Taita Agitation

A third organization that became closely linked to the KCA on the eve of the war was the Taita Hills Association (THA). This emerged early in 1939 under the leadership of Jimmy Mwambichi and Woresha Mengo. Government concern was immediately expressed, for by "June 1939 the disciples of the Kikuyu Central Association had so successfully fertilized the seeds of discontent by preaching a gospel of 'insecurity of native lands in Kenya' that between then and May 1940 Government's authority was flouted openly on numerous occasions."[106]

---

* KNA: DC/MKS 10B/15/1. The UMA used the KCA's offices and under the presidency of Elijah Kavula initiated a campaign against new government anti-soil-erosion measures, especially the demarcation of holdings with sisal. In 1939 the UMA sent another memorandum to the Secretary of State elaborating on its grievances.

At the root of this agitation were critical economic problems, which were especially serious in the "Dabida" part of the Taita Reserve. It was estimated that in this area the population was about 40,000, with a density of 476 persons per square mile of cultivable land.[107] In 1932 it was estimated that the rate of population increase was 4.5 per cent per annum.[108] The Taita, who had looked upon the plains beneath the Taita Hills as an overspill area, found these closed to them by the alienation of large areas for European sisal plantations. The Kenya Land Commission recognized their claims, which had been supported in evidence before them by both Government officials and missionaries, and recommended extensions amounting to 200 square miles to the "Dabida" part of the Reserve, increasing the area available by 40.5 per cent. They also recommended the provisional extension of a further 119 square miles, which could be made permanent "if the natives prove their need of it by conducting a vigorous campaign to destroy the tsetse fly."[109]

However, this did not satisfy a growing element among the Taita who were claiming all the land on the plains beneath their hills. This dissatisfaction crystallized into more active protest over the Government's policy toward a block of eleven square miles of European-alienated land which the Land Commission had recommended should be allocated in settlement of the "thorny" problem of the Kasigau.

The Kasigau, a tribe of some 400 people who occupied Kasigau Hill to the southeast of Taita District, were suspected of treacherously revealing the location of a British outpost to the Germans early in the First World War. They were immediately moved *en masse* to Malindi at the instance of the military authorities.* After the war, in 1920, they were allowed to return to Taita District but not to Kasigau Hill. Instead, "for administrative reasons"[110] they were settled at

---

* Three hundred and fifty Kamba were also moved back to Machakos from the same area at this time for similar reasons.

Mwatati in the northwest corner of what was to become LR.3880 (a vast block of 36,184 acres leased to Teita Concessions Ltd. in 1927). As this estate was developed they were slowly moved to the southern part of it near Sembe and the Vongoloni Hills.[111]

The Land Commission recommended that eleven square miles of LR.3880, roughly corresponding to the area they occupied, should be handed over to the Kasigau, and that the area should be linked with the Dabida Reserve by a narrow corridor. Teita Concessions Ltd. were not compensated for this, since they had already been given another large area (LR.6924) in compensation for the rights of the Kasigau and Taita, who were in actual occupation of land on LR.3880 at the time the lease was granted. However, in May 1937 the Kasigau decided to return to their original mountain home in Kasigau.

At this point "some of the better educated Taita" who were aware of the Land Commission's recommendations thought that "the Taita had a claim to the land vacated" by the Kasigau.[112] By March 1938 they had begun to "trespass" on the Teita Concession land at Mwatati. This encroachment was to continue. Between December 1938 and June 1939 "contacts were made with the Kikuyu Central Association and advice obtained as to the way to tackle government on land problems."[113] The District Commissioner notes that the Taita Hills Association "was formed to right what was considered to be a just grievance and failing to achieve its end—the return of certain land alienated to Teita Concessions Ltd.—became completely anti-government."[114]

Dissatisfaction and trespass continued and was not quieted by the arrest of Mwambichi and Mengo in May 1940 together with the leaders of the KCA and the UMA. In September 1943, Shirley Cooke, a former administrator and Member for the Coast, raised the Taita land claims in the Legislative Council. In his reply the Commissioner for Lands stated that both the Provincial and the District Commissioners were aware of "the claim of the Teita people for occupation rights over certain portions of Crown Land between Mwatate and Bura" and had set up a Committee to investigate and report on the claims.[115] This Committee, among whose members was F. O'B. Wilson, recommended that 10,000 acres should be added to the Taita Reserve, half of which were owned by Teita Concessions Ltd., the other half being unalienated Crown Land.

The NKCA, the UMA, and the Taita Hills Associations all represented a growth in political consciousness in different parts of the country. Although they had neither a broad base of support nor the political experience of the KCA, they nevertheless achieved three significant results. They introduced modern political methods and organization to important areas; they provided the opportunity for several new leaders, who were to play roles in the postwar development of the Kenya African Union (KAU) to serve their political apprenticeships; and they confirmed the leadership of the KCA in a wider political context.

The Kikuyu Central Association (1938)

Though the KCA sought to provide a focus for territorial organization,* Kikuyu grievances dominated its concerns. In 1938 the KCA was reconstituted as KCA (1938), with George K. Ndegwa as Acting General Secretary. It issued a stream of petitions, particularly on behalf of various groups of right-holders whose claims to land in the White Highlands had been extinguished by law upon the recommendation of the Kenya Land Commission. The number of claims for com-

---

* In a petition to the Secretary of State dated 11 September 1939, signed by George Ndegwa, Acting General Secretary of KCA (1938), this territorial concept is revealed: "We the Kikuyu, Wakamba and Wataita Central Association representing the Kenya Africans as a whole . . ."

pensation was far greater than had been envisaged. Indeed on investigation the numbers concerned proved "to be about ten times the number mentioned by the Commission," and a senior Government official noted that "it is unlikely a final and equitable solution of the problem will be easy."[116] A center of bitter dispute was the Tigoni area of Kiambu, where offers of other land by the Administration were refused by some right-holders. Their case became a central part of KCA protest and greatly strengthened the KCA's support in Kiambu.

The findings of the Kenya Land Commission had stimulated the Administration to look anew at the problem of soil conservation in the Reserves. Henceforth there was increased emphasis on terracing and similar measures and recourse to methods of compulsion to ensure that they were carried out. The KCA opposed this policy, as did the NKCA in Nyanza, and both found therein another easily exploited source of support. For example, in May 1938 in Embu (where a strong KCA branch had existed since 1930), after certain soil conservation rules had been passed by the Local Native Council, the women of Ndia division pulled up the grass they had been ordered to plant as wash stops and went to Nairobi to protest.[117]

During this period, Dr. Ralph Bunche, then a Professor at Howard University, visited Kenya, spending considerable time with Senior Chief Koinange and other Kikuyu leaders.[118] To the political leaders in Kiambu, Bunche's visit in early 1938 greatly reinforced their conviction of the justice and rightness of their grievances. He stimulated their pride in being African and symbolized the possibility of Africans rising to high positions and significant roles of leadership in a modern society. Like Dr. James Aggrey, who visited Kenya in 1924 with the Phelps-Stokes Educational Commission, Bunche represented contact with the outside world beyond the confines of the colonial framework; his stay became a part of the nationalist tradition, and was commemorated by his invitation to the 1963 Independence celebrations.

In 1938, with the return of Mbiyu Koinange* after receiving an M.A. from Columbia University, the idea took root of founding an African university. It may be that Bunche influenced Koinange's thinking on the need to improve educational opportunities in Kenya.

As we have seen, the impetus for the original KISA and Karing'a movement had come predominantly from cultural issues; the new Kenya African Teachers' College (KATC), however, was a response to a developing feeling that education was the key to political power, that it was a critical weapon for overcoming the barriers to political and economic advance. It was Mbiyu Koinange who thought to turn the Githunguri KISA school into a higher college, not just for the Kikuyu but for all Kenya Africans. Its name proudly proclaimed its transtribal aspiration.

Mbiyu's father, Senior Chief Koinange, had sent Mbiyu to America for education in 1927. On his return in 1938 he was offered a post in Government service at a salary much lower than that paid to Europeans with similar qualifications. He therefore rejected it. In winning support for the college, which he insisted must not become a tribal establishment. Mbiyu had a major ally in his father.

By the late 1930s Senior Chief Koinange had actively explored ways of fostering African advancement. He now felt that he could serve his people best by exploiting his good reputation with the Administration to further by all possible means the struggle for land, education, and freedom. In 1939 he petitioned the Governor not to move African rightholders from their land in the White Highlands, and asserted

---

* Originally christened Peter Mbiyu Koinange, he later dropped the "Peter."

that there were over fifty well-educated Africans fully capable of representing African interests in the Legislative Council, in the Municipal Council of Nairobi, and on the Land Boards.[119]

In 1938 Senior Chief Koinange brought together a number of age-groups to help raise funds for the new college. By this act the second major feature of Kikuyu social structure, the *riika*, was harnessed to modern politics. Kikuyu say, *Nyumba na Riika itiumagwo,* "you cannot get away from your family [the *mbari* or *nyumba*] or your age-group [the *riika*]." At the meeting Koinange announced to the representatives of the most senior age grades, collectively named *Njunge,* that "this school will be the grinding stone on which we will sharpen our children!"[120]

On January 7, 1939, the college was formally opened. The Government and all heads of departments were invited; however, only the Director of Education and the Acting Chief Native Commissioner attended. A Kikuyu elder, Muiruri Gatii, officiated at the opening ceremony. Holding a staff and leaves which symbolized that he had fulfilled all the tribal rites applicable to the highest office, he renamed the old KISA school the Kenya African Teachers' College.[121]

The opening of the College dramatically fulfilled a well-known prophecy of Mugo Kibiru, a famous Kikuyu seer who had once lived at Githunguri and whose sayings became a vital part of Kikuyu nationalist lore. When Kibiru was about to die, he called all the elders together to tell them what would happen to the country. As he handed over his responsibilities to Waiyaki he said, "Our land will be taken by some strangers whose skins are like red ochre (*ciengele*) and whose bodies are like moths (*ciihunita*) and from whose mouths comes out smoke. These people will come with a very big snake stretching from Mombasa to the lake of the uncircumcized in the west and this snake cannot be cut. They will pass by the stone cave of Chege wa Nyamu at

Limuru. But they will start to move from our country when the stone house with eight doors is built at Githunguri wa Irira and they will finally go when the fig tree at Thika bends and falls."[122]

Though the Government disliked the establishment of the College, it accepted that it had lost the initiative. Meanwhile, the age groups, elated by the successful opening, pressed on with the building fund. Each age group was asked to find 1,000 shillings. The collection of such amounts stimulated the formal organization of age groups by districts, with local chairmen and secretaries at all levels topped by a national committee. Although their organization was not completely established until after the Second World War, the age groups became a dominant part of the educational branch of the KCA organization. Just as collections for land petitions were carried out through the *mbari,* so collections for education were carried out through the *riika.* Githunguri, created out of nothing on the overwhelming emotional waves of the demand for education as an instrument of moderniza- tion, became in turn a powerful symbol for political con- sciousness.

Labor Unrest in Mombasa

The foundations of the growing militance in the character of African politics after the Second World War were to be found not only in the accelerating pattern of dissent in the rural areas but also among the developing African societies in the towns. It was ultimately to be in Nairobi that the political leadership became willing to use violence and other than constitutional methods to achieve reform. A spontane- ous series of strikes in Mombasa in July 1939 was a signifi- cant prelude to this new phase in Kenya politics, whereby the Administration's inability to resolve the increasingly complex range of urban problems in a racially stratified country was to be an important factor in turning men bitterly against the Government and the belief that reforms could be achieved by constitutional means.

On July 19, 1939, there was a "sit down, very orderly, strike"[123] among the laborers in the Public Works Department at Mombasa. From July 24, the strike spread rapidly to workers in the Municipality, the Electric Light and Power Company, the oil companies, and the Posts and Telegraphs Department. Employees of vegetable-growing firms and the town dairies were also involved. By August 1 the strike had spread to the dockworkers and on August 2 it "reached its height."[124] Pickets were out in force, and a crowd of 1,500 met that day at the Bonded Warehouse in the port area. In the town the police dispersed the strikers with baton charges; there were some instances of looting, and 150 people were arrested. However, by August 4 the strike was over and practically all the laborers had returned to work.[125] Two weeks later the Government appointed a Commission of Inquiry to examine labor conditions in Mombasa.

The strikers had chosen a dramatic moment—the beginning of the Second World War—to draw attention to Mombasa's role in the new Kenya. Up to the beginning of the twentieth century Mombasa was the dominant factor in the development of the East Africa Protectorate. It was the base of the Imperial British East Africa's Company's ventures. It was the springboard for much mission activity; indeed, it contained, in the colony for freed slaves at Freretown, substantial evidence of Christian success. Mombasa in these early years almost *was* mainland East Africa, and this state of affairs continued until the coming of the railway. Thereafter Mombasa declined in importance and receded into the political background. In much of West Africa the coastal areas became the focus of modernization and nationalist activities, but in Kenya this took place inland.

Yet the railroad also brought thousands of up-country

people to work at the port that has been so vital to the remarkable economic development of the southwest quadrant of the country. This influx in its turn slowly changed Mombasa's whole character. It is estimated that by 1939 there were at least 5,000 Luo, 5,000 Kikuyu, and 2,000 Kamba in the town, compared with at least 3,000 Arabs and Swahilis, 2,000 Coast Africans, and 3,000 Tanganyikans.[126] The Kamba connection had long been there, since they once controlled the inland trade routes, but twentieth-century Mombasa also filled up with dockworkers from Kisumu, vegetable sellers from Taita, and railway-workers from Kikuyu. Mombasa was no longer only an ancient Arab-Swahili city; it was now the critical port for the new Kenya.

Although Arab domination declined with the new industrial expansion, Mombasa remained legally part of the Zanzibar Protectorate, administered by Britain on behalf of the Sultan of Zanzibar. Nonetheless, it was politically and economically an integral part of the mainland. The European M.L.C.s from the Coast Province were often the odd men out in the Legislative Council. They represented the distaste of the cosmopolitan Coast for the rigid up-country racial attitudes. The freer environment and racial atmosphere in Mombasa also affected the growth of African politics there. The Kikuyu and Luo "colonies," far from their homelands, developed welfare organizations, as did many other groups.

Although Mombasa had not been a center of grievances, the labor unrest in 1939 illustrated the growing and critical problems of the urban areas. In the more fragmented commercial and industrial situation of Nairobi, with its rigid patterns of racial segregation, strike action by Africans was far more difficult to organize. But in Mombasa the concentrated strength of the dockworkers was to prove a powerful weapon; and their participation in the 1939 strike was the first tentative exploitation of their potential. The dockworkers' ability to create an economic crisis is today a significant factor in Kenya politics.

The Commission of Inquiry sat in public for 8 days and heard 119 witnesses, comprising 25 Europeans, 8 Indians, and 86 Arabs and Africans. The report discounted the general explanation of the strike as being due to "Kikuyu agitators" or the machinations of the Labour Trade Union of East Africa. At the same time it revealed the economic and social conditions under which the urban African in Mombasa existed. Fifty-two per cent of the total Railway staff at Mombasa received twenty shillings a month.[127] A considerable number of these people were not provided with a house or a housing allowance. In June 1931 daily wage rates for casual labor had been reduced because of the slump from two shillings to one shilling and fifty cents a day.[128] They had never been increased again. Road laborers working for the Municipality were paid sixteen shillings a month and lived in quarters that had been condemned.[129]

Housing was the particular problem on which the Commissioners concentrated. They found that the Government, the Municipality, and most of the private firms were evading the law by not providing housing, or an adequate housing allowance, for their workers. In the town dairies "the employees sleep on mats or pieces of corrugated iron, either above or amongst the cattle, and they have very little protection from the weather."[130] In those houses that were available for renting, the Commission noted that "cleanliness is almost impossible, latrines adjoin kitchens, light and ventilation are almost absent. In many rooms we visited it was impossible to read at any time during the day. Overcrowding seemed to be prevalent, and under such conditions as these the health of the occupants must suffer."[131]

One of the most significant witnesses at the Inquiry was Makhan Singh, General Secretary of the Labour Trade Union of East Africa. He told the Commissioners that his Nairobi-based Union had as members some 3,000 Indians,

2,000 Africans, and 2 Europeans. He also said that the Union had a Mombasa branch, and reminded them that the Indian workers of Mombasa had declared a small strike in December 1938, although the strike in Nairobi in 1937 had also made "the method of striking" known. It was not necessary, he argued, to seek manipulation by outsiders as the cause of the strike. There was more than enough reason in the working conditions in the town. "In some quarters responsibility for the strike has been laid upon some 'agitators.' We stress that there can never be a strike unless the conditions become unbearable. When workers declare a strike they select some of themselves to make speeches and to organize the strike. Now these speakers and organizers are called agitators and undesirables in the dictionaries of the employers." Makhan Singh also demanded a minimum wage of 50 shillings a month, an eight-hour day, and a 45-hour week.[132]

Although the strike did bring about certain small changes for the better in the port's working conditions, the outbreak of war inhibited any further action upon the critical problems the Report had revealed. But the strike remained important as the first indication of the extent and depth of these problems, a forerunner of the labor situation in postwar Nairobi. In the exploitation of these problems for both industrial and political purposes, Makhan Singh was to be a crucial figure.

Banning of African Associations

On the outbreak of the Second World War the Kikuyu Central Association, the Taita Hills Association, and the Ukamba Members Association sent a joint memorandum of loyalty to the Governor. But their opposition to Government measures and policies affecting land issues did not slacken.*

---

* Kenya Land Department, 30/11/3/1/11. In addition to petitions by the KCA in Kenya, Kenyatta in London requested in April 1940 an interview with the Secretary of State for the Colonies, to discuss in particular the question of the Tigoni right-holders.

However, an Administration anxiously viewing the threat of an Italian invasion from the north had little time for such distinctions, and by this time most administrators sincerely considered the activities of the KCA subversive. Colonialism implied certain norms of deference and subordination to established authority, and many of the activities of the KCA had the effect of continuously undermining these principles of behavior.

On May 27 and 28, 1940, twenty-three leaders of the KCA, the UMA, and the THA were detained under the Defence Regulations, 1939. The NKCA leaders at a meeting with the District Commissioner at Kakamega agreed to disband voluntarily for the course of the war. In fact the District Commissioner continued to use them to help with the recruiting campaign and other wartime measures. The detentions took place a week before Italy entered the war and in the same month and under the same law that was used for detaining Italian and German aliens in Kenya.

All twenty-three appealed under the regulations to an Advisory Committee consisting of Sir Charles Belcher, a former Chief Justice of Uganda, then farming in the Kinangop, Colonel L. K. Stanbrough, D.S.O., and W. C. Hunter,[133] a prominent early leader of the Convention of Associations. The Advisory Committee assembled in the District Commissioner's office, Naivasha, to hear their objections. The Government had to show that they had been or were likely to assist the enemy. The Provincial Commissioner, Central Province, about this time described their activities as "probably treasonable."[134] The records of the inquiry, which heard evidence for nine days and took ten weeks to report, are not available, but the appeal was rejected.

All the accused strenuously denied any association with foreign powers. The discovery of *Mein Kampf,* then on sale in the Nairobi bookshops, in a raid on May 20 on the KCA offices was one of the grounds for detention,[135] while another was alleged meetings with the Italian Consul. In a statement issued to the press, the Government claimed that the leaders of the Association "in spite of protestations of loyalty to the Government, have prevented their members from acting as loyal men, binding them by disloyal oaths."[136]

Twenty-two were sent to detention at Kapenguria, one Ndeti Matapaboi (a Dorobo) eventually being freed at Naivasha.[137] In 1942 the District Commissioner at Kapenguria noted: "It is worthy of record that the inmates of the Internment Camp voluntarily subscribed to the Sailors' Week Fund."[138] But they all refused to work, regarding themselves as political detainees not as ordinary criminals. The Kamba among them filled the boring hours by teaching the others how to make their famous wood carvings, and the detainees established a thriving cooperative business in this line.

In the Reserves the administrators all breathed sighs of relief. The District Commissioner, Fort Hall, noted in 1939, "Chief Michuki once said of an Association member that he was the louse in the Government's blanket and so made us all itch! There is a lot in that remark." In 1940 the same District Commissioner commented that "trying to administer a District infested with the KCA was rather like driving a motor car with a brake binding." However, in 1941 he recorded that the "detention of the Kikuyu Central Association leaders at Kapenguria has been a godsend but there have been signs latterly that this body is not dead and some of the more prominent of those not yet detained have been meeting secretly in Nairobi and this District during the past three months."[139]

Though leaderless and powerless, the KCA, which claimed a membership of 7,000 in early 1940, was still very much alive, and while the members were dutifully helping the British in their war in the day time, at night in their smoky huts they had started to talk again about the lands they had lost and the freedom they hoped to gain. By now some of them were getting bored with just talking.

CHAPTER 6

The Frustrations of Territorial Nationalism

The Second World War was a watershed in the growth and development of African nationalism in Tropical Africa. Prior to the war African political organizations neither commanded a mass following nor essentially challenged the legitimacy of the colonial state. The postwar years were to witness a new politics—mass political movements under a leadership determined to replace colonial rule with African majority rule. In West Africa, the National Council of Nigeria and the Cameroons, formed in 1944, was first in the field demanding new and radical changes, while in East Africa, the Kenya African Union, founded in the same year, was the pioneer organization. Although the tasks of building mass movements were formidable in West Africa, such movements did develop within those British and French colonial systems amenable to substantial political change. Nationalism remained within constitutional limits and was able to play a constructive role in the peaceful transfer of power from Europe to West Africa.

The aims and organizations of African nationalism in Kenya had much in common with the developments in West Africa, but at the same time opportunities for African participation in national institutions were severely limited.

The colonial goal in Kenya was not to create an African state, but rather a "western" state under multi-racial leadership. Postwar nationalism developed in an environment marked by the efforts of settler leaders, helped indirectly by the development policies of the local Administration, to consolidate their political power. The organizations and tactics employed by African leaders to change this restrictive situation took various forms, both overt and covert. Here we shall examine the overt, constitutional level of postwar African politics in Kenya. With the failure on this level to achieve substantial reform, militant leaders and covert organizations assumed the dominant role in challenging European and colonial control.

The Political Impact of the Second World War

When the Government declared the KCA, the UMA, and the THA "dangerous to the good government of the Colony,"[1] and detained many of the leading African politicians under the Defence Regulations, they undoubtedly hoped to contain political agitation. The Administration, depleted and over-extended by the pressing calls of a war now on Kenya's doorstep, intended to remove at least this one nagging worry from their crowded lives. The *East African Standard,* in an editorial about 'Fifth Columnists,' welcomed firm action against subversive associations "of every races."[2] Nevertheless, two important KCA leaders who were not detained—James Beauttah from Fort Hall and Jomo Kenyatta in England—were of some assistance in different ways to the British war effort.

Beauttah, elected in 1937 (along with Job Muchuchu) as a member of the Fort Hall Local Native Council, recalls that "elected members were in a majority at that time. I thought the L.N.C. a useful platform in that situation for airing grievances and I put forward a lot of motions in the L.N.C. to change and ameliorate conditions in the District. We discussed land questions. We had an L.N.C. Land Board. But politics were not allowed. The D.C. would stop us. I was not deported in 1940 because the D.C. of the time was friendly to me. . . . I went around talking to the people, urging them to volunteer to help in the war. I wanted them to fight. . . . After a motion on it [the war] had been passed by the L.N.C.,[3] I went around telling people to help buy the Spitfire to give to the King."[4]

Kenyatta spent the war years in the small Sussex village of Storrington, about forty miles south of London, where he found a job on a farm: "first on a general non-mechanized farm where he could learn the ropes thoroughly, and then in a tomato house. He was a terrific worker, popular company at the pub of an evening, and managed at the same time, to take a W.E.A. [Workers Educational Association] class . . . and keep chickens and grow vegetables."[5] He also lectured for over five years on African Affairs to the British Army, in various searchlight units and in military barracks.[6] Thus the KCA's representative in England, far from being detained under the Defence Regulations, was allowed to educate the British Army about Africa.

The critical factors in the selection in the Kenya detainees seem to have been official position in the KCA (1938), involvement in the organized Kamba resistance to compulsory destocking, and leadership in the resistance at Tigoni. But the detentions and the banning of political organizations, neither of which the Government even mentioned in the Legislative Council, could not destroy the KCA. By this time it was not so much dependent on individual men and efficient organization as on a body of people sharing common political ideas. During the war, when political activity was out of the question, the KCA continued to function intermittently through small local committees. Their prime task at this time was to organize collections for the families of those detained at Kapenguria.

Although these small spontaneous committees performed a useful function in keeping the spark of nationalism alive, of far greater importance in the postwar development of mass political activities was the wartime involvement of a new generation in the struggle against Germany, Italy, and Japan. Out of the First World War had come the East African Association. Out of the Second was to come the Kenya African Union (KAU).

At the beginning of the war the East African fighting forces consisted of seven battalions. From early 1940 this base was rapidly expanded to a final total in the neighborhood of 280,000 men, of whom Kenya contributed about 75,000.[7] Amid fervent assertions that the earlier tragedy of the Carrier Corps would not be repeated, a Military Labour Service and a Pioneer Corps were also raised. Even so the number of Kenya Africans directly involved was probably little greater than in the First World War. There was however, one important difference.

The decision in 1942 by which the King's African Rifles found themselves fighting for the first time outside Africa had far-reaching results.[8] It involved a radical change in principle from previous policy. For the first time Africans found themselves enlisting not to protect directly their own country, but in the service of an international cause, variously defined and expressed but usually called by some such phrase as "the preservation of liberty and democracy." A special Government committee set up during the war to consider the question of postwar African employment readily recognized that the African veteran of the Second World War would create a new set of problems. "In the last war the African fought only in East Africa amongst peoples speaking the same languages and practising similar customs. With few exceptions he was either an infantryman with rifle and bayonet or a carrier with a load. He had not yet acquired the habit of working for a wage and the home from which he was recruited was not in that state of economical and political flux in which it is today."[9]

Thus the new generation of ex-soldiers, a large proportion of whom had a smattering of elementary education, had absorbed all the same influences as had their fathers in the Carrier Corps, but they also had had certain significant additional experiences. For example, thousands of them saw service in India, whose politicians had been actively agitating for an assurance of a rapid advance to independence. Three postwar African leaders have described some of the effects of these experiences.

Waruhiu Itote from Nyeri (the "General China" of the Emergency) tells of a chance meeting at a railway station in India with an Indian girl brought up in East Africa; she told him of Britain's promise to India regarding self-government, and then, asking him what he thought he was fighting for, taxed him with his mercenary status. Itote has also described another meeting he had with an American Negro at a leave camp in India which resulted in lengthy political discussions centered on the color bar.[10]

Bildad Mwaganu Kaggia, a prominent activist in the postwar trade union movement and later in the Kenya African Union, said that while in the army he

> visited Egypt, Libya, Syria, and Israel, and in 1943 I went to England to establish a reception camp for African prisoners of war repatriated from Germany. I met Jomo [Kenyatta] while I was in England. I first became really interested in politics when I was in the Middle East. Previously I had been a keen student of religion, but after seeing the Holy Land I looked at Christianity in a different way. I saw the establishment of foreign religion through missions as a stepping-stone to colonialism, and I therefore thought that the first move in the struggle for independence must be liberate our people from foreign religious beliefs. These missions used slogans that supported the colonial authorities, such as "The Government or Powers that be are ordained by God." Many of our people,

fed by this, believed it and could not be expected to fight with their lives for their real rights while still believing it. The missions on their side also found certain advantages in the preservation of colonial rule.[11]

Kaggia had left the CMS primary school at Kahuhia in Fort Hall in 1939 and worked in the District Commissioner's office until January 1942, when he joined the Army as a clerk, reaching the rank of Staff Sergeant before demobilization.[12] The Bildad Kaggia of 1945 was a very different man from the recruit of 1940. On his return, after coming into conflict with the authorities at the Kahuhia mission, he began strongly attacking all missionary churches. His movement rapidly spread in Fort Hall, and elsewhere in central Kenya, ultimately even reaching Nyanza. Though he deliberately avoided naming this group, it became widely known as the *Dini ya Kaggia*.

Dedan Mugo Kimani, who was elected president of the All-Kikuyu Age Groups at a meeting at Githunguri in February 1947, has described how he became an instructor in the Army Hygiene Section, and later "joined 11 Division for fighting the Italian Army [and] became a Sergeant Instructor teaching Europeans (Majors, Colonels, all ranks in East African Medical Services) Swahili. I stayed one year in Ethiopia, visiting Addis Ababa and Asmara in 1941, returned in March 1942 to Kenya, and became Senior Sergeant Major W.O.II at Gilgil as Hygiene Instructor. I began to be a politician because the treatment of African non-commissioned officers was discriminating. Clothes, rations, quarters, were different from Asians and Europeans. I tried to agitate inside the Army but I was court-martialled for this in Gilgil in 1944 and sentenced to three months detention."[13] In December 1945 he was discharged on medical grounds and returned to Kiambu, where he was employed by the African Demobilization Unit. He became president of the Kenya Ex-Servicemen in September 1946, and was elected to the Kiambu Local Native Council in

October. In 1950 Kimani was convicted of administering an illegal oath in the first such case brought by the Government in Kiambu District.

These were but three among the many who during the years of demobilization from 1944 to 1946 flooded back to Kenya with new values and with their expectations raised by the war. An official Government report discussed the qualities shown by the African soldier during the war. "His capacity for taking responsibility and his skilled work have surprised those who knew him only as a manual labourer," wrote the members of the postwar African employment sub-committee. They followed with a warning:

> He has shown his worth and it will not be surprising if he expects to see it acknowledged. A second factor is the standard of life to which he has become accustomed. He has been well clothed and shod; he has been fed on a balanced and ample diet; and his medical and material needs have been carefully tended. His pay has been comparatively high and on discharge the habits of the standard of life he has acquired will not easily fall from him. His desires will be such that he will not generally be content with the low standard with which most Africans were content before the war.[14]

By comparison with other Kenya tribes, few Kikuyu were front-line soldiers; when assessing the military ability of various Kenya tribes, one senior administrative officer, with the tendency for stereotyping tribes so prevalent among colonial officials, disparagingly dismissed the Kikuyu in one line: "The contribution of the Kikuyu is mainly as clerks, signallers, hospital staff and personal servants."[15] But in total war such differences tended to be ironed out, and in desperate situations personal servants became as much involved as their masters. Those Kikuyu who served overseas came from a tribe that had been subjected to profound missionary educational effort and also had a history of twenty years of agitational politics, both of which factors greatly accentuated the impact of their various wartime experiences.

"White Man's Country"[16]

The "white man's country" to which the demobilized African soldiers returned had changed immensely. The most significant economic change had been in the growth and expansion of European agriculture, which was to continue to make tremendous strides in the immediate postwar years. In the crisis of war the European agricultural community had greatly strengthened their control over the country's economy, and, more particularly, increased their dominance in the organizational structure of the agricultural industry. Indeed, through the various interterritorial boards established to control production, they had achieved a degree of influence over the affairs of the whole of East Africa that they were never again to approach. Acute food shortages, caused not only by the curtailment of food imports owing to the lack of shipping space, but also by drought and the need to feed a large army, compelled the Government as a first priority to increase local production as rapidly as possible in order to make East Africa self-sufficient in foodstuffs. The brunt of this task fell on the Kenya settlers.

Throughout the war years, production in the country was controlled by the Agricultural Production and Settlement Boards, which directed a network of District Production Committees whose job was to tell every European farmer what and how much to plant and to make sure he did it. Patriotism combined with prospects of personal gain to ensure a magnificent response to the demands. Encouraged on the same pattern as England's farmers with grants for breaking new land, with guaranteed minimum returns per acre, and with fertilizer and seed subsidies, the settlers did all that was asked of them. In addition to cereal production, the acreage of coffee, tea, and sisal was expanded to the limit as wartime demands soared, owing to Japan's occupation of some former sources of production. During the war the value of domestic exports nearly doubled, reaching £7.1 million in 1946. European farmers had achieved a remarkable prosperity and were financially and psychologically more secure than they had ever been before.

Toward the end of the war the European leadership began to recognize the need for a different type of political organization to assert and advance their interests in the postwar period, sensing they would have old and new battles to fight in an era of postwar liberalism. Not only would Asian pressure again have to be contained, but African development also would have to be carefully guided. Moreover, Kenya's economy was no longer merely agricultural, but increasingly commercial and industrial as well. The former Convention of Associations (the "People's Parliament"), a loose confederation of District Associations primarily expressing farming interests, was moribund. Though it had been an effective vehicle in the past for expressing political demands in the most direct and forthright terms, many now recognized the need for a more sophisticated body, able not only to coordinate the activities and interests of the increasingly diversified European community in Nairobi with the rural District Associations, but also to provide a permanent source of information, guidance, support for, and pressure on, the European Elected Members. In a politics of growing cooperation and understanding between the Administration and the settler, different methods and techniques would be required.

After a number of preliminary meetings, a new body, the Electors' Union, came into being in March 1944. At the outset it declared that it was not a "party" organization, that it had no party purposes or aims, but was rather a "body at the disposal of the community for the common good."[17] A main function was to achieve and maintain European unity in coming situations of conflict that might well divide them. The Union hoped that Government would permit (as indeed they did) the heads of departments to attend and take part in conference meetings. In stating its objectives, emphasis was laid upon the long-established policy of safeguarding the White Highlands as a permanent home for Europeans and their descendants. Though they must work for increased white settlement, they must also develop an equitable and progressive policy to make European and African interests complementary. In this respect Europeans in the postwar era must repeatedly press their right to be consulted by, and associated with, Government in their joint responsibilities as trustees of Africans.[18] These were, of course, not new objectives, but the executive committee of the Union undertook to formulate a policy and strategy to achieve them in the new conditions of the postwar years.

In the subsequent *Outline of Policy* adopted at the conference of the Electors' Union in January 1946, the general principles governing political advance were set forth. Among them was the requirement that "leadership" remain in European control; moreover, the influence of settlers at the official level should be expanded in conjunction with a gradual move toward lessening the direct influence and intervention of the British Colonial Office. The settlers recognized the justice of "giving to the African reasonable representation" in the Legislative Council, but qualified this acceptance, contending that any expansion should be gradual and "in accord with the development of the African sense of civic responsibility." It was emphasized "that for very many years to come, the African community will be unfitted to exercise the privilege of election of its representatives."[19] Indian representation should also be limited and restricted.

In its organization, meetings, and publications, the Electors' Union presented to African eyes an image of European determination and power that went well beyond the reality of the situation. Europeans had become increasingly more concerned with consolidating and maintaining their influence than with achieving self-government. At this time few Europeans would really have welcomed independence; rather, they sought greater control over the machinery of Government. Though their ultimate political objectives remained conveniently vague, they seemed to envisage a kind of "Home Rule" for Kenya, involving a permanent relationship with Britain (similar to that of Ulster) and drawing upon British military, administrative, and financial strength. But while the Europeans were prepared to move forward slowly, they were not prepared to yield an inch of their gains.

Multi-Racialism

On December 12, 1944, Sir Philip Mitchell was sworn in as Governor, and he continued in office until June 21, 1952, four months before the declaration of a State of Emergency in the country. He came to the problems of Kenya after over thirty years in the Colonial Service, nearly all of it spent in East and Central Africa, none of it in West Africa. During this time he had built up a reputation as a liberal administrator with a flair for economics. He was the most experienced and trusted East Africanist the Colonial Office had. Both in Tanganyika and in Uganda, where he filled senior posts,* he had been exposed to the indirect effects of European political activity in Kenya and to the problems of racial pluralism. He came to Kenya convinced that he had a logical, integrated policy which would mold together all the various conflicting interests of the country into a new kind of multiracial nation, a light to Africa and the world. There is little doubt that his ideas and influence were to have a profound effect on British policy throughout East and Central Africa during the next decade.

---

* He became Chief Secretary of Tanganyika in 1934 and was Governor of Uganda from 1935–40.

In his memoirs, written shortly after he gave up his Governorship, Mitchell revealed much of the thinking that underlay his policy for postwar Kenya. He proceeds from certain fundamental propositions that he assumes are generally accepted. "It is common ground that the great mass of the people of this region [East and Central Africa] are still in a state of ignorance and backwardness, uncivilized, superstitious, economically weak to the point of near helplessness and quite unable to construct a civilized future for themselves, to 'pull themselves up by their own bootstraps.' " Universal suffrage or democratic government is unthinkable. If it were allowed, it would merely lead to a "twentieth-century model" of the slave trade whose abolition had in the first place been the motivation of "the great men who led the missionary venture of rescue"—the British colonization of Eastern Africa.[20]

If, therefore, retaining the British presence in Kenya is to be justified, it must be as trustees, and the Africans are "and must be, for a long time yet, wards in trust." The major aim of the trustee is then "to create conditions in which his wards can advance in civilization, knowledge and capacity, with all the help he can give, to the farthest point he can reach." The main essential must be "a radical transformation of the subsistence society in which the masses are still enmeshed."[21] This was the first, and major, plank of his program for postwar Kenya. Only a massive forward thrust of economic development could produce the required number of civilized Africans needed if the African was to participate responsibly in the processes of national government and ultimately to become an equal partner in the enterprise. It must be remembered that to hold even this belief—"that all human beings are inherently capable of civilization"—[22] was to place oneself on the liberal wing of European thought at this time.

The cornerstone of Mitchell's thinking, then, was that the political and social problems of the African in Kenya could best be approached through the medium of economic growth. If all communities concerned themselves with promoting the general welfare, then a new harmony would be achieved. European extremists and African "agitators," as all those who rejected this policy were defined, were equally disruptive. Mitchell had seen his primary political task to be the containment of both these groups and the development of a new kind of political community open to all civilized and moderate men. Under such a scheme the British Government should maintain its links with Kenya "for generations to come,"[23] although they would gradually become tenuous as the new community came into being.

Mitchell throughout his Governorship retained a firm belief in the concepts of multi-racialism—the multi-racial state or the multi-racial community—which were not yet common currency. He accepted from the first that there would have to be modifications in Kenya's political institutions. "I had long thought that where there was a problem of several communities, with political capacity in more or less inverse ratio to number, the only workable solution was the equal representation of them all without any regard to numbers." It can be assumed that in all the changes in political representation which he advocated during these years, whether in the Legislative or Executive Councils or during the critical 1951 talks with James Griffiths, then Britain's Labour Secretary of State for the Colonies, Mitchell was guided by this general principle. He had, after all, just spent two years as Governor of Fiji, where a similar system "seemed to me to work well."[24]

Faced with the dangers of an irresponsible European opposition, representing the major consent group in the country at the time, Mitchell sought to bring at least one influential representative of the settlers into the Government. At the same time he ingeniously created a more efficient governmental machine for economic development.

The inadequacy of the system whereby all branches of activity were concentrated in the hands of the Colonial Secretary had long been a matter of concern. In the years since the publication of Sir Alan Pim's report (1936) [25] a few minor changes had been initiated to remedy the more pressing defects. Mitchell introduced two major structural innovations. First he transformed the single line of authority stemming from the Colonial Secretary. Various departments of Government were now grouped under selected Members of the Executive Council in an embryonic cabinet system, though not all these Members had departmental responsibilities. Second, Unofficial representatives (Europeans, such as settlers and businessmen, who were in the Legislative Council but not in the Administration) could henceforth hold these portfolios, although an Unofficial had to resign his Legislative Council seat if he became a Member. In justifying this decision, the Government explained that it wished "to retain at its disposal the wide range of knowledge and experience outside the ranks of its own servants"[26] which had been so instrumental in the rapid wartime economic development. Finally, Mitchell offered Major (later Sir) F. W. Cavendish-Bentinck, heir-presumptive to the dukedom of Portland, a leading protagonist of white settlement and a former Secretary of the Convention of Associations, the important portfolio of Member for Agriculture, Animal Husbandry, and Natural Resources. His appointment was viewed with particular distrust by the leaders of the land-conscious Kikuyu.

Their suspicions were further aggravated when Cavendish-Bentinck was also made responsible for the £1.5 million postwar plan to settle more British (European) ex-soldiers in the White Highlands. Initiated by the Kenya Government, this scheme was supported and approved by the British Government. In Mitchell's eyes, further large-scale immigration was essential for the rapid development of the economy. In the Europeans' view it was equally essential to the expansion of European political power. The land and the life in this "white man's country" were described to would-be settlers in glowing terms. Leases under the scheme were for forty-four years, and it was accepted that for that period there would be no fundamental changes in the conditions governing them.

Europeans regarded this as a promise that there would be no moves adversely affecting their position in the political and social system during this time, and the strategy of the postwar European Electors' Union was based on this assumption. While no immediate threat to the White Highlands and its way of life appeared, in the decade following the war the British Government was continuously approached for reassurances to dispel European fears and insecurity regarding the future of white settlement. These fears were greatly enhanced by the emergence of a definite British policy for African self-government in West Africa.

There remained the problem of the African "agitator." Mitchell recognized that there was "a substantial and constantly growing body of Africans who must be distinguished from the great backward masses of the ignorant tribesmen." If these "politically mature groups" were willing to accept and "to collaborate without reserve" in his central policy, then there was no restriction of the roles they might play within the system. "But if they, or any one of them reject that policy, then they are in effect taking a position in opposition to high policy." Such people could not expect "to be accorded anything more than the representation reasonable for a minority" (presumably of the "civilized" inhabitants of the country, those who were not "civilized" having no political capacity).[27]

For the individual the doctrine was utilitarian. The individual African, by cooperating with all "Kenyans" regardless of race, could achieve his own greatest happiness, and incidentally that of the whole state, by putting his shoulder to the wheel of the production machine. Applied to the whole colonial state, the doctrine argued that economic growth would produce a new society in which racialist values would give way to those of class. As individual Africans achieved the economic status of the Europeans, so they would begin to identify themselves as fellow-members of the new community of "all civilized men," whether black, brown, or white. It was held that the possibility of advancement into this new status would give the African masses a continuing stake in the new community.

African Economic Participation

In practice the theory of multi-racialism, implemented by an Administration which had grown much closer to the settlers since 1929, when restrictions on administrators' buying land in the Colony were removed, served the general interests of the Europeans well. However, by concentrating on the importance of increasing economic *production,* while paying little attention to ensuring a more equitable economic *distribution,* it nullified any broad appeal it might have had to African leaders. The time-scale envisaged a gradualness in African development and participation that was no answer to the deepening intensity of their problems.

In the years prior to the Emergency in 1952, disparities between European and African income grew more pronounced. Between 1938 and 1952 the money value of domestic exports increased nearly sevenfold from £3.8 million to £25.8 million.[28] During the same period the African labor force doubled, reaching 438,702 in 1952 out of a total African population estimated at five and a half million.[29] The African dependence upon wage earnings for economic and social progress during this period was particularly striking. In 1951, 32.5 per cent of African real income was earned outside the African economy, three times as much as in Uganda. About two-thirds of Kenya African earnings were derived from wages, while less than 15 per cent of Uganda African income was dependent on this source. Whereas Uganda Africans had a *per capita* income of approximately £12 a year, in Kenya it was about £3. Moreover, in comparison with other white-dominated social and economic systems, in the Rhodesias and South Africa, African *per capita* income in Kenya was substantially lower than that of the African population in those countries.

In 1952, at a period of remarkable prosperity for European agriculture, the average wage for unskilled workers was 25 shillings per month. While it has been argued that inefficiency was a major reason for the consistently low wage scale for African workers, a Government committee set up in 1952 to investigate African wages reported that

> notwithstanding the generally low quality of African labour, a large section of the African labour force received an inadequate return in wages for the work which it performs. . . .
>
> We are left in no doubt, however, that *individual* Africans *do* attain standards of efficiency, industry and output equal to those of workers of other races and that, notwithstanding this, they continue to receive considerably *less* wages. As regards skilled and semi-skilled labour generally, it seems reasonable to assume that their wages will be largely affected, if not dictated, by the *lowest level* of wages, i.e. by that of the unskilled labour force.[30]

Ideally, in a free market economy changes in individual productivity and wages tend to be closely related. As productivity increases, so do wages, and the labor force becomes more integrated and specialized in the market economy. But in Kenya the Africans' increasing desire to be skilled and highly productive was incompatible with the settlers' wish to retain cheap and abundant supplies of labor. With wages kept at the lowest possible level, a permanent and stabilized labor force that commanded a high degree of skills and efficiency could not evolve. The African found himself trapped in a vicious circle. It was assumed that his productive capacity would have to rise in order to bring about real wage increases, but the low wages paid inhibited him from acquiring the training for the skills necessary for higher productivity.

One inherent consequence of this low wage economy was that nearly all African workers had to maintain an economic, social, and political stake in their own tribal areas in order to meet the minimum requirements of sustenance and security for themselves and their families. Approximately one-half of the urban workers in private industry, about one-quarter of those in the public services, and nearly three-quarters of the monthly contract labor in non-plantation agriculture were receiving wages in 1953 that were inadequate to satisfy their basic and essential needs. Moreover, this assessment was made only in respect of the worker himself, and "if, in assessing the adequacy of wages, we take into account not only the worker's own needs but also those of his wife and children, the picture becomes grim indeed."[31] Since workers had thus to depend on the rural areas, the vast majority were unable to commit themselves irrevocably to the towns. There was little hope that an independent, permanently settled, urbanized community would develop within such an economic system.

The Africans' handicap in the new economy had another facet: they had never developed any substantial independent source of income by growing cash crops in the rural areas. In contrast to the government of Uganda, Kenya's Administration had largely ignored African agricultural production for export; it had rather concentrated on the growth of a modern economy linked to European production. African rural areas were to provide a source of labor, while continuing to meet the subsistence needs of the African population. "Until 1923 the only attention given to the native areas by the Department of Agriculture was by means of occasional visits by officers in response to requests from administrative officers."[32] By 1937 there were only ten Agricultural Officers and seven Assistant Agricultural Officers stationed in the African Reserves.[33] After nearly twenty years in Kenya, Archbishop (then Archdeacon) Beecher, speaking in the Legislative Council in 1946 as a representative of African interests, maintained that African "poverty is to all intents and purposes as deep as it was when I first made the acquaintance of the Africans in this country."[34] Decades of neglect of African economic development had produced a situation whereby in 1952 only 6 per cent of Kenya's net geographical product came from African commercial activity. In Uganda in 1951 the figure was 63 per cent.[35] In general it can be estimated that the real value of African income from the market economy had grown at no more than 1 per cent per annum in the thirty years up to 1952. The rate of African population growth during the same period was probably near 3 per cent per annum. Perhaps more than any other data this provides a vivid demonstration that during this period the living standards of Africans did not improve but rather deteriorated.

In short, the low standard of living reflected not only low African wages, but the fact that adequate measures to improve and modernize the productivity and efficiency of African agriculture were not adopted. A European Member of the Legislative Council said in 1950 of the Reserves, "there are nearly one million Africans in land units to-day above the capacity of those lands to hold them."[36] An agricultural survey of Nyeri District in 1945 showed that twice as many families were living there as the land could support. Lack of governmental action in Kenya until the mid-1930s in these land units areas meant that the market or modernizing sector of the economy was almost entirely in the hands of non-Africans. Even after the war, when some increased governmental aid was made available for African agricultural development, no appreciable alteration took place in respect to Kenya's racially defined dual economy. Some of those most closely involved appreciated that "a real effort . . . must be made to change the agricultural economy."[37] However, the Director of Agriculture was advising as late as 1950 that obstacles to Africans' growing coffee in the southern Kikuyu areas should be continued.[38] He reported to the Member for Agriculture, Animal Husbandry, and Natural Resources that the Coffee Board were against "permitting Africans to grow coffee adjacent to the European areas at this juncture, as they hold my view that it might well be the cause of a rift in the present happy relations between European and African industries."[39]

As the country's economy continued to expand in the immediate postwar period, the African share in agricultural activity actually declined, while non-African (mostly European) agriculture increased its share of the geographical income between 1947 and 1951 from 13.6 per cent to 20.5 per cent. To many Africans involved in the market economy, the European was becoming richer and richer, while the African's status did not appreciably change. Though economic differentials between Africans existed, with a few Africans achieving substantial earnings, these were less important than the recognized fact that all Africans shared the lowest strata of the racial hierarchy. To most Africans race, economic position, status, and prestige were identical, and they began to form new organizations to bring about economic and political reform.

The Urban Bases of Postwar Nationalism

The major towns and other urban centers were important bases of operation for the new nationalism. The low wage levels in industry and commerce inhibited the development of a stable urban community, but did not discourage Africans from leaving the rural areas. Nairobi's African population nearly doubled between 1938 and 1947 from an estimated 40,000 to 77,000; by 1952 it was believed to be at least 95,000.[40] Whereas in 1936 60 per cent of Africans registered for employment were in European agriculture and 40 per cent in other spheres, in 1946 these percentages were reversed and African wage labor was no longer predominantly agricultural. More Africans, too, were employed in towns and were becoming part of the urban economy. The trend townwards, coupled with urban working and living conditions, inevitably stimulated the growth of a trade union movement among Africans.

The first to revive African trade unionism in the immediate postwar years was Chege Kibachia; his short trade union career illustrates some of the grave problems of organization that faced the new urban leaders. He was born in 1919 at Kiambu. After attending the KISA school at Githunguri, he went to a CMS primary school to learn Swahili in order to be eligible to enter the mission-run Alliance High School, near Nairobi. This was then Kenya's premier African school; it had been responsible for the education of the majority of the new leadership. At Alliance he was taught by James Gichuru, Eliud Mathu, and Joseph Otiende, all three of whom were to be major political leaders in the postwar period. He became senior prefect and school captain, but missed the opportunity of going on to advanced education at Makerere. Because of his secondary education he readily obtained a job as a clerk with a Kikuyu-owned company, the Kiambu Chicken and Egg Dealers, which in 1945 could afford to buy property in the Nairobi Bazaar for £8,000.[41] His salary of £9 a month was on a scale that few other Africans could then command. His employers represented one of the most successful groups of African traders, aiming to satisfy urban

African needs. The Kikuyu, living on the doorstep of Nairobi, naturally tended to dominate this type of commercial activity.

In 1945 Kibachia was for a short time assistant editor, under Tom Mbotela, of KASU's paper, *Sauti ya Mwafrika* —"The Voice of the African." His sympathies, however, were increasingly enlisted in the cause of the African labor force and their working conditions, and when he moved to Mombasa (the scene of labor unrest for several years) he became more actively involved in developing trade unionism. With three-quarters of the African labor force earning less than 40 shillings a month, a reasonable minimum wage was an immediate objective. The Commission of Inquiry had exposed the deplorable living and working conditions that had lain behind the Mombasa labor troubles of 1939, and these remained major causes of dissatisfaction, as were the color bar and the limited opportunities for advancement. Further unrest during the war culminated in 1945 in a minor strike, which the Administration settled through two Luo chiefs. But in January 1947 there was a general strike involving some 15,000 Africans—nearly the entire African labor force in Mombasa—led by Kibachia. The twelve-day strike was a success, for the Thacker tribunal award provided for a general minimum wage whose "implications were felt by the whole country."[42] Kibachia was the hero of the hour and was soon getting invitations from various parts of Kenya to help in organizing trade unions.

During the strike the African Workers' Federation was founded with Kibachia as president. Though he argued for a trade union movement divorced from politics, "since the workers must learn the specific functions of each," the Government viewed both him and the new Federation with considerable suspicion. Indeed, they regarded the Mombasa strike as "political in character," despite the acknowledged economic grievances, since it was "an attempt to coerce the

Government into raising the standard of living of the labourer to one far beyond the economic capacities of the country."[43]

Kibachia envisaged the Federation developing into a Kenya-wide trade union organization, and immediately sought to capitalize on his Mombasa fame. He traveled to Nairobi, Nakuru, Nanyuki, Gilgil, Naivasha, Uplands, and other places, "preaching trade unionism" and telling people "they should organize themselves and should not be frightened of the Government."[44] There was a rash of local strikes, even as far afield as Nyanza.[45] He was arrested in August 1947 and in September deported "on account of activities subversive of law and order."[46] With the arrest of other officers, the African Workers' Federation began rapidly to dissolve. The Federation offices while they existed had been known as *Afise ya Maskini*—the "Office of the Poor." For the Government to argue and insist that labor and politics could remain separate in a situation where Africans found themselves the bottom layer of a racially stratified economic pyramid was hardly realistic. As African leaders developed the skills needed to build mass organizations, these organizations, whatever their role or name, became part of the postwar nationalist movement. Politics became the means of achieving the social and economic goals that appeared to be unattainable in any other way.

In addition to the nascent trade union movement an array of other associations—tribal, vocational, social, and political—had come into being in the expanding urban centers. These tribal associations, such as the Luo Union, the Kikuyu General Union, the Kisii Union, the Taita and Taveta Union, the Masai Union, and the Akamba Union, founded to promote the social welfare of their members in Nairobi and Mombasa, became a further part of the infra-structure of the new nationalism. Vocational and trading associations were also important, the most prominent in the immediate postwar period being the Kenya Farmers' and Traders' Co-operative Ltd.⁴⁷ The early postwar years saw as well the growth and collapse of a number of African companies, many formed by ex-servicemen. Other groups were "Old Boys' Associations" of various schools, social and political clubs, such as the Kikuyu Club, and educational and residential societies. By 1948 there were over 60 African associations in Mombasa alone, forming a wide network of people and organized groups covering the life of the port. Many of these associations were branches of other bodies, which were also found in Nairobi and other towns. The development of a structure of organized African groups in the towns greatly helped the growth of a politics that went beyond the tribal context.

A decisive factor in fostering political action in Kenya's cities was the African press, which grew rapidly after 1945; many political leaders at various times edited one or more of the papers and news sheets. Some were published in Swahili and English, but many were written in the vernacular—Kikuyu, Luo, Luhya, or Kamba. The majority were published in Nairobi, though Mombasa could boast the *Coast African Express,* owned by the Coast African Association, and in Kisumu there was the *Nyanza Times* associated with Oginga Odinga and the Luo Thrift and Trading Company. In addition to KAU's *Sauti ya Mwafrika,* many other papers and news sheets were nationalist and militant in outlook. They expressed general dissent and bitterness over the color bar and the *kipande,* the insecurity and poverty of the Kikuyu squatter in the Rift Valley, the need for greater African representation in central and local government, and the hope for tribal and national unity. Though the mortality rate was high, new papers were always being published.

Without question, Kikuyu country received the most benefits from this new press; not only were there a large number of Kikuyu papers, but the Kikuyu were closest to Nairobi; they did not meet such severe circulation difficulties as elsewhere. The most influential paper, since the Government had not allowed *Muigwithania* to resume publication after the war, was the militant *Mumenyereri* ("He who looks after"), edited by Henry Muoria, who during 1946 was KAU's Assistant General Secretary. A weekly with an average circulation of 10,000, it was widely distributed throughout Kikuyuland. Considered the paper of Kikuyu patriotism, it published a mixture of real and imagined grievances. As tension grew in 1951 and 1952, it became uncompromising in its nationalism. Invitations to political meetings, called under the guise of "tea parties" (which usually included secret oathing ceremonies) at the Kikuyu Club, in Nairobi's Pumwani Location, became a regular feature of the paper. ("Tea-parties" could not be legally controlled by the Administration since technically they were not held in "a public place."[48]) As a channel of communication and an instrument of political education, *Mumenyereri* and other like-minded papers were vital to the rapid postwar spread of nationalism.

The Development of the Kenya African Union

Though Africans had long sought and recognized the importance of direct representation in the country's legislature, it was not until October 10, 1944, that their first member, Eliud Mathu, was nominated to the Legislative Council.* Since the beginning of the war the Government had not objected to the principle of an African representing "native interests," though they had continued to believe that African political development "could best be attained through the

---

* Mathu, a Kikuyu educated at Alliance High School and Oxford University, had founded the first Kenya African Teacher's Union at Kikuyu in 1934 and was well known in government and missionary circles. At the time of his nomination, he was Principal of the Kikuyu Karing'a school at Waithaka. See *Baraza*, Oct. 7, 1944.

medium of Local Native Councils."[49] In January 1950, C. E. (later Sir Charles) Mortimer, the Member for Health and Local Government, said in the Legislative Council that "the development on right lines of our local government system in African areas from the broad base in the location councils, up through the African district councils to the Standing Committee for Local Government in African Areas, is of far greater importance to the Africans of this Colony than the addition of further African members to this Council."[50] The Government ignored the fact that rapid social and economic change had produced a crucial range of issues which were of territorial or national concern to African interests and welfare.

Mathu's appointment was generally well received by Europeans and Indians. No one, however, looked upon it as a first step toward African self-government. Indeed, it was believed that it would be generations before Africans would be competent to assume any significant governmental responsibility. Europeans still regarded the Indians, not the Africans, as the major political threat to their interests and aspirations. But soon insistent African clamor for greater and elected representation in the Legislative Council was to awaken European fears for the future, especially as the increase in 1948 to four members, far from assuaging African demands, merely stimulated them further.

The African campaign to secure the pending Governor's nomination stimulated political action and brought a new African leadership to the fore. There was now a substantial body of men who had received at least some secondary eduction, as well as a nucleus who had been to Makerere College in Uganda for higher education, including diploma work. A few possessed university degrees, including Eliud Mathu and Mbiyu Koinange, who had been the most prominent candidates in the indirect contest for the first African seat in the Legislative Council. Local Native Councils had each forwarded three names for the Governor to choose from. To support Mathu in his new task and to provide a transtribal organization for the advancement of African interests, thirty-three Africans, reflecting in part a new educated leadership from various tribal backgrounds, met in Nairobi on October 1, 1944, and formed the Kenya African Union (KAU). The interim office-bearers appointed included Harry Thuku as Chairman, Francis J. Khamisi (Coast) as Secretary, Albert Awino (Luo) as Treasurer. The Committee consisted of John Kebaso (Gusii), James Gichuru (Kikuyu), F. M. Ng'ang'a (Kikuyu), J. Jeremiah (Taita), Simeon Mulandi (Kamba, former leader in the banned Ukamba Members Association), Harry Nangurai (Masai), and S. B. Jackayo (Luhya).

A month later, under pressure from the Government, the organization was renamed the Kenya African Study Union (KASU). At this point Government was not unfriendly to the new body. Indeed, it had been started "with the encouragement of a former, very able and experienced, Chief Native Commissioner, who hoped thereby to interest serious-minded Africans with some education in a form of study group, through which he might be able to help them to understand public affairs."[51] It was regarded as an inevitable step in the political development of educated Africans. Moreover, since the KCA had been banned it was desirable to have some alternative outlet for political expression.[52] Though the Government grew increasingly critical of the organization, it permitted civil servants to join it until 1949.

Thuku resigned in January 1945, and at the first delegates' conference on February 3, James S. Gichuru was elected President. He was representative in many ways of the new élite, having been educated at Makerere and become a school teacher at the Alliance High School, Kikuyu. Gichuru energetically seized the chance to give direction and purpose to KASU. Under his leadership it acted less like a Government-sanctioned study union and more like a political party, championing such long-standing African grievances as "the abolition of the *kipande,* the restoration of our lost lands and more representation in the Legislative Council. We were not demanding independence."[53]

Within a year it had dropped all pretense of being a study union, and at the second annual delegates' conference in February 1946, it reverted to its original title of the Kenya African Union (KAU). This did much to remove doubts held by leaders of the proscribed KCA after Thuku's appointment as first chairman. Thuku had become more suspect than ever to KCA leaders since his KPA had passed a resolution appreciating the guarantee against further land alienation conveyed in Section 3 of the Kenya (Native Lands) Order-in-Council of 1939.[54] At the second conference, J. D. Otiende was elected Vice-President and W. W. W. Awori became Treasurer; both were Luhya.

The return of Jomo Kenyatta in September 1946 and his assumption of the presidency of KAU on June 1, 1947, legitimized the credentials of the new Union in the eyes of those long faithful to the KCA, which had raised the funds for his passage. Many KCA members had been reluctant to give up their proscribed organization and indeed had continued meeting secretly. In 1945 and 1946 George Ndegwa had constantly but unsuccessfully tried to persuade the Administration to allow it to function again. With Kenyatta's return KAU at last had a real opportunity to develop into the dominant vehicle for African nationalism. Though its infrastructure of organization in Kikuyu country and the Rift Valley was still largely controlled by KCA leaders, in Nairobi a militant, younger, and uncompromising leadership was emerging, which at first expressed itself politically through the budding trade union movement and finally after 1951 in KAU's Nairobi Branch.

Kenyatta came back as the unquestioned leader of the new nationalism. To many he represented the chance of unity, which was essential in the struggle for land and equality. He himself had spent sixteen years in England transmitting the aspirations and troubles of his people. They had subscribed liberally to keep him there and they looked to him for the solution of their problems. He summed up their hopes and gave new life and confidence to the struggle. His absence abroad had enabled him to avoid the strains and faction-alism of Kikuyu politics. To the old he was not too young, to the young he was not too old; to the illiterate he was not too educated, to the educated he was nobody's fool. He had a knowledge of the British political system possessed by few Kenya Africans. He had written a book which cried out its faith in the dignity of his people and their way of life. His passage back, subscribed for by them, brought him to a land where he was all things to all men. His political problem was how to maintain this in a situation where the prospects for African political advancement were hardly hopeful.

Mitchell rejected the validity of African nationalism and saw in the activities of African politicans a threat to the smooth running of his administrative rule and the slow evo-lution toward the multi-racial community. He seldom rec-ognized its potential as a creative force capable of being channeled into constitutional forms of national expression. When, soon after his return, Kenyatta indicated a desire to take an active part in national affairs, Mitchell's response was that he should first take part in the business of his Local Native Council.[55] To a Governor who regarded "the creation in Africa of an entirely African self-governing state" as "fan-tastic,"[56] this seemed the right and proper way to begin. To many European settlers, however, Kenyatta was not merely a political threat but also a danger to society. By early 1948 an extreme group centered on Limuru was actively working for his deportation.

Kenyatta's problems in building a coherent mass movement were formidable. Among them was the great unevenness of political awareness through the country, widespread tribal parochialism, the small number of educated English-speaking leaders, and the inadequacies of social communication that could enable them to function as a national élite. In the next few years Kenyatta's great achievement was to articulate the concept of a "Kenya people" and to extend KAU's foothold in Nyanza and on the coast and its growing strength among the Kamba. His efforts were aided by the cumulative social changes which in many ways challenged the meaning of the tribe as the highest political ideal. Emphasizing Kenyatta's important role, Oginga Odinga says, "With the arrival of Kenyatta, Luo people began to think in terms of the whole country for the first time. Up to the Second World War, teachers taught in terms of the tribe; they did not think in terms of a nation. Kenyatta's role was one of political education."[57] Though structurally the party remained weak even in parts of central Kenya, the leadership of Kenyatta came to command territorial recognition.

Under Kenyatta's leadership, KAU attempted to organize branches in as many parts of Kenya as possible. Initially there was some success. Among the politically conscious Kikuyu on their own land unit and in the towns and on the farms of the White Highlands, it was relatively easy. In many instances existing KCA networks of leadership could be readily employed. But on the coast and in the west political organization was far more difficult. For the most part there were few English-speaking and educated leaders, and the leaders were often unwilling to commit themselves to a nationalism still full of uncertainties.

Apart from the pastoral tribes of the Rift Valley, who showed little interest in politics, there did not exist as yet even among the agricultural Luhya, Luo, and Gusii a realistic basis for mass political organization. Politics continued to reflect parochial clan issues instead of any larger unity. Even Nyanza urban organizations in Nairobi and Mombasa were focused in great part on clan and location structures. Among the Luo in Nyanza, KAU commanded little substantial support, though a few leaders, especially Walter Odede, Achieng Oneko, and Oginga Odinga, proved valuable contacts. The immediate postwar opportunities for gaining a following among the Bantu Luhya of North Nyanza were greater.

In the 1930s there had been intermittent links between the KCA and the North Kavirondo Central Association. As we have seen, parts of North Nyanza faced a land problem that promoted sympathy for the intense feelings of the Kikuyu. Although the NKCA had gone into voluntary liquidation at the time the KCA was banned,[58] nonetheless, they still "came with a deputation on an average about once every two months," the District Commissioner reported in 1942, adding that "I always give them a patient hearing and try to answer their requests."[59] In 1946 a revived NKCA showed "signs of becoming a definite political party with their eyes on the Indian Congress party. Their recent attempts to oust Chief Amutala and to put in their own man as ologongo [sub-chief] in S. Kitosh indicate the line that their activities are likely to take."[60] There existed personal contacts and leadership bonds between these Bantu people which could be exploited for political purposes. Yet although KAU was able to hold a few very successful meetings in North Nyanza, the foundations for sustained and effective organization were lacking in terms of leadership, mobilization, and political awareness. But, as with the Luo, some Luhya leaders, particularly Joseph D. Otiende, John Adala, and W. W. W. Awori, played valuable roles in developing the KAU organization among their people.

In Kisii, where by 1950 there were some 600 Kikuyu families,[61] Kikuyu immigrants, led by Njoroge Kagunda, had become highly organized in a branch of the proscribed KCA. They made some converts among the Gusii until the Administration, alarmed by their success, began a campaign against them. The Chief Native Commissioner said that some 50 families had tried to set up "a separate Kikuyu enclave in the Kisii land unit."[62] In 1950, seventeen were prosecuted and ordered to leave the district; their huts were demolished and their crops destroyed by grazing stock over them. But Kikuyu infiltration continued. They were not finally removed until the Emergency broke.

Under the leadership first of Gichuru and then of Kenyatta, KAU also sought to establish and maintain inter-territorial contacts with African leaders in Tanganyika and Uganda. In 1946 and 1947 Khamisi and Gichuru visited Dar es Salaam and Kampala to make contact with leading politicians. There was even talk of forming an East African National Congress under Kenyatta's leadership in 1950. In 1951 KAU sent F. Kubai, M. Koinange, and Munyua Waiyaki to help the Meru of Tanganyika (who had formed themselves into the "Meru Citizens Union, Freemen") with the preparation of their land case against the Tanganyika Government and local settlers before the United Nations.

Despite the massive socio-political changes impelled in part by urbanization and a militant nationalist press, a colony-wide nationalist organization was slow to take root and indeed had hardly done so by the outbreak of the Emergency. While Kenyatta realized the necessity of maintaining a national executive with a transtribal membership, few facilities for an effective country-wide mass party existed. Though the ideology of African nationalism commanded widespread support, the organizational base was communal. It is not at all surprising that KAU was attacked by its critics as being primarily a Kikuyu union, since only among the Kikuyu did the requisites of leadership and social communication exist to the extent needed to support a mass move-

ment. The Kikuyu became the spearhead of the nationalist movement, and inevitably at KAU meetings in Nairobi,
Central Province, and the Rift Valley great use was made of
issues, slogans, songs, symbols, and values derived essentially
from Kikuyu experiences, which had limited meaning elsewhere.

During the years before the Emergency, in addition to
addressing meetings in various parts of the country, Kenyatta
also busied himself with the management and direction of
the Kenya Teachers College at Githunguri in Kiambu.
Githunguri also became the focus of the Kikuyu age-groups
organization and the proscribed KCA General Council, the
apex of the Kikuyu spiritual renaissance and of Kikuyu
nationalism. The age-group organization had soon proved
itself a successful adaptation of a traditional structure for
modern social and political objectives. Kenyatta, living at
Githunguri, found himself in the middle of the deep agrarian crisis and at the center of educational dissatisfaction.
From here he came under increasing pressure as attempts to
achieve constitutional reform became discredited and were
replaced by militant politics emanating from Nairobi by
those willing to employ direct action and violence and ultimately enveloping the rural areas of central Kenya.

Failure to Achieve Economic and Political Reform

Between 1945 and 1953, KAU engaged in a long and futile
struggle to achieve political change by reform. In addition to
the commanding issue of land and to its demand that the
report of the Kenya Land Commission be revised, KAU's
policies were directed toward achieving equality with Europeans. Its influence upon Government policy, however, was
negligible. A major petition to the British Government, for
example, was described by the colonial administration as
"immature," in places "untruthful," and, "as to be expected,
presents a one-sided picture in its criticism of Govern-

ment."[63] More important and damaging to the African hopes for political reform was the defeat of the principle of equal representation among racial groups in the Central Legislative Assembly of the proposed East African High Commission.

In December 1945, the British Government published for "discussion only" proposals for an inter-territorial organization of the three territories of East Africa—Kenya, Uganda, and Tanganyika.[64] The new Governor, Sir Philip Mitchell, although rejecting political federation, was reluctant to lose the progress made during the war in regional cooperation; the proposals he drafted sought to institutionalize that cooperation in an East African High Commission.[65] They embodied the principle of equal representation of Africans, Indians, and Europeans from each territory in a Central Legislative Assembly. The majority of European leaders categorically rejected the proposals, essentially because they regarded equal representation as a threat to their continued political predominance. The European constitutional position inside Kenya should be secured before there was any tie-up with Tanganyika or Uganda.[66] They resented as well the fact that they had not even been consulted, and it seemed to them that this was one of a series of measures designed by the new Labour Government in Britain to reduce their influence. For example, it had recently been suggested that an area in the White Highlands be turned over to the Kamba for cultivation,* and that the title of Teita Concessions Ltd. to large landholdings in the White Highlands be abrogated in favor of the Taita. In addition to these signs of "bad faith," the British Government now wished to establish a legislature based on racial equality. The Europeans clung tenaciously to the *status quo,* and were determined to oppose any concept of political advancement based upon equal representation.

Africans, however, widely welcomed the proposals. For

---

* The Ithanga Hills.

them it seemed a great advance. In February 1946 KAU accepted them and opposed the grant of self-government to Kenya until Africans shared full responsibility; they put forth as well a claim for at least six representatives in the Legislative Council. But after months of hostile European opposition, revised proposals for an inter-territorial organization in East Africa were published in February 1947.[67] While the British Labour Government denied that the principle of equal representation had been abandoned, it was clear to all that it had been qualified in the face of European pressure at least as far as Kenya was concerned. Here the composition of the Legislative Council was such that there would be two elected Europeans and two non-European representatives from Kenya in the Central Assembly. These proposals, which were regarded as a victory for the Europeans, were accepted both by the colonial government and by the settler community. But the East African Indian National Congress argued that their acceptance had created a dangerous precedent by allowing a small European community to veto the implementation of the British Government's original proposals for equality of representation. KAU declared: "We have lost the battle,"[68] and "Two Ten" (the revised proposals were issued as "Colonial No. 210") henceforth became a term of abuse among Kenya Africans.

Linked with the acceptance by Kenya Europeans of the proposals in Colonial 210 was the establishment of an unofficial majority composed of all races in the Kenya Legislative Council. This would now comprise fifteen officials and twenty-two unofficials, of whom eleven would be European, five Indians, four Africans, and two Arabs. The increase in African representation was something of an achievement for Archdeacon Beecher, who had represented African interests in the Legislative Council since 1943. He had consistently urged that no two people could adequately represent African interests, and had pleaded with the Governor to examine the situation in the hope that in 1947 six seats on the Legislative Council would be made available to representatives of African interests. This plea had been endorsed by the African legislator, Eliud Mathu, and ultimately the Governor had agreed that African representation should be increased to four in the new Legislative Council of 1948. These four Africans would each represent African interests for a separate area, namely the Nyanza Province; the Central Province, including Nairobi; the Coast Province; and the Rift Valley and remainder of the Colony. But the Governor's practice of nominating individuals after seeking advice from the Local Native Councils would continue.

A similar rigidity in government policy prevailed throughout 1950 and 1951. Decades of representation on the land question and the economic and social grievances it symbolized culminated in KAU's major land petition in 1951—the last significant petition before the declaration of the Emergency. This "Prayer for the Restoration of our land," a version of which was handed to the Secretary of State, James Griffiths, on his visit in May 1951, listed the consequences of Kenya's land policy as "severe overcrowding of the territories in which Africans are permitted to live," "the creation of a population of over 250,000 squatters—with no rights of security, in the European areas," "the exodus of large numbers of Africans to the towns to serve as cheap labour," and lastly "the increase of poverty, malnutrition, crime and moral degradation among the Africans." It stated that the effect of the Crown Lands Ordinance passed in 1938 had been "to establish a European aristocracy based not on moral or mental superiority, but on an artificially created monopoly of fertile land situated in a climate giving the greatest opportunity for health. In contrast a large part of the African population is compelled to live in dry, hot and unhealthy areas insufficient in extent and fertility to maintain existence. In the rural areas the result has been overstocking, soil erosion and deplorable agricultural conditions; in the urban areas overcrowding, vice and ghetto-like conditions." As an unequivocal expression of dissent, it stated: "The African people in Kenya do not recognize the moral authority of either the Crown Lands Ordinance or the Native Lands Trust Ordinance. Their land has been taken from them without their consent."[69]

In the Legislative Council in May 1951, Mathu made a forthright attack on the 1934 Kenya Land Commission Report. Calling for a new Land Commission, this time with African representation, he asked whether the original Commission's recommendations were "going to be taken as sacrosanct, something that cannot be touched for 9½ centuries to come" (this was a reference to the 999 year leases under which much European land was held).[70] In November 1951 Mbiyu Koinange and Achieng Oneko went to Europe to present another version of the land petition directly to Members of the British Parliament and the Economic and Social Council of the United Nations in Paris. The petition had 67,000 signatures[71] and great hopes were placed in its outcome. Men continued to believe that if only Britain could be made aware of their grievances and troubles, redress would be forthcoming.

Kenya's colonial government, however, far from seeing this land petition as revealing a near-crisis in economic affairs, regarded it as an irresponsible attempt by an unrepresentative minority to reverse established economic policies and to reopen land issues that had been justly settled. In 1950 Mitchell had acknowledged that some of "the most intractable grievances" in Kenya arose from "the land Settlement in this colony, resulting from the Carter Commission." But that had been "the result of historical causes and events, and history will not go into reverse: and what can be done in that field is strictly circumscribed."[72]

The attitude of the Kenya Government with respect to KAU's demands for land and economic reform was made clear to the Colonial Office in 1952. The Administration argued that the land the Europeans had occupied had been empty and unused, consisting of "enormous tracts of grass and bush, uninhabited save for wild animals and periodical visits by savage herdsmen with their herds of cattle." The Masai had moved by agreement. It was now "difficult to find any land in the European area which is not either fully productive or in the process of development." The Kenya Land Commission had disposed of the Kikuyu claims of right "along the edges of the old Masai grazing lands," rights which in the old days "were far from secure and far from fully established, being liable to frequent upset by tribal raids and fighting." Only the Kikuyu were opposed to the Kenya Land Commission, and their attack "has been organized mainly by the so-called 'Kenya African Union,' which it should be noted is still, despite assertions to the contrary and efforts to enlist support from other tribes, an almost entirely Kikuyu organization. The majority of Africans of other tribes are indifferent to it, many with just cause and suspicions; and others openly hostile." Not only do the Kikuyu try to reopen the claims already adjudicated by the "comprehensive and final" Kenya Land Commission, but they also try to extend it to the whole area of European settlement. "Since the basis of the economic development of Kenya is European capital and European enterprise," the proposed solution of replacing European farms by Kikuyu peasants "would at best provide only very temporary relief of overcrowding and in the long run it would destroy the whole basis of the Colony's economy and put an end to development."[73]

Though the economic plight and aspirations of the Kikuyu had long supplied the main drive behind African nationalism, KAU leadership realized that the real key to the future lay in the political control of the country. By 1950 KAU had launched a campaign to gain substantial repre-

sentation in the colony's Legislative Council, initially requesting twelve elected members, as compared with the
European settlers eleven, and African appointees to the posts
of Assistant Secretary and Deputy Chief Native Commissioner. As we shall see, the dramatic demands by ultra-
militant urban groups in 1950 and 1951 for self-government
"now," while representing a growing revolutionary force, did
not dominate KAU's policy until 1952. At this time KAU
leadership concentrated most of their energies on strengthening the African position *vis-à-vis* the European oligarchy.
Nonetheless, implicit in their expressed goal of a common
electoral roll for all races was the ultimate objective of an
African self-governing state.

Mitchell did not at first see African nationalism and the
growing body of dissent it represented as the most important
threat to his vision of a multi-racial community. More important in his calculations was the intransigence of the European settlers. Some consideration had to be given to African
views, but essentially their nationalism was an "emotional
movement rather than a rational policy," led by so-called
educated men, "with the sort of education our children have
by the time they are 12 years of age."[74] Settlers, on the other
hand, as part of the governing élite, had to be consulted, and
no advance to the ideal would be possible without their
agreement. In a sense they *were* "Kenya," possessing a
nationalism with its own distinct symbols and legends rooted
in the history of pioneering endeavor of each district in the
Highlands. Mitchell was therefore prepared to make such
concessions to them as were necessary to gain their cooperation and support and as were consonant with his ultimate
objectives.

Though the settler leadership recognized that European
self-government was no longer possible, they sought the
greatest possible executive authority within the apparatus of

the constitution and the maximum amount of local autonomy in the towns and in the White Highlands. Thus they
looked upon the granting of a Royal Charter to the European controlled Municipal Council of Nairobi in 1950 as a
great symbolic landmark toward permanent European dominance in Kenya's affairs. Similarly they regarded the up-
grading in late 1952 of the District Councils in the White
Highlands to the status of County Councils as a further
significant step in this direction.

Yet, despite these apparent achievements, most Europeans
retained a deep distrust of British colonial policy—particularly as administered by a Labour Government and in the
light of rapid African political development in the Gold
Coast and Nigeria. They therefore reacted vigorously to the
changes in the Tanganyika Constitution proposed in 1949.
These reflected Mitchell's ideas of political representation in
a multi-racial community, but the suggestion of equality of
representation of Africans, Asians, and Europeans in the
Tanganyika Legislative Council conflicted with European
objectives. Moreover, European settlers felt bound to oppose
policies which appeared to show the African that his best
chance of advancement lay in the national political sphere.
Rather, the first essential was to encourage Africans to take a
full part in the economic development of the country.
Addressing the Electors' Union in June 1950, the Chairman
defined the European position in these words: "To the
Africans we offer the sympathetic tutelage which will lead
them to full participation in the Government of this country.
But we have made our position clear. We are here to stay and
the other races must accept that premise with all it im-
plies."[75]

European opposition and agitation against the proposed
changes in Tanganyika drew forth public protests by African and Indian leaders. In April 1950, KAU and the East
African Indian National Congress sponsored a joint protest

meeting opposing European political aims. African speakers called for direct elections on a common roll and rejected the contention that they did not understand the ballot box. Eliud Mathu thought that experiments in democratic elections should take place in local government. He called on non-Europeans to form a united front. A. B. Patel, leader of the Asian elected members, blamed the Europeans for the political controversies, saying that they were unaware that a new age had dawned and that the old age had died, and were blind to the unmistakable awakening of Asia and Africa, which must inevitably demolish their power and privileges. Any attempt to build a society in East Africa on the basis of South African racialism would lead to conflict. He contended that no non-European had any confidence in the leadership of any unofficial European in East Africa. Even these remarks, however, were moderate in contrast with the militant mood of the audience, which overwhelmingly supported the demand of the trade union leaders, Makhan Singh and Fred Kubai, for the immediate independence of the East African territories.[76]

In addition to the controversy over the Tanganyika constitutional proposal and the alarm created among Africans by the publication of the Electors' Union *Kenya Plan* in 1949,[77] there was a bitter campaign early in 1950 by Europeans against the new National Registration Ordinance, which had been approved by their representatives in the Legislative Council. This ordinance, which replaced the old one under which only Africans had to carry a *kipande* or identity certificate, entailed fingerprinting for all races. European resentment at the fingerprinting as "the mark of the criminal" was expressed in heated meetings and letters of outraged protest appeared in newspapers; there even sprang up a European Society of Civil Rights, described by a liberal European M.L.C. as "that subversive body." The Society's leaders—L. Vigar, a builder, two lawyers, J. Gledhill and

Walter Shapley, and Col. C. E. Thornton, formerly of the Indian Army—were later to take an active part in the march by Europeans on Government House in 1953 after the murder of the Ruck family on the Kinangop.

A commission set up by the Legislative Council to examine the Registration question reported in February 1950. Sir Bertrand Glancy, the Commissioner and formerly a member of the Indian Civil Service, recommended that those who could fill in a form in English and provide two photos of themselves need not be fingerprinted. Eliud Mathu and B. A. Ohanga, African Legislative Council representatives, rejected this surrender by the Administration to Europeans. In African eyes this was further evidence of the decisive power that Europeans could exercise. In the face of organized European protests, the Administration would always give way.

Governor Mitchell's announcement in October 1950 of proposed increases in African and Indian representation in the Legislative Council immediately stimulated an uncompromising stand by Europeans against any erosion of their political power. They stood firm upon the so-called permanence of the privileged position granted them in the 1923 White Paper. Though increased African representation had made serious inroads into the European hegemony of the Council since then, none of the increases had been so fundamental as the new proposals. Europeans held that their parity of representation with non-Europeans should not be altered unless there was a full enquiry into, and a complete reappraisal of, the existing constitution. European leaders were willing to concede increased African representation, but any increase in non-European representation must be matched by additional European increases.

The "growing uncertainty" in the minds of the communities of East Africa was the subject of an important policy statement by James Griffiths, the Secretary of State for the

Colonies, in December 1950. The differing patterns of constitutional development in Kenya, Uganda, and Tanganyika indicated that it would be best if changes were made "separately in each territory rather than on a general East African basis." The ultimate objective for all three would remain self-government within the Commonwealth. The task now was to create conditions in which fear and suspicion between the communities would disappear; moreover, "in any constitutional changes in the direction of self-government, care must be taken to safeguard the proper rights and interests of all the different communities." Griffiths maintained that Africans must be helped forward in their development, so that they might take their full part in the economic and political life of the territories. Final authority would be retained by Britain until the "goal of true partnership" among the communities was attained.[78]

On instructions from Griffiths, Mitchell held preliminary constitutional talks with representatives of each racial group. In February 1951 he announced that no substantial alterations were intended. What was being discussed was an increase in the number of Indian representatives by one, and a request by Africans for greater representation. Arabs had also asked for an additional seat, and Africans wanted their interests in the Executive Council represented by an African. With regard to KAU's goal of a common electoral roll for all races, Mitchell held this to be impracticable at the present stage. He also rejected the demand for direct elections of African representatives, maintaining that it was essential to continue the old system, whereby each African L. N. C. submitted a panel of three names for him to make a final choice.[79]

Neither the European elected members nor the African nominated members of the Legislative Council were happy with this announcement. The African members stated their demand had been for half the total unofficial members to be

Africans. They held that racial proportions should be along the lines of the Uganda arrangements, by which African members were equal to the total of Europeans and Indians.[80] In a carefully guarded statement, the European elected members declared that no changes in representation were necessary, except to give the Muslim Indians two communal representatives. If parity between European elected members and non-Europeans was retained, they would not approve increases in African representation. However, they regarded the colony's existing constitution as unsuited to the needs of the country. Suggesting that only minor adjustments in representation be made for the present, they declared that they would take the lead in initiating discussions on a new constitution. "Principles of the liberal traditions of western civilization" should be the guide in preparing it. The constitution should also allow for a considerable period, "the length of which it is impossible to state at this stage," during which European "leadership" would be necessary. While the constitution should provide opportunities for the legitimate aspirations of all people, it must recognize that "the advances of any people towards a full share in the direction of public affairs must be dependent upon the character and ability of the people concerned." The pace at which this policy was to be carried out should be decided by "those in authority locally" and not accelerated by "ill-advised pressure from abroad."[81]

In May 1951 Griffiths briefly visited Kenya, and again the leaders of the communities advanced their views. On the assumption that non-African representation would remain unchanged, KAU sought twelve elected parliamentary members to represent particular areas of the Colony. The Arabs pressed for an additional member, and, like the Africans, a seat on the Executive Council. Asians urged the adoption of equal representation of all racial groups, while the European elected members restated their stand on parity.

At the end of May Griffiths made a statement in the House of Commons which contained the last British policy intervention in Kenya's affairs before the outbreak of the Emergency eighteen months later. Sometime before May 1953, "a body should be set up representative of all groups in the Council under an independent Chairman from outside Kenya, to consider what constitutional changes should be made."[82] In the transitional period the Africans would have a member on the Executive Council, while in the Legislative Council their representatives, still appointed by the Governor, would be increased from four to six, the Asian elected members from five to six, and the European elected representation from eleven to fourteen. To reduce the disparity between the Government and representative sides of the Legislative Council, Griffiths also increased the members on the Official side. These changes would come into effect in 1952. Griffiths hoped the Constitutional Conference would produce an agreed solution, but failing this, Britain would decide new constitutional arrangements before 1956.

Europeans received the statement with relief, for it accepted their demand for the maintenance of the *status quo* in the allocation of communal seats. A sub-committee of the Electors' Union, known as the Vincent Constitutional Committee, was set up to ascertain the views of the European community and to put up definite proposals to the Conference proposed by the Secretary of State. While the European community recognized their inability to maintain indefinitely their past predominance in shaping policy, they continued to act as if there was no need in the foreseeable future for major political and social reform. As the politically dominant community, they refused the role of a protected, but privileged, minority within the framework of the multiracial colonial state.

Griffiths' proposals were not political reforms, rather mere interim adjustments. The country was rapidly approaching a political and social crisis, yet neither the Administration nor the Labour Government recognized it. Race relations were regarded as good, and economically the country was more prosperous than ever. Apart from European fear of change, the Administration saw African nationalism as an expression of deviant behavior, a psychological aberration, and were unable to conceive that the political structure itself might be at issue. May 1951 was a turning point, and the insensitivity of the Government to African political demands was a contributing factor to a rapidly developing crisis. Those African leaders who believed that it was possible to achieve political development by a steady and rapid increase of the representation of African interests began to lose influence, giving way to men who were prepared to employ direct action and violence.

CHAPTER 7

The Growth of
Militant Politics

In the postwar period in both the rural and urban areas of central Kenya, Kikuyu resistance and opposition to European dominance became increasingly militant and gradually more committed to the employment of non-constitutional means to achieve social, economic, and political change. The gap between the colonial government and the politically conscious Kikuyu had constantly widened as each rejected the assumptions on which the other based his actions. At the same time there was a growing lack of confidence in the good faith of the colonial government and an increasing distrust of its motives and policies. While some African leaders continued to work toward constitutional reform within this situation, others turned to and found support for political activity which directly challenged the laws and institutions of the colonial state. These activities assumed various forms, and included mass resistance to government agricultural policies in the rural areas, urban strikes and political demonstrations, and selective political violence. To mobilize support for such tactics and to raise the level of political commitment, secret oaths were employed on an ever wider scale, and clandestine organizations developed for their administration and control. By the summer of 1952, disagreement between Kikuyu political leaders and the leaders of other major peoples, over the intentions of the colonial government and the role of violence in changing the system, had weakened the national organization and effectiveness of KAU. As the European settlers and the colonial Administration perceived the growing militancy in Kikuyu politics and the decline of support for moderate leaders in KAU, they sought a declaration of a State of Emergency and the neutralization of all African political activity. In October 1952 a State of Emergency was proclaimed, which in itself led to more widespread disorder and violence.

Opposition and Dissent

After the war the critical lack of confidence in Government intentions was immediately illustrated by the events that led the Administration to shut down a dried-vegetable factory in Nyeri District. In the first year of the war a factory had been established at Kerugoya in Embu to dry carrots, cabbages, cauliflowers, and potatoes for the troops in the forward areas.[1] At the time, the decision to locate the factory in an African Reserve had been strongly criticized by some European settlers on the grounds that such an industry was eminently suitable for them to undertake. Their arguments were rejected both because of the complexity of the drying process and because costs would be much lower in an African area where a price was offered which was "very fair and attractive to the native grower, but which would certainly not be so to a European farmer."[2]

Starting in 1940 with 1,300 acres, by August 1941 the Kerugoya factory was producing 50 tons a month. In August 1943, a second factory was opened at Karatina in Nyeri, and during the year the two factories produced 826 tons. The project was clearly a commercial and agricultural success. In 1944 12,519 growers sent 16,000 tons of vegetables to the factories, which were then employing 36

Europeans, 53 Asians, and 5,615 Africans. By the time the factories were closed down in December 1946, a total of 6,614 tons of dried vegetables valued at £1,221,769 had been produced, and the gross return to growers and workers had amounted to £384,812.[3]

In 1945 a visiting Colonial Office official was enthusiastic about the scheme and the part it might play in solving Kenya's growing agrarian problems. It offered "a prospect of utilising the land in a way that will enable it to support a far larger population than was possible under the former conditions, thus affording some solution for the problem of overcrowding."[4] It might, then, alleviate some of the effects of the agrarian problem, a problem intensified by Kenya's rigid agrarian color bar.

The Kikuyu had viewed the project suspiciously from the start. Indeed, only the powers of compulsion available to the Government under wartime conditions had persuaded the local Kikuyu to allow the scheme to take over large areas of their swamps and other irrigable land, and the leases were due to expire one year after the war's end.[5] The Government assumed that the Kikuyu would wish to continue a project so profitable and in their best economic interests. But while the Kikuyu did agree to its continuance, they also insisted that it come under their control. They formed the United Companies of Mumbi (largely financed by ex-soldiers' gratuities) and sought to purchase it from the Government for £30,000.[6] The Government rejected this offer, proposing a revised scheme in which the Kikuyu and a European company would each have a 49 per cent interest, while the Government retained 2 per cent. Though propaganda for this scheme was carried out, it was to no avail. The campaign mounted by the Nyeri KAU leaders revealed an unwillingness to accept anything less than a complete hand-over of the factory and all its assets to the United Companies of Mumbi.

The Government refused these conditions, and the factory

was closed down. In commenting upon the impact of the ex-servicemen whom the Administration regarded as the critical core of the opposition to their offer, the Provincial Commissioner wrote that "they have developed a definite racial feeling resenting the presence of Indian Traders in the Reserves and the control of other matters, more especially the Karatina Dried Vegetable Products factory, by Government."[7] This was not the only time that political dissent was to be misinterpreted simply as an example of racial antagonism.

A more far reaching and bitter conflict with the Administration came over soil conservation and cattle dipping, which reached its peak in Fort Hall and Nyeri. Before the Second World War, as we have seen, the Administration had recognized the seriousness of the increasing depletion of fertile soil in many of the African rural areas and had begun a campaign against erosion. By the end of the war the productive capacity of much of Kikuyuland was estimated to have fallen by at least 50 per cent as a partial result of unprecedented overcropping. With the emphasis, owing to the Kenya Land Commission settlement, on the responsibility of the Reserves to feed a rapidly expanding population, the conservation problem commanded immediate attention. The rehabilitation of the denuded areas rapidly became the prime objective of postwar agricultural and administrative policy.

Conversely, opposition to the various measures associated with this policy became a major element in the strategy of political leaders in both Nyeri and Fort Hall. Their motives were not so irrational as they were generally made out to be. Dustbowls and red hillsides scarred with finger erosion dramatized, as little else could at this time, the inadequacies of the Government's unacceptable land policy. As the economic difficulties of their people grew, the leaders criticized all the more strongly the racially defined system on which land policy was based. In their view, neatly terraced hillsides were not only a poor indication of real economic well-being, but served to distract from the nagging problems of over-population and resettlement, which were becoming the Administration's nightmare. "Terracing" thus became to both sides an index of the Government's general control of the situation, and the field on which some of the new leaders chose to do battle with the old system. Indeed the graphs of monthly terracing and wash-stop figures became indicators of victory as anxiously awaited in the offices of the Provincial Administration as any wartime communiqué.

There were signs elsewhere, however, that militant opposition was not confined to the two northern Districts, Fort Hall and Nyeri. In particular, the pressure was rising in the crowded northwest area of Kiambu, the critical area in the "stolen lands" dispute. A strike at the Uplands Bacon Factory near Lari on September 5, 1947, ended in violence; the police opened fire on a riot that developed, killing three of the strikers and wounding six others. In another incident on February 1, 1947, 250 Rift Valley squatters came from Limuru to protest on the lawns of Government House. Six arrests were made. At a *baraza* the Governor held with them, he asserted that the only way out of their present trouble "was to find themselves work." He said, "It is no good coming and asking me to do things which cannot be done. The important thing is for each man and his family to go back to the farms and behave like sensible people, and sign a contract with someone who wants to employ them, and so get a roof over his head and food to eat, and give me time to study their problems."[8]

These points of open conflict were part of a persistent and developing pattern of dissent to Government policy and authority. But Government officials continued to interpret these events as the result of agitation by irresponsible and self-seeking leadership, rather than of critical weaknesses in economic and political policy. (The Government had suspected Kenyatta as well as other militants as the driving force behind opposition to its agricultural rehabilitation program.) In January 1948 the Legislative Council debated a motion by S. V. Cooke, a European elected member for the Coast, "that this Council, believing that often agitation is a symptom and not a cause of unrest, views with grave concern the political situation in many of the native areas today."[9] Eliud Mathu seconded. The motion only obtained two votes, and during the debate the Chief Secretary told Cooke that he "should not forget that agitation is often a cause of unrest."[10]

The colonial government's attitude did not appreciably change in the critical years that followed. They saw the activities of most African leaders as destructive, and continued to believe that the solution to the country's problems lay in effective administration and economic growth under European leadership rather than in any substantial reform of the political structure. The complacency of this viewpoint was soon to be most militantly challenged in Nairobi, by the spokesmen for the thousands of homeless and unemployed now living in the city.

After the War economic pressures and rural underemployment drove ever larger numbers of Africans to Nairobi. Neither the Government nor the European-dominated Municipal Council faced up to the massive social problems that this enormous influx of Africans presented. By 1949 and 1950 there was increasing resort to strong police action in vain attempts to clear the city of the unemployed. However, as fast as the "vagrants" were returned to the Reserves they flocked back in again. The chronic problem of the dispossessed was an essential factor in Nairobi's postwar history. Among these elements were to be found many of the most politically militant and committed men, in terms of a willingness to employ direct action against the colonial regime. Their organization and activities were to be the vital focus for impelling political action along an ultra-radical path.

At first after the war many of these men had been organized in a loose association known as the "Forty Group" *(Anake a 40)*, largely though not exclusively composed of ex-servicemen of the age group circumcised in 1940, most of whom had campaigned in Ethiopia, Madagascar, India, or Burma. Their leaders included such men as Fred Kubai and Charles Wambaa from Kiambu, Mwangi Macharia, Eliud Mutonyi, and Isaac Gathanju from Fort Hall, and Stanley Mathenge and Domenico Ngatu from Nyeri. Though their activities were centered upon Nairobi, they took an active part in stimulating opposition to the Government's conservation measures in Fort Hall and Nyeri. Increasingly, however, this "ginger group" was absorbed into the African trade union movement, which rapidly became the most militant force for protest in Nairobi.

In 1947 Makhan Singh, who had returned to India in December 1939, was persuaded to come back to Kenya.* Upon his return he immediately sought to develop the political potential of the nascent African trade union movement, linking up with Fred Kubai, then General Secretary of the Transport and Allied Workers Union,[11] later the Kenya African Road Transport and Mechanics Union, and Bildad Kaggia, then president of the Clerks and Commercial Workers Union. On May 1, 1949, these leaders announced the formation of the East African Trade Union Congress (EATUC), with six unions affiliated to it and with Makhan Singh as General Secretary and Kubai as President. The EATUC rapidly gathered strength in Nairobi, openly eschewing the possibility of any genuine separation of politics and labor in a colonial situation. By late 1949 the trade

---

* According to James Beauttah, then visiting India; interview, April 23, 1964.

union movement had become for them a far more militant vehicle for championing African aspirations than KAU. Though the Government refused to register the EATUC (that is, grant it legal recognition) on the grounds that it did not represent any single trade, the organization continued to operate.

The Oath as an Instrument for Achieving Unity

In late 1949, the Electors' Union published their *Kenya Plan,* which African leaders interpreted as an authoritative restatement of European intentions to create a white-dominated British dominion in East Africa. A liberal European, Derek Erskine, held that prominent Africans looked upon the Plan as "a carefully considered blueprint for European domination in perpetuity."* Its impact upon African leaders was immense and immediate. Its publication convinced them of the urgent need for far more effective political organization, and, above all, unity, if their goals were to be achieved. Although KAU fulfilled an array of vital functions in seeking a territorial base for postwar nationalism, in presenting African demands and grievances to the Administration, and in trying to secure support overseas in Britain, India, and in the councils of the United Nations, its weaknesses in the context of Kenya's politics were apparent to many. With the Kenya settlers determined and organized to maintain their position of dominance, constitutional nationalism had achieved few African victories; indeed, white economic and political power seemed continually to expand. Though there was no questioning of the role of KAU as the vehicle of territorial nationalism, certain Kikuyu leaders came to believe that an additional, more strategic, instru-

---

* Interview, Sir Derek Erskine, February 1965. See *EAS*, Sept. 9, 1949. The Plan was a statement of European intentions to maintain the paramountcy of their position. African advancement must only take place by merit, ability, and appreciation of responsible British citizenship.

ment was necessary. If political action was to be effective in bringing about essential changes then some means had to be found to overcome the disunities within African society and to raise and sustain commitment to specific political actions.

Although the Kikuyu people were the most politically conscious section of the African population, with an intricate network of leadership and organization, there were many factors inhibiting the attainment of overall unity within the tribe. Two generations of rapid social change had accentuated those features of traditional Kikuyu culture that tended to emphasize individualism and self-achievement. In addition, new patterns of social stratification had evolved, based upon a combination of education, land, and wealth. Among those at the top of the pyramid were the African administrative class, progressive farmers, some teachers, and businessmen. Most of these were adherents of a Christian mission. They were people who had clearly benefited from the British presence and feared the implications of radical political change. Constitutional nationalism was the limit of their political involvement. But for the overwhelming mass of the population, economic anxiety and social frustration had become increasingly prevalent. Yet, though aspiration for change existed, there seemed no immediate prospect for economic and social reform.

Apart from this major economic division among the people, there were other factors inhibiting political unity. Uneven levels of development between and even within Kikuyu districts tended to affect the intensity of grievances and the will for political action. Links with militant groups in Nairobi were stronger in some areas than in others. Some chiefs effectively dominated their areas, whereas others exercised merely nominal control. Moreover, there existed a bitter legacy of personal antagonism between former KCA leaders and Kikuyu mission church leaders, which had its roots in the female circumcision controversy.

In addition, colonial policy had confined the struggle for achievement and status within very narrow economic and geographical limits. This struggle had increasingly eroded traditional social norms and sanctions. The dramatic increase in land litigation was merely an outward sign of major social disintegration.* Beauttah has vividly captured how Kikuyu political leaders viewed the results of this process. "Our society had broken down and the unity that we had in our old structure had been replaced by everyone fighting for himself, everyone on his own against all the troubles that had been brought to us. There was a fundamental growing disunity that was our weakness." Yet, "we had had so many wishes and ambitions awakened in us and then always the door slammed in our face. This is worse than never having the ambitions wakened in the first place, far, far, worse." However, "it is very very difficult for us to unite and put common interests above our individual interests."[12]

Within the recent experience of the Kikuyu people there had been one occasion in which unquestioned unity had been achieved and resistance to the power of the Government raised to an unprecedented level. In the early postwar years among the broken *mbari* of the landless Kikuyu settled by the Government at Olenguruone, above Elburgon in the Rift Valley, a secret mass oath had been employed to create the discipline and will for sustained resistance in the face of great hardships. This episode had a profound effect on Kikuyu leaders, who were soon to adopt a similar kind of mass oath of unity to resolve problems of organization, to raise the commitment of their people, and to bind them together in a common struggle. Olenguruone was not, how-

---

* *EAS*, August 11, 1950, reported 8,000 cases of litigation in Kiambu alone within the previous year. See also *Baraza*, August 19, 1950.

ever, the first occasion on which an oath had been used in modern Kikuyu political organization. Nor can the importance of a political oath of unity be understood in isolation.

In many societies, the taking of an oath is both a sacred and a social event. In this sense, many of the purposes served by oaths in African and non-African societies are comparable, for one of the most common features of oaths is the presence of symbols related to the supreme values of a society. In western practice, for example, Bibles and national flags have frequently sanctified oaths of allegiance or fidelity to a government or its laws. In taking an oath, an individual associates himself with certain sacred symbols and rituals; the behavior or beliefs to which the individual is bound by the oath thereby acquire a sanction that goes beyond immediate and personal obligations and that links the individual to a larger social entity, whether a secret society or a nation.

Further, the taking of an oath is in itself a social act, done before witnesses, and thus its most general effect is to renew or to clarify an individual's position *vis-à-vis* a group and its values and norms. Loyalty oaths in the United States, for example, were designed to distinguish trustworthy from untrustworthy employees; those who took the oaths stated explicitly and publicly their loyalty to the government. Similarly, oaths of initiation and allegiance to secret societies, such as the Freemasons, represent an acknowledgment by the individual adherent that he understands the meaning and obligations of membership. Participation in oaths helps to draw the line between "friends" and "enemies," or members and non-members.

By binding a person to the values of a group, and by clarifying the boundaries between groups, oaths are important factors in establishing social solidarity and in overcoming anomie. A reciprocal function of this is that the oath-taker becomes more receptive to the demands of the group. Whether the sanctions for breaking an oath are rooted in belief (e.g., "may this oath kill me") or in law (e.g., punishment for perjury after swearing to tell the truth), they probably combine with a positive allegiance to the group to produce a high level of conformity. This is important in situations of political conflict, where ordinary people may be called upon to defy laws and to face violence or imprisonment. In such situations, oaths may reassure individuals that they are not alone, that many others are committed to the same values and behavior. The sacred and social nature of oaths may help to clarify individual duties and obligations in situations of social conflict or confusion.[13]

Although during the postwar period in Kenya the use of oaths in African politics served mainly the two functions of building social solidarity and raising the level of political commitment, oaths had played important roles generally in traditional African society and were employed on many occasions for many different reasons. One oath might sanctify a land transaction, another might be taken to stiffen the resolve of a group involved in fighting, another to purify a person or group who had broken some taboo, and still others acted as a form of trial by ordeal. With the coming of the Europeans, all such oaths were increasingly condemned and suppressed by missionaries, while administrators adopted an ambivalent attitude, privately and sometimes publicly disparaging their effectiveness, while at the same time often encouraging their use to decide difficult legal cases.

The earliest use of an oath in a modern political context seems to have occurred shortly after 1925, when leaders of the Kikuyu Central Association decided to introduce an oath of loyalty to their Association; the transtribal character of the East African Association had probably militated against the use of oaths in that organization. The KCA leaders, however, seem to have been inspired by an oath of loyalty to the King which was taken in the new Local Native Councils. It is perhaps not surprising that the first KCA oath, flourishing among the groups of Kikuyu who had most accepted western culture, should contain few traditional elements. Then the only way to become a *good* African was to become *less* African. The oath was therefore taken with a Bible. Significantly, however, a handful of soil was also held to the navel while the words of loyalty to the Association and to Kikuyu land were repeated. During the thirties, the wording of this oath became more nationalistic and it was given to all KCA members. Yet its link with traditional practice was maintained in that in general no one who was not a married man with his own *nyumba* could be given this oath. As the Second World War drew to a close, the inner group of KCA leaders in Kiambu, who had been released from their restriction at Kapenguria, devised a new oath of allegiance relying upon Kikuyu symbols alone; the meat of a goat, for example, replaced the Bible as a central symbol. The new style oath generated its own exhilaration, not by breaking traditional taboos but by breaking those of western civilization. One of the KCA leaders detained at Kapenguria during the war described in this manner how he was given the new oath on his return.

> I held the blood in a calabash in my right hand and the meat in my left hand and as I took them I repeated these words to my people. "If I become an enemy of my land or my people and if I become lazy in working for my country, let this meat and blood kill me straight away. If I am ever bribed to abandon my people, if we have changed our minds since we went to detention may this oath kill us." First they gave it to me and then we served each other and we eight were all reunited. This was a political oath to reunite us. After we had finished the meat we sat down and we decided that all previous members of the KCA must do the same, but that no one should be forced to take it against his will.[14]

The new oath, beginning at Kabete in Kiambu before Kenyatta's return, gradually spread during the immediate postwar years among much of the leadership in the district. An influential political leader and oath administrator in Kiambu has described its evolution up to 1950.

> I gave it to leading Kikuyu government servants, Christian leaders and politicians, businessmen, chiefs, police inspectors, and so on. . . . I did not give the oath to children or to young men who did not understand what they were doing. I did, however, give it to grown-up women. What I did was to move everywhere in the country and I selected people to be given the oath on the advice of the local KCA leaders. The oath could be given after a private tea-party in someone's house or in schools. I even asked the local leader to show me who were his strongest opponents and I would go to persuade them amicably to take the oath. . . . We wanted to oath slowly, so that people understood and to people who could understand. We did not want mass oathing.[15]

After 1950, however, as oaths began to be used on a wider scale, important regional variations in their function and content emerged. In Kiambu, with its long history of KCA control and organization, the goat oath had been administered for several years on a selective basis (as above) and with great care by a few experienced elder nationalists. Their policy was slowly to persuade the élite to join the nationalist movement through taking an oath.* In most parts of Kiambu, even during the Emergency, oaths remained an instrument of moderation and indeed control. In Nyeri and Fort Hall, however, few people had taken an oath by 1950, although in that year an acceleration in its administration began, increasingly directed from Nairobi. Oaths in these

---

* Kiambu politicians saw the importance of converting the élite; however, since the oath challenged many the élite's European-oriented values, this took time. In Fort Hall and Nyeri there was no time and hence the divisions were more marked there between the élite and others during the Emergency.

two districts quickly developed into an instrument of mobilization for violent action, and their administration and direction came increasingly into the hands of relative newcomers to the political scene. The content of oaths in these two districts became increasingly divorced from Kikuyu traditions, and the speed with which it was spread produced a situation much more likely to explode into violence than in Kiambu.

However, even in Kiambu by mid-1952, the control element in oaths of unity was directly threatened by the "batuni" oath, brought by the dispossessed of the Rift Valley, an oath which in both content and form proclaimed the need for commitment to violence. It is significant that Lari, where in 1953 the most dramatic single instance of a breakdown of control occurred, was both the nearest point of entrance to Kiambu District for squatters returning from the Rift Valley and one of the most heavily populated locations in central Kenya.

Oaths underwent further transformations after the start of the Emergency and the exodus to the forests. The forest forces used them much as they had been used in Kikuyu traditional military practice—to renew the forces' loyalty to the nationalist cause. Oaths were taken before and after any engagement, and for many of the "generals" became an essential element in their efforts to sustain morale in increasingly difficult circumstances.

In tracing the development of the political role of oaths in the postwar period, there is no more significant event than the Olenguruone affair, in which an oath was first employed not only to reinforce mutual confidence and trust, but also to raise the level of political commitment, so that those who took it would accept any sacrifice in the pursuit of their just ends. The behavior of the Kikuyu settlers at Olenguruone, though incomprehensible to the Administration, was to influence profoundly the course of the emerging crisis in central Kenya. The background for the events at Olenguruone in 1949 is to be found in the changing attitude of Europeans to the "squatters."

From as early as 1904 European settlers had encouraged families to come on to their farms, in order to obtain the labor that was essential to their development.[16] The Native Labour Commission of 1913 considered that squatters should be encouraged in every possible way "on the understanding that a squatter takes his wife and family and sheep and goats with him, but no cattle, on to the farm."[17] At the same time they suggested that there must be some control, and by 1916 discussions were proceeding as to the best means of achieving it. In 1918 an ordinance appeared whose preamble could still state "Whereas it is desirable to encourage resident labourers on farms . . ."[18] In these early days the arrangements made individually by European farmers were vague but usually amounted to a loose tenancy agreement by which the African laborer came on to the farm with his family and stock and occupied an undeveloped portion of it with or without some payment of rent. This "sort of crofting system"[19] fitted in well enough with prior Kikuyu attitudes to a frontier situation and to the traditional position of *ahoi* in their own system of land tenure. It also reduced the population pressures; an administrative officer commented that when "at Dagoretti in 1925 on a rough calculation I ascertained that the increase in population about balanced the numbers who went out as squatters."[20] However, by 1930 the economic disadvantages to the European farmers were becoming increasingly apparent.

The African population and stock on the farms was growing at an alarming rate. At this time of acute agricultural depression the farmer had no need of the extra labor. Rather, he found himself facing the problems of an excess of farm workers. Secondly, he found it very difficult to rid himself legally of any of his "tenants" or their descendants. Although this problem affected many tribes, it was particularly intense among the Kikuyu, and especially among those from southern Kiambu where population pressures were felt most deeply. In 1935 a District Commissioner recognized another problem "arising from the squatter situation, and that is the ultimate position of the numbers of squatter children who have grown up or are growing up, and who are to all intents and purposes detribalized. They know no other homes beyond the farms where they were born. The Kikuyu on the farms appears to be a colonist and not a squatter."[21]

At the time of the Kenya Land Commission hearings there was a movement among Europeans to ease the way by which "squatters" could be evicted. A memorandum to the Commission conservatively computed the number of Kikuyu residing outside their Reserves at 110,000.[22] The Commissioners conceded that there was some truth in the Kikuyu case that a returned squatter family might find itself without land because its *mbari* holdings had been alienated to Europeans or "because other right-holders on their *githaka* have extended the area of their cultivation and there is no room left for them."[23] Furthermore "when one reflects that the three Kikuyu districts are only 1,931 square miles in extent, even with the addition of Mwea, it is apparent that the possible return of 110,000 squatters would augment by 57 to the square mile a population which is already dense enough to cause embarrassment." Nevertheless, they recommended that District Commissioners should have power to require "any landless family to be received on any *githaka* where there is room, but preferably on a *githaka* of the same clan in an area which is comparatively sparsely inhabited."[24] Should this not be sufficient, the squatters would have the alternative of going to other land outside the Reserves and Highlands where land would be leased on certain conditions to Africans.[25] It can thus be fairly said that the Commissioners were aware of the dangers in viewing the Reserves as a kind of dustbin into which every inconvenient human being could be put. In theory at least senior Government officers agreed. Answering a question from Archdeacon Burns, one of the two representatives of African interests, on December 14, 1936, in the Legislative Council, the Chief Native Commissioner acknowledged that there was insufficient land in Kiambu to accommodate squatters being returned from farms on which they had been living under agreements made under the Resident Native Labourers Ordinance.[26]

But even while the Land Commissioners were sitting, squatters were being evicted. "The occupiers of the Rongai Valley (near Nakuru) have by mutual consent rid themselves of practically all squatter cattle, contracts being strictly observed in respect of notice of termination,"[27] and during the next few years the Kikuyu squatters evicted in the Nakuru-Naivasha area spilled over into some of the undeveloped parts of the vast Masai Reserves,[28] where they joined other Kikuyu, some of whom had been living there since the time of the Carrier Corps press gang raids in 1917. Sometimes the Tribal Police literally smoked them out by burning the huts; at other times they achieved a reasonable *modus vivendi* with the Masai. The majority of the evicted Kikuyu squatters joined the KCA, which by 1940 had penetrated most corners of the Rift Valley. There was also a marked growth of Karing'a and KISA schools, which, since many farms even in 1938 provided no educational facilities,[29] moved in to fill the vacuum.

The general recommendations of the Kenya Land Commission had led to a revised Resident Labourers Ordinance, which was passed in 1937 but which as we shall see did not come into operation until August 1940. This Ordinance made it clear that squatters on a farm were no longer tenants, and had rights only so long as they were working for the farmer. It gave the seven European-run District Councils* (which would not even accept African Advisory Councils, let

---

* Nairobi, Naivasha, Nakuru, Aberdare, Uasin Gishu, Trans Nzoia, and Nyanza.

alone direct African representation) the power to limit the
acreage permitted for cultivation, to eliminate squatter stock,
and to increase the number of work days from 180 to 240 or
270 per year for all farms in their areas. There was no
compensating increase in wages. New agreements had to be
signed under the Ordinance with each laborer, and those
who turned down the new terms or who were redundant
were to be evicted, with their families. But the Secretary of
State for the Colonies refused to allow the implementation of
this Ordinance until alternative land had been found on
which to put the squatters who were evicted.

At a meeting of the Kenya Government Executive Council
on February 17, 1939,[30] some 52,500 acres of land, including
the area known as Olenguruone, were made available in
various parts of Masailand for settlement by the ex-squatters.
The Olenguruone portion covered an area of 34,700 acres at
an altitude of 8,000 feet on the southern edge of the Mau
plateau just inside Masailand. It had a yearly rainfall of
about 70 inches.

In 1940 the Provincial Commissioner, Nyeri, was considering putting some original right-holders there. "When all the
available land had been allocated, I think that future
landless people, if their claims to be landless are proved to
the satisfaction of the Sub-Committee of the District Commissioner, Kiambu, should be accommodated in the Mau
area."[31] It became uncertain, then, whether Olenguruone
was for ex-squatters, or whether it was land given in exchange for land lost by their *mbari* in the early days of
European settlement in Kiambu. Several of the Olenguruone settlers, sent there as squatters evicted under the 1937
Ordinance, believed that the new land was to replace their
Kiambu *ithaka* alienated to Europeans and that the Olenguruone land was now their *mbari* land under Kikuyu custom.
The fog of ambiguity and misunderstanding over the exact
status of the land was present from the start. The Olengu-

ruone affair soon reached a point where the Government and the Kikuyu were simply not talking the same language or about the same things.

The legal position was that at Olenguruone the Government bought 30,000 acres for £6,000 from the Masai and also obtained from them approximately 3,500 acres by exchange. Later, when the total block acquired was surveyed it was found to contain 34,700 acres, i.e., an excess of 1,200 acres. It was originally proposed to proclaim the whole area as Native Reserve since it had been excised from the Masai Native Land Unit. Owing to technical difficulties this was not done, and the position was finally legalized by creating a Native Settlement Area, a new category established by the Kenya Land Commission, by the enactment of an amendment to the Crown Lands Ordinance.[32] It was also decided that the Kikuyu "who, for a number of years, had created a problem by their residence in the Masai Native Land Unit,"[33] should be put on the surplus 1,200 acres.

The Olenguruone settlement therefore would contain squatters who were about to be evicted and squatters who had already been evicted but had found a temporary home at Mellili in Masailand, where they were not necessarily unwelcome to the Masai but were most undesirable in the eyes of the Administration, especially after the Kenya Land Commission had entrenched tribal land boundaries. There were also some original right-holders from Kiambu where the numbers were proving vastly larger than the Land Commission had estimated. The Government had agreed that all these groups must be found alternative land, as their rights in the Kikuyu Reserves could not now be satisfied even where their *mbari* land had not been alienated, and the Reserves could not anyway absorb their large numbers. The Kenya Land Commission had accepted that the status of such alternative land would be "native leasehold areas" and would be subject to certain development rules, but the

Kikuyu assumed that it would be their property in the same sense as the lost land in southern Kiambu had been their property.

They had some justification for this. The land given at Lari and Kerita, near Uplands, to satisfy *mbari* claims to the Tigoni "island" in the middle of a "white" area near Limuru had been given unconditionally and was being farmed without special rules.[34] The Government looked upon Olenguruone as a controlled settlement, and the Kikuyu looked upon it as new *mbari* land replacing what had been lost to white settlement.

The Kikuyu version subsequent of events is given by Samuel Koina, appointed a Court elder in Narok in Masailand in 1936 and in 1940 unanimously chosen by the new settlers as their official chief.

> We agreed to go . . . to Olenguruone in place of our shambas which had been taken from us in Kiambu in 1902. The first Settlement Officer . . . whose father had taken my family's land in Kiambu, changed all this. . . . [He] was very tough. He said they [the Government] could not allow Olenguruone to become like a reserve. If we still believed this silly stuff about Kiambu lands then we must be given an oath and they brought up elders from the Court at Nakuru in 1943 and we were all given a *githathi* oath. We then said that we must rub out this oath with one of our own. . . . [He] said that if we stayed in Olenguruone like a reserve we would claim all the land between Olenguruone and the Kiambu District.[35]

Samuel Koina himself had been one of the founders of KCA in the Rift Valley, becoming a member at Limuru in 1928 and opening a Karing'a school in the 1930s on Lord Delamere's Soysambu Estate. Koina's point—that the rules were imposed on the Kikuyu settlers after they had been living there without them for a year—is confirmed elsewhere, and it seems that at the original *baraza* in Masailand at which the emigration was discussed, the Government officials, in their eagerness to get acceptance of the move, did not make the status of the settlement clear beyond all possible doubt. Resistance to the Settlement Officer's attempt to impose these rules on the settlers intensified the unity of their opposition to the Government, which was now threatening to evict those who did not obey them. Koina denied that it was merely the ordinary terracing and agricultural laws to which the settlers objected. Rather, it was the insistence on special crop rotations and other advanced agricultural practices, which, for example, meant they could not plant maize. Resistance grew and expressed itself through the goat oath. Koina stated that

> our oath was given to everyone, man, woman and child. There were 11,800 of us there at the time. . . . If a stranger came to Olenguruone he was given our oath. Olenguruone people paid twelve shillings and fifty cents (this was for lawyers to fight for our land) and the goat, but strangers paid one shilling for putting their names in the book. We told them that they would pay the goat and the money at their home places. They used to visit us because people wondered at our wonderful unity and how we all stood together. No stranger was ever oathed by force. It was not an oath for fighting. We wanted the land.[36]

In the development of the oath there was perhaps no more critical moment than its successful transformation from a symbol of selective membership and loyalty to its employment at Olenguruone as an instrument to ensure mass obedience in a situation of open defiance to constituted authority. By early 1946 the whole population of the settlement had been oathed, and in April 1946 several hundred led by Koina walked 150 miles to Kiambu to discuss the situation with Senior Chief Koinange.[37] There the Chief Native Commissioner and Eliud Mathu also spoke to them. Mathu was at this time a member of the Board that passed the rules under which the settlement was run. Koinange, who had attended the original *baraza* in Masailand, took up their case through the Kiambu Local Native Council, which formed a special sub-committee for the crisis. But the Government was not prepared to budge, and for a time affairs were at a standstill.

In 1947 the administration of the settlement was transferred from Masai to the Rift Valley Province, where it was attached to Nakuru, the main European district. This move was greeted with further suspicion by the Kikuyu leaders. The Provincial Commissioner of the Rift Valley held a *baraza* at which the gulf between the two sides was revealed. He offered larger individual acreages but insisted on holders' abiding by the settlement rules. If they could not follow the rules, they should go to the Kamba settlement scheme at Makueni, in dry tsetse-fly country. The Kikuyu by now were demanding the removal of the European Settlement Officer. They claimed he had no right to be there, since this was *their* land, just as the Kiambu Reserve was *their* land. The Government then issued notices to depart within fourteen days. Koina's tactics changed. He tried to delay the implementation of these notices while he applied pressure elsewhere. A first extension of three months was granted, during which the Kikuyu sent a deputation to the Chief Native Commissioner, Wyn Harris,* who gave a further three months' extension. In 1948 50 settlers with lapsed permits were summoned to court at Nakuru, where the case quickly developed into a restatement of the Kikuyu rejection of the Government's land policy and the Kenya Land Commission settlement. Koinange and Kenyatta both gave evidence. The Olenguruone settlers took their case right up to the Court of Appeal, but the Government had introduced new settlement rules that made summary eviction possible together with the

---

* Later Governor of the Gambia and a member of the Devlin Commission on Nyasaland.

forfeiture of property, the demolition of houses, and the impounding of cattle.

After a pause in the operations caused by bad weather and holidays, in October 1949 new eviction orders were issued under the amended rules. These, too, were ignored, and in November a strong force of armed police moved in to start "the depressing and unpleasant task of evicting the Wakikuyu."[38] "All stock was impounded and on November 2nd demolition of buildings and sequestration of crops commerced." At the end of December all their stock was sold.[39] The evicted tenants were again offered free transport either to the Reserve, where they were expected to claim space from their *mbari* or to the Yatta where a reception camp had been established. Neither alternative was attractive, for the Bı Yatta was one of the waterless dry areas suggested by the Kenya Land Commission as suitable for Kikuyu overspill, and the Reserves, according to a Government Report in September 1947, "themselves need relief rather than additional pressure," for "there are limits to which further people and stock can be re-absorbed without grave social and economic distress."[40] The remnants of the Kikuyu settlers and their wives hung on grimly for a few more weeks, but by March 3, 1950, police and court action had removed them all. Many of the 11,800 returned of their own accord to the southern part of Kiambu, though others, refusing to move until the bitter end, were forcibly removed with their families to the special reception camp set up for them in the Yatta.

The District Commissioner at Nakuru significantly commented in July 1949: "I have always considered that, whatever the merits of their case, the Olenguruone settlers should have an alternative area to which they may go if they wish. Otherwise this District—for which I am directly responsible —will be inundated by a flood of wandering Kikuyu of an

undesirable type whose presence will be a menace to law
and order. Cromwell offered the dispossessed Irish the unpal-
atable choice of Hell or Connaught and I would now
suggest Hell or the Kikuyu Bi Yatta for these people."[41] The
District Officer in charge of the evictions described the
scheme as "a disastrous failure which may have long and
unforeseen consequences."[42]

To higher government officials, the sternest measures
appeared justified. Here was an apparently deliberate and
short-sighted attempt to sabotage a resettlement scheme that
might go some way toward solving one of the more intractable consequences of white settlement. Had the Kikuyu
accepted the settlement under rules, as indeed a few of them
did, then this could be a fine pattern for the future. But to the
Kikuyu leaders, herein lay the real difficulty. If they accepted
the regulations, then they accepted that this was a just
settlement of the problem of the Kiambu alienated lands.
Moreover, they would be accepting Kenya's agrarian color
bar, and the fact that Olenguruone was not theirs to do with
as they liked in the same way that their former *mbari* lands
in Kiambu had been. These deeper principles were never
clearly articulated, however, and became submerged in
other issues, such as whether or not they should be allowed
to plant maize at 8,000 feet.

The political effects of the Olenguruone resistance were to
be immense. When the evicted settlers came by truck on
their way to the camp at Yatta, they passed through several of
the most populated centers of central Kenya. As they
traveled they sang the Olenguruone songs, which joined the
Kanyegenuri and the *Muthirigu* as anthems of nationalist
resistance, and raised the Masai place name of Olenguruone
into a national symbol of sacrifice and martyrdom. They also
brought with them a tradition of unity and defiance of
Government on the part of men, women, and children, all of
whom had been oathed and had stood firm.

On February 20, 1950, toward the end of the Olenguruone expulsions, an important meeting of influential KAU and trade union leaders from many parts of central Kenya was held at ex-Senior Chief* Koinange's home at Kiambu just outside Nairobi. These leaders recognized to a greater extent than ever before the immense potential of an oath as an instrument for achieving unity and concerted action. They decided that the pace of oathing must be increased and its coverage greatly extended. However, they faced difficult and continuing problems of security and manpower in rapidly achieving this goal. The task was easiest in Kiambu where there was a history of postwar oathing. In Fort Hall and Nyeri it took some time to get underway. But by August 1952 secrecy had become less important and mass oathing ceremonies in Nyeri involving over 500 people were being reported. By the outbreak of the Emergency oathing was also widespread in the Rift Valley and Nairobi.

For an oath to be an effective instrument in overcoming social fragmentation and re-establishing a central loyalty, it had to employ the symbols that all Kikuyu recognized as common to their people. Thus there was a constant emphasis in the ritual on "Gikuyu" and "Mumbi," the traditional founders of the tribe; there was the appeal to the legendary period of *"Ndemi na Mathathi"* as the golden age of tribal unity and prosperity; there were the prayers to Ngai, the God of the Kikuyu, and the symbolic act of facing Mt. Kenya, the traditional attitude for prayer; and there was the renewed use, among those who had taken the oath, of traditional age-group greetings and other Kikuyu customs. Though the roots of an oath's ritual lay in Kikuyu traditional religion, this did not reflect an escape from modernity but rather the employment of common symbols at a time of intense national crisis for the Kikuyu people. Its sanctions

---

* Koinange became a Senior Chief after the death of Kinyanjui in 1929; he retired in 1949.

lay not only in the fear of reprisals from the secret organization controlling it, real though this was, but also in the potential ostracism from the new brotherhood it was creating. Yet it was also regarded as a nationalist oath, and to foreswear it was to foreswear one's nationalism. Its administration was usually accompanied by a political lecture, outlining the objectives of KAU and the nationalist version of Kenya's history. In short, the oath constituted the consummatory means to achieve the instrumental end of viable political unity.

As oathing spread, KAU's public meetings became fervent emotional gatherings of a deeply committed people. The fervor was heightened by the public use of traditional Kikuyu symbols and songs (often sung to Christian hymn tunes). Kinuthia Mugia, the most famous Kikuyu songwriter, has vividly described their political use: "Songs win over speeches every time. They are easily remembered and enter the head more quickly and more lastingly. If a child cries loudly his mother comes quickly, if he merely whimpers she lets him be. People have to be surprised somehow. Songs are a great prayer to God because he hears them quickly as a mother hears a loud cry from her baby. . . . A singer is someone very well trusted by people."[43] Oaths, the songs, reminders of Kikuyu culture, and the charisma of Kenyatta gave an unparalleled spirit and quality to KAU's meetings in central Kenya by 1952.

The use of an oath for the purposes of political unity and mobilization had as its outstanding feature the demand for a total commitment that transcended other obligations. It defined friends and enemies and sharply delimited the boundaries of the movement. It sought a total subjection of the individual to the commands of the new community. No longer was one taking part in politics solely within the rules laid down by the colonial state. It was this absolute commitment, symbolized in the act of taking a secret oath of unity, that became the critical factor in the extraordinary strength of militant nationalism. Moreover, oathing intensified the Kikuyu confrontation with the Europeans and locked both groups in bitter conflict. The hostility and apparent revulsion which Europeans displayed toward oaths probably encouraged their further use by Kikuyu nationalists. The great fear that oath-taking seemed to inspire among Europeans may in itself have reflected their awareness of the long traditions of binding oaths in European society. At the same time, the use of an oath by Kikuyu nationalists was used by the Europeans as the most important element in the thesis that Kikuyu politics at this time had reverted to primitive atavism.

Though total unity was never achieved among the Kikuyu by means of oaths, especially with respect to much of the African administration personnel, mission church leaders, members of the Christian revival, and others, nonetheless the unity-building quality of oaths acted to prevent political fragmentation among the overwhelming part of the population in a situation of growing pressure and frustration. But while oaths eliminated apathy as an alternative to political action, they also dangerously isolated certain Christian elements in the tribe as well as a small group of Kikuyu traditionalists who disapproved of the participation of women and children in the rituals.

In addition, oathing accelerated the isolation of the Kikuyu from other African peoples in Kenya. Apart from some Kamba, few other peoples had been oathed by October 1952, though plans existed to create an oath suitable for other tribes. Outside Kenya, oath-taking seemed inexplicable to overseas liberals and thereby may have jeopardized support for Kenya African nationalism. More significantly, however, mass oathing created insuperable problems of discipline and control for the leadership of the nationalist movement, for by raising the commitment of the masses in central Kenya and by forging a unity between rural and urban protest, oathing made it possible for those most willing to employ violence to come to dominate the situation. Thus, while the advantages of an oath as an organizational tool in a crisis were immense, a high price was paid for its use.

Politics of Direct Action

As mass oathing became a significant factor in the dynamics of the politics of central Kenya, it increasingly affected the character of political organization. KAU remained the public forum of nationalism, but the widespread use of a secret oath for mobilization and unity could only be carried out by an equivalent structure for communication and action. By late 1952 in central Kenya and other Kikuyu dominated areas, the leadership of these structures had become almost synonymous with those of KAU, much of the membership of KAU also having taken an oath.

The initial focus of conspiracy was Kiambu, which had clearly emerged in the postwar period as the center of Kikuyu political leadership. Politics in Kiambu had always been dominated by the land issue. Kiambu, in terms of development the most favored district in Kikuyu country, had thrown up a remarkable proportion of nationalist leaders, including such figures as Kenyatta, Gichuru, (G. K.) Ndegwa, Mathu, Kubai, and ex-Senior Chief Koinange and his son Mbiyu Koinange. The district also had an array of lesser known leaders, who had long played important roles in KCA and KAU politics. Among these were Charles Wambaa, Dedan Mugo Kimani, Ng'ang'a Ngoro, Kinuthia Mugia, Mugo Muratha, Marius Ng'ang'a Karatu, Ishmael Mungai, and Mbugwa Ngahu. The single-minded concern of this Kikuyu leadership with the land issue had had a disproportionate effect upon the strategy and policy of KAU. At the popular level Kiambu also supplied the nationalist movement with most of its impetus and financial support.

During the last two years or so preceding the declaration of the Emergency, the organization that sought to control and coordinate political action within Kiambu and influence development elsewhere was called "Parliament." The heart of this secret body was the General Council of the proscribed KCA, which had reactivated itself shortly after the release of the KCA detainees from Kapenguria. The original General Council had been established in Kiambu in the mid-thirties after the split within the KCA following Thuku's return. It had representation on a territorial basis from the various locations in the district. Each location also had its own committees with representation from sublocations. By the time "Parliament" had evolved, representatives were also coming from the KCA secret committees in the Rift Valley, Olenguruone, and the Kilimanjaro region in northern Tanganyika. KCA and KAU leadership in these committees tended to be identical, though there were KAU branches elsewhere that were not controlled by KCA leadership, as in Thika and Nairobi after 1951, as well as, of course, in other tribal areas. "Parliament" also had as official members representatives of the KISA and Karing'a schools, and representatives of the Kikuyu Land Board Association—the *Mbari* committee in Kiambu.

There was greater flexibility of leadership choice than this formal structure conveys. The growing band of committed leaders would have easy access to the meetings of "Parliament" or its related bodies, KISA, Karing'a, and the KLBA. Moreover, there was a considerable degree of overlapping, for the same leaders often played important roles in more than one organization.

Before "Parliament" came into being, the secret KCA General Council tended to meet at Githunguri in the grounds of the Kenya Teachers' College, while the *Mbari* committee was centered upon Banana Hill at Koinange's home outside of Nairobi. With the growing lack of security at

Githunguri in the face of police observation, Banana Hill became the center of organization as "Parliament" evolved. Chief Koinange took a prominent part in the activities of "Parliament" and contributed immensely to its authority by the influence and prestige he commanded among the people. Kenyatta and Mbiyu Koinange were unlikely to attend its deliberations since their presence would attract the attention of the Administration to the organization. Nevertheless their pervasive leadership undoubtedly affected the policies and decisions of the "Parliament."

Prior to the establishment of "Parliament," Ishmael Mungai had been Chairman of the KCA General Council in Kiambu since the mid-thirties. About 1949 he was succeeded by Mbugwa Ngahu who became the first Chairman of "Parliament." In late 1952 Ngahu was arrested for failing to terrace his land, and Joshua Mucheru, the Treasurer, took over. Ngahu Ng'ang'a was the "Parliament's" first Secretary, and in 1951 Mugo Muratha became Assistant Secretary and early in the Emergency, Secretary.

Until the latter half of 1951 "Parliament" provided the main stimulus for both conspiratorial and constitutional politics in Kenya. The central feature of the conspiratorial function of "Parliament" was the extension of a secret oath of unity to all parts of central Kenya. To this end it offered KAU leaders in both the rural and the urban areas any assistance they required. "Parliament's" concern in the use of an oath was to ensure an overwhelming solidarity on the widest possible scale among all Kikuyu. The leaders of "Parliament" believed that if they could achieve committed mass support then the real source of power in Britain would be bound to heed their petitions. The employment of violence played little part in their plans, although the situation might entail the use of techniques of civil disobedience as developed in India. At the same time the belief in the power of petition to bring about reform was never fully abandoned. Much of the strategy and tactics of the national executive of KAU during this period had its origin in ideas discussed by the "Parliament." But the use of a secret oath of unity on a mass basis among rural and urban Kikuyu and the increasing radicalization and conspiratorial character of the politics that followed, created insuperable problems for constitutional and territorial nationalism.

Already among the thousands of unemployed and low-wage earners in the "hopeless congestion"[44] of Nairobi, there was a radical character to social and political protest. The trade union movement had become the organizational focus of urban African politics. Alienated from the Government, in early 1950 the East African Trade Union Congress led by Kubai conducted a bitter campaign attacking the granting of a Royal Charter to the City of Nairobi. They called upon all Africans in the city to boycott the celebrations. The campaign was reinforced by widespread rumors that the occasion would be marked by an extension of the city boundary to include Limuru, Thika, Machakos, and Ngong, thus bringing these areas under the "hated" rule of the European-controlled city government. Protest exploded into violence. An attempt was first made to shoot Tom Mbotela, a moderate KAU leader, but the main target was Councillor Muchohi Gikonyo, a Kikuyu chosen by the Nairobi African Advisory Council to present the Duke of Gloucester with a Kamba stool, a Masai fly wisk, and a Kikuyu hat—to symbolize Nairobi as the meeting place of these three peoples. Both attempted assassinations failed, but the line had been drawn between the moderates and the militants.

On the first anniversary of the founding of the EATUC, a large May Day rally was held in Nairobi. The Congress picked up the radical demands of Makhan Singh and Fred Kubai for the immediate independence of the East African territories announced at the joint April meeting of KAU and the East Indian National Congress, and pledged "to do their utmost for the achievement of workers' demands, complete freedom and independence of East African territories and lasting peace of the world as a final solution to the problems of the workers in East Africa."[45]

Ten days later Makhan Singh and Fred Kubai were both arrested for being officers of an illegal trade union, and on May 16 the remaining officers of the Congress called a strike in Nairobi demanding their release, recognition of the Congress, and incidentally a 100 shilling minimum monthly wage. Large crowds attempted to hold mass meetings in Pumwani, which were broken up by the Police. The general strike lasted for a week, and the intimidatory methods used by the pickets marked a new mode of violence in the city. Makhan Singh was put under restriction, and Kubai was fined 110 shillings. On May 19 Kubai was rearrested and charged, together with another member of the Transport and Allied Workers Union, with the attempted assassination of Nairobi Councillor Muchohi Gikonyo on April 1. Committed for trial in August, he was finally acquitted on February 16, 1951, after spending nine months in jail on remand.

Although this militant action in Nairobi was supported by some of the leadership within KAU, the strike was at variance with the main concerns of the nationalist movement. It did reveal, however, the frustrations felt by the trade union leaders with the moderation of KAU under the domination of "Parliament," and the constitutionalists in Nairobi, such as Tom Mbotela, KAU's Vice-President, Joseph Katithi, the General Secretary, and Ambrose Ofafa, the Treasurer, as well as the African nominated members in the Legislative Council. For the next few months the militant urban elements would be contained as a result of strong Governmental action, but with the return of Kubai and the spread of oathing through the locations and peri-urban slums of Nairobi, a new and more powerful instrument for political action had been forged that was to have far reaching and momentous results.

Kenyatta himself opposed the strike in May as inconsistent with the main strategy of KAU. KAU's problem as an omnibus African movement was to contain all elements and build support not only in Kikuyu areas but also throughout the territory. Overt extremism in an urban environment especially on the part of a predominantly Kikuyu trade union movement could not fail to alienate other groups, particularly other tribes, and the more educated Africans whose support KAU wished to command. Moreover, with prospects for a revision of Kenya's constitution and a need for support from sympathetic individuals and organizations overseas, the image of KAU as the embodiment of constitutional nationalism had to be maintained.

The appointment of Apa B. Pant as Commissioner for India in East Africa in 1948 had encouraged the hope that independent India would be a source of support for African nationalism. Pant developed close ties with prominent KAU leaders, giving advice and providing new avenues of communication. Sympathetic to African aspirations, he sought as well cooperation between local Indian and African leaders. Mbiyu Koinange spent three months in India in late 1949 and associated closely with Pant on his return. Githunguri students were given scholarships to study in India. The visit of Fenner Brockway, a British Labour Member of Parliament, also gave some hope for international support and assistance through the Congress of Peoples Against Imperialism of which he was chairman. Within East Africa, contacts were established with Tanganyikan and Baganda political leaders in the expectation that this cooperation would increase the effectiveness of African nationalism. Mbiyu Koinange drafted a Constitution of the Republic of East Africa, but this pan-African approach was premature and brought few results.

With the outlawing of the "Mau Mau" Association by the

Government in August 1950* and the worsening of race relations, another effort was made in the latter part of 1950 to advance the cause of constitutional nationalism by developing a dialogue with Europeans. Mbiyu Koinange took the initiative in asking Sir Charles Mortimer to summon and preside over a meeting of representatives of all three races. Mortimer had recently retired from the Government and had a liberal reputation gained from playing a prominent part on the Race Relations Committee which had been established under Protestant missionary auspices in the thirties. (Mathu and Beauttah, Arthur and Owen, had been members of this earlier body at various times; it had split in July 1938 over an argument about whether Europeans could effectively represent the "interest" of Africans, some of whom were like "children."[46]) Mortimer agreed with Koinange's suggestion, and the inaugural meeting of the Kenya Citizens Association took place on October 23, 1950.[47] Although Kenyatta, Mbiyu Koinange, ex-Senior Chief Koinange, and other prominent KAU leaders attended its meetings, the Europeans present represented merely the marginal liberal fringe of their community. A dialogue with settler political leadership never developed.

An oath of unity was now being taken on an increasingly large-scale and was beginning to be an important factor on the political scene. Mbotela saw oathing as dividing the Kikuyu into two groups, and as a direct threat to constitutional nationalism. With the consent of the Administration, he held numerous meetings denouncing "Mau Mau." The committee of the Kenya Citizens Association called upon Kenyatta to condemn it as well, and on February 4, 1951, in the African locations of Nairobi he held the first such meeting, which in the next year and a half was to be followed

---

* The Government believed that an association called Mau Mau existed whose object was to drive the Europeans from the country. An oath was employed to achieve secrecy. The association was probably the proscribed KCA. See Chapter IX.

by others. Kenyatta said he did not know of the word "Mau Mau" or in what language it occurred, but that nonetheless it was a bad thing. Since an oath of unity was not referred to by Kikuyu as "Mau Mau," this kind of denouncement may have meant little. In an environment of growing racial isolation, restrictions strictly limiting the holding of KAU meetings and bitterness over such recent issues as the Beecher Report, which was interpreted by African leadership both as critically limiting opportunities for African educational advancement and as an attempt to bring the independent schools under government control, oathing and conspiracy in politics marched ahead.[48]

The release of Kubai after his acquittal in February 1951 was to be a critical factor in the developing crisis. Kubai returned to find the trade union movement disintegrating, with many leaders having fled to Uganda and Tanganyika. In a radical reappraisal, it was decided to use the trade unions for industrial issues only, and to bring the force of the African workers into KAU.[49] A branch of KAU had been established in Nairobi and was under moderate leadership, and to control this branch became the objective of Kubai, Kaggia, John Kali, John Mungai, James Njoroge, Aggrey Minya, Paul Ngei, and other militant urban leaders. For the next few months the struggle for political leadership in Nairobi went on. On June 10, Kubai's group swept the board at the Nairobi KAU branch elections, supervised by Kenyatta, in Kaloleni Hall. Kubai was elected Chairman, John Mungai Vice-Chairman, Kaggia General Secretary and Ngei Assistant Secretary. All the former office bearers lost their posts. Though they were educated, they were "not hot enough" as one militant put it.[50] A demand by Kubai at the meeting for independence within three years dramatically reflected the mood of this radical urban nationalism.

The urban radicals were committed men, absolutely convinced of the justice of their cause, intolerant of moderation in politics, and possessing little faith in the prospects of constitutional reform in the immediate future. "Africa for the Africans" infused their mood, and self-government "now" was their objective. If peaceful change was not possible, they were prepared to employ violence. They could entertain no thought of overthrowing the colonial Government, particularly since it could also command the armed might of Britain. But they could hope to bring about a crisis in which the British Government might well have to intervene in such a way as to cause a dramatic re-evaluation of its policies in Kenya. They were tired of unanswered petitions, and rejected the arguments of the educated constitutional nationalists for a program of eventual self-government built upon the gradual social and economic advance of the African peoples. Unable to attract to their militant course of action the educated nationalists, such as Mathu, Mbotela, and Katithi, they repudiated them, attacking them in public meetings.

From June to November 1951, the urban militants consolidated their hold on power in Nairobi and began to extend their influence in the national movement on a country-wide basis. The strength of this revolutionary force within KAU could now not be ignored. Even Kenyatta found his powers of manoeuver increasingly restricted, and felt a need to adopt a more militant attitude; in a speech at Thika in August, for example, he said that blood might have to be shed in the nationalist cause. He toured central Kenya and Nyanza with Kubai and other political militants. In October Kenyatta produced a flag for KAU and by implication for a self-governing African Kenya. After substantial pressure, the Nairobi KAU branch finally received Kenyatta's approval to organize a national party conference, the first to be held since October 1949.

The militant leaders had some initial difficulty in persuading delegates that the conference was constitutional, but they dominated its proceedings from the start. Though Kenyatta insisted on multi-tribal representation among the national office bearers, the radical militants succeeded in ousting the constitutional nationalists and gaining virtual control of the national executive committee. They were represented on it by Kubai, Kaggia, Beauttah, James Njoroge, and Charles Wambaa. Other members of the committee were ex-Senior Chief Koinange, Jesse Kariuki, Jesse Kitabi (Kamba), and Jonathan Njoroge. J. D. Otiende (a Luhya) became General Secretary, Paul Ngei (leader of the Machakos Kamba) the new Assistant Secretary, P. H. Okondo (a Luhya) the Auditor, and H. L. Nangurai (for many years the chief KCA contact among the Masai) Treasurer. Mbotela, Katithi, and Ofafa all lost their posts. The conference provided an excellent opportunity for the militants to press their point of view.

During the latter part of 1951 the pace of oathing in Nairobi mounted significantly. It was therefore decided to bring urban oathing under the control of the executive committee of the KAU Nairobi branch. The fact that some people had made a money racket out of giving oaths, and some leaders were taking independent action, were contributing factors to this move. As this took place a secret committee (originally known as the *Muhimu* (Important) and later as the Central Committee), composed of the inner-core of KAU Nairobi branch's executive committee, was formed. Additional representatives were brought in over the next year, until the secret Central Committee ultimately contained two members from each secret committee that the people from Fort Hall, Nyeri, Embu, Meru, and Machakos districts living and working in Nairobi had established. In addition, Nairobi itself had two representatives, Eliud Mutonyi and Kaggia, while Charles Wambaa and John Koinange were delegates from the Banana Hill "Parliament." Other dominant members were Fred Kubai and J. D. Kali, Hiram Kingeru and Kanyeki Wathega (Nyeri), Willy

George Njui Kamumbo (Embu), Isaac Gathanju, and James Njoroge (Fort Hall).[51] When both *Muhimu* and the subsequent Central Committee were formed, all the members took a special leaders' oath together.

When the state of Emergency was declared, the Central Committee thus controlled five district committees in Nairobi, while the sixth district, Kiambu, had a special relationship through the Banana Hill liaison officers. Each district committee within Nairobi had developed its own subordinate organization. In some instances, notably among people from Nyeri, an intermediate divisional structure controlling groups of locations had emerged both in Nairobi and in Nyeri by the beginning of the Emergency. Fort Hall at this time had fifteen location committees in Nairobi, with sub-location committees working under them. Before the Emergency began, Machakos did not have any location committees in the home district, although there were a few Kamba locations that had secret committees (i.e. Kangundo, Matungulu, Kilungu, and Mukaa) in Nairobi. As the secret movement grew, it was particularly susceptible to infiltration by criminal elements, who were also used for acquiring guns and other supplies. Courts were also established at various levels of the organization to instill some degree of discipline. By October 1952 the organization was more advanced in some districts and locations than in others, but the tremendous impetus given by the declaration of the Emergency undoubtedly stimulated its rapid consummation in the early months of the ensuing struggle. This is not to imply that the Central Committee completely dominated the situation in the Nairobi area, for at least in one slum area—Kariobangi—the situation after the declaration of the Emergency rapidly developed into a reign of terror, despite efforts by the Central Committee to re-establish their control over this shanty village.

As the secret movement strengthened its grip on Nairobi,

it began to have an increasing impact upon the rural Kikuyu areas. It probably had least effect upon the squatters in the Rift Valley as contrasted with the Reserves, which were vital areas for militant mass support. The secret movement in the Rift Valley had stronger links with the Kiambu "Parliament" than with the Nairobi Central Committee. Though farm workers posed problems of security for the Administration and the settlers, difficulties of communication and their comparative isolation reduced their influence on political action. While Kiambu remained under the influence of "Parliament," their control in some locations of the district was being threatened by alternate Kiambu militant leaders based on Nairobi. "Parliament," rooted in the long Kiambu tradition of the politics of petition, was at variance with the growing readiness of the Nairobi Central Committee to employ violence. Except for the special case of violent vengeance at Lari in 1953, Kiambu remained outwardly quiescent even after the declaration of the Emergency. Comparatively few men went to the forest, and "Parliament" continued to control resistance from inside the district. Though it changed its name to the Kiambu War Council during the Emergency and operated from secret underground headquarters, it continued to draft petitions, and collect funds for the defense at Kenyatta's trial at Kapenguria as well as seeking out defense witnesses.

In the districts north of Kiambu the growth of the secret and radical movement in Nairobi had a more dramatic effect. Following the meeting in February 1950 at Banana Hill an oath of unity had been spreading, and by late 1951 Nairobi militants were taking an increasingly active part in accelerating its coverage. This increase in oathing was reflected in a resurgence of direct action in Fort Hall and Nyeri. In November there was large-scale agrarian disobedience by women in Fort Hall followed by wholesale arrests. In the same month Beauttah was convicted for collecting money without issuing receipts, and in February 1952, together with Andrew Ng'ang'a, Petro Kigondu, and Kimana Njuku (prominent KAU leaders in the district), he was sentenced to two years in prison for conspiracy. These men were to remain behind barbed wire until after the end of the Emergency. Nyeri saw an outbreak of arson in January and February which led to strong reinforcements of police being posted to the district.

Oathing not only raised the ordinary person's commitment, but also bound together the rural north and the radical leadership of the urban center. Henceforth the influence and effect of the "Parliament" on events outside Kiambu declined. Though the decision to create solidarity through an oath originated in Kiambu, it was the Nairobi radicals who had taken it over and made it an instrument in fostering militant, and if necessary, violent political action. The KAU committees in Nyeri and Fort Hall had now secretly become the driving force behind a renewed campaign of agrarian disobedience. The alliance of these northern districts with Nairobi, supported by an organized movement of mobile oathing groups issuing regularly from the city, was a crucial factor in rapidly intensifying African commitment to conflict. By August 1952 some Nairobi committes were sending special organizers up to the districts to prepare for resistance in the forest. Prior to this the Nairobi Central Committee had already accepted the necessity to eliminate police informers and was slowly building up its supplies of guns and ammunition.

The mass meeting at Nyeri of some 25,000 Kikuyu on July 26 powerfully demonstrated the dominance of the militants. While this meeting emphasized the magnetic nature of Kenyatta's leadership, it also showed that no one man could control the disintegrating situation. In a real sense radical and conspiratorial politics had greatly enhanced the solidarity of the Kikuyu behind Kenyatta, but it had also critically narrowed his effective control. The direct linking of his name with an oath gave authority to the movement. The symbolic role of his leadership was prominent but greater power probably lay in the hands of the militants willing to employ violence.

A month later a very different kind of public meeting was held in Kiambu with the approval of the Administration. Present were the élite of the district, Kenyatta, ex-Senior Chief Koinange, Mathu, Thuku, Gichuru, Senior Chief Waruhiu, and other political and governmental leaders. The long struggle between the Kikuyu and the European oligarchy was moving toward a climax of violence which these leaders sought to contain. Many spoke, although Kenyatta's words commanded the greatest authority. Speaking of the harm that "Mau Mau" was causing KAU as it sought to achieve the legitimate aspirations of Africans, he condemned it by employing a traditional Kikuyu curse *"Kura Na Miiri Ya Mikongoi."* This phrase, which was to be featured in Kenyatta's trial at Kapenguria, is literally translated as "to be lost in the roots of the Mikongoi tree."* In *Facing Mount Kenya,* Kenyatta himself translates it as to "be driven to the unknown corners of the earth"[52] or "Oblivion."[53] Though the Administration could believe that he had again evaded any denunciation, shortly afterwards he is reported to have been called before the secret Central Committee, who remonstrated with him over the strength of his denunciation. If he continued to denounce "Mau Mau" in this manner who, the militants asked, would lead the fight for the country when he was arrested?

Faced by the mass emotion exhibited at KAU rallies and by an expanding pattern of violence (arson in Nanyuki, cattle maiming in Timau, and a campaign of selective

---

*In a major rally in Kenya's "Little General Election" in June 1966, Kenyatta consigned the opposition party to the *miiri ya Mikongoi.*

assassination), the settler leaders demanded the declaration of an Emergency in the country. Within the Government there were differences of opinion. Mitchell, nearing the end of the second extension of his term of office and the climax of a most distinguished career in the Colonial Service, believed that the Government faced essentially just another *dini* or fanatical religious movement. He did not feel that the "Mau Mau" activities up to date merited any such drastic action. He had, however, recognized the growing gravity of certain economic problems in the colony, which might, with profit, be subject to close study by a Royal Commission. He left the colony on final retirement in June 1952. His successor did not arrive until the end of September.

The provincial administrators were more impressed with the seriousness of the situation. One of their first reactions, however, since they, too, agreed it was probably some sort of *dini*, was to organize "cleansing," that is, counter-oathing ceremonies by witch-doctors, and to press for powers to detain the leading "agitators." Indeed, in late August Jesse Kariuki was arrested and in September he was detained under the Deportation Ordinance.

But on October 7, 1952, Senior Chief Waruhiu, the leading government spokesman in Kikuyu country and one of the most prominent Christian leaders in Kiambu, was assassinated. This event finally united all shades of European opinion behind the settlers' demand for immediate and drastic action. The declaration of the Emergency and the coming of the Security Forces brought a dramatic change in the situation. As the full weight of Government power was brought to bear on the Kikuyu, the assertive character of their radical politics was transformed into desperate resistance as they sought to preserve their hopes and ideals as a people under increasingly severe siege conditions.

CHAPTER 8

Violence and Reform

The dramatic assassination of Senior Chief Waruhiu just outside Nairobi was a direct and serious challenge to the authority of the colonial state. The new Governor, Sir Evelyn Baring, who had previously served in Southern Rhodesia and the British High Commission Territories in southern Africa, decided that his first duty was to restore law and order. After a short interval for completing certain troop movements and drafting the necessary legislation, on October 20, 1952, he signed a proclamation declaring that "a public emergency has arisen which makes it necessary to confer special powers on the Government and its officers for the purpose of maintaining law and order."[1]

The declaration of the Emergency did not head off an incipient mass revolution, but rather precipitated further mobilization for small-scale, violent resistance in the rural areas, along with increased violence in Nairobi. In this respect, much of the violence that occurred during the Emergency was not simply a continuation of either pre-Emergency political tactics or the Government's security measures but derived from the conditions of the Emergency itself. The deployment of British and East African troops and the strengthening of the police introduced a new element of violence into the situation, as this Chapter will show. Most Europeans strongly believed that they were opposing an evil and barbaric movement. Some of them saw the need for economic and social concessions, but few recognized the necessity for far-reaching political reform. Moreover, they felt that the nature of the organization they faced justified both personal and public violence.

Thus, the "siege" of Kikuyuland and the formation of units of resistance in the forests, led for the most part by men not associated with the leadership of pre-Emergency political groups, altered the scope of violence qualitatively, bringing it to a level far beyond the capacity of pre-Emergency organizations, whether African or governmental. And, at the same time, the Emergency provided a context for the implementation of the myth of "Mau Mau."* The trial of Jomo Kenyatta at Kapenguria was an effort to provide legal justification for it, while wholesale arrests and detentions and the Government's adoption of the philosophy of confession and "rehabilitation" emphasized the psychological rather than the social bases of African political opposition.

Yet during these years, in which the Europeans seemed to be achieving their greatest influence since the time of Grigg, their position was slowly being eroded by other factors over which they had little or no control. The apparent strength of the British military action at the outset of the Emergency masked its real importance as a confirmation of the long-term weakness of the European position in Kenya. For the sending in of British troops was a reassertion of the British presence in, and responsibility for, Kenya. Though it was some years before the full consequences became apparent, British troops did not leave the country again until a year after Independence had been achieved; during the intervening period, dramatic steps were taken to bring about political reform in the country. Thus, to a large extent, the radical leaders of KAU and the trade unions had their objective fulfilled—namely, to produce a situation of social discontent and a climate of endemic hostility that would bring the

---

* See Chapter 9.

conditions under which Kenya Africans lived directly to the attention of the overseas colonial authority.

In the years following the declaration of the Emergency, growing international appreciation of the African political mood and the triumph of nationalism on the West Coast supported a new political context in which Tom Mboya and others were able to achieve constitutional reform despite persistent administrative obstruction. The Europeans continued to attempt to retain elements of the Kenya they had known by forging new alliances. Nevertheless, the release of Jomo Kenyatta and his acceptance as the father of an African Kenya nation finally exploded the myth under which the country had been governed for so long.

Kapenguria and Lari

Sir Evelyn Baring's analysis of the situation he faced was as simple as his solution to it. He accepted the argument that he was confronting a movement called "Mau Mau," an atavistic and secret cult almost wholly confined to the Kikuyu, designed to drive out the European and to turn Kenya into a land of "magic and murder."[2] At the head of the movement stood Kenyatta, supported by most of the Kikuyu political leaders. These men, through an oath and by exploiting certain grievances, were manipulating the mass of the Kikuyu population to build a nefarious and conspiratorial movement. On October 9 he cabled the Secretary of State that "quite apart from their political views most of the Kenya African Union leaders, including Kenyatta, are the planners of the *Mau Mau* movement." He recommended the immediate removal of "Kenyatta and several of his henchmen." Unless this was done the Kikuyu chiefs, headmen, civil servants, and missionaries would soon cease to support the Government. The trouble would spread to the Kamba and even to Nyanza, and lastly, "there will be reprisals by Europeans."[3]

At 12:45 a.m. on October 21, Assistant Superintendent of Police Benton and some 80 police arrested Kenyatta at his home at Gatundu in the Kiambu Reserve. They took him and a ton and a half of documents to police headquarters on the Athi River Road.[4] This was part of Operation "Jock Scott" with which the Emergency opened and which entailed the detention of the major KAU leaders in central Kenya.

At this point the Government apparently believed that if it locked up the KAU leaders it would simultaneously remove the organizers of "Mau Mau." Since the mass of the people had merely been deceived, it should be possible to restore discipline very soon both in the Reserves and in the settled areas and to persuade the Kikuyu to follow responsible European and African leadership. No political changes were considered necessary. It would be sufficient to bring about stricter control of the masses by reasserting "tribal" discipline through the Government chiefs and headmen, who would be given strong support. The economic problems would be investigated within an East African context by a Royal Commission. But within six months, the implementation of this policy, as the Security Forces slowly invested the Kikuyu rural areas, helped to bring about violence on an increasingly large scale.

Together with this policy of stricter control the Government accepted the necessity to justify in a court of law the reasoning behind its actions. If "Mau Mau" was a secret organization with criminal intentions, then Kenyatta, Achieng Oneko, Paul Ngei, Fred Kubai, and Bildad Kaggia of the KAU national executive committee and Kungu Karumba, chairman of the Chura Divisional Branch of KAU in Kiambu, should be brought to trial on criminal charges. The inclusion in this national organizing committee of "Mau Mau" of Oneko (a Luo) and Ngei (a Kamba), probably the most outspoken politicians among their respective peoples at this time, confirmed another Government tendency to equate all radical politics with "Mau Mau."

In the Government's view, after the verdict the people of Kenya and, indeed, of the world would understand the real character of "Mau Mau." Just as the previous generation of administrators had hoped that the judgment of the Kenya Land Commission would produce a final and permanent settlement of the land question, so too their successors hoped that by directly attributing responsibility to these six there would be a final and permanent settlement of the "Mau Mau" question. It could be proved, so the Administration argued, that a small coterie of desperadoes had attempted to pervert Kikuyu traditions for their own criminal ends.

The trial opened at Kapenguria, where the western edge of the Rift Valley escarpment drops down to the plains of Pokot. A peaceful and beautiful setting, it could hardly have been more inconvenient for a major trial of international importance. Communications with Nairobi, let alone the outside world, were appalling, and the trial was held in a cramped old red-roofed structure normally used as the schoolroom of an agricultural training college.

Defense counsel gathered from all over the world. Leading them was D. N. Pritt, Q. C. from Britain. The judge was Ransley Samuel Thacker, Q. C. Thacker, who had officially retired from the Service on August 15, 1952,[5] was especially recalled to take the case. For five years he had been a Senior Puisne Judge in Kenya and on two occasions he had acted as Chief Justice. Since the war he had presided at some trials involving Africa leaders in Nairobi, including the charge, which had been dismissed, of attempted murder against Fred Kubai, one of the accused at Kapenguria.

The Defense maintained throughout that this was no ordinary criminal trial but that African nationalism itself stood accused. The determined opposition of the Prosecution to this position immediately injected a bitter undercurrent into the proceedings. The trial opened on November 24, 1952, and the extraordinary security precautions, which had turned Kapenguria into an armed camp, belied the Prosecution's claims as they opposed bail: "These people are perfectly ordinary people and are arraigned on ordinary criminal charges, about which there is no mystery."[6] Guards covered all entrances to the building, the East African Armoured Car Squadron patrolled the earth roads, barbed wire was everywhere seen, and the constable outside the door to the courthouse stood with fixed bayonet; a spotter airplane circled overhead.

But it was the Prosecution who first broke down the distinction between politics and crime by announcing that they proposed to establish "that Mau Mau is part of KAU—a militant part, a sort of Stern Gang."[7] In all the histrionic cut and thrust of this remarkable trial this distinction remained the fundamental point at issue. Pritt's tactics and methods, which so affronted the Judge and the Prosecution, were designed to force the trial and these deeper issues onto the headlines of the Kenya and world press. In this the Defense undoubtedly succeeded, and the seeds of doubt sown at Kapenguria remained in the background of informed discussion on Kenya's problems. Thacker might dismiss Kenyatta's recitation of Kikuyu land grievances with "I gather grievances have nothing to do with Mau Mau, and Mau Mau has nothing to do with grievances,"[8] but others did not.

Thacker attempted to have the final word on this issue in his judgment delivered on April 8, 1953. The trial had lasted from November 1952 to March 1953, with 58 days in court; 44 witnesses were heard for the Crown and 35 for the Defense. Thacker left no room for doubt of his views: "Another point is the allegation by defence counsel that this trial savours of a political trial, and the Court has been reassured by the Deputy Director of Public Prosecutions that it is not a political trial. It happens, of course, that the six accused have engaged in politics over a number of years, but that does not make this trial a political trial. It is an ordinary criminal trial on ordinary criminal charges." But he was too late. Kapenguria had already become a political trial, and no one judge could end the debate it had started.

As Thacker sat down in the packed room to deliver his judgment, which culminated in Kenyatta and the other five accused being sentenced to the maximum penalty of seven years' hard labor, the curious hoped in vain that he would shed some light on the crowning mystery of all—what was this thing called "Mau Mau"? The still stricter security measures, the sandbags protecting the entrance to the court, the police officer with his Sten gun who sat near the judge, two airplanes overhead instead of one, were more an indication of the consequences of Kenyatta's arrest than of the reasons for it. Step by step Thacker traced out his analysis.

Jomo Kenyatta, and five others, had been charged before him for managing, or assisting with managing, and being members of "an unlawful society, that is to say, the society commonly known as Mau Mau, which society had been declared . . . to be a society dangerous to the good government"[9] of the Colony. They were also charged with conspiring to compel persons to take an oath, conspiring to excite disaffection against the Government, and conspiring to raise discontent and "to promote feelings of ill will and hostility between different classes of the population."[10]

The Prosecution had elaborated on the charges: "as a result of the prosecutions which took place in 1950 the society's name was changed to Mau Mau . . . you [Kenyatta] elevated Mau Mau into the position of a religious cult."[11] Furthermore, "it is a society which does not have records or appear to have official lists of members or to carry banners or insignia,"[12] and "looking at Mau Mau quite dispassionately and quite objectively and quite outside this trial there can be no one who can say that it does not do the most appalling criminal things and that it appears to be a purely barbarous movement negative in everything it does and accompanied by circumstances of revolting savagery."[13]

Although Thacker had previously confirmed that he was not to "take any account of what I have read or what I have in my mind, what I think that the society known as Mau Mau stands for other than what appears in the note" [record],[14] he could not have remained unaware of the increasing deterioration in the security situation in the country, and must have known of the "Lari massacre," which had occurred two weeks before. In his judgment he first found as a fact that there was a society known as "Mau Mau."[15] He further found that when Kenyatta returned to Kenya in 1946 he "commenced to organize this Mau Mau society, the object of which was to drive out from Kenya all Europeans, and in doing so to kill them if necessary."[16] Thacker stated that he was firmly convinced that "the accused, who formed part of the Executive Committee of KAU were also the Executive Committee of Mau Mau."[17] "They have taken advantage of the uneducated or primitive African in order to further their own ambitious purposes and their lust for power."[18] But Thacker failed to define any more closely the organization of the society.

Kenyatta, during his cross-examination, maintained that the Government "wanted, I think, not to eliminate Mau Mau, Sir, but what they wanted to eliminate is the only political organization—that is KAU—which fights constitutionally for the rights of the African people."[19] In a last exchange with Somerhough of the Prosecution, he said:

> KENYATTA: I have done my best and if all other people had done as I have done, Mau Mau would not be as it is now. You made it what it is, not Kenyatta.
> Q.: What "you," the Europeans, the Crown or who has made it what it is?

KENYATTA: The Government not handling Mau Mau in the proper way and you blame it to me.

Q.: It is the Government's fault that Mau Mau exists and goes on?

KENYATTA: Well, I say yes.

SOMERHOUGH: I will take that answer. Thank you.[20]

By the time the trial ended there had indeed already been indications that the Government's "handling" of the situation had brought its own problems. The Reserves were the focus of the re-institution of firm "tribal discipline," in which the chiefs and headmen played a primary role. But they were being underpinned by a network of new police posts stretching across the Kikuyu Reserves, which were manned by young Europeans from the Kenya Regiment, the Kenya Police, and Kenya Police Reserve. As a result of increased police sweeps in Nairobi and other towns, hundreds of Kikuyu young men were "repatriated." Rather than face the "tribal discipline," many moved straight into the forests to reinforce the nucleus already there.

In the Rift Valley the declaration of the Emergency created a crisis for the Kikuyu laborers and squatters and their growing numbers of dependents. New Emergency regulations were introduced making it compulsory for them to be photographed. The local leaders of KAU immediately decided that these regulations should be opposed. To many squatters the regulations implied compromising a belief that they might eventually acquire the land then occupied by European settlers. To others it raised the same issues as the *kipande* controversy. Thousands of squatters refused to be photographed, and the Government decided they, too, must be "repatriated." Transit camps were established whose reputation was such that many Rift Valley Kikuyu decided to make their own arrangements rather than be processed through them. Thus in the early months of the Emergency the Kikuyu Reserves, already bursting at their seams, had to receive a further influx of refugees, some of whom were second and third generation inhabitants of the Rift Valley. Indeed some families had had only a tenuous contact with the Reserves for thirty or forty years.

So they came, by the tens of thousands, on foot, by bus, by truck, and by train, many leaving behind all they had—goats, maize, beds, and houses—to be sold by the Government, who would forward the proceeds to their "district of origin." They arrived with their pots and pans, the clothes they stood up in, and small packs of the beans or maize they had salvaged. Some of the children got lost on the way. Many of the young men walked straight from the point of arrival to the sanctuary of the forest. Those who remained in the Reserves found, after the warmth of the initial greetings from long-forgotten relatives, that the burden of existence grew rapidly beyond all human strength. By the end of 1953, the Government estimated their numbers at 100,000, of whom perhaps a third required Governmental aid for subsistence.[21]

But it was not until March 26, 1953, that two incidents on the same night dramatically closed the initial phase of the Emergency. The first, a successful raid on Naivasha Police Station, in which the attackers drove away a truck containing ammunition, rifles, and automatic weapons, prompted a more professional military approach by the Government to the problem of restoring law and order. The second incident, known as the "Lari massacre," reinforced Government thinking that it was faced with "an advanced form of group insanity."[22] The violence at Lari had its roots in the land conflicts with Europeans on the Kikuyu frontier.

Lari itself is situated on the edge of Kikuyu country, high in the cold bamboo lands of the escarpment forest some 30 miles from Nairobi. It is eight miles above Limuru, one of the original European settlement areas, which had also been a thriving center for a more intensive post-1945 European influx. At Limuru and nearby Tigoni, former members of the Indian Civil Service and the Indian Army mingled with ex-missionaries and retired Kenya administrators. It was an ideal retirement area with a perfect climate, cheap servants, and suburban amenities.

When the Limuru farms were originally alienated, the transaction was never accepted by the Kikuyu as legitimate. By an oversight the part known as Tigoni, comprising 945 acres, "remained as an island of unalienated Crown Land in the middle of the farm area."[23] In 1916 the District Commissioner of Kiambu proposed that the area be made a township, and in 1925 a successor decided to remove all the Kikuyu living there and to compensate the *githaka* owners. In 1923 there had been 312 people on the land, but by 1932 this had increased to 607 people, a density of 411 to the square mile. The Kenya Land Commissioners agreed that at the time of the original land alienation "there appears to have been a small village or possibly only one hut near where the Police Station is now and a few other huts dotted about the neighbourhood, but few or none of them were within the boundaries of the area in question."[24] But the Kikuyu held that there were 10 *mbari* with *githaka* rights on the land. The Land Commissioners eventually decided that while there were some Kikuyu rights in the land before the great famine of 1898, their occupation up until then was never very effective and that "when the famine occurred they left the area and did not return to it in any considerable numbers until after the surrounding farms had been alienated."[25]

By the thirties the pressure from the Limuru and Tigoni settlers to remove this island of Kikuyu had intensified. The Kenya Land Commissioners proposed that the Tigoni land should be surrendered in exchange for a block of forest land which would join that other isolated "island," the Lari

Native Reserve, with the main Reserve and so eliminate two "islands" by a single tidy exchange. Three *barazas* were held, and the representatives of six of the ten *mbari* agreed with their decisions, although later the *githaka* owners "for the most part" withdrew their consent. The terms of the exchange were generous and were eventually made more so. The Commissioners held it "to be to the advantage of these natives and the reserve as a whole that they should be ordered to quit Tigoni" with suitable compensation.[26] The three most prominent leaders among the ten Tigoni *mbari* were Luka Wakahangara, John Mbugwa, and Marius Ng'ang'a Karatu. For some time they all refused to move, on the grounds that the land they were offered at Nyamweru in Lari was already claimed by three other *mbari*.[27] Acceptance would mean accepting the political basis of the Kenya Land Commission Report, the extinction of all other Kikuyu land rights, and specifically the claim of the Lari *mbari* to the land being offered in exchange.

In late 1936 the Government began to insist on the implementation of the decision of the Commissioners. Kenyatta, in England, was informed by the KCA and protested to the British Government. By 1937 Wakahangara had persuaded some groups to go to Lari but others remained obdurate. Mukoma, the local chief and a long-time KCA supporter, is reported to have told Wakahangara that "now you have made all your *mbari* to become poor for life and you have opened the home and let the hyena [European] get in the house."[28] Wakahangara's own *mbari* was split on whether to accept the Government's proposals. In May 1940 the moment of crisis came. The Chief Native Commissioner gave the residents one week's notice, and in the last week of May the Government acted. A District Officer arrived bringing prisoners, police, and Tribal Police with orders to burn or demolish all the houses in the area. Karatu, one of the leaders of those who totally rejected the Administration's proposals, watched from a hiding-place as his own house was demolished. All crops were also uprooted or destroyed. Wakahangara's group had already been moved by truck with their housing material to Nyamweru at Lari, where they were allotted large individual farms and allowed to sell off any trees on the forest land. Wakahangara himself became chief of the new settlement at Lari. Karatu and Mbugwa were arrested on May 27 and detained with the other KCA leaders at Kapenguria until December 1943. Many of the Tigoni refugees tried to make a living as *ahoi* elsewhere in Kiambu or became squatters in the Rift Valley. The Tigoni land claims remained an enduring theme in KAU politics, and the opponents of Wakahangara at Lari and Tigoni were among KAU's strongest adherents in Kiambu. After the war, KAU continued to forward petitions about Tigoni to both the Kenya and the British Governments.

This long-drawn-out dispute over land meant that even before the Emergency the population at Lari was divided into two bitterly opposed groups. KAU's support for the anti-Wakahangara faction drove Wakahangara and his group into the opposition. By 1952, however, there were other factors raising tensions in the area to dangerous levels. European District Councils were critically affecting the economic well-being of squatters by enacting orders under the Resident Labourers Ordinance restricting the size of squatters' plots on European farms, thereby limiting the number of stock that squatters could keep. In some areas during the year a determined effort was made to bring about the "total elimination" of their stock.[29] By mid-1952 there was firmer and more sustained police action against squatters. Lari, a pivotal area in the constant interaction between the Reserve and the White Highlands, became a refuge for many of those who were uprooted and landless. The continued influx of economically desperate people, some of them related to the original claimants of the land on to which

Wakahangara had moved, greatly intensified the conflict situation.

Increasingly the majority of people living around Lari had come to look upon Wakahangara, his family, and his followers as the root and symbol of all their troubles, owing to both their feeling of betrayal at Tigoni and his acceptance of land claimed by the local *mbari*. By March 1953, the majority had taken both the first oath of unity and the second, *batuni*, oath. As we have seen, the second oath, which had started in mid-1952, bound those who took it to violent action if necessary. Wakahangara, now an ex-Chief, was wholly committed to and dependent upon the Government. It is scarcely surprising that of the only two initial Home Guard "Loyalists" posts in Kiambu District, one was at Lari supported by Wakahangara.

The militant leaders of the area set out to destroy Wakahangara and his group as well as Chief Makimei and the "Loyalists," regarding them as implacable enemies. They met for four days preparing plans, the final committee session being held in a house in the Railway quarters at Limuru. It was decided to kill all the chiefs, headmen, and Home Guards in the area on the night of the twenty-sixth of March. Moreover, anyone who might be able to give evidence in court afterwards would also have to be killed. This would inevitably mean women and older children. At least ten young men, six from the Rift Valley and four from Nairobi, were brought in to strengthen their ranks. *Pangas* or knives would be used; the group had only one gun. Money was collected and left in a shop at Limuru so that it could be drawn on by anyone forced to escape, but the plan was that every man in Lari who had taken the *batuni* oath would join in the affair. Afterwards everyone would return to his own house so that the Government would think that fighters from the forest were responsible. Preliminary arrangements were made with the Naivasha secret committee ("War Council") to synchronize the operation with the attack on the Naivasha Police Station.

On March 24 the leaders of the raid were chosen from each sub-location. Two days later at 7 p.m. some 3,000 people assembled in a large open space known as *Rurii rwa Tharau* and were quickly and brusquely marshalled and given their final orders. The burning of Home Guard huts and the killing of those on the list, as well as others, started soon thereafter.[30] Ex-Chief Wakahangara and 26 members of his family died. Chief Makimei and his headmen succeeded in fighting off attacks, but others did not. A total of at least ninety-seven "Loyalists" or their dependents died, while the casualties of the attackers "in the battle and pursuit after the massacre far outnumbered those of the loyalists and Security Forces combined, in what was the most extensive *Mau Mau* attack of the Emergency."[31]

Lari was clearly a terrible tragedy. Intense socio-economic conflict was precipitated into violence in an area bereft of the moral constraints of older settled communities. Against the broad context of anti-Government feeling among the Kikuyu, we have sought to describe this disintegration into organized killing in terms of the belief, held by the majority of the people in a single location, that it was no longer possible to resolve immediate problems within the framework of law and order. That the motives for Lari were largely specific to the place and the situation, however, was not the interpretation accepted by the Government. The official position was that "the general motive of the Lari massacre was to murder all loyalists in the area and so to frighten everybody throughout the Kikuyu country into joining *Mau Mau.*"[32] This implied that the affair was not organized locally, and indeed the Government seems to have gone out of its way to demonstrate the questionable proposition that virtually all who took part in the attack came from outside the location. Of the 1,400 arrested following the attack, the claim was made that some 50 per cent came from the adjacent Githunguri Location, the rest from other nearby locations, the forest, and Nairobi.[33]

Probably no other single episode had a greater effect upon the conduct and course of the Emergency. Like the oath, Lari divided men into hostile camps and critically widened divisions within Kikuyu country. Exploited by the Government for propaganda purposes, it had the effect of further alienating sympathy outside Kenya for the African position and strengthening the feeling among the Security Forces that their cause was just.

Law and Order

During the first phase of the Emergency neither the Government nor the militant Kikuyu leaders understood very well the full implications of the new situation. The kind of panic that led to the declaration of a State of Emergency and the lack of any real preparation for military action on either side gave an unreal, improvised air to the early operations. However, Lari and the raid on the Naivasha Police Station did much to crystallize the Government's thinking on its problems. It now seemed clear that the minds of a large majority of the population in central Kenya had been infected. Indeed, the only healthy areas seemed to be in the immediate neighborhood of a few strong chiefs and Christian mission stations. It was as if a half-century of administration and civilization had been wiped out. It would therefore be necessary to "rehabilitate" the Kikuyu people, using the few who could be trusted—the "Loyalists"—as a nucleus for creating a new society. The process would take time, and for it to succeed it was essential to re-establish Governmental control throughout Kikuyu country and provide maximum support to the "Loyalists."

General Sir George Erskine arrived in June 1953, as

Commander-in-Chief, East Africa. He produced an overall military plan designed to restore control to each area, section by section, in Central Province, ignoring at first such outlying areas as Mbere in Embu or Tharaka in Meru, where political activity was still rudimentary. As each district was invested, the leaders of the "passive wing" (the term used by the Government for the organization in the "Reserves" supplying food, money, ammunition, clothing, and information to the groups in the forest) would be arrested and put in detention camps, and the rest of the population would gradually be placed in guarded villages. Meanwhile the forest groups would be contained by heavy bombing from RAF Lincoln bombers attacking campsites previously located by infra-red reconnaissance photography. Erskine calculated the bombers would save him another brigade.

There could hardly be any doubt that Erskine would achieve his military objectives. The Government was prepared to detain up to 80,000 people, and the military envisaged doubling or tripling this figure if necessary.[34] Every month the Security Forces gradually became stronger and better trained, the appreciations of the Intelligence branch more valuable, and restrictions on the movement of Kikuyu more effective. Provincial and District Emergency Committees responsible for coordinating the activities of the Army, Police, and Administration in the field were organized. A massive injection of Europeans into the districts brought a degree of direct administration of the Kikuyu unparalleled among any other people in the history of British colonial Africa. In March 1954, a small War Council was formed in Nairobi which gave a new decisiveness to the machinery of Government.

By 1955 military control of the Reserves was secured and communication between the "passive wing" and the forests became increasingly hazardous. The siege of Kikuyuland, from Muguga in the south to Nyeri in the north, had turned the country into an armed camp. Nearly every hill was capped with a small fort, complete with a tall watchtower, a deep moat full of needle-sharp spikes, extensive barbed wire defenses, and thick earth ramparts. Nestling below was a newly built village with sheds for all the cattle and goats. The whole population had been removed from their former homes to these new encampments. Many shops and markets were closed. For months at a time recalcitrant villages were put under 23-hour curfews, the inhabitants being allowed out for one hour a day, under armed guard, to get food. A strip a mile wide along the forest edge had been made a prohibited area in which no cultivation was permitted and anyone moving could be shot on sight. Finally, the population had been set to work digging a wide, deep ditch along more than a hundred miles of forest boundary. The isolation of the forest fighters was complete. In 1955 the troops were withdrawn from the Reserves, and the Security Forces moved the siege into the forests, using greatly improved techniques, including the "pseudo-gang" (a Government organized forest group). By mid-1956 even in the forests the operations had dwindled down to a private man-hunt for Dedan Kimathi, who was eventually tracked down on October 21, 1956, four years to the day after the arrest of Jomo Kenyatta.

In late 1953 Erskine publicly announced that military measures would not solve the country's problem which was "purely political." The Administration had already outlined the basis of its future political thinking for the Kikuyu. Political activity for the Kikuyu must be totally banned while the disease of "Mau Mau" was rooted out. In time, when the tribe had been carefully nursed through its period of convalescence, a new and responsible politics might be shaped round the elements that had not been affected—the "Loyalists." This "tiny individual flicker of resistance to Mau Mau"[35] comprised a few scattered groups of people who were for various reasons out of sympathy with militant and radical nationalism. These included a few of the tougher chiefs and other Government servants, some businessmen and teachers, and others, together with a large number of Christians who looked at least in part for religious, not political, solutions to their problems.

Many Christians had been genuinely offended by the use of the oath and by the KCA's "most bitter persecution"[36] that earlier had followed the female circumcision controversy. Especially antagonistic were the members of the Revival movement within the Church. This movement challenged "people who are nominal Christians with their need to know Jesus as a personal Saviour. When, through His blood, they find this new relationship, they surrender the whole of their lives and possessions to Him."[37] The Revival movement is described in terms reminiscent of Beauttah's description of the moral effect of the oath in restoring honesty and loyalty to society. "Stolen property has been restored, lies have been acknowledged, immorality and drunkenness have been brought into 'the light' and confessed, reparation is made wherever possible."[38] Many followers of the Revival subsequently died rather than obey the commands of the political movement. But those whom the European missionaries viewed as *Kikuyu* martyrs were *Christian* martyrs to the Kikuyu.

Self-defense led some of these people to join together in isolated groups. In March 1953, the Administration decided to issue them some arms. Senior Government officials had originally opposed this step, on the grounds that it might subsequently prove difficult to disarm the groups. It was therefore decided that they must be strictly controlled by European District Officers, advised and helped by a senior Army Officer with experience in Malaya. The "Loyalists," who had had no close contact with KAU, would be the hard core of the new society, of the "reconstruction of the Kikuyu people."[39] They would be the new élite cadre round which the District Officers could shape the future of the tribe. Their advice would decide whether a man should be detained and when he should be allowed to return from detention. The concept of "loyalty" was exemplified by such diverse elements among the "Loyalists" as the Christian martyrs and the old chief who nailed the Union Jack to his flag post near the forest edge in defiance of "Mau Mau." These were "the salt of the Kikuyu earth, the peers of the Kikuyu realm," as one administrator put it.

In the Government's view, not only did a new social structure have to be created, but all traces of the past must be destroyed. Baring and the Secretary of State publicly committed the Government to a promise that Kenyatta and many other leaders would never be allowed to return to Kikuyu country. The land of many known "terrorists" was legally confiscated, their houses and shops pulled down. The KISA and Karing'a school buildings were razed to the ground or converted into mission schools. Githunguri was transformed into a Divisional Administrative Centre. Nearly all African newspapers were banned and copies destroyed. Finally, while the process of "reconstruction" went on, the Central Province was legally closed to visitors, and sealed off from the outside world for six years.

The Administration structured the ideology of the Emergency around the "Loyalist" as the true Kikuyu. When the first African elections to the Legislative Council were held in March 1957, the franchise among the Kikuyu was restricted to those who possessed "Loyalty Certificates." But although the "Loyalists" continued to wield immense power and influence in the "Reserves," they never assumed the commanding political leadership roles that the Administration had hoped.

Kikuyu Nationalist Resistance

The young militant nationalists who found themselves in the forest after August 1952 were at first as unsure as the Government about how to handle the situation. Though the exact number of people in the forest will never be known, it is estimated that by mid-1953 something like 15,000 were living there. In the physical siege of Kikuyu country, the forest had become the innermost keep, the ultimate point of resistance. But the forest fighters lacked the training required for sustained military action or effective guerrilla warfare. Moreover, they were daily and without warning inundated by new, untrained recruits in the first year of the Emergency. Among their leaders, however, were several ex-servicemen who had campaigned in the jungles of Burma. To cope with the organizational problems of their "Land Freedom Army," they employed models drawn from their military and civil experience, organizing forest camps, known as "BUSH NO. I," and so on, along military lines. During the early part of the Emergency, when the Security Forces were occupied with immediate problems in the Reserve, they had a breathing space to develop this organization. As their confidence grew, they began to set up workshops in the forests to make crude guns and even grenades.

Geographical factors greatly aided the resistance. The magnificent indigenous forests of Mt. Kenya and the Aberdares Range, frequented usually only by a handful of honey hunters and, near the edges, by the Forest Department laborers growing maize and vegetables in newly planted coppices, made superb natural hiding places. It was a land whose steep hills and deep valleys were squashed so closely and tightly together that the inhabitants say God must have made them on Saturday. The precipitous slopes were clothed in a tangle of giant bamboos, which could be swiftly cut into snug, waterproof bivouacs or rapidly split into poles to carry water. Men on the run could disappear as quickly and permanently as a needle in a haystack. Their heavy-booted, heavy-breathing pursuers could be heard crackling the bamboo a mile away in the still, clear, champagne air of these high hills. The huge forest sweeps mounted by the military in the early days of the Emergency were more likely to stampede a herd of elephants than to flush any of the fighters. This was the country in which the men in the forests over the next two years tied down a whole division of British troops in a grim game of hide-and-seek.

Dedan Kimathi[40] and Waruhiu Itote ("General China"[41]) were generally acknowledged as the senior leaders on the Aberdares and Mt. Kenya forests respectively. They had little communication with each other. The need for food, funds, and medical supplies meant that "Bushes" could effectively maintain themselves only opposite those parts of the Reserve whence their members originated. Within each sub-location in the Reserve there was a different level of commitment to the movement. In some parts the Home Guard was strong, in others weak. In some areas the chief was sympathetic, in others he was a dedicated "loyalist." Within the "Bushes" themselves there were some daring leaders— men like Kimathi himself, Stanley Mathenge, China, and Tanganyika in Nyeri, Matenjagwo, Kago, and Mbaria Kaniu in Fort Hall, and Kimbo, the cattle raider, operating between Nanyuki and Naivasha—but others were more passive. The difficult terrain prevented easy lateral communication within the forest itself, and the campaign soon developed into a series of local battles of attrition, ridge by ridge.

The most intense battles took place between April and August 1953 in the Fort Hall District and to some extent in Nyeri District. Here the main targets were the newly built "Loyalists" guard posts, the chiefs, headmen, and Tribal Police, as well as other Government supporters. Many on both sides died in these raids and encounters. On May 8, 1953, for example, a group of raiders led by Stanley Mathenge made a determined night attack on the Othaya Divisional Police Station in Nyeri District, "blowing a bugle as they approached and opening fire with a Bren gun captured from the 4th K.A.R. in an ambush a month before."[42] They

lost the Bren gun and 16 of their men were killed. Raids
were also made on European farms, but the struggle with the
Security Forces was primarily carried on in the Reserves.
Slowly the Security Forces established their dominance and
by mid-1954, large-scale raids ceased.

Though defeated in the Reserves, and with some sur-
rendering to the Security Forces, nonetheless many men and
women in the forest continued their resistance. Their aim,
apart from surviving and carrying on the struggle for freedom and land, was to attract international attention to their
cause. No outside help was forthcoming, and the Emergency
was not itself to give rise to a major political investigating
commission from Britain.

At least from 1953 to 1955 Kimathi sought to provide an
overall perspective of the resistance in the forest. He spent as
much time as possible touring the various "Bushes," where
he discussed the conduct and aims of the campaign with
other leaders. In these and other meetings, he also expressed
much of the ideology that motivated the resistance. At one
point, while in the forest, Kimathi was reported to have said,
"I do not lead rebels but I lead Africans who want their self-
government and land. My people want to live in a better
world than they met with when they were born. I lead them
because God never created any nation to be ruled by
another nation forever."[43] At another time, in a letter to his
former (African) teacher, Kimathi wrote, "we are not
fighting for an everlasting hatred but are creating a true and
real brotherhood between white and black so that we may
be regarded as people and as human beings who can do each
and everything."[44]

Nderitu Thuita, a commander in the forest, also argued at
a meeting that "war does not mean everlasting hatred
between whites and blacks, but chiefly means the need for
urgent investigations for a peaceful settlement that would
make each and every one satisfied."[45] A similar thought runs

through the observation of Karari Njama, one of the few, if not the only, African in the forest with a secondary education, that "peace is hidden in the big words JUSTICE and cooperation where all the inhabitants of a country live without discrimination of any kind."[46] Throughout Kimathi's writings and speeches, and in the reports of meetings held by forest groups, there is a consistent emphasis on the need for justice, on the possibility of reconciliation, and on the right to self-government. Though the leadership that emerged in the forests was basically a new leadership, not a part of those élites involved in KAU, the trade union movement, or the rural political organizations in Kiambu, it was infused by many of the same ideals and objectives as the more articulate and generally better-educated élite of the pre-Emergency organizations.

Kimathi also tried to organize regular meetings of a body that came to be called in 1954 the "Kenya Parliament." It represented the ideal of a central organization, rather than an effective legislative and executive body. One ambitious session of the "Kenya Parliament" was held on October 23 and 24, 1954, in the Aberdares.[47] It was attended by 37 leaders, including four from Kiambu, an area that had been causing Kimathi some concern, owing to the Government's containment of Nairobi and the arrest of most of the remaining leaders of the "Parliament in Kiambu." After renewing the oath, various financial and kindred matters were settled. The "Kenya Parliament" then discussed organizational problems and passed certain resolutions that illustrated the constant pressure toward fragmentation among the forest groups. It was decided that no group would be recognized without a minimum of 500 names on its books. No group could divide into two unless it had at least 2,000 members. It was resolved that there should be no branches of the "Kenya Parliament" and that no leader had permission to promote his men without the authority and confirma-

Published by permission of the Commissioner of Police, Kenya.

Crowd amassed near police lines opposite Norfolk Hotel, Nairobi, protesting Thuku's detention, March 1922. Shooting took place shortly after this photograph was taken, as crowd moved toward police lines in rear.

Early meeting of Kiambu Local Native Council, about 1925.

Senior Chief Koinange, probably taken in late 1940.

Paramount Chief Kinyanjui about 1925.

Ambu H. Patel, *Jomo the Great*. Nairobi: Desai Printers Ltd., 1961.

Members of the KCA who received Kenyatta on his arrival from Europe, Fall to 1930. Left to right: Benedeto Wamutito, Josphat Kamau, Amos Wagacha, Jomo Kenyatta, Job Muchuchu, James Njoroge.

KCA leaders, 1963. Back row, left to right: Suleiman Miano (Kirinyaga, Ndia), M. Siolo M'Regu (Meru), Stafani M'Ituire (Meru), Muthakie Ngariama (Embu), Josiah Thindi Kiuna (Rift Valley), Njora Kamau (Rift Valley), Mwangi Kamau (Rift Valley), Kiriba Ichangai (Rift Valley), Mugo Kimaburi (Kinani Forest), Thoga Githachuri (Masai). Middle row: Donali M'tu Magimbi (Meru), M'tu Mwirichia M'tu Mwenda (Meru), Kiruri Kiiru (Kiambu), Musa Kibue (Kiambu Git-hunguri), Jesii M. Kagonge (Embu), Kangaru Ngari (Nyeri), Kamuchengo Njihobwe (Embu), Kamochere Thiga (Embu), Nathaniel Mahingo (Rift Valley), Isaac Mwalonji (Machakos Ngerani). Front row: Ng'ang'a Ngoro (Kiambu Kikuyu), Marius Ng'ang'a Karatu (Kiambu Limuru), Wanjama Ngururi (Naivasha), Joseph Kange'the (Mugang'a Fort Hall), George K. Ndegwa (Kiambu Karura), Jesse Kariuki (Murang'a, Fort Hall), Paulo-Nguru (Nyeri), Ernest Ole Sokoyian (Narok Massai), Sogoyiyo Ole Ndega (Massai Ngong).

Pan Africa (Nairobi), Dec. 12, 1963, p. 41.

Kenyatta with Samuel Muindi, the Kamba leader, shortly after Muindi's release from restriction in 1947.

Kenya African Teachers' College in late 1940's, with Kenyatta reclining in foreground in grey trousers.

KAU leaders, about 1951. Left to right: Jesse Kariuki, Achieng Oneko, Kenyatta, Fred Kubai, ex-Senior Chief Koinange, Oginga Odinga, Dedan Kiamathi, Bildad Kaggia, Muinga Chokwe.

Griffith's visit, 1951, with Eliud Mathu, Koinange, Mbiyu, and Kenyatta in background.

Kiambu meeting just prior to the Emergency, August 1952. Speaker is
Senior Chief Waruhiu. Front row, left to right: James Gichuru, Harry
Thuku, ex-Senior Chief Koinange, Eliud Mathu, Kenyatta, Chief Josiah
Njonjo, and another Kiambu leader.

Kenyatta addressing Kiambu meeting just prior to the Emergency,
August 1952.

A Kikuyu guard post close to the edge of the prohibited forest area in Fort Hall district (with Aberdares mountains in the background).

Kikuyu village, Kiambu, during the Emergency.

Outside the courthouse at Kapenguria during the trial. Left to right: Paul Ngei, Fred Kubai, Kenyatta, Achieng Oneko, Kungu Karumba, and Bildad Kaggia.

Dedan Kimathi soon after his capture in 1956.

"General" China after his capture.

"General" Kago

East African Newspapers Ltd.

KANU airport rally, 1961. Mungai Njoroge and Tom Mboya (in white hats),
with idealized portrait of their detained leader, Kenyatta.

East African Newspapers Ltd.

Kenyatta restricted at Maralal, April 11, 1961.

tion of the "Kenya Parliament." No one could attend the "Kenya Parliament" as a member unless he had been chosen by his group at a General Meeting. If leaders made mistakes, they could be impeached before the "Kenya Parliament."

Such meetings, however, did not result in any greater coordination of activity. The geographical and logistical obstacles were too overwhelming, the build-up against them too immense. Communication among the various leaders grew increasingly spasmodic. Moreover, there had been for some time along the forest edges and in the Reserves small atomized bands of men, called *Komereras,* who owed allegiance to no one except the leader of their group and who operated outside the control of the "passive wing." Kimathi had scathingly attacked them in late 1953: *"Komerera* is an outlaw or deserter's group of cowards who desert from hunger, in search of money by force . . . [They are] chiefly the group generally killed by the enemies. *Komerera* have no real dwelling places. *Komerera* generally roam from village to village and from one place to another."[48]

As the isolation of the forest groups became more absolute and the disintegration more complete, the small groups that were left in this inner "keep" came increasingly to rely on the use of prophets for predictive purposes. New oaths were employed to maintain morale and discipline. With food from the "Reserves" virtually denied to them, they lived off the roots and berries of the forests, trapped deer on the moorlands for meat and skins, or caught the trout with which the Europeans had stocked the mountain streams. When China was captured wounded on January 1, 1954, the Government began a series of attempts to negotiate surrender terms with the forest leaders. But the factors that had impeded the growth of any effective unified forest command equally precluded the probability of any overall surrender, and, while the negotiations achieved some piecemeal results, individuals and small groups continued to live outside the law in the forests up to, and even beyond, the granting of Independence to Kenya.

Just as Nairobi had been the capstone of the secret organization, so too the Security Forces saw the control of the city as the decisive piece in the operational jigsaw. Although minor police and military sweeps were periodically carried out in the capital, it was not until April 1954 that the Government mounted a major operation (codename "Anvil"), aimed at arresting and screening the Kikuyu in the city. The Nairobi Central Committee had found their headquarters, Kiburi House, under close police observation after the start of the Emergency. Those who had not been arrested began to vary their rendezvous, holding meetings at a variety of places.

After the Emergency began the Nairobi Central Committee, now known as the "War Council," regarded itself as the central coordinating body of the whole movement. Direct contact with the groups in the forest was intermittent, although Stanley Mathenge is reported to have twice visited their meetings in 1953 in Nairobi's Shauri Moyo Location. As members were arrested or killed, the secret Nairobi district committees supplied replacements. They also supplied three members to a central communications group whose task it was to ensure that the links between the Central Committee, the network of district committees in Nairobi, and "Parliament" in Kiambu were kept open. The Nairobi group defined their primary tasks as the supply of recruits and medicines to the forest, the collection of funds for legal representation, and the maintenance of discipline in the movement in Nairobi itself. They sought to act as the final court of appeal on all matters within Nairobi and could require full reports on all activities of the lower committees, including assassinations. Eliud Mutonyi, a trader from Fort Hall, remained their leader until his arrest in November 1953.

Under "Operation Anvil" the Government was prepared to detain as many Kikuyu from Nairobi as was necessary to crush the underground organization. As a result some 27,000 Kikuyu went into the detention camps. "Anvil" essentially ended the major military phase of the Emergency, save for a few minor actions against small gangs. The official casualties up to the end of 1956 were 11,503 Kikuyu killed, 1,035 captured wounded, 1,550 captured unwounded, 26,625 arrested, and 2,714 surrendered. On the Government side (including both civilians and armed forces) the casualties were 95 Europeans killed and 127 wounded, 29 Asians killed and 48 wounded, and 1,920 Africans killed and 2,385 wounded.[49] The unevenness of the battle and the violence of the campaign is well attested by these figures.

Agrarian Reform

The Government recognized early in the Emergency the need for economic reform if the measures taken to re-establish law and order were to be effective. Apart from soil conservation, settlement and land betterment schemes, agricultural education, and some assistance to individual progressive farmers, a beginning had been made in permitting and encouraging Africans to grow what had been European cash-crops—essentially coffee, tea, sisal, pyrethrum, and pineapples. The need now was to accelerate this production and find a way of providing employment for the thousands of landless peoples—particularly among the Kikuyu. Experts were not lacking who said this could be done. Three kinds of programs ultimately came into being: (1) a renewed attack on the perennial problem of soil conservation and the rehabilitation of eroded areas; (2) a much more efficient use of the available high-potential land within the African rural areas, through a rapidly expanding program of cash crop development; and (3) a maximum encouragement of a process called land consolidation, whereby various pieces of land an individual owned would be brought together into one farm. It was axiomatic that this development would take place within the existing agrarian racial boundaries.

The "Swynnerton" plan,[50] hastily produced in late 1953 and based on programs designed by district and provincial teams, became the key to African agricultural development. With British economic aid, great strides were taken in the next few years toward African economic betterment. While major emphasis was placed on a rapid increase with respect to a number of cash crops, the expansion in African coffee production was perhaps the most significant. Between 1954 and 1959 African coffee planting increased from about 4,000 to 26,000 acres. Some 89,000 Africans were now growing coffee, and a considerable portion of these were Kikuyu producers. These changes, together with those in other sectors of the economy, acted to mitigate the pre-Emergency barriers to participation by Africans in the growing prosperity of the country and helped to provide a new basis for European-African relations.

Land consolidation was to have immense implications for economic development, but the immediate aims of policies associated with it were political as well. A few individual *mbari,* particularly Chief Muhoya's in Tetu and Chief Eliud's in Iriaini in Nyeri, had with Government encouragement consolidated the land within their areas before the Emergency. During the Emergency the Government gradually realized that land consolidatation also had political and social advantages. Between 1953 and 1955, hundreds of thousands of Kikuyu homesteads that had been scattered over the countryside were destroyed for security reasons, and 950,000 people were moved into villages. A major redistribution of land boundaries suddenly seemed more practicable. Just as suddenly, it also seemed to supply the answer to many other problems. In the future the new villages could be much more effectively policed than the scattered huts they replaced. Villages could be more easily provided with social services and could themselves provide homes for the landless and retired squatters from the White Highlands. Lastly they could become the center for the reconstruction of Kikuyu society around the new élite, the "Loyalists." In early plans, it was held that only "Loyalists" with a considerable acreage of land would be allowed to leave the village and reside on their farms, but later this idea was abandoned as the emphasis shifted from creating a two-fold élite-mass division to a three-fold stratified structure, consisting of an élite, a settled peasantry, and a laboring class.

It was early realized that consolidation and the issue of freehold land titles would reduce the traditional rights of *ahoi* on the new farms. But the landless could now be accommodated in the villages and would become laborers on the consolidated farms. Administrative and agricultural officers believed that landowners with three acres of land would be able to employ up to three of these laborers. Thus there would indeed actually be a *shortage* of labor in the Kikuyu areas for the foreseeable future.[51] As late as 1957 C. M. Johnston, the Special Commissioner for Kikuyu, Embu, and Meru, was reported as stating that between 40 and 60 per cent of the total population would remain in the villages, which would be developed into thriving townships with their own industries. The inhabitants would be at the bottom of a "squirearchy" dominated by a wealthy middle class "sufficiently intelligent to see where its future lies, and strong enough to exert a counter influence "to political agitators.[52]

As the plan for consolidating all the land in the three Kikuyu districts was implemented, there were some significant shifts in emphasis to ease its general acceptance and remove grounds for grievances. The initial notion of using land consolidation to reward "Loyalists" was abandoned, although in a number of ways they were in a position to profit most from the new economic opportunities that accompanied consolidation. Special care was taken to see that detainees in the camps knew what was happening and had their interests looked after. Some ex-detainees were even allowed on the consolidation committees sharing out the land, although the "Loyalists" were usually a dominant majority. Yet the Administration realized that this scheme, designed to make Kenya's racially organized agrarian system better equipped to handle its economic consequences, would be fundamentally unacceptable to nationalist leaders committed to breaking that system. As the pressure grew for the release of detainees, so did the pressure grow from the Administration for more staff and money to carry through consolidation more rapidly. Consolidation in Kiambu, originally planned to take five years, was completed in half that time, by September 1958. In Nyeri it was finished by the end of 1959. Fort Hall, however, presented some problems: a swelling volume of complaints had forced investigations that led to admissions of corruption and inefficiency. In large parts of the district the operation had eventually to be done over again and had not been completed by the end of the Emergency.

Although law and order had been re-established by 1956, the Emergency Regulations, which allowed no visitors into Kikuyuland and no Kikuyu out of it without a pass from the Administration, were kept in force until the beginning of 1960. Despite the authoritarian powers wielded by the Administration, the inequalities and injustices associated with aspects of the land consolidation program stimulated the emergence of a new underground movement—*Kiama kia Muingi*—the People's Party (KKM). A Committee set up to investigate the detention camps supported a description of this movement as "primarily a protest against abuses of powers taken under the Emergency Regulations, particularly in regard to land consolidation and the disposal of property," and commented that its activities had been largely "confined to the expression of legitimate grievances."[53]

The newly elected African members of the Legislative Council recognized the economic advantages of land consolidation, but were critical of many of the methods that had been employed by the Administration. Following a debate on this issue in the Legislative Council, a special committee of Unofficial Members was set up to investigate the program. Composed mainly of Africans, they warned the Government in their report that many Africans viewed the program as a "child of the Emergency." They regarded this as a "fatal mistake." Though land consolidation was not imposed upon the Kikuyu people, it has not been "fully and voluntarily accepted." Justice has often been sacrificed for the sake of completing "self-imposed deadlines," and opposition to consolidation has been "viewed as a sign of anti-government attitude or form of behaviour bordering on subversion." Moreover, "many suspect that to oppose or criticize land consolidation is to commit a wrong under Emergency regulations." They saw the danger of a new class of landless peoples coming into being as a result of land consolidation and proposed a program of rural industrialization, land reclamation, and the settlement of landless Africans in the unused portions of the White Highlands and elsewhere. Furthermore, there was recognized a need to make available the facilities of the essentially European Land Bank to Africans.[54]

Far from stabilizing a new political society in Kikuyuland, land consolidation could easily have become a major focus of attack by African nationalism once the Emergency had ended. This assault failed to develop principally because of the political changes adopted in 1960 which were to lead to African majority rule, and the beginnings of the gradual removal of land barriers in the White Highlands. African settlement schemes in the Highlands would help remove the pressure in the Reserves, while British economic assistance would help to maintain land values of European farms. Land consolidation, as a political policy tied to the maintenance of the Colony's rigid agrarian color bar, was doomed to fail. But, with the achievement of African rule, land consolidation could cease to be a political issue to Africans and stand on its own economic merits as a far-reaching measure of agrarian reform.

Political Reform

The arrest of Kenyatta together with nearly all the national office-bearers of KAU, as well as many branch officers in central Kenya, did not lead to the immediate banning of the party. For some months, the Government accepted that a purge of Kikuyu influence might be sufficient to enable KAU to function as a moderate party. Following a meeting of leaders who had not been arrested, a provisional executive of KAU was announced in which F. W. Odede was appointed Acting President, Joseph Murumbi Acting Secretary, and W. W. W. Awori Acting Treasurer. Odede, a Luo, and Awori, a Luhya, were nominated African members of the Legislative Council at the time. Odede was also a member of KAU's national committee, while Awori was a former national Treasurer and Vice-President of the party. Murumbi, of Masai-Goan descent, was relatively new to KAU, having spent many years in school in India and in the British Military Administration in Somalia. Together with Mbiyu Koinange, he was to spend the next decade in exile, working in England for Kenya's independence. Among others that came forward at this time to fill the leadership void were C. M. G. Argwings-Kodhek, the first Luo lawyer, and Tom Mboya, a young Luo trade unionist; both were to play leading roles in the fulfilment of KAU's objectives.

Within a week of the declaration of the Emergency, the new provisional leadership issued a statement. While reiterating in detail many of KAU's past demands, they also called for "the release or immediate trial of all persons arrested since 20 October." Among the other demands made were the ending by law of racial discrimination; parity in African and non-African unofficial representation on the Legislative Council, with representatives elected by means of a common voters' roll for all races; the ending of permanent European and Asian immigration; the extension of social and economic programs for African advancement; freedom in political and trade union organization and activities; and equal elected representation by all three races to the proposed "Griffiths" constitutional conference which was to meet by May 1953. If this conference failed to achieve agreement, a constitutional commission should be sent from Britain. They requested, as well, that African needs for land be met.[55]

The importance of this statement lay not in any expectation that it might effect a change in Government policy, but rather that KAU's objectives had support among leaders who were not Kikuyu.* Though these new leaders did not publicly condone violence, they identified themselves with the cause of nationalism as expressed in KAU's political, economic, and social program. But as the Emergency developed they had scant hope of influencing policy, for neither the Government nor the settler community was prepared to negotiate while violence continued to spread. Increasingly this new KAU leadership was seen as supporting the same objectives as the old and to be providing ideological support for those resisting in the forest and the Reserves. The association of some of them with the Defense at the Kapenguria Trial, and the refusal of KAU to denounce publicly the detained leaders, confirmed the Government's suspicions that the organization was too deeply affected by the "Kikuyu malaise" for it to be allowed to continue. This attitude of

---

* One was a Goan, Pio Gama Pinto, who was detained in 1954 because of his close relations with "Mau Mau" leaders. He was assassinated in 1965.

the Government to the remaining African politicians was
enhanced by the marked reluctance on the part of the African members in the Legislative Council to support the increasingly severe measures deemed necessary by the Government for the prosecution of the Emergency.

On March 10, 1953, Odede was detained. A week earlier
he had made Pritt an honorary Kikuyu elder at a large
African meeting in Nairobi. Awori became Acting President. Later in the month Murumbi, traveling as the official
representative of KAU, went to India, where he was received
by Pandit Nehru. But the end of KAU was in sight, and on
June 8 it was formally and finally proscribed. In a broadcast
explaining the reasons for its banning, the Acting Chief
Native Commissioner announced that "the Kenya Government can never again allow such an association as the Kenya
African Union." In future the Government would only
permit those "local associations which have been reasonable
and sincere in the interests of their own people."⁵⁶ Henceforth, the tone of speeches and statements emanating from
African nominated members of Legislative Council was more
conciliatory toward the Government's policies.

For two years during the critical period of the Emergency
no African political association whatsoever was permitted to
function in the country. Then in June 1955 with the fading
away of effective resistance in the forests, the Government
announced that political associations could now be formed,
but that their organization had to be restricted to the district
level. At this time, however, among the Kikuyu, the Embu,
and the Meru of the Central Province only an advisory
council composed of "Loyalists" was permitted. The new
politics would require careful guidance in order that a
responsible and mature African electorate could evolve. As
the norms and values of parliamentary government became
understood, district organizations and later constituency
conventions could play an important role in political devel-

opment in association with the African member in the Legislative Council representing the area. Though the primary task now was to create responsibility in local affairs, at some future date a country-wide convention of associations might possibly be permitted. But in building the new policy, territorial nationalism with its appeal to emotions rather than reason had no place and its growth and development had to be restricted and contained.

Within a broader framework the principles of multi-racial government sought to regulate African political participation. Embodied in the "Lyttelton" constitution of 1954, these principles included the preservation of separate representation in the executive and legislative institutions by each of the three main racial groups, with European participation equal to non-Europeans, and the establishment of ministerial government with multi-racial representatives and a strong ruling majority in the Legislative Council. Apart from the six Official Ministers, and two nominated Officials appointed from the local community, there were six Unofficials—three elected Europeans, two elected Asians, and one nominated African representative drawn from the Legislative Council. Though the Council of Ministers was the chief instrument of government, final authority remained with the Governor and ultimately with Britain. It was envisaged that these constitutional arrangements could endure until 1960, and that during these six years there would be no change in the racial basis of representation or in the proportion of unofficial representatives of the three racial groups unless agreement was achieved among all parties concerned. Moreover, no minister could propose or support legislation affecting the land rights of any group.[57]

While the constitutional arrangements entailed no reduction in European influence in national affairs, they did implicitly raise questions about the future and thereby encouraged a rift in the settler community. This was to grow

despite efforts to maintain unity. The immediate future of
the Europeans was secure, but many sensed that new developments might result in actions and policies not favorable to
continued European dominance in the political, social, and
economic life of the country. The appointment of an African
nominated member, B. A. Ohanga, as Minister for Community Development, caused little concern, since this portfolio
mainly affected African interests, but the appointment of
two Asian ministers was viewed much more unfavorably. Far
more significant for the future, however, was the prospect of
having *elected* African representatives in the Legislative
Council.

W. F. (later Sir Walter) Coutts, a former Fort Hall
District Commissioner, returned to Kenya in 1955 to investigate the basis for an African franchise. He produced a report
much in keeping with liberal thinking on multi-racialism at
this time, recommending qualifications for the vote that
essentially harmonized with the new "loyalist" concept of the
responsible African. There were additional votes for those
having qualifications making them more "responsible" than
others, while among the Kikuyu, the Embu, and the Meru
only those holding Loyalty Certificates would be eligible for
any vote at all.

Despite the efforts of the Government to shape and control
the pace of political development, the granting of the
franchise was to provide a constitutional vehicle whereby
African leaders could make politically effective their overwhelming numerical strength and radically alter the plan to
build a multi-racial state in Kenya under European leadership. Until the first African elections in March 1957 (for
eight representatives in the Legislative Council) African
influence on public policy was limited. Apart from the
continuing resistance in the forests, there had emerged,
however, new African sources of criticism and opposition to
Government policy. One was within the revived trade union

movement organized by Tom Mboya, a young, dynamic leader with exceptional organizational ability. In October 1953 he became General Secretary of the Kenya Federation of Registered Trade Unions (later renamed the Kenya Federation of Labour) ; he was soon in the forefront of industrial conflict and political action. "As general secretary of the Federation, Mboya criticized various aspects of government policy concerning the prosecution of the Emergency, inadequate representation of Africans on all government bodies, the encouragement of tribal associations, and the continued restrictions on the formation of a new African political organization on a colony-wide basis."[58] The reforms that Mboya and the unions called for were much the same as those demanded by the proscribed KAU. In addition there was criticism of the restrictive character of the proposed African franchise and the limited character of African participation in the Legislative Council.

As Mboya's Federation became increasingly aggressive on political issues, the Government decided to act against it. Thus, in early 1956, the Government threatened to withdraw the registration (legal recognition) of the Federation. As Kubai had found in 1950, there were severe limitations in a colonial situation on the employment of a trade union in the advancement of African political aspirations. To avoid the loss of registration the Federation had to agree to restrict its activities to industrial affairs.

Though the explicitly political role of the trade union movement was curbed, an alternative focus for political organization and action was now being developed through the district associations. By 1957 a few had been formed in various parts of the country and their numbers were to increase rapidly during the next three years. They represented many areas where KAU had not been able to organize and therefore were new sources of support for African nationalism. Most important was the role of Luo leadership, which had come into prominence with the neutralization of the Kikuyu. Not only was Nyanza rapidly developing as a significant base for a new rural nationalism, but also Luo leadership in the trade union movement and political organization in Nairobi came to the fore. One of the earliest and most important of the district associations was the one led in Nairobi by Argwings-Kodhek, who had been a member of KAU's national committee in 1952. Drawing support from the large concentration of urban Luo workers, and reflecting the nationalist spirit of other urban groups, the Kenya African National Congress was formed in late 1955. Not until the name and the scope of its activities was narrowed to the Nairobi District African Congress did Government permit its registration, in April 1956. Despite all attempts by Government to restrict the influence of Nairobi in mobilizing and coordinating African nationalism, new channels were to be developed in an effort to build a colony-wide movement and achieve the goal of an African-governed Kenya.

The first direct African elections in March 1957 were the turning point in the search for self-determination and dignity. The struggle for power was now channeled into the Legislative Council, bringing a realism to its proceedings that had long been absent. Six of the eight former nominated African members were defeated by men who rejected the "Lyttelton" constitutional arrangements for multi-racialism and saw Kenya's future in an African perspective. Though the new members represented diverse parts of the country which had experienced different patterns of development, and though they were not subject to the discipline of a country-wide party, nonetheless they were all united in demanding fifteen new African seats on the Legislative Council. By refusing to accept any ministerial position and thereby challenging the whole concept of multi-racial government, they brought about in a matter of months a

political crisis which resulted in a new constitution being
imposed.

The "Lennox-Boyd" constitution of 1958 recognized the
imperative of greater African representation by increasing
the number of elected members from eight to fourteen—but
it endeavored as well to preserve multi-racial government.
The essential principles of the "Lyttelton" constitution were
retained, with the Council of Ministers continuing to be
drawn from the Administration or their appointees and the
elected European, Asian, and African members on a basis of
their having respectively four, two, and two representatives.
Other arrangements were designed to ensure the continuance and development of a multi-racial political system
during the next decade. These included a strong governmental majority in the legislature, a new system of selection
of some representatives on an equal proportionate basis
between the three main racial groups by the Legislative
Council acting as electoral college, and constitutional safe-
guards that sought to protect racial or religious groups
against discriminatory legislation. For the foreseeable future
ultimate control of Kenya would be maintained by Britain.

These constitutional arrangements, however, were not to
last for long. With increased representation and parity with
Europeans in the Legislative Council, African political
power had been greatly increased. While the innovation of
"specially elected" members, four from each racial group,
would guarantee the election of at least some politically
moderate Africans, among whom the Governor could find
someone willing to become a minister and thereby allow the
Administration to claim that the Council of Ministers was
multi-racial, the control of the direction and pace of political
change was moving into African hands. Not only could
nationalism now claim that it was transtribal in scope and
purpose, but there was also a growing body of international

opinion which recognized the legitimacy of its aspirations. Overseas liberals might argue with Africans in terms of the ideals of multi-racialism, but few of these could deny the necessity for African political advancement. In Britain, in the United States, and elsewhere, African leaders and particularly Mboya, through travel, speeches, and personal contacts, strove to build an international constituency favorably disposed to African demands for "one man, one vote." In the councils of pan-Africanism in West and East Africa, Kenya nationalism became linked with the continental struggle for the ending of colonialism. A new era was coming into being in which men no longer accepted the legitimacy of the rule of whites over non-whites.

Following the 1957 African elections, which resulted in Argwings-Kodhek's defeat by Mboya for the Nairobi seat in the Legislative Council, the Nairobi Peoples' Convention Party (NPCP) gradually came to dominate African political life in the city. By late 1958 it was the most dynamic expression of Kenya nationalism, possessing a remarkable élan and buoyancy associated with the expectations of rapid political change. *Uhuru* (freedom) was its cry, and Kenyatta, the father of Kenya nationalism, its hero. The resurrection of Kenyatta's name and its identification with the new nationalism was begun by Oginga Odinga, who had built up a mass following in Central Nyanza first through his reorganization of the Luo Union between 1953 and 1957 and then in the African District Association (Central Nyanza). In June 1958 he electrified the Legislative Council and horrified the settlers and the Administration by referring to those who had been convicted at Kapenguria as "still the political leaders" and comparing Kenyatta with Makarios the exiled leader in Cyprus.[59] Kenyatta, then isolated in detention in Kenya's remote north, had been an unmentionable name since 1953, but henceforth his image was increasingly to dominate the Kenya scene.

While the Administration continued its policy of promoting leadership in Kikuyu country by means of "Loyalist" groups, other Kikuyu elements were now beginning to play more prominent roles. Gikonyo Kiano, though elected to the Legislative Council in March 1958 by those Kikuyu holding loyalty certificates, spoke of Kenyatta as a freedom fighter at the Accra Pan-African Conference in December 1958. Within Mboya's multi-tribal NPCP was a new generation of young, educated Kikuyu who helped spread the party's influence and ideas into the Kikuyu rural areas. In early 1959 the Administration, alarmed by its apparent strength and assertive character, decided to clamp down on its activities. Many of the prominent Kikuyu leaders, including Josef Mathenge, Gerald Mahinda, and Sammy Maina were restricted to their districts. Efforts by the Administration to contain African nationalism could now only have a temporary impact.

In the spring of 1959 the Secretary of State accepted the African demand for a constitutional conference. This found support as well in the Legislative Council from Michael (later Sir) Blundell's newly formed multi-racial New Kenya Group. European unity had been shattered, with Group-Captain Briggs ultimately leading those in the Council opposed to Blundell's multi-racialism. As progress toward an African majority became increasingly apparent, the African elected leaders also split into two groups. Leadership conflicts contributed to this disunity, but more fundamental were the growing fears of the leaders of the pastoral and smaller agricultural tribes of being dominated by a coalition of the large agricultural tribes with the achievement of self-government. This division expressed itself in the emergence of two short-lived parties. The Kenya National Party, founded in July and multi-racial in character until November, attracted the support in the main of the small tribal groups who were represented by eight of the fourteen elected members—prominent roles being played by Masinde Muliro, commanding substantial following among the Luhya; Ronald Ngala, with unquestioned allegiance from the coastal tribes; and the forceful Kalenjin leader Daniel arap Moi. In opposition to the defensive attitude of these leaders who functioned in a parliamentary multi-racial framework, stood the aggressive Kenya Independence Movement, founded in August but never registered by the Government as the ban on Kenya-wide African parties still persisted. It not only drew support among the rural Kikuyu, Luo, Kamba, and Taita but also controlled the militant urban nationalism of central Kenya. Mboya, Odinga, and Kiano were its outstanding leaders, but as the date of the promised constitutional conference approached, all African leaders recognized the critical need for unity in order to grasp the chance to alter fundamentally the course of sixty years of Kenya's history. That unity was maintained in the constitutional conference in London in early January, which for the first time charted the course for African majority rule in Kenya. Following the conference the fragile unity that had existed dissolved into the basic divisions which had previously manifested themselves. Two parties were formed—the Kenya African National Union (KANU), led by Gichuru, Mboya, and Odinga (since the Government refused to register the party under the presidency of Kenyatta) and the Kenya African Democratic Union (KADU), led by Ngala, Muliro, and Moi.

The myth of "Mau Mau" with Kenyatta as the leader of an atavistic cult, however, was to create major problems for the Administration as Kenya entered the terminal phase of colonialism. For the new Governor, Sir Patrick Renison, was advised by men with long experience in Kenya, men who saw Kenyatta as a leader into "darkness and death" and were allegedly prepared to resign en masse if he should ever come to power. Following the first general election in early 1961,

Renison tried to construct a government with KANU, which had won over two-thirds of the votes. But KANU's chief slogan during its campaign had been "Uhuru na Kenyatta" ("Freedom with Kenyatta"), and the party was not prepared to take office with its leader still in detention in a remote area. KADU, however, with less than a fifth of the vote, was persuaded. With constitutional power in their hands, KADU leaders began to feel that they could lead Kenya to independence. Even with Kenyatta's release in August 1961 they did not drop this illusion. Renison's policy resulted in two years of fruitless constitutional arguments and political manoeuvering as KADU sought to entrench their minority position. Although this interlude had one benefit, in providing the structure for an African administration which had been so long delayed in Kenya, it encouraged tribal fears and suspicions over land and power to such an extent that it raised grave doubts over the stability of an independent Kenya. Only with the coming into power for the first time in June 1963 of an African majority government under the leadership of Kenyatta could Kenya go forward with confidence and security to a new future as an independent African state building a new nation.

The Myth of "Mau Mau"

"Mau Mau" has been represented as a phenomenon that could not be interpreted mainly in terms of a political movement, but required a more fundamental explanation of deviant and irrational behavior. In part, reports of oathing ceremonies and the very secrecy and militancy of the movement gave support to this view, while the "Lari massacre" in the early months of the Emergency tended to remove any doubt that "Mau Mau" was an atavistic flight from reason and the processes of modernization. During the Emergency, many people were brutally killed, cattle were maimed, and the discipline of men was on occasion strained to the breaking point. The siege conditions under which the poorly educated forest groups operated were conducive to acts associated with the image of "Mau Mau." They were increasingly cut off from communication with labor on European farms and kith and kin in the Kikuyu rural areas, and the organization of these groups was subjected to intense internal stresses and strains. The use of tradition with respect to symbols and organizational methods became more marked, and leadership had to rely on whatever measures it could to maintain morale in situations of increasing adversity.

But the myth of "Mau Mau" goes beyond this specific evidence of precipitating conditions and overt activity associated with the resistance movement. It claims that "Mau Mau" instigated a movement designed to achieve Kikuyu dominance, and that the symbols and traditions of the movement—its "Kikuyuism"—were not so much instrumental means as consummatory ends that were essentially evil.

Ethnocentrism has been an important element behind the general acceptance of this myth. At a more immediate level of explanation, we may observe a concrete set of interrelated beliefs held by Europeans in Kenya. The most important of these were (1) an implicit conviction that the colonial system was perfectly capable of responding to the legitimate social and political grievances of Africans; (2) the belief that "Mau Mau" was but another manifestation of earlier African religious movements; (3) and the belief that in employing secret oaths, the African was rejecting modernity and reverting to primitive behavior patterns.

An essential factor which prompted colonists and administrators to view "Mau Mau" as a rejection of progress was an unquestioned belief that the existing political system was ultimately flexible and responsive. Though the political system demanded deference to its authority structures, gradual political change—a norm of British political culture—would occur as Africans acquired western political skills and moral responsibility. Indeed, the single most universally held assumption of the Kenya European was that accepting the legitimacy of the colonial system was in the enlightened self-interest of the individual African. In the colonial mind, the African's choice was simple. Either he chose the colonial system and its premises of modernization and rationality or he reverted to an inherently irrational and inward-looking tribal collectivity. The colonial system, it was argued, was fully capable of meeting those political, economic, and social demands of Africans which were legitimate. Some Europeans

were prepared to admit that Africans had legitimate grievances, but these, it was usually argued, were either the
product of inefficient administration or else birth-pangs of
the metamorphosis from traditional to modern society. Few
doubted that, *vis-à-vis* the African population, the colonial-
settler system was beneficial. This belief became overwhelmingly powerful in the postwar context as colonial policy gave
more attention to schemes for economic and social reform.
The "real" problems of Kenya, it was argued, were economic
problems and economic prosperity could resolve them.

While the concept of an African state was regarded as
fantastic, the new doctrine of multi-racialism advanced by
Sir Philip Mitchell held out the prospect of a new society in
which the allocation of social, economic, and political roles
would depend not on color but on ability. If Africans would
only cooperate with administrator and settler in furthering
the total economic growth of the country, then all would
benefit. What was most incomprehensible of all to Europeans was the deliberate obstruction of schemes designed by
a benevolent administration to further the development of
the Reserves. What possible rational objection could there
be to terracing land and to the enforcement of other good
agricultural practices?

But the policies that Sir Philip Mitchell sought to popular-
ize with the settler population were not acceptable to most
African leaders for several reasons. First, the new ideas of
multi-racialism sought to interpret the doctrine of the paramountcy of African interests in terms of European culture.
Mitchell believed that traditional Africa was evil and barbaric; he could see no merit in a tribal society in which man
lived in a Hobbesian state of war of all against all. Hence the
Leviathan of the colonial state represented the enlightened
self-interests of the African in which the new educated man
could remove himself completely from the darkness of his
barbaric origin into the sun of the white man's culture. For

those politicized Kikuyu who fifteen years before Mitchell's arrival in Kenya had fought a partially successful battle with the missionary churches for the right to selective modernization, this doctrine was anathema.

Second, the multi-racial doctrine gave permanence and respectability to the existing power structure and also tended to consolidate the relationship between the European settler and the colonial administrator, both of whom would retain indefinitely their roles as leaders of the country. A community of interests between these two groups had not always prevailed; the first generation of administrators in Kenya, including such men as John Ainsworth, had in most instances been sympathetic to the need to develop the African areas of Kenya, and doubtful of the wisdom of white settlement. They did not look forward to retiring in the country, and often clashed with the policies of the settlers. Then in 1929 Colonial Regulations were altered to allow civil servants to acquire land in the country. Henceforth social contact and intermarriage brought an increasing identity of viewpoint. By 1951 even the Governor could buy a farm in Kenya to which to retire, and it was stated that it "is the public policy to encourage civil servants to retire to Kenya, where their intimate experience of African affairs can be of the greatest value to Government and public alike."[1] A growing number of civil servants were taking advantage of this, including members of the Provincial Administration and the Medical, Agricultural, and Veterinary Departments.

At this time the Administration itself had probably never been further from the ordinary people. The District Commissioner in the Reserves was increasingly kept in his office by the growing complexity of government. In the settled areas, with the consolidation of the policy of separate development, there was almost no contact at all except for a few *barazas* held on farms by Labor Officers. In 1947 the European District Councils had agreed at a joint conference that the pattern of African Advisory Councils then being implemented in Kenya's towns would not be applied in the White Highlands. Thus the Kikuyu "squatters," the marginal section of society most torn by anxieties, among whom the mass oath was spreading with the greatest rapidity, were the most isolated from the Administration.

Third, the qualified optimism about the future arising from the belief that economic development within an economic system dominated by European settlers could "assimilate" the African to European culture appeared to Kikuyu leaders to have no basis in reality. Postwar Kenya witnessed rapid economic development in the "settled" areas, but the "trickle down" effects to African workers and squatters seemed negligible.

Fourth, the Administration's schemes to develop African rural areas by reclaiming land lost by soil erosion, and improving crops and cattle were admirable, in the abstract. But in practice they occurred within the context of the structure of the colonial state and were part of Mitchell's scheme to help make the African rural areas self-supporting. And just as the pacifist sees civil defense as a part of a war mentality, so many Kikuyu saw such improvement schemes as part of the mentality of Kenya's racially organized economic and social system. To participate in such schemes implied not only accepting the racial land barriers, but also accepting a doctrinaire political development, guided and led by Europeans, according to an economic blueprint.

A second factor in Kenya's colonial experience that shaped the European perception of "Mau Mau" was a tradition of nativistic and messianic religious movements. These were often confused in the European mind with the African separatist churches that emerged out of disagreements on various points with Christian missionary bodies. This confusion arose in part from the African as well as European use of the omnibus Swahili term *dini* to describe all kinds of African religious phenomena.

Among the Kamba there had been nativistic movements with strong overtones of messianism before the First World War, movements the Administration characterized as "mania." After the war, in 1922 in Machakos (a month after Thuku's arrest), one Ndonye Kauti had asserted that he was God's chosen instrument to bring about the deliverance of the Kamba and the expulsion of the Europeans. His doctrine comprised an "imperfectly assimilated assortment of Biblical references interlarded with various ideas of Ndonye's own of a more or less inflammatory nature."[2] God would send him *simiti* (cement) with which to achieve his objectives. After an unsuccessful attempt to have him certified insane, he was eventually deported to Lamu in 1923. But coinciding with these nativistic-messianic movements in Ukambani was the growth of a strong independent church, the African Brotherhood Church, which originated in a splinter group from the AIM.

Among the Luo in Central and South Nyanza there had been the religious movement of "Mumbo." Starting in Alego in 1913,[3] it had spread into South Nyanza during the war. It, too, prophesied the expulsion of Europeans and preached "opposition to government in all its manifestations —tax collection, the orders of Government officers, Chiefs and headmen."[4] Adherents in Central Nyanza believed that Mumbo, a great serpent from Lake Victoria, had swallowed up the first priest, Onyango Dunde, and had spat him out on the lake shore to proclaim the message.[5] In South Nyanza the movement became associated in 1920 with the name of Sakawa, a powerful local pre-colonial leader who had died in 1902. One of the priests, a woman called Bonareri, was certified. Four others were deported to Lamu in 1921, while in 1934 another ten, including the most influential leader, Mosi Auma, were restricted.

Growing parallel with these movements there were also, in both Central and North Nyanza, many independent churches, most of which originated from dissension within missionary societies. Central Nyanza, dominated for many years by the CMS, saw the foundation in 1910 of the Nomia Luo Mission by John Owalo. He soon had 10,000 followers and had begun his own primary educational program.[6] In North Nyanza, too, where there had been a greater proliferation of missions, the thirties and forties had seen the emergence of several independent churches, especially in the highly populated southern locations of the district. In 1934 the *Dini ya Roho* split from the African Anglican Church (CMS) and later itself developed three local factions (one emerging from among former adherents of the American Friends African Mission). In 1941 the African Israel Church split from the Canadian Pentecostal Assemblies of East Africa, and itself split again in 1948 to form the African Divine Church. During the fifties a splinter group of the African Divine Church was to form the Local African Divine Church. In 1946 the African Interior Church separated from the American Church of God Mission in Bunyore. The Rev. Arthur Gatungu's African Orthodox Church also came into North Nyanza from Kikuyu, being brought there by Bantu Bunyore adherents who left the Luo Nomia Mission.[7] Most of the churches split over questions of church discipline, or issues of leadership or control of schools. There was also on occasion straight Luo-Luhya tribal conflict. The liturgy of all these independent groups was increasingly marked by the use of drums, and there was a strong emphasis on locally comprehensible forms of worship. The European missionary deplored and condemned such manifestations of independence and rejection. The European administrator anxiously watched for the signs of hysteria, which might lead to disorder. The European settler tended to look upon them as unchristian and bizarre, examples of the continuing backwardness of all African peoples.

In 1934 and 1947 two messianic-type movements among the Kikuyu had ended in violence and death. In Kikuyu religion one of the most important figures was the *murathi* (pl. *arathi*) or prophet. It was his job to advise whether or not the circumstances were propitious for certain actions, such as a military patrol. In the upheaval in Kikuyu following the female circumcision controversy, several of these *arathi*, known in Swahili as *Watu wa Mungu* (God's People), appeared in 1930 and 1931 in Kiambu and Fort Hall.[8] They deserted their homes and wandered about serving God, relying on the traditional obligation of the people to a *murathi* to feed them. These *arathi*, whose followers numbered 400 in Fort Hall in 1931,[9] wholly rejected missionary teachings. They built their own church on a hill at Ruchu in Fort Hall. "They were forbidden to use European clothes or money, etc. and were not allowed to sleep in anything but a Kikuyu hut belonging to a member of their faith. . . . They preach against the white religion saying it is false and they seem to be of the opinion that the whites will eventually leave this Colony."[10] According to Kenyatta[11] they armed themselves with bows and arrows "as a symbol of their fight against the evil spirits." The police considered them a threat to peace. They began to hunt them down, ultimately killing three in the Ndarugu Forest in 1934.

In December 1947, at Gatundu, near Kenyatta's home some 30 miles from Nairobi, there was more violence. Reuben Kihiko, leader of a similar group of *arathi* known as *Dini ya Jesu Kristo,* asked a tailor called Stephen Muhinja to sew a flag for his group. Muhinja refused and there was an altercation. A few days later some of Kihiko's group met the tailor and forced him to go with them. A passerby told the police, who sent an unarmed patrol to release the tailor. The patrol freed Muhinja, but as they were returning to the station to get reinforcements to arrest Kihiko and his group, there was a clash, and two African constables and a European inspector were killed. Seventeen of Kihiko's group were brought to court, and four, including Kihiko, were executed.

But in the period just prior to the Emergency, the incidents uppermost in European minds concerned the *Dini ya Msambwa,* which had been involved in a major clash at Kolloa in Baringo on April 24, 1950. The founder, Elijah Masinde, a Vugusu, was born about 1910, at Kimilili in Elgon Nyanza District.[12] He was a fine football player, representing Kenya in a game with Uganda in 1930. Originally a member of the FAM, in 1935 he had to leave the church when he took a second wife. About this time he was working as a process-server at the Kavujai Native Tribunal (Court). In 1943 Masinde founded the *Dini ya Msambwa* (*Msambwa* is the name used by many peoples in western Kenya for the spirit of an ancestor). He preached a return to the traditional Vugusu (Kitosh) religion. In 1943 at a District Commissioner's *baraza* at Kimilili, he abruptly questioned Government policy, especially soil conservation and other agricultural measures. Thereafter he increasingly came into conflict with his local chief, refusing to attend "civil conscription *barazas"* in 1944 or to allow an Agricultural Instructor to enter his land to inspect it for the Mexican marigold weed that had by law to be eradicated. The local Assistant Agricultural Officer had been conducting some intense agricultural campaigns at this time. On October 30, 1944, Masinde and ten other men at first repelled a Government party sent to arrest him, though the whole group were later arrested. While they were in jail the Assistant Agricultural Officer's house was burned down. Masinde was widely believed to have prophesied that this would happen. He was convicted and ordered to enter a bond of 500 shillings to keep the peace. When he refused to sign this, he was sent back to jail. While there, he was committed to Mathari Mental Hospital on April 26, 1945. Two years later, in May 1947, he was discharged against the advice of the Provincial Commissioner.

On July 13, 1947, Masinde went to Kimaliwa and told a crowd of some 400 that all Europeans must be expelled from the country and an African king, governor, and administration appointed. In August at another meeting he urged the Vugusu to make guns with which to drive out the Europeans who had stolen their land. He attended a chief's *baraza* on September 15 and protested against soil conservation. Four days later he led a crowd of "about 5,000 followers" to the old fortified encampment near Lugulu where Hobley had fought a major battle with the Vugusu in the "pacification" period. A sheep was killed, and a piece given to each man present. Soon after the Administration decided to re-arrest him. Masinde went into hiding, moving about in the Eldoret farms and even crossing into Uganda. On February 7, 1948, some 800 Vugusu gathered outside Kibabii Roman Catholic Mission, demanding that the missionaries abandon the station. On February 8 the District Commissioner dispersed a large crowd at Sangalo. On February 10 another crowd, armed with sticks, marched on the temporary police post at Malakisi to release three tribesmen who had been arrested. Provoked by actions of members of the crowd, the police opened fire, killing 11 and wounding 16. On February 16, Masinde was arrested by the police without any trouble, in a cave at Chesamis where he was living with some 200 followers. He was deported to Lamu* and the *Dini ya Msambwa* was declared an unlawful society. But these actions did not bring an end to the movement.

On March 10, 1949, came the first of a wave of sixteen cases of arson affecting farm buildings, churches, and schools in the Trans Nzoia District. By the end of 1949 the Government considered the activities of the sect to be on the increase. Indeed, more violence was in the offing, in another tribe under another leader. In 1946 Lukas Pkiech from Suk

---

* Later he was moved to Marsabit.

(Pokot) was converted by Masinde and returned to proselytize. On August 18, 1948, he was convicted of being a member of the *Dini ya Msambwa* and sentenced to two and one-half years' imprisonment. Twelve days later he escaped from detention. For nearly a year the Administration hunted him. At length, on April 24, 1950, at Kolloa in Baringo District, they caught up with him and a group of some 200 followers armed with spears. A violent and bloody battle followed. On the Government side three Europeans and one member of the Tribal Police were killed; several Suk were killed and 50 were believed to have been wounded. No further incident or disorder of any kind occurred later. A Police Levy Force, costing £22,000 a year to be paid by the Suk, was put in the area.[13]

These African religious movements formed an intrinsic part of the ethnic perspective and mental heritage of the Kenya administrators, missionaries, and settlers. As African politics grew more radical and secretive in the early 1950s, officials, colonists, and missionaries tended to adopt a common view that developing unrest among the Kikuyu followed an old pattern. They discerned in "Mau Mau" a similar kind of emotional, irrational, and atavistic response to problems of rapid social change. Their view was reinforced by certain characteristics of Kikuyu politics at this time—the emotionalism exhibited at the mass KAU rallies and the use of religious symbols and hymn tunes. Europeans became convinced that they were faced with a secret, tribal cult, led by unscrupulous agitators, mere confidence tricksters who stirred up the primitive masses in order to line their own pockets and further their own ambitions. The cult was essentially anti-European and sought Kikuyu domination of the whole of Kenya. The mastermind of the conspiracy was Jomo Kenyatta.

Such a cult appealed to a large majority of the Kikuyu people, they felt, since there existed "a spiritual vacuum" in which "Satan could find work for empty souls."[14] To the head of the Church of Scotland in Kenya, "Mau Mau" was "a resurgence of the old pagan faith reacting not only against Western civilisation which [was] breaking down the old pattern of life, but against a new religion which cannot and will not come to terms with it."[15] The evil influences and forces that were expressed in the female circumcision crisis of 1929 were abroad once again. For L. S. B. Leakey the strength and support that "Mau Mau" attained among the Kikuyu derived essentially from the fact that it was a new religion that had the force of "turning thousands of peace-loving Kikuyu into murderous fanatics."[16]

A third factor which served to reinforce the colonial community's conviction that "Mau Mau" was essentially an irrational rejection of modernity was the widespread use of oaths and oathing ceremonies. For Kenya's Europeans, no other single feature of "Mau Mau" so clearly and unequivocally symbolized the atavistic and primitive character of Kikuyu politics. The very word "Mau Mau" probably contributed to this impression.

The term "Mau Mau" made its first official appearance in 1948, when the District Commissioner of Nakuru in the Rift Valley noted the arrival of another "politico-religious sect" with branches at Naivasha and Ol Kalou similar to the *Watu wa Mungu*, "probably affiliated to the Kikuyu Central Association," called "Maumau" and "emanating from the Kikuyu reserve."[17] It is noteworthy that at its official debut the term was understood as one word, not two, and could easily have been a corruption of the Kikuyu word for an oath —*muma*. F. D. Corfield, who was appointed by the colonial government on October 17, 1957, as "Government Commissioner (History of *Mau Mau*), to carry out an enquiry into the origins of the Mau Mau movement," traces the phrase to police discussions with witnesses during a case brought against Kikuyu farm laborers at the Ngata Estate of Lord Egerton of Tatton in Njoro, in March 1948.[18] There was certainly an oath involved in this episode, but both the newspaper account and the District Commissioner in his Annual Report ascribed this incident solely to KCA, and neither mentioned "Mau Mau."[19]

By mid-1950, the Government had decided to mount a campaign against oathing. Beginning in June, a spate of cases were brought from the Lake farms at Naivasha,[20] where some of those evicted from Olenguruone had found work. In addition to the oath to join the "Mau Mau Association" to chase the Europeans out of Kenya, participants were alleged to pay 62 shillings and 50 cents and contribute a ram at the secret meetings at which the oaths were given. Parmenas Kiritu, an English-speaking shopkeeper, later head of the "Loyalist" Torchbearers Association in the area during the Emergency, and the person to whom many African sources ascribe the first public use of the words, gave evidence that he had known of the existence of the "Mau Mau Association" since 1948 and that it had a bad reputation among honest people. "It is a Kikuyu word which means that you want to do something very quickly."[21]

Cases against people allegedly involved in secret oathing were also being brought in 1950 in the Kiambu Reserve. But at this time in these Kiambu cases there was no mention of "Mau Mau." On each occasion the charge was concerned with taking or giving a KCA oath. In the most famous of these early Kiambu cases, Dedan Mugo, president of the All-Kikuyu Age Groups, was accused of oathing Johanna Njuguna Kamau "to obey the orders of the proscribed Kikuyu Central Association" whose main aims were "the flouting of British rule and authority."[22] In September the first case was taken at Nyeri where Nahashon Munyori and fourteen others, including the vice-president and treasurer of the Nyeri KAU branch, were accused of taking a KCA oath at a so-called tea-party at Kiandu in Nyeri on August 26, 1950.[23] Again in October 1950, a case was brought against four Kikuyu in Nairobi for being "members of the proscribed KCA."[24] But by August 1950, on the basis of the oath cases alone, the Government believed that there was sufficient evidence of the dangerous nature of "Mau Mau" for the movement to be legally proscribed.

Europeans' stereotyped views of the Kikuyu character also help explain their assumption that the oath was central to the "Mau Mau" movement. Long isolation behind forest barriers was held to have given the Kikuyu a "forest psychology"[25] and to have made them endemically secretive, irrational, and predisposed toward barbarism. Unlike the gay, dancing and drinking Kamba, or the noble, brave, and extrovert Masai, they were a sour, inward-looking people, perpetually grousing, with little music in their souls.[26] But they were also very quick, industrious, and clever—East Africa's Jewry. Even if they did revolt, they could be quickly crushed, since their leaders were merely agitators and the population had none of the qualities necessary for sustained and gallant resistance. A troublesome people, their politics had been one of constant subversion. "Kikuyuism" was its dominant characteristic, a mysterious and sinister emotion probably only comprehensible in the light of the peculiar religious beliefs of the tribe.

Rejecting political explanations of Kikuyu disaffection from the colonial-settler system, explanations of "Mau Mau" were sought in terms of the peculiarly intense identity problems of the Kikuyu—the lack of congruity between their traditional values and status and success within the new, modernizing society. They possessed "a subconscious realisation of their inability to compete with the new world thrust upon them."[27] People joined because "Mau Mau" offered a new alternative, a new set of precepts and rules, that were to be rigidly enforced and blindly obeyed. Therefore, to explain "Mau Mau" was to account for leaders being able to exact this slavish obedience; the explanation ignored the particular acts or goals which that leadership sought.

According to the European myth of "Mau Mau," taking the oath was a decisive event in the personality development of the individual Kikuyu. Before taking the oath the individual Kikuyu—despite his peculiar psychological characteristics as a member of the Kikuyu tribe—was a rational being, or at least amenable to the process of rational argument and persuasion by members of the African élite and its African local officials. After having taken the oath, he underwent a profound metamorphosis. He was henceforth immune from rational thought processes; he underwent a psychological regression by which he cast out the white culture and bound his "will" to the secret association. He became an automaton, a mere tool in the hands of the oath-givers. He became an object with whom no rational dialogue could take place until he had been psychologically cleansed.

"Rehabilitation"

The Government's "rehabilitation" program was designed specifically to remove the "disease" of "Mau Mau" from thousands of Kikuyu detainees. This program led eventually to its own negation in the Hola camp incident, described below. After Hola, the Government abandoned its theory that "rehabilitation" was a prerequisite to re-entering normal society, and the restriction of senior political leaders for the next two years was instead based mainly on arguments of security.

The "rehabilitation" program had its ideological roots in the European myth of "Mau Mau," but its development and application were a consequence of the Government's military and security measures. By the end of 1953 there were some 16,000 people in detention as a direct result of the Emergency. These were in addition to the normal prison population of the country. Some 12,000 of these had been convicted before the ordinary courts, mostly for taking an oath. There were also 1,400 people in Special Detention Camps, the majority under detention orders signed by the Governor for lack of sufficient evidence to sustain criminal charges, and there were some 2,500 men, women, and children in various Works Camps and Screening Centres under short-term detention orders.[28] During the first year of the Emergency more urgent matters precluded any priority consideration being given to the problems of the future of these detainees and prisoners.

However, during 1954 the implementation of the military plan to restore order in the Kikuyu Reserves and Nairobi had brought the swelling flood of assorted detainees to proportions so unmanageable that their treatment became the overriding problem facing the Government. By the end of 1954, partly as a result of "Operation Anvil," there were some 17,000 convicts and 50,000 detainess in prison.[29] Whereas in 1953 a significant proportion of the detainees were felt to be so sick with the "disease" that they would require permanent isolation in exile settlements, this could not be said of the majority of those picked up in late 1953 and 1954. Most of these were regarded as passive supporters who had been hypnotized by agitators and who might well be amenable to cure.

Accordingly, in 1953 T. G. Askwith, an experienced and liberal officer who had been Municipal African Affairs Officer in Nairobi and an enthusiastic supporter of the Kenya Citizens Association, was sent to Malaya to study "the work of rehabilitation amongst the Communists, Chinese and Malays."[30] On his return he submitted a report which formed the basis for the discussions of a special committee that had been set up by the Government to report on "the sociological causes underlying Mau Mau" and to make proposals "on the means for ending it." Among its members

were L. S. B. Leakey and Harry Thuku, and it was advised
by Dr. J. C. Carothers, for many years in psychiatric charge
of the Mathari Mental Hospital on the outskirts of Nairobi.
This committee confirmed the accepted theory of "Mau
Mau," out of which arose the ideology of "rehabilitation,"
carried out initially by Askwith's Department of Community Development and Rehabilitation.

The Sociological Committee endorsed Askwith's general
analysis that "Mau Mau is a dangerous obsession based not
on intellect, but on feeling and emotion which has been
worked up over many years by certain leaders exploiting
grievances in which, whether real or imagined, they themselves genuinely believe. To overcome this obsession mere
argument and persuasion is not enough, and an attack must
be made on feelings and emotions."[31] Askwith felt that the
Bahati and Subukia "Resistance Movement Centres" in the
Rift Valley, run by local European settlers, had evolved a
successful method of attack, by inducing fear "similar to that
engendered in the schoolboy who has been called for an
interview with the Headmaster."[32] That the fear was on
occasions greater than this has been shown by Michael (later
Sir) Blundell, who quotes the Commandant of one camp
(who screened 7,000 Kikuyu and trained five more teams for
other districts) as saying that since "Mau Mau was built on
fear we had to create a greater fear of our camp than that of
Mau Mau . . .

"We, ourselves, started rumours regarding the atrocities
supposed to be committed in the camp, and these stories lost
nothing in horror value as they were passed on.

"Another trick was to walk into the camp at dead of night
with a hurricane lamp, handcuffs, rope and a gun, select a
prisoner who had been difficult to screen, handcuff him and
march him out, all without a word. Shortly afterwards there
would be a series of screams and shouts from the forest,
followed by a shot, then complete silence. In the morning I

would walk into the camp dangling a pair of handcuffs, rope and gun, throw them on to the office table, say nothing, and then start the day's screening, when a remarkably improved atmosphere was evident amongst the Mau Mau prisoners. The prisoner, of course, had not been shot, but quietly transferred to another and remote screening camp."[33]

The pressure of fear thus induced could only be alleviated by confessing the oath. Confession was the first and most vital step in getting rid of "the poison of Mau Mau."[34] Without it "rehabilitation" could not start. Askwith felt that the Government should not even concern itself in the first place with trying to "rehabilitate" those who did not confess. The Sociological Committee agreed that "full and complete confession" was essential, and noted the psychological "parallel in the Catholic confessional and in psycho-analysis."[35] Such confessions, however, would be most effective "if freely and voluntarily made" in the presence of people who knew the person concerned well. The Committee did not believe that rumor of beatings, which anyway "could not be sustained unless real beatings took place from time to time," was the right way to induce fear. They suggested instead "the prospect, for instance, that Mau Mau is bound to lose, that public opinion is bound to turn against it and round on their oppressors, that many of them may never be allowed to return to their homes and that those who do so will find themselves shunned. Constant reminders of the foulness of the oath which they have taken, should, in time, produce nausea and self-disgust." Confession, by whatever means induced, was to remain the foundation stone of "rehabilitation" policy until after the events at Hola in March 1959.

After confession the detainee must be prepared for reabsorption into the reconstructed Kikuyu society. Accordingly, he would slowly move down "the pipeline" through a series of camps until, in the last one, in his Home District, a committee of local "Loyalists" pronounced him cured and fit to rejoin them. The process of building up new attitudes in the detainee during his progress was called "rehabilitation." In essence it involved both religious and political re-education. Since most of Kenya's administrators owed their original selection to their comparative success within the British public school system, it is not surprising that much of the emphasis in the process should have been on hard work, washing, discipline, and games. Askwith noted that "hard physical labour has a very cleansing influence" and also recommended the development of crafts and agricultural work. He advised that the Christian churches should be brought in to re-establish moral values. Cooperators should be allowed to have their families with them, although Askwith warned that "wives have in many cases persuaded their husbands to take the oath and are often very militant. They are also said to be bringing up their children to follow the Mau Mau creed. It is therefore probably more important to rehabilitate the women than the men if the next generation is to be saved."[36]

Askwith proposed that general re-education should be based on his booklet, *The Story of Kenya's Progress*.[37] In his report he maintained that "Africans, and particularly the Kikuyu, have been misled and the Government and Europeans have been vilified. This has done much to encourage the growth of the obsession which has induced the Kikuyu to believe in the crazy notion that they could manage their own affairs without the European. African instructors are now being recruited and will be trained for this purpose."[38]

The Story of Kenya's Progress is a kind of multi-racial primer. It describes the "evolution of government based and controlled very largely by economic development." It tells how the missionaries "persevered in their efforts to civilize the backward people of Africa, in spite of all difficulties," how European farmers and Indians were encouraged to come to Kenya to develop the country and thereby help to repay the money borrowed to build the Uganda Railway, which was constructed "to help the missionaries in their civilizing work, to establish law and order, and abolish the slave trade," because there "was little possibility of the African inhabitants being able to produce crops for exports, as they could hardly grow enough for their own needs, owing to their primitive methods of agriculture." The detainee could learn how "unoccupied land which lay between African tribes who were frequently at war with each other was reserved for farming by Europeans or Indians. In this way a barrier was placed between the tribes, and fighting was prevented."

The booklet also taught correct social behavior. "At the end of a programme given by the mobile cinema you hear the song God Save the King or God Save the Queen. Those who understand that this is a prayer for our Sovereign, whom they respect and honour, will, you find, always stand quietly at attention when they hear this song." The detainee could also learn that it "has taken hundreds of years" for Britain to reach the stage of democratic elections and full responsible government. Indeed, when elections were first introduced only those with education and property could vote. The system of electing African Members of Legislative Council by having the District Councils select three names to send to the Governor for his consideration is favorably compared with the system of electing the American President. This is a good system because "the African section of the population which is still the largest in number is the least experienced in political matters" and the Europeans and Indians "understand better what democratic government means." On Africanization Askwith warily states that "the European officers are patiently training African officers to take more and more responsibility for administration in the districts and in many cases their efforts are being successful," but it "will be a slow process, made more difficult because government is becoming daily more complicated."

Askwith emphasized the vital part that the missions play in Kenya's system, and noted that "there are a number of Africans who have forgotten all the missionaries have done for them and are still doing in spite of the ever-increasing burden, and are filled with ingratitude." The most important part of the teaching of the missionaries "was not how to read, write and do arithmetic, but how to live better lives, how to behave towards parents and those in authority like chiefs and the Government, and finally, of course, how to follow God."

The booklet concludes with some comments on freedom.

> Freedom is a great privilege. It cannot be given but can only be earned. It is only safe in the hands of those who know how to use it. . . . It is the policy in British territories to give the inhabitants much freedom, some say too much is given and the people are not yet ready or responsible enough to receive it. Nevertheless, people are allowed to criticize the Government and provided they do not do things that are likely to cause a disturbance or prevent the operation of the Government, they have far more freedom than ever existed in the old Africa.

The Christian Council of Kenya and the Roman Catholic Church supported the new Government policy and, assisted by Government grants, organized a chaplaincy service throughout the growing network of camps and prisons. Indeed "a large proportion of the elders posted to the camps were selected with the help of the churches,"[39] and the Government noted that the "rehabilitation" process afforded "an undoubted opportunity for the churches to re-establish Christian values."[40] By October 1955 Askwith was responsible for "rehabilitation" in 53 camps, and had 36 Rehabilitation Officers, 83 Rehabilitation Assistants, 17 African Probation Assistants, and 237 elders working with his organization.[41]

On their side, the most militant detainees reacted in two ways. They refused to regard themselves as criminals, insisted that they were political prisoners, and stood upon their rights under the Geneva Convention. They also refused to confess their oath. This last became the symbol of a continued adherence to nationalism.

Until 1956 there was no commanding pressure on the Government to release detainees. There was still much to be done to restore law and order in the Reserves and the forests. Nevertheless special "I" teams were formed to start obtaining confessions and generally sort out the camp into various categories, "White" significantly being the color chosen for instant release, "Grey" for the doubtful, and "Black" for the hard core. Between 1956 and 1958 increasing pressures came from the British Government to speed up the rate of releases. With the resistance in the forests limited to small groups bent on survival, the focus of the struggle had shifted to the Detention camps, where at the end of 1956 there were 20,016 detainees in 39 camps, and 7,825 "Mau Mau" convicts scattered among 21 prisons.[42]

After 1956 the Government increasingly accepted the legitimacy of the use of force to extract the vital initial confession from a detainee in order to accelerate the rate of release. But at least one warning had been made that the pace might be too quick for proper "rehabilitation" of the more militant elements. The District Commissioner, Kiambu, maintained that the liquid being pumped along the pipeline "is of an increasingly heavy *Mau Mau* specific gravity, and may become too black and glutinous to pass freely."[43] The six camps on the Mwea plains in Embu District, some 50 miles from Nairobi, became the center for accelerating the production of confessions, on which the pace of releases depended. Great care was exercised, and special hair-splitting instructions on the difference between "compelling" and "overwhelming" force issued from the Attorney General's office. "Compelling" force was legal—moving detainees against their wishes, hair-cutting, shaving, medical examination, forced feedings if necessary, and dressing them in the authorized detainee uniform. "Overwhelming" force, which was illegal, was applying force to a detainee in order to break his moral resistance to a lawful order. Under these definitions it would be legal to use such force as was needed to take one set of clothes off a recalcitrant detainee and put another set on. On the other hand it would be using "overwhelming" force, and therefore illegal, to hit the same detainee with a baton to make him comply with an order to change his clothes. In the Mwea camps the system was concentrated into a routine known as "Intake Procedure." On arrival the prisoners or detainees were first asked to confess. If they did not confess they were then given a lawful order, such as being told to change their clothes. Since putting on the new clothes implied giving up their status as "political" detainees, some refused. "Compelling" force was then used to make them obey and was continued until they confessed.

By the beginning of 1959 the Government could look with considerable satisfaction on the statistics of "rehabilitation." More than 77,000 had been released by February 1959,[44] with only some 1,100[45] people left in the camps by August. These included those who had not been amenable to "rehabilitation" and had been returned up the pipeline, those "whose records were so black, or whose crimes were so brutal, that they would not be accepted back by their own communities" (represented by the "Loyalist" committees), and those who were "the organizers and managers of the Mau Mau society."[46]

That some provision would have to be made for permanent segregation had become apparent early in the Emergency. It had once been thought that there might be as many as 6,000 in this category, and it was decided to open an exile settlement for them. Hola, remote, virtually uninhabited, was chosen. It was on the Tana River, in an area long projected for an agricultural irrigation scheme, which the detainees could work on. As a result of the apparent accomplishments of the "rehabilitation" program by 1959, the estimate of detainees "who would require settlement was reduced to some 500."[47] Within the exile settlement there would have to be different arrangements for "the cooperators," who had been "rehabilitated" but were not acceptable to the "Loyalists," and the non-cooperators, who had refused to confess their part in "Mau Mau." The cooperator would be given a hut and rationed and paid until he harvested his first crop, when his family would be allowed to join him. The non-cooperator, who remained a moral danger even to his own children, could not have his family with him. There was talk of opening, in due course, a special "isolation ward" section of the settlement for these non-cooperators who would then have no contact with the outside world. Until this development there should be as little association as possible between the two groups.

During 1958 the complex of camps scattered all over the colony began to close down. Many of the remaining detainees were sent to Hola. As more and more arrived, a decline in discipline and cooperation with Government became apparent. The Minister for African Affairs and the Commissioner of Prisons visited Hola toward the end of the year, and it was decided to strengthen discipline. But the decline continued, and on February 7, 1959, Senior Superintendent Cowan, the foremost Detention Camp expert in the Kenya Prisons Service, arrived at Hola with instructions to investigate the situation and propose remedies.

Cowan had been working in Detention camps in Mwea for two years, where he had been closely involved in the development of the "Intake Procedure" and the "rehabilitation" method known as the "dilution technique."

> The essence of this technique was the division of recalcitrant detainees into very small and manageable parties and the dilution of these parties with a number of co-operative detainees

who greatly outnumbered the recalcitrant detainees. The whole technique was supervised by a comparatively very large number of Prison staff, both European and African. This technique involved the use of highly co-operative detainees to persuade their fellow detainees to confess and respond to rehabilitation. This dilution technique had been markedly successful and had resulted in very large numbers of detainees being released to freedom.[48]

Before returning to Nairobi Cowan drew up a plan: "A numerically greatly superior warder staff, under the control of all available European officers, should be paraded. The group of recalcitrant detainees in one compound should then be given the order to work on the scheme."[49] Since work on the irrigation scheme implied cooperation with the Government, Cowan expected that any violent resistance would occur at this stage where his superior force of warders could easily manage it inside the compound. Should the detainees simply refuse to march to work, they would be picked up and carried there. When they arrived they would be given a pre-arranged "work task" which did not require the use of tools (which could become weapons), such as weeding by hand.

> If any detainee refused to comply with a lawful order to weed, Cowan's plan was that two warders should be allocated to that detainee and, by holding his hands, physically make him pull weeds from the ground. From Cowan's experience he was convinced that once such token work had been performed by the detainee he would have considered that he had broken his Mau Mau oath which had, by superstitious dread, previously prevented him from cooperating. Experience shows that once a detainee has cleared this psychological hurdle, he will probably become co-operative and thus start on the road to freedom.[50]

On February 19 Cowan flew to Britain on leave. At the end of the month Takwa Camp on Manda Island, which housed most of the top KAU leaders arrested during and after Operation "Jock Scott" and included many members of the Kiambaa "Parliament" and the Nairobi Central Committee, was closed down and its occupants transferred to Hola. Discipline and cooperation at Hola continued to deteriorate; it was felt the attitudes of the new arrivals were beginning to contaminate the whole camp. During the following week there were anxious discussions between the Ministry of Defence (responsible for the Prisons Department) and the Ministry for African Affairs (now responsible for Rehabilitation). The Commissioner of Prisons minuted the Minister of Defence, "We must either let them stew and risk the contamination" or introduce the Cowan Plan "with the risk of someone getting hurt or killed." The Minister for African Affairs considered "it was essential, if there were to be any prospect of successful rehabilitation, to try to carry out the operation, as planned by Cowan, without further delay."[51] Although he agreed that the operation was a serious one, similar operations, involving the dilution technique, had been carried out on a number of occasions without miscarriage.[52] Accordingly the Officer in charge at Hola was authorized by the Minister of Defence to implement the Cowan Plan as soon as possible.

On March 3, 1959, an operation based on the Cowan Plan was carried out and ended in disaster. Out of 88 detainees involved in the operation, eleven died and others were seriously hurt. Ten of those who died were Kikuyu and one was a Turkana. Next day the Government issued a Press statement which implied that the deaths were due to poison in water drunk by the detainees from a water cart.[53] A week later this explanation was withdrawn, and it was announced that there would be a proper Coroner's Inquest. An investigation of the remaining Detention camps and the complaints of the detainees also took place.

This was carried out by a small Committee, headed by R. D. Fairn, one of Her Majesty's Prison Commissioners, which was admirably equipped to conduct a microscopic technical examination of the Detention camps and rehabilitation. It was no part, however, of the Committee's duty to examine Kenya's political problems. Impressed by the strong determination of many of the remaining detainees "that nothing shall move them or their followers into any admission of guilt or any co-operation with Government," the Committee, which had a former Kenya missionary as another of its members, felt that the problem needed psychiatric treatment, ideally by a Christian psychiatrist, with a knowledge of the Kikuyu language.[54] This was, in some ways, the last assertion of the "psychological" approach to the problem of "Mau Mau." Five years earlier the then Bishop of Mombasa had led a deputation to a psychiatrist in London to discuss the oath. The results were somewhat discouraging, although the specialist had seen some evidence of "a communal psychosis."[55] The Committee recognized that after seven years of detention some individuals might well have developed psychological problems and become "morbidly bound up with their own condition." Everything must be tried to coax them out of it. "For example, we have heard of a Kikuyu 'comic entertainer.' Why not invite his services?" The policy should no longer be to cut detainees off from the world, they must be brought into it again. For these reasons the Committee deplored the confinement of these hard-core resisters at the Athi River detention camp "in darkened cells . . . there must be at least a window into the free world, through which his imagination could range."[56]

On the use of "lawless violence" in the camps the Commissioners were uncompromising. They had "seen and talked with injured men in the camps and we have had impressive testimony from responsible people on all sides that violence, not just corporal punishment, was often used in the past by the 'screening teams' to compel confessions."[57] They also strongly advised the discontinuance of the use of "shock" treatment involving corporal punishment.

The tragedy at Hola was to have other far-reaching

consequences. After it, for the first time, the Administration quietly accepted that detainees could be released without confessing the oath or being rehabilitated, thus invalidating the basic propositions on which the ideology of rehabilitation had been constructed. Henceforth they almost begged detainees to go home, and many were carried, mute and unconfessed, from Land Rovers back to their families in the Reserves.

But, perhaps most important of all, the lengths to which the Kenya Government had been driven to maintain its apolitical analysis of "Mau Mau" led to a profound reappraisal of Kenya's problems in Britain. Within a period of six weeks, in June and July 1959, there were two major debates in the House of Commons on the Hola affair. The Labour Party in opposition predictably condemned the conduct of all those responsible. But it was a leading Conservative, J. Enoch Powell, who made the most damaging attack in his assessment of the affair as "a great administrative disaster."[58] Iain Macleod, Colonial Secretary at the critical Lancaster House Constitutional Conference in 1960, has said "Hola helped to convince me that swift change was needed in Kenya."[59]

Though Kenya rapidly moved into an African oriented political system, few Europeans, whether settlers, missionaries, or administrators, ever doubted that "rehabilitation" was a complete success. This perspective, stressing the elements of moral turpitude and psychological breakdown in African politics, was reinforced in 1960 by the publication of the official *Historical Survey of the Origins and Growth of Mau Mau*, the most exhaustive attempt to probe the motives and legitimacy of African politics in Kenya.[60] The interpretation of this "rehabilitation" thesis in the minds of some has indeed continued into the post-independence period, when it has been claimed by some to account for the responsible discharge of political roles by former militant African leaders.

CHAPTER 10

Conclusion

This study of African social and political responses to alien rule in Kenya has essentially been an exploration into variant aspects of colonial nationalism. Though the patterns of social mobilization and political organization reflected many distinct features, the objectives and ideology of Kenya colonial nationalism were broadly similar to African nationalist movements elsewhere. To elaborate this argument, it is necessary first to discuss some of the diverse usages of the term nationalism in the context of colonial Africa.

Nationalism was initially a European concept which occurred in a given historical context and led to the emergence of political systems that have been referred to as "nation-states." It has been argued that nationalism as an analytical concept relates to certain *objective* criteria, such as a common historical experience, language, and culture, as well as clearly articulated ideologies and myths. Since the criteria suggested by Western experience have seldom been applicable to the African environment, there have been some who have rejected the concept; notably Lord Hailey, who spoke of "Africanism."[1] Most observers, however, have employed the concept of nationalism in describing African protest in the colonial context, though they have differed in the need for rigor and precision of definition. Thus Thomas Hodgkin has considered every social movement of protest against alien rule as nationalism.[2] In criticism of this all-embracing definition, it has been argued that to include all social protest as a part of nationalism obscures the concept's political meaning, for nationalism must be predicated on at least the aspiration of a future self-governing nation.

Though significant differences have existed in respect to the rigor of definition, these differences have not essentially encumbered analysis, for all were concerned with describing a somewhat similar colonial situation of alien domination and African assertion—to employ Professor Emerson's exceedingly useful term.[3] Indeed, most analysts have come to similar conclusions, for they were employing the concept of nationalism not so much as a conceptual tool but as a means of describing common processes of political and social mobilization and the search for power and dignity by Africans within a highly structured colonial framework. This monolithic situation, in which African leaders were concerned with a limited number of political functions and choices associated with the acquisition of power and the definition of the new nation, has facilitated the making of propositions by reference to readily comparative situations.

The analysis of this book, as well as much of the literature on nationalism in other parts of colonial Africa, points to two major perspectives in the evaluation of pre-independence African politics: ideology and organization. The development of the ideology of African nationalism during the colonial period may be seen as taking place along a continuum whose opposite poles (in value terms) were acceptance of a subordinate role with the deference values fostered by the colonial system, and total rejection of subordinate status and the assertion of a distinct African personality. The first expression of political demands in the colonial context was, essentially, a demand for assimilation. In insisting upon equality before the law, African élites spoke the language of civil liberties in the search for human dignity. In demanding personal and civil liberties, social protest movements paid little attention to the problem of territorial political control and directed their demands to the local agents of the metropolitan powers. The crucial turning-point in colonial nationalism was the rejection by the protest movements or political parties of the legitimacy of the colonial system. At this point there occurred a marked shift from a limited civil-liberties ideology to demands for the acquisition of political power and ultimately for a monopoly of coercive powers—a shift in which the values of civil liberties became instrumental rather than consummatory.[4]

The general ideological problem of African political leaders was to apply western liberal nationalism—ideas of social justice and self-determination—to their local conditions and to define membership in terms of a new political community and territory. In Kenya, African leaders had not only to confront a European political and cultural élitism demanding conformity to the rituals of deference, but as European racialism gave way to multi-racialism, they had the additional ideological problem of combatting a doctrine which appeared both liberal and to some extent nationalist. The language of multi-racialism—of racial equality, of "partnership," of equal rights of all civilized men, of the Protestant ethic—was superficially similar to that of African nationalism. In opposing the multi-racial ideology as it came into prominence in the 1950s, African leaders were prone to lay themselves open to charges of tribalism or racialism. "Multi-racialists" demanded that all liberals of whatever race work together under white leadership to create the economic and social conditions of a non-racial society. But African leaders emphasized social and personal discriminatory treatment that coexisted with this manifest ideology; a solution to their problems, they urged, required not individual representation but political power. This different emphasis was vital and, in laying such stress on it, African political leaders were frequently castigated as racialists.

Though African nationalism in colonial Kenya shared many common ideological perspectives with other nationalist movements, Kenya protest movements failed to become vehicles for territorial integration. Not only was meaningful political organization primarily limited to the Kikuyu in the pre-Emergency period, but also some tribal groups were little concerned with the ideology of colonial nationalism. Given this essentially organizational or building-block approach to the study of pre-independent African politics, did what occurred in central Kenya—culminating in violence in the early 1950s—constitute nationalism?

It is a central assumption of this study that such an organizational approach can only provide a partial answer to this question. To understand more fully both the meaning and impact of African politics in this crucial period, we must combine both the objective indices of nationalist organizational development with the subjective intentions of the actors involved.

African nationalist organizations have had infrequent success in projecting their ideological aspirations toward the objective of a united territorial political community. In certain parts of West Africa and in Tanganyika in East Africa, the search for political power and the building of party organization for national integration tended to be congruent. An array of factors associated with the character of social mobilization, ethnicity, and the presence of permissive colonial authorities amenable to radical political change fostered the simultaneous pursuit of both. In many parts of Africa, the characteristics of a successful "acquisition" movement have been quite different from those fostering an "integrational" movement. Indeed, the organizational forms and techniques employed to advance what may be called the "acquisition" function of colonial nationalism have in a number of situations militated against the solutions of the "integration" problem. For the main task of nationalism in a "colonial situation" of alien rule has been the acquisition of political power and authority in the colonial state; to this, all other tasks have been secondary, including the development of organizations capable of fostering territorial integration.

Uneven patterns of African social mobilization have been a common variable in obstructing the integrative function of nationalism in colonial Africa.[5] In Kenya the differential rate in social mobilization among the diverse cultural sectors of African population was very marked and was crucial in restricting the development of transtribal political organization. Though significant segments of the subordinated African population possessed a community of grievances, the rapid social mobilization of the Kikuyu in response to the colonial experience meant that the quality and intensity of their demands on the settler-oriented colonial system were immeasurably greater than that of the less mobilized groups.

White settlement rapidly created a crisis for Kikuyu traditional culture, limiting many of the evolutionary adjustments to the new colonial system that other tribal groups were able to make. The quantity of Kikuyu land alienated for white settlement, as contrasted to the Masai, was relatively small. But we have seen that in ecological and social terms the Kikuyu could least afford to lose land. Moreover, their social system, which was closely linked to pioneer land settlement, now found barriers placed on its expansion. As the population expanded and internal conflict deepened, the cry for the return of the "stolen land" emerged as the salient political issue for the Kikuyu masses. But this issue was of sight appeal to such groups as the Luo or the Luhya, which had been little affected by the pattern of European land settlement.

Though their traditional value made the Kikuyu very receptive to the acquisitive and achievement-oriented values of the new white power élite, there was little opportunity for mobility for thousands who sought to enter the market economy. At nearly every point in the European-dominated hierarchy, barriers appeared to advancement and to positions of prestige and status. Lack of technical skill, education, and capital were factors inhibiting mobility within the colonial society, but politically more significant was the character of the white-settler-oriented economy, which essentially restricted the role of the African to that of a low wage earner. Deeply enmeshed in a colonial state characterized by segregation, racial discrimination, and separate development, and bitterly frustrated by their marginal economic, social, and political roles, Kikuyu leaders relentlessly attacked the racial barriers to upward mobility.

While in the immediate postwar years KAU strove to achieve a country-wide organizational structure representing the interests of all the Africans in Kenya, the Kikuyu areas of central Kenya not only provided the hard core of leadership, but also the vast bulk of protest against colonial rule. As the Kikuyu demands for change intensified, the willingness and capacity of the colonial-settler élite for reform seemed to diminish. Increasingly, in the early postwar period, the Administration, the settlers, and the missionaries had drawn together to the extent that, in most Kikuyu eyes, they were regarded as part of a single, permanent, and integrated racial coalition.

The inability of KAU to obtain any significant redress of economic, social, and political grievances led to the adoption of new organizational means to achieve the cohesion and unity required for militant and prolonged resistance. In the politicized environment of central Kenya, the oath was a simple weapon. It emphasized rural and traditional characteristics in Kikuyu culture, and served as well to bind together militant urban and rural protest. However, as we have argued, it is part of the myth of "Mau Mau" to fail to distinguish between the form and meaning of the oath. Preoccupation with the ritual and traditional aspects of the oathing procedure obscured the deeper significance of the oaths as an organizational weapon in a context of mass mobilization.

Although oathing strengthened the Kikuyu organizational ability to challenge the colonial state, it nonetheless had the additional effect of limiting the institutional spread of the national movement to non-Kikuyu groups. This dilemma was not unrecognized by the Kikuyu leadership, for they envisaged the creation of other tribal oaths which would serve to mobilize and commit non-Kikuyu people to their style of militant nationalism. Lack of sufficient time and the Administration's success in compartmentalizing and controlling African political activity were two important factors that prevented this from occurring in any extensive manner. Thus, the pattern of nationalism as it unfolded stemmed from a rationally conceived strategy in search of political power within a context of structural conditions which severely inhibited the growth of a country-wide national organizational movement.

In contrast to the nationalism of the pre-Emergency period, that of the late 1950s possessed several distinct advantages in its assertion for political power. Foremost among these was a colonial situation far more amenable to rapid change owing to a competitive international situation and shifts in British policy as well as to the existence of a greater number of educated African leaders drawn from an array of tribal groups. Nonetheless, only in part was this new nationalism able to advance national or territorial integration. Organizationally, nationalism remained fragmented and dominated by tribal parochialism—a condition encouraged by Administrative policy. Though the goal of African independence was achieved and the immediate crisis of stability was overcome by a consolidation of power and Africanization of the institutions of state management, the complex problems and issues of national integration will long endure.

CHAPTER 1

1. The same census gave the Asian population as 176,613; European, 55,759; and Arabs, 34,048. The tribal populations given in this chapter are found in this source. *Kenya Population Census, 1962. Advance Report of Volumes I & II* (Nairobi, 1964), pp. 5, 45.

Before Indian Independence in 1947, the term "Indian" referred to all peoples whose origin was the subcontinent. After partition, however, the term Asian was used to refer to those of Indian and Pakistani origin.

2. See D. A. Low, "The Northern Interior, 1840–84," Chap. IX in Roland Oliver and Gervase Mathew, eds., *History of East Africa*, Vol. I (Oxford, 1963), for an excellent account of the Masai role during this period.

3. There is a vivid account of an expedition against the Kamasia in 1897 in Brigadier-General Trevor Ternan, *Some Experiences of an Old Bromsgrovian* (London, 1930), pp. 284–94.

4. Colonel R. Meinertzhagen, *Kenya Diary, 1902–1906* (Edinburgh, 1957), pp. 196–265.

5. Lt. Col. H. Moyse-Bartlett, *The King's African Rifles: A Study in the Military History of East and Central Africa* (Aldershot, 1956), pp. 197–211.

6. Kenya National Archives (hereafter referred to as KNA): ELGM/7 Elgeyo (Tambach) Political Record Book, vol. 1.

7. Sir Frederick Jackson, *Early Days in East Africa* (London, 1930), pp. 196–98 and p. 230. This Pangani was on the Tangankia Coast.

8. We are much indebted to A. T. Matson, formerly of the Kenya Medical Department, for both his long discussions and his numerous articles, particularly in the *Kenya Weekly News* and the *Uganda Journal*, covering this period.

9. We are indebted to Dr. B. A. Ogot for this information.

10. M. G. Whisson, "The Rise of Asembo and the Curse of Kakia," *Proceedings of the Conference of the East African Institute of Social Research*, 1961.

11. C. W. Hobley, *Kenya From Chartered Company to Crown Colony* (London, 1929), pp. 82–86; W. Robert Foran, *The Kenya Police, 1887–1960* (London, 1962), p. 27; Moyse-Bartlett, *The King's African Rifles*, p. 208; W. Lloyd-Jones, *K.A.R.* (London, 1926), pp. 107–12.

12. Robert Foran, *A Cuckoo in Kenya* (London, 1936), pp. 177–78.

13. Foran, *The Kenya Police*, p. 29.

14. KNA: TTA/6, Political Records 1909–34, p. 2.

15. *Ibid.*

16. KNA: Coast Section, 5/336, C. Dundas, "Report on the Giriama Rising," 25 October 1914. See also Norman Leys, *Kenya* (London, 1924), pp. 128–30.

17. KNA: Coast Section, 20/138, "Political Prisoners from Giriama. Deportation of a woman Me Katilili and Elder Wanji wa Madori."
18. KNA: Coast Section, 5/336. "Giriama Rising 1914–1915," A. M. Champion, "Summary of Incidents on Outbreak of Giriama Rising."
19. KNA: Coast Section, 16/38, "Giriama Affairs 1915–16," Report from F. Traill, D. C., Nyika, to P. C., Mombasa, August 30, 1915.
20. KNA: Dundas, "Report on the Giriama Rising."
21. KNA: Coast Section, 5/336, "Memorandum. Giriama Rising."
22. KNA: Dundas, "Report on the Giriama Rising."
23. Rev. Dr. J. Lewis Krapf, *Travels, Researches, and Missionary Labours, during an Eighteen Years' Residence in Eastern Africa* (London, 1860), p. 552.
24. C. W. L. Bulpett, ed., *John Boyes, King of the Wa-Kikuyu* (London, 1911), pp. 178–88.
25. *The Life Story of a Kenya Chief*, The Life of Chief Kasina Ndoo as told to J. B. Carson (London, 1958), p. 16.
26. For a definitive account of Lugard in East Africa, see Margery Perham, *Lugard: The Years of Adventure, 1858–1898* (London, 1956).
27. For a British version of this episode, see Major J. R. L. Macdonald, R. E., *Soldiering and Surveying in British East Africa, 1891–1894* (London, 1897), pp. 111–21.
28. Letters of Francis George Hall to his father, Lt. Col. Edward Hall, late 52nd Bengal Native Infantry, II, 1892–1895, 48. From a typescript in the possession of Hon. Joseph Murumbi M.P., Kenya. The original letters are deposited in Rhodes House, Oxford, England.
29. Letters of Francis George Hall, II, 162–64.
30. *Ibid.*, p. 112.
31. Letters of Francis George Hall, III, 1896–1901, 71. At this time the word village seems to have been used to describe a single family homestead rather than a complex of such homesteads.
32. Meinertzhagen, *Kenya Diary, 1902–1906*, p. 146.
33. Foran, *The Kenya Police*, p. 26.
34. A description of the founding of early missions is to be found in R. Oliver, *The Missionary Factor in East Africa* (London, 1952), pp. 168–71; see also T. J. Jones, *Education in East Africa* (New York, 1925), pp. 120–33.
35. An early venture in 1894 had failed; see E. Richards, *Fifty Years in Nyanza, 1906–1956* (Maseno, 1956), pp. 8, 9, 10.
36. Kapenguria Trial, Verbatim Transcript, p. 1023, in the Kenya Supreme Court Archives, and speech by President Kenyatta at the opening of a new ward at Kikuyu Hospital on April 17, 1965.
37. *Report of the Land Committee, 1905* (Nairobi, 1905), p. 50.
38. *Report of the Kenya Land Commission*, Cmd. 4556 (1934), p. 14 and pp. 95–101.
39. Sir Charles Eliot, *The East Africa Protectorate* (London, 1905), p. 104.
40. KNA: DC/MKS 10A/1/1, Machakos Land File, 1903, and Machakos Land File, 1912; East Africa Protectorate, May 15, 1912.
41. See Elspeth Huxley, *White Man's Country: Lord Delamere and the Making of Kenya* (London, 1935), vols. I, II.
42. See M. Dilley, *British Policy in Kenya Colony* (New York, 1927), for a well-documented study covering the period 1900–1935; see also George

Bennett, *Kenya, A Political History: The Colonial Period* (London, 1963), for a more recent scholarly account.

43. For a good discussion of some of the economic effects of white settlement in Kenya, see E. Brett, "Economic Policy in Kenya Colony: A Study in the Politics of Resource Allocation," *Proceedings of the Conference of the East African Institute of Social Research,* January 1965.

44. Norman Leys, *Kenya* (London, 1924), p. 195.

45. See Thomas Hodgkin, *Nationalism in Colonial Africa* (London, 1956), pp. 63–83.

46. Dr. E. Boedecker, "Early History of Nairobi Township" (Kabete, 1936). Typescript in Macmillan Library, Nairobi. The Uganda Railway reached Nairobi on May 18, 1899, according to R. O. Preston, *Oriental Nairobi* (Nairobi, 1938), p. 1, but Lt. Col. J. H. Patterson, Divisional Engineer at the time, states that the railroad reached Nairobi on June 5, 1899. See his *The Man-Eaters of Tsavo* (London, 1934), pp. 295–96. M. F. Hill quotes official records as showing May 30, 1899, to be the date; see his *Permanent Way* (Nairobi, 1950), pp. 190–91.

47. KNA: DC/NBI 1/1/1, p. 4. Nairobi District Political Record Book.

48. Letters of Francis George Hall, III, 1896–1901, 105.

49. Kibera, begun in 1912, was handed over to the civil Administration in 1928. See *Kenya Land Commission: Evidence and Memoranda,* I, 1160, 1168. Hereafter *KLC: Evidence.*

50. Mary Parker, *Political and Social Aspects of the Development of Municipal Government in Kenya, with Special Reference to Nairobi* (London: Colonial Office, n.d. [1949]) (Mimeograph), p. 2.

51. *Ibid.,* p. 80. Still in existence in 1928.

52. *Native Affairs Department Annual Report,* 1925, pp. 34, 35.

53. Parker, *Municipal Government in Kenya,* p. 80.

54. *Ibid.*

55. *KLC: Evidence,* I, 1124.

56. *KLC: Evidence,* I, 1129–30, gives 247 Moslem, 12 Christian, and 34 Pagan out of 293 householders. Inhabitants came from twelve different Kenya tribes and from Uganda, Tanganyika, Abyssinia, Nyasaland, Zanzibar, Belgian Congo, Italian Somaliland, Sudan, Madagascar, and Mozambique.

57. *The Leader of British East Africa,* Nairobi, September 3, 1921, p. 126, hereafter referred to as *LBEA.*

58. Parker, *Municipal Government in Kenya,* p. 80.

59. Lt. Col. Charles Hordern, Compiler, *Military Operations, East Africa,* vol. I, August 1914—September 1916 (H.M.S.O., 1941), pp. 22–23.

60. "Report on the period from August 4, 1914 to September 15, 1919 by Lt. Col. O. F. Watkins, C.B.E., D.S.O.," Director of Military Labour to the B.E.A. Expeditionary Force (Typescript, Kenya Government Library), p. 14. Watkins was later to become first editor of *Baraza,* a Swahili newspaper started in 1939.

61. *Ibid.,* pp. 23–24.

62. Under the Native Followers Recruitment Ordinance, 1915.

63. *Minutes of the Proceedings of the Legislative Council,* 26 October 1923, p. 20.

64. KNA: NZA 1/12, Nyanza Province Annual Reports, 1916/17 and 1919.

65. T. R.'s or Tribal Retainers were the bodyguard, messengers, and strongarm men of the Government-appointed Chiefs. They received low pay

at best. This encouraged the practice of extortion and bribery among their ranks. In later years they were slowly regularized into the Tribal Police Force. Capiteni were "village" headmen. Muturi was a headman.

66. KNA: KBU/77, Dagoretti Political Record Book (1913–19), vol. II, fol. 87.

67. Watkins, "Report," pp. 4–5.

68. Leys, *Kenya*, p. 287.

69. Editorial: "Diet for Native Africans," in *The Journal of the Kenya Medical Service*, vol. I, no. 10 (March 1924), p. 2.

70. W. McGregor Ross, *Kenya From Within: A Short Political History* (London, 1927), pp. 152–3.

71. *Kenya Land Commission Report: Summary of Conclusions Reached by His Majesty's Government*. Cmd. 4580 (1934), paras. 27, 28.

72. See a description in L. S. B. Leakey, *White African* (London, 1937), pp. 42–43.

73. Seventeen thousand is also the figure mentioned in the Nyeri Political Record Book, vol. I (KNA. NYI/9, fol. 211).

74. C. P. Groves, *The Planting of Christianity in Africa*, vol. IV, 1914–1954 (London, 1958), pp. 68, 69.

75. Interview: Marius Ng'ang'a Karatu, January 6, 1964.

76. Interview: Jonathan Okwirri, March 1965.

77. KNA: NYI/9, Nyeri Political Record Book, vol. I.

78. *Minutes of the Proceedings of the Legislative Council of East Africa*, 10 October 1916. *Third Session*, p. 3.

79. *Report of the Special Committee on Elective Representation, June 1917*, quoted by George Bennett in "Imperial Paternalism: The Representation of African Interests in the Kenya Legislative Council," Kenneth Robinson and Frederick Madden, eds., *Essays in Imperial Government* (Oxford, 1963), pp. 141–42. See *Minutes of the Proceedings of the Legislative Council of East Africa*, 19 June 1917. *Second Session*, pp. 19–22.

80. The so-called War Council, comprising mainly settlers, was concerned with the impact of the war on East Africa rather than its conduct; see Ross, *Kenya From Within*, pp. 80–81.

81. *KLC: Evidence*, I, 68.

82. Foran, *The Kenya Police*, p. 54.

83. *KLC: Evidence*, III, 2461. C. Tomkinson, D. C., Kericho.

84. Huxley, *White Man's Country*, II, 88.

CHAPTER 2

1. There are letters from him in the *East African Standard*, Nairobi, on May 16, 1921 and May 28, 1921. Referred to hereafter as *EAS*. "K. Mukasa of Uganda" is also named as a member in Kibaara Kabutu, *Jinsi Kenya Ilivyookolewa* (Nairobi, 1964).

2. J. Sabluoni of Nyasaland is mentioned in *ibid.*

3. See the letter from I. S. Mukibi in *EAS*, December 12, 1921, p. 3. Also H. D. Hooper, *Africa in the Making* (London, 1924), pp. 35–38.

4. *Ibid.*, p. 36. Articles in *Sekanyolya* on the Indian Question and Wage Reduction are reprinted in *LBEA*, July 9, 1921 (p. 24), and August 6, 1921 (p. 8), respectively.

5. Ngara, a main Asian residential and shopping quarter, is named after

Ngara Gaitho, a Kikuyu who had a homestead there at the time Nairobi was founded. See questions addressed by Chief Josiah Njonjo to Mr. T. A. Wood, CMG., MBE., *KLC: Evidence*, I, 743. There is a picture of Ngara Gaitho in *Nairobi Charter Celebrations 1950: A Pictorial Record (EAS*—no date). See also KNA: DC/MKS 10A/1/4, Ukamba Province Land File, 1906, Part II, Letter from Ngara Gaitho to Ainsworth in which he says he was given 20/- compensation (16 January 1906).

6. Gathirimu was also the grandfather of Lenana, the Masai *Laibon* instrumental in the peaceful acceptance of British over-rule by his people. Interview: Harry Thuku, October 31, 1963, and evidence of Chief Koinange, *KLC: Evidence,* I, 170.

7. Interview: Harry Thuku, October 31, 1963.

8. *LBEA,* July 9, 1921, pp. 1 and 12.

9. Statement by the Convention of Associations, *LBEA,* November 5, 1921, p. 24.

10. *Economic Commission Final Report, Part I* (Nairobi: March, 1919), pp. 20–21.

11. *Ibid.*

12. Estimated non-African population figures in 1921 were: European 9,651, Indians 22,822, Goans 2,421, Arabs 10,102, Other 627. *Report on the Census of Non-Natives, 24 April 1921* by C. E. Spencer. The quote is from Huxley, *White Man's Country,* II, 118.

13. Chanan Singh, "The Historical Background," in Dharam Ghai, ed., *Portrait of a Minority: Asians in East Africa* (Nairobi, 1965), p. 7.

14. See George Bennett's pioneering article on early African political associations, "The Development of Political Organizations in Kenya" in *Political Studies,* vol. V, no. 2 (June 1957), p. 119.

15. For a fuller explanation of *mbari* land, see below, Chap. V, pp. 145–52.

16. Interview: Matthew Njoroge, November 1963.

17. *Report of the Land Settlement Commission, 1919,* p. 11.

18. *Economic Commission, Final Report, Part I* (1919), pp. 18–19.

19. Letter from I. M. Mungai, "Secretary, Kikuyu Association, Nairobi," in *EAS,* May 31, 1921, protesting against the move to reduce African wages.

20. In his testimony before the Native Labour Commission. See *Native Labour Commission, 1912–13. Evidence and Report* (Nairobi), p. 72.

21. *Ibid.,* pp. 326–31.

22. *LBEA,* August 6, 1921, p. 13.

23. *Ibid.*

24. KNA: DC/MKS 5/1/2, Local Native Council Minutes 1922–34, "Minutes of Meeting of Ulu District Council, March 22, 1922," p. 2.

25. *LBEA,* September 3, 1921. In a faded photograph in the *Leader* only about a hundred people appear to be present.

26. KNA: NYI/9, Nyeri Political Record Book, I, "Events of 1922."

27. *LBEA,* October 29, 1921, p. 8.

28. *LBEA,* December 17, 1921, p. 12b. Two days earlier Thuku had written to the *East African Standard,* reporting on the resolutions taken at the Nov. 29 meeting. See *EAS* December 15, 1921.

29. Church Missionary Society Office, Nairobi: *Log Book of CMS Station at Weithaga,* p. 96.

30. *Papers relating to Native Disturbances in Kenya* (March 1922), Cmd. 1691, p. 5.

31. *LBEA*, April 1, 1922, p. 25.

32. *EAS*, March 16, 1922, p. 5, states that Thuku was arrested on March 14 at "his residence in Pangani."

33. Interview: Jesse Kariuki, April 6, 10, 1964.

34. Foran, *The Kenya Police*, p. 57.

35. See the Official Inquest Report printed in *LBEA*, April 1, 1922, p. 10, and *EAS*, April 1, 1922. Also KNA: R. W. Hemsted, "Short History of the Kikuyu Province 1911–1927," NYI/9, Nyeri Political Record Book. The evening of the fourteenth is also given as the date of the arrest in *Native Disturbances in Kenya*, Cmd. 1691, p. 8.

36. *EAS*, March 16, 1922, p. 5.

37. For the Indian meeting, see *LBEA*, March 18, 1922, p. 12a. The memorial was to Major Wavell, Commander of the Arab Rifles and a Muslim.

38. Foran, *The Kenya Police*, p. 57.

39. *LBEA*, April 1, 1922, p. 10.

40. *Native Disturbances in Kenya*, Cmd. 1691, p. 10.

41. Stated at the inquest into the subsequent violence; see *LBEA*, March 25, 1922, p. 19.

42. This figure is confirmed in *Native Disturbances in Kenya*, Cmd. 1691, p. 7.

43. Interview: Job Muchuchu, May 1964.

44. McGregor Ross, *Kenya from Within*, p. 233, states that at least 25 were killed or died of wounds.

45. *EAS*, April 1, 1922.

46. *EAS*, May 23, 1922; appeal of Abdullah R. Tairara against sentence of two years' imprisonment.

47. *LBEA*, September 3, 1921, copy of letter from Alfred Muthuri of CSM, Kikuyu, to D. C., Kyambu.

48. KNA: PC/CP 18/3/1, Political Deportees, "George Mugekeni-Deportee."

49. *EAS*, May 23, 1922.

50. Interview: Jesse Kariuki, April 6, 10, 1964.

51. *Native Disturbances in Kenya*, Cmd. 1691, p. 8.

52. *EAS*, August 11, 1923. *EAS* spelled his name as Karioki.

53. The new Government Swahili newspaper, *Habari*, had recently expressed some views on the marriage issue. The status of Kenya had been changed from Protectorate to Colony in 1920.

54. *EAS*, August 11, 1923.

55. *EAS*, March 25, 1922.

56. KNA: CN/51, Native Affairs, 1908–1922, letter from Acting Governor P. C., Kisumu, to D. C., Kisumu, October 19, 1917.

57. Rev. Canon H. K. Binns of the Church Missionary Society who started work in Mombasa in 1876.

58. Interview: James Beauttah, April 23, 1964.

59. For Basudde's further political activities, see F. B. Welbourn, *East African Rebels* (London, 1961), pp. 20–22.

60. *LBEA*, February 25, 1922, p. 12.

61. J. M. Lonsdale, "Archdeacon Owen and the Kavirondo Taxpayers Welfare Association," *Proceedings of the Conference of the East African Institute of Social Research*, 1963.

62. The meeting was called by the Provincial Commissioner; see *ibid.*

63. Nyanza Province Annual Report, 1922, quoted by Lonsdale, "Archdeacon Owen and the Kavirondo Taxpayers Welfare Association," pp. 1, 2.

64. *Native Labour Commission 1912–13. Evidence and Report.* Evidence of M. W. H. Beech, p. 75.

65. KNA: PC/NZA 3/31/1/2, Native Affairs North Kavirondo, quoted in letter from P. C., Nyanza, to Colonial Secretary, Nairobi, dated 6 July 1930.

66. *Kenya Law Reports,* Vol. IX Part II (1923), pp. 102–5. In this case Isaka Wainaina Gathomo and Kamau Gathomo filed an action for trespass against Murito Indangara and Ng'ang'a Munito on land alienated to a European settler but which they claimed was theirs.

67. Interview: James Beauttah, April 17, 23, 1964.

68. *Economic Commission Final Report, Part I* (1919), p. 22.

69. Huxley, *White Man's Country,* II, 126.

70. Quoted in Huxley, *White Man's Country,* II, 131.

71. George Bennett, *Kenya: A Political History: The Colonial Period* (London, 1963), p. 50.

72. Huxley, *White Man's Country,* II, 135.

73. Quotes that follow are from *ibid.,* pp. 135, 136.

74. *Ibid.,* p. 138.

75. The Earl of Lytton, *The Desert and the Green* (London, 1957), pp. 114–15.

76. See George Bennett, "Paramountcy to Partnership: J. H. Oldham and Africa," *Africa* (October 1960), p. 357. See also Oliver, *The Missionary Factor in East Africa,* pp. 260–63.

77. *Indians in Kenya: A Memorandum,* Cmd. 1922 (1923), p. 9.

78. *Report of the Land Settlement Commission,* 1919, p. 5. They also recommended the excision of the Wakamba and Suk Reserves.

CHAPTER 3

1. M. Sorrenson, "The Official Mind and Kikuyu Land Tenure, 1895–1939," *Proceedings of the Conference of the East African Institute of Social Research,* 1963, p. 4. For a more inclusive treatment of land policy in Kenya during the period 1895–1945, see his Appendix I to Vincent Harlow and E. M. Chilver, eds., *History of East Africa,* Vol. II (Oxford, 1965), pp. 672–89.

2. Fenner Brockway, *African Journeys* (London, 1955), pp. 87–88.

3. Kenya Ministry of Agriculture Archives: File on "Coffee Growing in African Areas."

4. The Church of Scotland Mission and the Church Missionary Society.

5. KNA: NYI/9, Nyeri Political Record Book.

6. *Ibid.*

7. *Ibid.,* p. 2.

8. *Ibid.,* p. 1. They were Swanson and J. MacDougall.

9. S. H. La Fontaine and J. H. Mower, *Local Government in Kenya: Its Origins and Development,* (Nairobi, 1955), p. 15.

10. KNA: DC/MKS 4/5–6, Machakos District Political Record Book, 1911–1914, III.

11. *KLC: Evidence,* I, 744.

12. Literally "son of a baboon."

13. KNA: KBU/63, "Chiefs' Character Book." See Karen Blixen, *Out of Africa* (London, 1954) for a description of Kinyanjui.

14. *KLC: Evidence,* I, 637.

15. KNA: KBU/63, "Chiefs' Character Book."

16. George Bennett, "Kenyatta and the Kikuyu," *International Affairs,* Vol. 37, No. 4 (October 1961) , p. 482.

17. *KLC: Evidence,* I, 378.

18. KNA: KBU/16, Kiambu District Annual Report, 1923. Also see *EAS,* June 7, 1923: Letter from Josiah Njonjo, Koinange Mbiu, and Philip Karanja James.

19. Sir Robert Coryndon, Legislative Council *Minutes of Proceedings* (May 15, 1924) , Session I, pp. 11, 12.

20. KNA: PC/CP, 8/5/1, Kikuyu Association 1921–1931, letter of January 12, 1928.

21. In 1931 the Association was still referred to as the Kikuyu Association: Chief Koinange's evidence before the *Joint Select Committee on Closer Union in East Africa: Minutes of Evidence,* II (1931) , p. 418; by 1932 the Association is referred to as Loyal Patriots Kikuyu and Loyal Kikuyu Patriots, and in 1933 as Kikuyu Loyal Patriots Association. *KLC: Evidence,* I, 128, 171, and 381.

22. See below, pp. 115–16.

23. 172 H. C. *Debates,* April 8, 1924, cols. 351–95.

24. Later Secretary of State for the Colonies and Lord Harlech.

25. Two other members were Major A.C. Church, D.S.O., M.C., M.P. (Labour) and Mr. F. C. Linfield, J. P., M. P. (Liberal) . The Report was published in 1925 as *Report of the East Africa Commission 1924,* Cmd. 2387 (1925) .

26. KNA: KBU/58, Land Tenure-Githaka System, "Memorandum presented by the Kikuyu Association, Kenya Colony, to the Members of the E. A. Commission, November, 1924."

27. *Ibid.*

28. *EAS,* June 7, 1923.

29. *Ibid.,* June 23, 1923.

30. Kenya Director of Education, quoted in Thomas Jesse Jones, *Education in East Africa* (New York, 1925) , pp. 124–25.

31. *Ibid.,* p. 124.

32. *EAS,* November 19, 1924. The NCU continued to function for some years. The D. C., South Kavirondo, in 1927 described the branch in his district as "non-political, orderly and entirely under the control of the Church." KNA: PC/NZA, 3/1/9, The Legislative Council Ordinance, 1919, letter from D. C., South Kavirondo, to P. C., Nyanza, December 31, 1927.

33. KNA. DC/NN 10/1/3, Political Associations, letter from Secretary of Native Catholic Union, Mumias to D. C., North Kavirondo, June 20, 1943.

34. "Memorandum of the Kavirondo Taxpayers Welfare Association to the Parliamentary Commission, 1924." See also Lonsdale, "Archdeacon Owen and the Kavirondo Taxpayers Association," in *Proceedings of the Conference of the East African Institute of Social Research,* 1963.

35. Interview: James Beauttah, April 17, 23, 1964.

36. *Memorandum of The Kikuyu Central Association, Fort Hall: To be presented to The Hilton Young Commission.* Printed in Nairobi by the Kikuyu Central Association. They stated the Association was founded in 1922 and had 3,000 members "on its rolls." See also *EAS,* January 14 and February 4, 1928.

37. Recorded minutes of proceedings of oral evidence given to the Hilton Young Commission, Colonial Office, London.

38. *Ibid.*

39. Letter of James Beauttah to Johnstone Kenyatta, September 24, 1926, in possession of Ambu H. Patel, Nairobi.

40. Kenyatta himself wrote a short life of Wangombe, entitled *My People of Kikuyu and the Life of Chief Wangombe* (published by the United Society for Christian Literature, London, 1944).

41. *EAS*, December 31, 1927, p. 56.

42. *Native Affairs Department Annual Report, 1926*, p. 13.

43. KNA: PC/NZA 3/1/9. The Legislative Council Ordinance, 1919, letter from D. C., North Kavirondo, to P. C., Ryanza, December 20, 1927.

44. Interview: James Beauttah, April 17, 23, 1964.

45. Interview: Joseph Kang'ethe, April 22, 23, 1964.

46. Kang'ethe was quickly dismissed from the Council. KNA: NYI/9, Nyeri Political Records, "Political Development 1925–27," memo by A. M. Champion.

47. KNA: PC/CP 8/5/2, Kikuyu Central Association, letter to Governor, December 31, 1925. See also *EAS*, January 2, 1926.

48. *Ibid.* Petition signed by Danieli Kamau, John Mbuthia, Henry Mwangi Gichuiri, James Njeroge, Abdullah Tairara, Henry D. Maturukia, Petro Njuguna Kigondu, Joseph Kang'ethe.

49. KNA: PC/CP 8/5/2, Kikuyu Central Association, letter to Governor, December 31, 1925.

50. KNA: NYI/9, Nyeri Political Records.

51. KNA: PC/CP 4/1/2, Kikuyu Province Annual Reports, 1927.

52. KNA: PC/CP 4/1/2, Kikuyu Province Annual Reports, 1928.

53. Interview: Joseph Kang'ethe, April 22, 23, 1964.

54. Interview: Marius Ng'ang'a Karatu, January 6, 1964.

55. Kapenguria Trial, Verbatim Transcript, p. 998.

56. Interview: Joseph Kang'ethe, April 22, 23, 1964.

57. Translated by Gabriel Gathendu, 1963.

58. See Bennett, "Development of Political Organizations in Kenya," in *Political Studies*, Vol. V, No. 2 (1957), p. 121, when he quotes the approval of *Muigwithania* by the Chief Native Commissioner.

59. KNA: (G.H.) –64 III, "Records of Interviews with His Excellency," fol. 2. See *The Times*, February 21, 1929, for reference to his departure.

60. This petition was printed as pamphlet together with some other KCA items and the Secretary of State's answer: *Correspondence between KCA and the Colonial Office, 1929–1930.*

61. George Delf, *Jomo Kenyatta: Towards Truth About 'The Light of Kenya'* (London, 1961), pp. 70–71.

62. Interview: Jesse Kariuki, April 6, 10, 1964.

63. Interview: James Beauttah, April 17, 1964, and *Report and Constitution: Kikuyu Independent Schools Association* (Nyeri, 1938), p. 3.

CHAPTER 4

1. Canon H. J. Butcher, "Memorandum on Spheres and Alliances," Presbyterian Church of East Africa, General Secretary's Office, Nairobi (hereafter: PCEA, Nairobi).

2. Evidence of Mr. W. P. Knapp, in *KLC: Evidence*, I, 772.

3. *Kenya 1898–1948*, pamphlet published by Church of Scotland Foreign

Mission Committee, p. 19. Between 1914 and 1944 there was a remarkable growth of the Christian Church in Kenya, with about 8 per cent of the population Christians in 1938. See Roland Oliver, *The Missionary Factor in East Africa* (London, 1952), pp. 234–35.

4. *Ibid.*, p. 225.

5. Quoted in Rev. M. G. Capon, *Towards Unity in Kenya* (Nairobi, 1962), p. 16.

6. "Minutes of a Meeting of the Representative Council of the Alliance of Missionary Societies in Kenya Colony, held 31 August and 1 and 2 September 1922," quoted in *ibid.*, p. 28.

7. "Minutes of a Meeting of the Representative Council, 25 to 27 April 1921," p. 3 (PCEA, Nairobi).

8. Quoted in F. B. Welbourn, *East African Rebels* (London, 1961), p. 128.

9. Capon, *Towards Unity in Kenya*, p. 27.

10. "Minutes of the Meeting of a Conference of Representatives of Native Churches in Southern Kikuyuland, held at the Church of Scotland Mission, Kikuyu, July 5 and 6, 1916," p. 3 (PCEA, Nairobi).

11. KNA: DC/MKS 10B/12/1, Circumcision of Women, Circular No. 36 (September 21, 1925).

12. The North Kavirondo Local Native Council led the way in 1925.

13. *Conference of Governors of the East African Dependencies 1926: Summary of Proceedings*, p. 20.

14. Statement made by Dr. H. R. A. Philp before the Committee for the Protection of Coloured Women in the Crown Colonies, 10 April 1930; file on Female Mutilation, KCA, and other Native Political Matters, 1929–30 (PCEA, Nairobi).

15. H. R. A. Philp, "Native Gynaecology," *The Journal of the Kenya Medical Service*, vol. I, no. 8 (January 1924), pp. 3, 4; and "Artificial Atresia in Kikuyu Women," *Kenya Medical Journal*, vol. II, no. 3 (June 1925), pp. 86, 87.

16. Interview: Willy Jimmy Wambugu Maina, May 1964. They were Maina himself, Meshak Matu, Joseph Kanua, Gideon Michuki, Ezekiel Kobora, Grishon Watitu, and Simeon Wambugu.

17. In 1921 the custom was forbidden in "Laws of the Native Church (Church of Scotland)."

18. Statement made by Dr. H. R. A. Philp . . . , p. 9.

19. *Ibid.*, p. 10.

20. Church of Scotland, *Memorandum prepared by the Kikuyu Mission Council on Female Circumcision* (Kikuyu, 1931), p. 27, 31. Hereafter: CSM, *Memorandum*.

21. Quotes are from the Statement made by Dr. H. R. A. Philp . . . file on Female Mutilation (PCEA, Nairobi).

22. KNA: NYI/9 Nyeri Political Record Book, Section H.

23. *Ibid.*

24. *Paper relating to the Question of the Closer Union of Kenya, Uganda, and Tanganyika Territory*, col. 57 (1931), p. 14.

25. "Minutes of a Conference of Kikuyu Church Elders, held at Tumutumu from March 8 to 12, 1929," p. 2, file on Female Mutilation (PCEA, Nairobi).

26. Kiambu D. C.'s Court Criminal Case No. 1 of 1929. See KNA: DC/MKS 10B/12/1, Circumcision of Women, Memorandum on "The Political Situation" by D. C., Kiambu, January 12, 1930.

27. CSM, *Memorandum*, p. 42.

28. *Ibid.*, p. 42; see also *EAS*, February 8, 1930.
29. KNA: DC/MKS 10B/12/1, letter to CNC, Nairobi, October 1, 1929.
30. Interview: Ng'ang'a Ngoro, January 28, 1964.
31. L. S. B. Leakey, "The Kikuyu Problem of the Initiation of Girls," *The Journal of the Royal Arthropological Institute of Great Britain and Ireland,* vol. LXI, 1931 (January to June), p. 279. In 1924 the whole New Testament appeared for the first time.
32. Arthur, "Safari Diary," file on Female Mutilation (PCEA, Nairobi).
33. KNA: DC/MKS 10B/12/1, D. C., Kiambu, Memorandum on "The Political Situation," January 12, 1930.
34. CSM, *Memorandum,* Appendix V.
35. "The Crisis at Kikuyu." Typewritten article written by J. W. Arthur, dated November 17, 1929, p. 9. Also KNA: DC/MKS 10B/12/1: D. C., Kiambu, Memorandum on "The Political Situation," 12 January 1930.
36. CSM, *Memorandum,* p. 47.
37. "The Crisis at Kikuyu," p. 10.
38. *The Times,* February 27, 1930, p. 13.
39. "Letter from the Bishop of Mombasa to all the Clergy and Members of Pastorate Committees in the Diocese, 12 October 1931;" file on Female Mutilation (PCEA, Nairobi).
40. *KLC: Evidence,* I, 1100.
41. *Native Affairs Department Annual Report 1930,* p. 4.
42. *KLC: Evidence,* I, 1100.
43. Interview: Johanna Karanja, April 1964.
44. *Report and Constitution: Kikuyu Independent Schools Association* (Nyeri, 1938), p. 3. It is here stated that KISA was established in 1929.
45. Welbourn, *East African Rebels,* p. 147.
46. "Presbytery of Kenya: Minutes of Meeting of 25 September 1934, regarding relations with the Independent Schools;" file on Female Mutilation (PCEA, Nairobi).
47. Interviews: Johanna Kunyiha, December 1960, and Willy Jimmy Wambugu Maina, May 1964.
48. "Confidential Circular to the Members of the Allied Missions from the Bishop of Mombasa, dated 4 January 1935;" file on Female Mutilation (PCEA, Nairobi).
49. See Welbourn, *East African Rebels,* pp. 77–102, for an excellent account of Reuben Spartas' leadership in the development of the African Greek Orthodox Church in Uganda.
50. Interview: James Beauttah, April 17, 23, 1964.
51. Welbourn, *East African Rebels,* p. 238, n. 9.
52. George Delf, *Jomo Kenyatta,* pp. 99–100.
53. Jomo Kenyatta, *Facing Mount Kenya* (London, 1938), p. xviii.
54. *Ibid.*, p. 153.
55. *Ibid.*, p. 133.
56. *Kikuyu News,* September 1938, pp. 175–76 (PCEA, Nairobi).
57. KNA: DC/MKS 10B/12/1, D. C., Kiambu, Memorandum on "The Political Situation," January 12, 1930.

CHAPTER 5

1. *Joint Committee on Closer Union in East Africa, Minutes of Evidence,* H. C. Paper 156, II (1931), 254.
2. See Lord Altrincham, *Kenya's Opportunity: Memories, Hopes and Ideas*

(London, 1955), pp. 106, 278–83; also *Speeches by His Excellency, Lieut. Colonel Sir E. W. M. Grigg, 1925–1930* (Nairobi, n.d.), pp. 338–39.

3. Quoted in Delf, *Jomo Kenyatta* (London, 1961), pp. 72–73, a letter to *The Times* (London), March 26, 1930.

4. *Ibid.*

5. KNA: PC/CP 18/3/2; Political and Other Deportees, "Minutes of Meeting held on 19 January 1931 at the camp of Chief Waruhiu." Present were the P. C., the D. C., Waruhiu, Thuku, and Waiganjo.

6. See *EAS*, May 27, 1933; also, Interview: Harry Thuku, October 31, 1963.

7. Lord Hailey, *Native Administration and Political Development in British Tropical Africa, 1940–42* (London, Colonial Office), p. 221.

8. *Rules and Regulations of the Kikuyu Provincial Association* (Nairobi, 1939), p. 2.

9. On November 23, 1939, the D. C., Kiambu, wrote that the KPA "was founded after Harry Thuku had quarrelled with the Kikuyu Central Association. I have heard it stated that the quarrel took place because he disagreed with their anti-government policy. This may be partly true but I should imagine the real truth was that he preferred to be No. 1 in his own association." The D. C. said that the KPA seemed to have little influence in Kiambu. See KNA: PC/CP 8/5/6 Kikuyu Provincial Association, letter of D. C. Kiambu to P. C. Nyeri, November 23, 1939.

10. KNA: PC/CP 8/5/6 Kikuyu Provincial Association; letter from Thuku to District Commissioners, Fort Hall, Nyeri, and Embu, Feb. 8, 1941. For a discussion of these measures, see below, pp. 163–64, 237–8.

11. *Ibid.,* letter dated September 30, 1941.

12. Kenya Govt. Library: "Handing Over Report, Kiambu District, H. E. Lambert to W. Perreau, 23/10/43."

13. Parmenas Githendu Mockerie, *An African Speaks For His People* (London, 1934), pp. 11 ff.

14. *Muigwithania*, Vol. IV, No. 5 (May 1931).

15. *Joint Committee on Closer Union*, II, 404.

16. *Ibid.*, p. 418.

17. KNA: PC/CP 8/5/1; Kikuyu Association 1921–1931, fol. 16.

18. *Joint Select Committee on Closer Union in East Africa, Report*, I, (1931), 73–74.

19. *Correspondence (1931–1932) arising from the Report of the Joint Select Committee on Closer Union in East Africa*, (1932), p. 30. See also Kenya Legislative Council *Debates* (24 April 1934), I, 79–80.

20. *Correspondence (1931–1932)*, p. 55.

21. See George Bennett, "Imperial Paternalism: The Representation of African Interests in the Kenya Legislative Council," in Kenneth Robinson and Frederick Madden, eds., *Essays in Imperial Government* (Oxford, 1963), pp. 141–69.

22. *East Africa Royal Commission 1953–1955: Report*, Cmd. 9475 (1955), p. 53.

23. *Report of the Land Commission of 1925* (Salisbury, Government Printer, 1926), p. 4, quoted in the *Second Report of the Select Committee on Resettlement of Natives to the Southern Rhodesian Legislative Assembly* (Salisbury, Government Printer, 1960).

24. See *KLC: Evidence*, I, 147, for evidence of Ng'ang'a Ngoro as a "representative of the Kikuyu Land Board Association."

25. Interview: Ng'ang'a Ngoro, January 28, 1964.

26. J. E. Goldthorpe, *Outlines of East African Society* (Kampala, 1958), p. 58.

27. *Native Land Tenure in Kikuyu Province, Report of Committee* (November 1929), p. 17.

28. John Middleton, *The Kikuyu and Kamba of Kenya*, Ethnographic Survey of Africa (London, 1953), p. 35.

29. Kenyatta, *Facing Mount Kenya*, p. 198.

30. A. H. J. Prins, *East African Age-Class Systems* (Djakarta, 1953), p. 52.

31. Kenyatta, *Facing Mount Kenya*, p. 103.

32. *Ibid.*, p. 115.

33. Prins, *East African Age-Class Systems*, p. 100.

34. *Ibid.*, pp. 100–01; Kenyatta, *Facing Mount Kenya*, pp. 157–58.

35. See L. S. B. Leakey, *Mau Mau and the Kikuyu* (London, 1953), p. 35.

36. Middleton, *The Kikuyu and Kamba of Kenya*, p. 37.

37. Lucy Mair, *Primitive Government* (London, 1962), p. 100.

38. Prins, *East African Age-Class Systems*, p. 125.

39. Dr. H. A. Boedeker in *KLC: Evidence*, I, 708.

40. John Patterson in *KLC: Evidence*, I, 746.

41. An exception was Mervyn H. Beech, "Kikuyu System of Land Tenure," *Journal of the African Society* (1917), pp. 44–59, 136–44.

42. In Civil Case No. 576 of 1919 and Civil Case No. 132 of 1920, quoted in the Memorandum by the Commissioner of Lands in *KLC: Evidence*, p. 32.

43. *KLC: Evidence*, I, p. 55.

44. George Bennett, *Kenya: A Political History*, pp. 23–24.

45. Quoted in *Ibid.*, *Correspondence relating to the Tenure of Land in the East Africa Protectorate*, Cd.4117 (1908), p. 33, Elgin to Sadler, 19 March 1908.

46. These were:
   (a) The Kenya (Highlands) Order in Council, 1939, which set up the Highlands Board and defined boundaries of the Highlands.
   (b) The Kenya (Native Areas) Order in Council, 1939, which set up the Native Lands Trust Board, eliminated "Crown Land" definition.
   (c) The Native Lands Trust Ordinance, 1938 (No. 28), which defined all lands found to be native lands by reason of historic right. Section 70 provided for the extinguishing of all native rights in the White Highlands.
   (d) The Crown Lands (Amendment) Ordinance, 1938 (No. 27), which made provision for other areas to be Native Reserves, temporary Native Reserves, and Native Leasehold Areas.
   (e) The Crown Lands (Amendment) Ordinance, 1942 (No. 19), which set up Native Settlement Areas—Olenguruone, Kichuini, Digo, and Gedi.
   (f) The Land Control Ordinance, 1944 (No. 22), which set up the Highlands Board.
   (g) Resident Labourers Ordinance, 1937 (No. 30), as amended by No. 18 of 1939 and No. 38 of 1941, which gave District Councils in the Highlands powers to control laborers on farms.

47. Kenya Legislative Council *Debates* (19 October 1934), II, 608.

48. *EAS*, June 16, 1934, pp. 34, 35. Letter from J. M. Kamau.

49. Kenya Legislative Council *Debates* (19 October 1934), II, 595, 596.

50. *KLC: Evidence*, III, 2169.

51. *Ibid.*, pp. 2144–47.

52. Günter Wagner, *The Bantu of North Kavirondo* (London, 1956), II, p. 175, for a discussion of the North Kavirondo Chamber of Commerce.

53. KNA: NN/32, January 4, 1941, a letter from Police to District Commissioner, North Nyanza.

54. *Ibid.*, March 18, 1937, D. C., North Nyanza, to P. C., Kisumu.

55. *Ibid.*, "An English translation made at the Kaimosi Mission of the North Kavirondo Central Association pamphlet entitled 'Avaluhya'-'kinship.'"

56. Lord Hailey, *Native Administration and Political Development in British Tropical Africa*, p. 221.

57. Kenya Legislative Council *Debates* (21 April 1939), cols. 284–87.

58. Kenya Land Department: LND 30/11/–40.

59. *The Times*, February 27, 1930, p. 13.

60. KNA: DC/MKS 4/9, Machakos District Political Record, vol. VII, 1930–1938, p. 3.

61. *Report of the Kenya Land Commission*, para. 743.

62. *EAS*, August 5, 1938, and August 8, 1938.

63. *Ibid.*, August 20, 1938.

64. "Overstocking in Kenya," *The East African Agricultural Journal*, vol. I (July 1935), p. 18.

65. *Ibid.*, p. 16.

66. Kenya Legislative Council *Debates* (24 October 1934), II, 679.

67. *Ibid.*

68. "Land Usage and Soil Erosion in Africa," Supplement to the *Journal of The Royal African Society* (January 1938), p. 11.

69. KNA: DC/MKS 14/3/2, Machakos District Agricultural Gazeteer, p. 10.

70. Kenya Legislative Council *Debates* (16 April 1930), I, 330.

71. *Report of the Kenya Land Commission*, para. 2040.

72. "Overstocking in Kenya: II—Overstocking in Native Reserves and Disposal of Surplus Stock," *The East African Agricultural Journal*, vol. I (January 1936).

73. Colin Maher, *Soil Erosion and Land Utilization in the Ukamba Reserve (Machakos)*. 1937 (Report in the Library of the Ministry of Agriculture, Nairobi.)

74. C.A.C. 345, Colonial Office, July 1937.

75. *Report of the Kenya Land Commission*, para. 761.

76. *EAS*, April 22, 1939.

77. *Ibid.*, October 19, 1938.

78. KNA: DC/MKS 4/9, Machakos District Political Record, vol. VII, 1930–1938, p. 85. Typed copy of Governor's speech, 14 July 1937.

79. *Department of Agriculture, Annual Report* (1938), p. 66.

80. KNA: DC/MKS 14/3/2, Machakos District Agricultural Gazeteer, p. 16.

81. Quoted in *Department of Agriculture: Annual Report* (1938), p. 67.

82. *EAS*, August 20, 1938.

83. KNA: DC/MKS 10B/15/1, fol. 8, 9, Destocking Campaign and General Correspondence on Political Affairs," 1938–39. Also Kenya Legislative Council

Debates (17 August 1938), cols. 230–33, where Isher Dass quotes the petition in full.

84. *Manchester Guardian,* May 26, July 2, July 13, August 11, October 1, 1938. He also used the correspondence columns of the "New Statesman."

85. Quoted in *Ibid.,* May 26, 1938. It is also reproduced in KNA: DC/MKS 10B/15/1, fol. 9, Destocking Campaign and General Correspondence on Political Affairs, 1938–39.

86. KNA: DC/MKS 10B/15/1, fol. 12, Destocking Campaign and General Correspondence on Political Affairs, 1938–39.

87. *EAS,* August 20, 1938.

88. *Manchester Guardian,* July 2, 1938; letter from Jomo Kenyatta.

89. KNA: DC/MKS 10B/15/1, fol. 14.

90. *Ibid.,* fol. 38.

91. *Muigwithania,* Vol. I, No. 2 (June 1938), pp. 15–16, published a letter from Samuel Muindi and two others to the President of KCA appealing for help.

92. *EAS,* August 6, 1938.

93. Hailey, *Native Administration and Political Development in British Tropical Africa, 1940–42,* p. 221.

94. KNA: DC/MKS 4/9, "Handing Over Report, Machakos District, A. N. Bailward to D. O. Brumage" (no date), fol. 18.

95. Quoted in *EAS,* September 30, 1938.

96. Kenya Legislative Council *Debates* (August 17, 1938), cols. 229–41.

97. *EAS,* August 1, 1938.

98. *Ibid.,* August 18, 1938.

99. *Ibid.,* August 20, 1938.

100. *Ibid.,* August 27, 1938.

101. *Ibid.,* September 9, 1938.

102. KNA: DC/MKS 10B/15/1, fol. 35.

103. *Ibid.,* fol. 37.

104. *Department of Agriculture: Annual Report* (1938), p. 67.

105. *African Affairs Department: Annual Report, 1953,* p. 123.

106. KNA: Coast Section 108/63, Taita Hills Association and Taita Lands, letter from D. C., Voi, to P. C., Mombasa, May 23, 1942.

107. Evidence of W. Slade-Hawkins in *KLC: Evidence,* III, 2793.

108. *Ibid.,* p. 2770, evidence of Dr. D. Bell.

109. *Report of the Kenya Land Commission,* para. 1277.

110. *Report of the Kenya Land Commission,* para. 1265.

111. *KLC: Evidence,* III, 2722.

112. KNA: Coast Section, 108/63, letter from D. C., Voi, to P. C., Mombasa, dated May 23, 1942.

113. *Ibid.*

114. *Ibid.*

115. Kenya Legislative Council *Debates* (14 September 1943), XVII, col. 6, 7.

116. *Annual Report of the Commissioner of Lands and Settlement, 1938,* p. 4.

117. *Annual Report on Native Affairs,* 1938, p. 14; also H. E. Lambert, *Kikuyu Social and Political Institutions* (London, 1956), p. 100.

118. Ralph J. Bunche, "The Land Equation in Kenya," *Journal of Negro History* (January 1939), pp. 33–43.

119. Kenya Land Department: LND 39/11/3, letter dated 7 May 1939.
120. Interview: Ng'ang'a Ngoro, May 11, 1964.
121. *EAS*, January 16, 1939, letter by Andrew Gathea, secretary of the Kenya African Teachers College.
122. Interview: Gathuri Chege, November 1963, paraphrased in part. The fig tree obliged in 1963, having been propped up by the Thika Town Council for a few years.
123. See *Report of the Commission of Inquiry appointed to Examine the Labour Conditions in Mombasa*, 1939, hereafter referred to as *Mombasa Labour Report 1939*, p. 35; and KNA: Coast Section 106/58, "Evidence: Mombasa Labour Commission of Inquiry," p. 273.
124. *Mombasa Labour Report 1939*, p. 36.
125. *Ibid.*, p. 37.
126. *Ibid.*, p. 60.
127. *Ibid.*, p. 5.
128. *Ibid.*, p. 4.
129. *Ibid.*, p. 6.
130. *Ibid.*, p. 8.
131. *Ibid.*, pp. 8, 9.
132. KNA: Coast Section, 106/58; "Evidence: Mombasa Labour Commission of Inquiry," pp. 199, 202; quoted from p. 194; for his demands, see p. 195.
133. *Proclamations, Rules and Regulations*, 1939, Government Notice No. 660, p. 526.
134. Kenya Government Library: "Handing Over Report, Central Province," S. H. La Fontaine to C. Tomkinson (1940), p. 2.
135. *Ibid.*
136. *EAS*, June 5, 1940.
137. Interview: Marius Ng'ang'a Karatu, 6 January 1964.
138. KNA: WP/3, West Suk District Annual Report, 1942.
139. KNA: DC/FHI/18, 19, 20, Annual Report, 1939; 1940; 1941.

CHAPTER 6

1. Government Notice No. 465 of 1940 (P.R.R., p. 441), dated May 31, 1940.
2. *EAS*, June 1, 1940.
3. *Report on Native Affairs, 1939–1945*, p. 3. Following the suggestion by Chief Njiiri, a sum sufficient to purchase two Spitfires for the Royal Air Force was contributed from the reserve funds of the Local Native Councils of Central Province.
4. Interview: James Beauttah, April 23, 1964.
5. Quoted in Delf, *Jomo Kenyatta*, p. 118.
6. Kapenguria Trial, Verbatim Transcript, p. 996.
7. *Report on Native Affairs, 1939–1945*, p. 58; but see *Manpower, Demobilization and Reabsorption, Report—1945*, p. 6, where it is estimated that the total number recruited for the army from Kenya was 97,000.
8. Lt. Col. H. Moyse-Bartlett, *The King's African Rifles*, p. 685.
9. *Report of the Sub-Committee on Post-War Employment of Africans, 1943*, p. 4.
10. Interview: Waruhiu Itote, November, 1963, and his *'Mau Mau' General* (Nairobi, 1966).

11. Interview: Bildad Kaggia, October 31, 1963.

12. Kapenguria Trial, Verbatim Transcript, pp. 1707 ff.

13. Interview: Dedan Mugo Kimani, January 4, 1964.

14. *Report of the Sub-Committee on Post-War Employment of Africans, 1943*, pp. 5–6.

15. Quoted in *Report on Native Affairs, 1939–1945*, p. 59.

16. This phrase is taken from the title *White Man's Country* by Elspeth Huxley.

17. *EAS*, March 27, 1944.

18. *EAS*, March 24, March 31, 1944.

19. Electors' Union, *Outline of Policy*, p. 22.

20. Sir Philip Mitchell, *African Afterthoughts* (London, 1954), pp. 219–20.

21. *Ibid.*, p. 220.

22. *Ibid.*, p. 223.

23. *Ibid.*, p. 276 (from a speech made by Sir Philip Mitchell in 1947 to the Nairobi Rotary Club).

24. *Ibid.*, p. 219.

25. *Report of the Commission Appointed to Enquire into and Report on the Financial Position and System of Taxation of Kenya*, Colonial No. 116 (1936), pp. 70–78.

26. *Proposals for the Reorganization of the Administration of Kenya*, Sessional Paper No. 3 (Nairobi, 1945).

27. *African Afterthoughts*, p. 221.

28. *East Africa Royal Commission 1953–1955: Report*, Cmd. 9475 (1955), p. 460.

29. *Labour Department Annual Report, 1952*, p. 6.

30. *Report of the Committee on African Wages* (Nairobi, 1954), p. 33.

31. *Ibid.*, p. 32.

32. *Memorandum on Native Agricultural Development in the Native Reserves* (Kenya Department of Agriculture, n.d.), p. 3.

33. *Ibid.*

34. Kenya Legislative Council *Debates* (25 September 1946), vol. XXV, col. 64.

35. *East Africa Royal Commission, 1953–1955: Report*, p. 478.

36. S. V. Cooke; see Kenya Legislative Council *Debates* (19 January 1950), vol. XXXV, col. 971.

37. Kenya Govt. Library: "Post-War Five Year Development Plan, Central Province," p. 22.

38. *KNA:* Ministry of Agriculture Section. COFF/2/2/2. Vol. III–Coffee: Cultivation by Natives: Central Province. Arabica, fol. 11, 13.

39. *Ibid.*

40. City Council of Nairobi, *African Affairs Department Report, 1952.*

41. Mary Parker, *Political and Social Aspects of the Development of Municipal Government in Kenya with Special Reference to Nairobi* (Colonial Office, n.d.), p. 22.

42. *Labour Department Annual Report, 1947*, p. 15.

43. *Ibid.*, p. 16.

44. Interview: Chege Kibachia, April 1964.

45. *EAS*, April 21, 1947, Report on Strikes in Kisii and Kisumu.

46. *Labour Department Annual Report, 1947*, p. 14.

47. Parker, *Municipal Government*, p. 22.

48. The Supreme Court upheld this view. See KNA: KBU/43, **Kiambu** District Annual Report 1952, p. 1.

49. Kenya Government Library: "Minutes of the Executive Council," July to December 1939, p. 141.

50. Kenya Legislative Council *Debates* (19 January 1950), vol. XXXV, col. 987.

51. Mitchell, *African Afterthoughts*, p. 258.

52. Kenya Land Department: LND. 30/11/3/1. Letter to Creech-Jones, M.P., Secretary of State for the Colonies, 11 February, 1947.

53. Interview: James S. Gichuru, October 25, 1963.

54. Lord Hailey, *Native Administration and Political Development*, p. 221.

55. Mitchell, *African Afterthoughts*, p. 259.

56. *The Times*, December 4, 1948. See also "Communism in Kenya: Note by Governor," (n.d.-1949?) in possession of Joseph Murumbi, M.P.

57. Interview: Oginga Odinga, August 1957. See also *Baraza*, Nairobi's major Swahali paper, between 1947–52 for reports of numerous KAU meetings held by Kenyatta throughout Kenya.

58. *Report on Native Affairs, 1939–1945*, p. 3.

59. Kenya Government Library: "North Kavirondo Handing Over Reports, K. L. Hunter to P. J. de Bromhead (30 December 1942)," p. 2.

60. *Ibid.*, L. E. Whitehouse to C. H. Williams (1946), p. 2.

61. Kenya Legislative Council *Debates* (19 January 1950), vol. XXXV, col. 976.

62. *Ibid.*

63. Kenya Land Department: LND 30/11/3/1, Letter to Creech-Jones, M.P., Secretary of State for the Colonies, 11 February 1947.

64. *Inter-Territorial Organization in East Africa*, Colonial No. 191 (1945).

65. Mitchell, *African Afterthoughts*, pp. 219–21.

66. Letter from C. E. V. Buxton in *EAS*, April 11, 1947.

67. *Inter-Territorial Organization in East Africa, Revised Proposals*, Colonial No. 210 (1947).

68. *EAS*, August 8, 1947.

69. Kenya Land Department: LND 30/11/3/1, II. See also Mbiyu Koinange with Achieng Oneko, *Land Hunger in Kenya* (London: U. D. C. Publication, 1952).

70. Kenya Legislative Council *Debates* (10 May 1951), vol. XLII, cols. 66–67.

71. Fenner Brockway, *African Journeys* (London 1955), p. 89.

72. *EAS*, January 27, 1950.

73. Kenya Land Department: LND 30/11/3/1, II. Comments by Government on *Land Hunger in Kenya*, a pamphlet by Mbiyu Koinange in collaboration with Achieng Oneko.

74. *EAS*, January 27, 1950, p. 6.

75. *Ibid.*, June 16, 1950.

76. *Ibid.*, April 24, 1950. See also *The Times*, April 25, 1950.

77. Kenya Legislative Council *Debates* (17 May 1950), vol. XXXVII, col. 166.

78. 482 H.C. *Debates* 55, (13 December 1950), cols. 1167–69.

79. *EAS*, February 16, 1951.

80. *The Times*, March 5, 1951.

81. *EAS*, March 2, 1951.
82. *EAS*, June 1, 1951.

CHAPTER 7

1. *Department of Agriculture: Annual Report, 1940*, p. 4.
2. V. A. Beckley and Violet E. Notley, "Drying of Vegetables," *The East African Agricultural Journal* (July 1941) , p. 6.
3. This information is from the *Department of Agriculture: Annual Report*, for the years 1941; 1943; 1944; and 1946, p. 11.
4. *Labor Conditions in East Africa*, Colonial No. 193 (1946). Report by Major G. St. J. Orde Brown, p. 23.
5. Elspeth Huxley, *The Sorcerer's Apprentice* (London, 1948) , p. 349.
6. *Ibid.*, pp. 349–50.
7. Kenya Govt. Library: *"Nyeri Provincial Handing-Over Report* (25 August 1946) ," p. 1. For account of the final public meeting at Karatina see *Baraza*, February 22, 1947.
8. *EAS*, Feb. 3, 1947.
9. Kenya Legislative Council *Debates* (8 January 1948) , col. 684 ff.
10. *Ibid*.
11. The first upcountry African trade union to be registered; see *Labour Department Annual Report, 1946*, p. 15. There were a number of other "unofficial unions"—workers' associations.
12. Interview: James Beauttah, April 23, 1964.
13. We are indebted to David Koff for his suggestions in the above paragraphs.
14. Interview: Charles Wambaa, January 15, 16, 1964.
15. Interview: Dedan Mugo Kimani, January 4, 1964.
16. Kenya Govt. Library: "A Discussion of the Problems of the Squatter," Labour Commissioner, February 1946.
17. *Native Labour Commission, 1912–1913. Evidence and Report* (Nairobi, n.d.) , p. 328.
18. The Resident Natives (Squatters) Ordinance, 1918 (No. 33). This was replaced by the Resident Native Labourers Ordinance, 1925 (No. 5).
19. Sir Philip Mitchell, *The Agrarian Problem in Kenya* (Nairobi, 1948) , p. 19.
20. Kenya Govt. Library: "Post-War Five Year Development Plan," Central Province, p. 3.
21. *Native Affairs Department Annual Report, 1935*, p. 163.
22. *Report of the Kenya Land Commission*, p. 466.
23. *Ibid.*, p. 467.
24. *Ibid.*, p. 468.
25. *Ibid.*, p. 379.
26. Kenya Legislative Council *Debates* (14 December 1936) , II, 775.
27. *Native Affairs Department Annual Report, 1933*, p. 109.
28. *Native Affairs Department Annual Report, 1936*, p. 162.
29. *Native Affairs Department Annual Report, 1938*, p. 89.
30. Kenya Govt. Library: "Minutes of the Executive Council," January to July 1939, p. 25.
31. Kenya Govt. Library: *"Handing Over Report,* May 1940, S. H. La Fontaine, P.C., Nyeri," p. 2.
32. The Crown Lands (Amendment) Ordinance, 1942 (No. 19).

33. KNA: NKU/23, Olenguruone, "Memorandum from Acting Native Courts Officer to Chief Native Commissioner, dated 8.3.50."

34. See below, Chapter VIII.

35. Samuel Koina: Interview, January 1, 1964.

36. *Ibid.*

37. *EAS*, May 1, 1946.

38. KNA: NKU/23 Olenguruone, Letter from Settlement Officer to D. C., Nakuru, dated 21.3.50.

39. KNA: NKU/34, Nakuru District Annual Report, 1949, p. 23.

40. Kenya Govt. Library: "Resident Native Labour Problem in Kenya, Revised Draft Statement of Policy discussed by the Ad Hoc Committee Appointed under the chairmanship of Major the Hon. F. W. Cavendish-Bentinck on the 9th September 1947."

41. KNA: PC/RVP, 6A/1/17/2. Olenguruone, fol. 98A.

42. KNA: NKU/23 Olenguruone, "Letter from Settlement Officer to D. C., Nakuru, dated 21.3.50."

43. Interview: Kinuthia Mugia, April 8, 1964.

44. Kenya Legislative Council *Debates* (27 November 1947), col. 520.

45. *EAS*, May 3, 1950.

46. "The Minutes of a Meeting of the Christian Council on Race Relations held at Bishopsbourne, Nairobi, on 20th July, 1938," File 6, 5/A, Christian Council on Race Relations, CCK Offices, Nairobi.

47. Interview: Sir Charles E. Mortimer, December 1, 1964.

48. *African Education in Kenya: Report of a Committee Appointed to Inquire into the Scope, Content and Methods of African Education, its Administration and Finance, and to Make Recommendations, 1949.*

49. Interview: Fred Kubai, October 19, 1963.

50. Interview: Eliud Mutonyi, January 22, 1964.

51. Interview: Eliud Mutonyi, December 27, 1963; Mutonyi was chairman of the Central Committee.

52. *Facing Mount Kenya*, p. 294.

53. *Ibid.*, p. 323.

CHAPTER 8

1. Proclamation No. 38 of 1952, Kenya Proclamations, Rules and Regulations, 1952, p. 490.

2. Title of Chap. 13 in Sir Philip Mitchell's *African Afterthoughts*.

3. *Historical Survey of the Origins and Growth of Mau Mau*, Cmnd. 1030 (1960), pp. 274–75.

4. Kapenguria Trial, Verbatim Transcript, Supreme Court Archives (Nairobi), p. 381.

5. *Judicial Department Annual Report, 1952.*

6. Kapenguria Trial, Verbatim Transcript, p. 11. For an excellent account, see Montagu Slater, *The Trial of Jomo Kenyatta* (London, 1955).

7. Kapenguria Trial, Verbatim Transcript, p. 10.

8. *Ibid.*, p. 931.

9. *Ibid.*, Charge Sheets.

10. *Ibid.*

11. *Ibid.*, pp. 1293, 1294.

12. *Ibid.*, p. 8.

13. *Ibid.*, p. 2063.

14. *Ibid.*, p. 176.

15. Kapenguria Trial, Judgement, p. 7.

16. *Ibid.*, p. 111.

17. *Ibid.*, p. 99.

18. *Ibid.*, p. 103.

19. Kapenguria Trial, Verbatim Transcript, p. 1298.

20. *Ibid.*, p. 1296.

21. Press Office Handout No. 1217 (October 20, 1955). "Kenya Government's Rehabilitation Programme," p. 5.

22. Sir Philip Mitchell, "Mau Mau," in C. Groves Haines, ed., *Africa Today* (Baltimore, 1955), p. 490.

23. *Report of the Kenya Land Commission*, p. 115.

24. *Ibid.*, pp. 115–16.

25. *Ibid.*, p. 116.

26. *Ibid.*, pp. 117–18.

27. Interview: Marius Ng'ang'a Karatu, January 6, 1964.

28. *Ibid.*

29. *Labour Department Annual Report, 1952*, p. 11.

30. Interview: Daniel Mwangi Kego, January 21 and May 1964.

31. *History of the Loyalists: A Tribute to the Tribal Police, African Guards and All Loyalists of the Kikuyu, Embu and Miru tribes who resisted the Mau Mau Revolt* (Nairobi, 1961), p. 31; unpublished printed booklet, Kenya Government Library.

32. *Ibid.*, p. 32.

33. *Ibid.*, p. 31.

34. Sir Michael Blundell, *So Rough a Wind* (London, 1964), p. 167.

35. *Ibid.*, p. 132.

36. The Church of Scotland Foreign Mission Committee, *Mau Mau and the Church* (Edinburgh, 1953), p. 3.

37. E. M. Wiseman, *Kikuyu Martyrs* (London, 1958), p. 8.

38. T. F. C. Bewes, *Kikuyu Conflict* (London, 1953), p. 49.

39. Blundell, *So Rough a Wind*, p. 136.

40. See the "Dedan Kimathi Papers" for his activities in 1954. The Security Forces found these papers on January 26, 1955, in the Aberdare Forest above Nyeri, and had them translated. They comprised letters between Kimathi and other leaders in the forest, minutes of various meetings, rules of conduct and organization, and letters to chiefs, the Administration, newspapers, and "passive wing" leaders in the Reserve.

41. British military titles were used by the forest fighters; some adopted aliases.

42. *History of the Loyalists*, p. 45.

43. Kimathi Papers, EFI/3/3/620. We are indebted to an unpublished paper by David Koff for some of the following ideas.

44. *Ibid.*, EFI/3/3/132.

45. *Ibid.*, EFI/3/3/390.

46. *Ibid.*

47. *Ibid.*, EFI/3/3/645, October 23–24, 1954.

48. *Ibid.*, EFI/3/3/601, from Dedan Kimathi's Note Book.

49. *Historical Survey of the Origins and Growth of Mau Mau*, Cmnd. 1030 (1960), p. 316.

50. *A Plan to Intensify the Development of African Agriculture in Kenya, 1955*, compiled by R. J. M. Swynnerton, O.B.E., M.C., Assistant Director of Agriculture.

51. M. P. K. Sorrenson, "Counter Revolution to Mau Mau: Land Consolidation in Kikuyuland, 1952–1960," *Proceedings of Conference at the East African Institute of Social Research*, June, 1963.

52. *EAS*, February 27, 1957.

53. *Report of the Committee on Emergency Detention Camps* (Nairobi, 1959), p. 15.

54. *Draft Report of Unofficial Members, Land Consolidation Group* (1958), pp. 19–22, Typescript.

55. A complete statement of KAU's demands on October 27, 1953, is reproduced in "Opportunity in Kenya," *A Report to the Fabian Colonial Bureau*, Research Series No. 162 (London, 1953), App. I.

56. Quoted in *ibid.*, p. 3.

57. See Carl G. Rosberg, Jr., "Political Conflict and Change in Kenya" in *Transition in Africa*, ed. Gwendolen M. Carter and William O. Brown (Boston, 1958), pp. 95–98.

58. George Bennett and Carl G. Rosberg, *The Kenyatta Election: Kenya 1960–1961* (London, 1961), p. 32.

59. Kenya Legislative Council *Debates* (26 June 1958), cols. 2402 and 2406.

CHAPTER 9

1. *The Times* (London), March 5, 1951.

2. KNA: Machakos District Annual Report, 1922.

3. Bethwell A. Ogot, "British Administration in the Central Nyanza District of Kenya 1900–1960," *Journal of African History*, vol. IV, No. 2 (1962), p. 257.

4. Evidence given by C.E.V. Buxton in Criminal Case No. 7 of 1924, Supreme Court, Nairobi.

5. Ogot, "British Administration," p. 257.

6. *Ibid.*, p. 256.

7. *Report of the Committee on African Religious Bodies in North Nyanza*, African District Council of North Nyanza (Kakamega, 1951). (Mimeograph)

8. KNA: Fort Hall District, File No. 62 ADM. 15/1/6 Box 5, False Prophets (Watu wa Mungu), letter from Colonial Secretary (Nairobi) to P. C., Nyeri, dated February 19, 1934.

9. *Ibid.*, letters from D.C., Fort Hall, to P.C., Nyeri, February 27, 1934.

10. *Ibid.*, statement of Watenga wa Kapera, February 26, 1934.

11. *Facing Mount Kenya*, pp. 278–79.

12. Much of the information that follows on the early career of Elijah Masinde is taken from a paper called "Elijah Masinde" written by E. C. Eggins, District Officer, North Nyanza, dated August 13, 1949. See also *Report of the Commission of Inquiry into the Affray at Kolloa, Baringo* (Nairobi, 1950).

13. *Report of the Commission of Inquiry into the Affray at Kolloa, Baringo* (Nairobi, 1950).

14. *The Kikuyu Tribe and Mau Mau* (Nairobi, n.d.), p. 6.

15. The Rev. R. G. M. Calderwood, "The Christian Churches' Role in Combating Mau Mau," Government of Kenya, Press Office, September 24, 1953.

16. L. S. B. Leakey, *Defeating Mau Mau* (London, 1954), p. 43.

17. Kenya Govt. Library: Nakuru District Annual Report, 1948. See also The Church of Scotland Foreign Mission Committee, *Mau Mau and the Church* (Edinburgh, 1953), p. 5.

18. *Historical Survey of the Origins and Growth of Mau Mau*, Cmnd. 1030 (1960), p. 77.

19. *EAS*, July 17, 1948.

20. *Ibid.*, June 3, 1950 and June 25, 1950.

21. *Ibid.*, June 3, 1950.

22. *EAS*, July 14, 1950.

23. *EAS*, September 29, 1950.

24. *EAS*, October 20, 1950.

25. J. C. Carothers, *The Psychology of Mau Mau* (Nairobi, 1954), p. 4.

26. *Ibid.*, p. 5.

27. *The Kikuyu Tribe and Mau Mau*, p. 3.

28. Commissioner for Community Development and Rehabilitation, "Rehabilitation," January 6, 1954, unpublished.

29. *Department of Community Development and Rehabilitation. Annual Report, 1954*, p. 21.

30. *Department of Community Development and Rehabilitation. Annual Report, 1953*, p. 2.

31. Commissioner for Community Development and Rehabilitation, "Rehabilitation," unpublished.

32. *Ibid.*

33. Blundell, *So Rough a Wind*, pp. 198–99.

34. "Rehabilitation" (January 6, 1954).

35. "Report on the Sociological Causes Underlying Mau Mau with some Proposals on the Means of Ending It" (May 24, 1954), unpublished.

36. "Rehabilitation" (January 6, 1954).

37. Tom Askwith, *The Story of Kenya's Progress* (Nairobi, 1953).

38. "Rehabilitation" (January 6, 1954).

39. *Department of Community Development and Rehabilitation. Annual Report, 1954*, p. 22.

40. *Ibid.*, p. 24.

41. "Kenya Government's Rehabilitation Programme." Press Office Handout No. 1217 (October 20, 1955).

42. *Ministry of Community Development, Annual Report, 1956*, p. 3.

43. *African Affairs Department, Annual Report, 1956*, pp. 37–38.

44. "Report of the Committee" set up under Colonial Regulation 60 to inquire into disciplinary charges against Superintendent Michael Gerard Sullivan and Assistant Superintendent Alexander von Coutts of the Kenya Prison Service, p. 6. (Mimeo). See also *Documents relating to the death of eleven Mau Mau detainees at Hola Camp in Kenya*. Cmnd. 778 (1959).

45. *Report of the Committee on Emergency Detention Camps* (Nairobi, 1959), p. 10.

46. "Report of the Committee," p. 6.

47. *Ibid.*

48. *Ibid.*, p. 10.

49. *Ibid.*, pp. 12–13.

50. *Ibid.*, p. 13.

51. *Ibid.*, p. 23.

52. *Ibid.*, p. 25.

53. Kenya News. Press Office Handout No. 142: "Death of Ten Detainees at Hola."

54. *Report of the Committee on Emergency Detention Camps*, p. 10.

55. Leonard Beecher (The Archbishop of East Africa), "Hope in Place of Hopelessness," in *Which Road for Kenya? A "Guardian" Symposium* (Nairobi: 1961), p. 7.

56. *Report of the Committee on Emergency Detention Camps,* p. 11.
57. *Ibid.,* p. 12.
58. 466 H.C. *Debates* (27 July 1959), col. 232.
59. *The Spectator* (London), March 20, 1964, p. 366.
60. This British Command Paper, popularly known as the "Corfield Report," is in many ways the most complete and authoritative available analysis of the growth of the European myth of "Mau Mau." While all main elements of the myth can be found in the "Corfield Report," a major emphasis was on the use of the oaths and the role of Kenyatta. Specifically, the *batuni* oath, sanctioning the use of violence, by "combining magical forms with unheard of bestialities, has transformed a human being into a new frame of mind which has rarely, if ever, been witnessed before" (p. 163). The result was that "the people of Kenya were faced with a terrorist organization not of ordinary humans fighting for a cause, but of primitive beasts who had been made to forsake all moral codes in order to achieve the subjugation of the Kikuyu tribe and the ultimate massacre of the European population" (p. 169). For Corfield and many others "*Mau Mau* . . . was developed by Kenyatta as an atavistic tribal rising aimed against western civilization and technology and in particular against Government and the Europeans as symbols of progress" (p. 220). Kenyatta, "the architect of *Mau Mau*" (p. 219), had returned from England in 1946 "with the outlines of a plan to enslave the Kikuyu and subjugate them to his will" (p. 169). The "positive telling oath" which "signalized the final ostracism of the oath takers from their tribal affinities" could "only have been instituted by Jomo Kenyatta, their known and accepted leader" (p. 170). Kenyatta "was able to blend the technique of revolution, undoubtedly learnt while he was in Russia, with an appeal to superstition . . . In this way *Mau Mau* gradually but inexorably assumed the character of a tribal religion, albeit a religion based on evil, which bore remarkable resemblance to the witchcraft and black magic practised in Europe during the Middle Ages" (p. 52).

NOTES TO CONCLUSION

1. Lord Hailey, *An African Survey.* Revised 1956. (London, 1957) pp. 251–54.
2. Thomas Hodgkin, *Nationalism in Colonial Africa,* p. 23. Here Hodgkin refers to James S. Coleman's pioneering paper, "Nationalism in Tropical Africa" 1954), in which he argued that the term nationalism should be limited essentially to political movements whose objective is self-government or independence of a recognized African nation or potential. See also James S. Coleman, *Nigeria: Background to Nationalism* (Berkeley and Los Angeles, 1958), p. 425, and Martin Kilson, "The Analysis of African Nationalism," *World Politics,* April, 1958.
3. Rupert Emerson, *From Empire to Nation: The Rise to Self-Assertion of Asian and African Peoples* (Cambridge, 1960).
4. See David E. Apter, *The Political Kingdom in Uganda* (Princeton, 1961), pp. 85–91, for this use of the consummatory-instrumental distinction.
5. Karl Deutsch, *Nationalism and Social Communication* (New York, 1953).

Selected Bibliography

The literature and documentation relating to the study of Kenya nationalism in the colonial period is extensive and is being augmented as private and public papers are increasingly made available. In Kenya, attention has been given to the establishment of a National Archives, and in anticipation of this organization we have referred to Kenya Government Archives and records as Kenya National Archives (KNA). A few of the documents used have been since re-numbered or organized in another manner. In Britain the Rhodes House Library has played a leading role in collecting manuscript materials.

An important source of information has been interviews. In recording and citing these interviews we have often had to paraphrase, especially when the interviewee was speaking in Swahali or Kikuyu.

Of necessity this bibliography is selective. Some books listed below have bibliographies, such as M. Dilley, *British Policy in Kenya Colony,* a scholarly political study covering the period of 1900–1935, and the bibliography compiled by Alison Smith in *History of East Africa,* Vol. II, edited by Vincent Harlow and E. M. Chilvers. In addition, see particularly Roland Young and J. Gus Liebenow, Jr., "Survey of Background Materials for the Study of the Government of East Africa," *American Political Science Review* (March, 1954). For a guide to Kenya's Provincial and District Annual Reports, see *Archives Microfilming Programme,* Government of Kenya, compiled by D. Charman (1964). Some of the interviews and the unpublished materials are cited in the notes and are not catalogued in the bibliography.

The literature on colonial nationalism in Africa has grown rapidly in the last decade. See the following books for bibliographical references: Thomas Hodgkin, *Nationalism in Colonial Africa* (London: Frederick Muller, Ltd., 1956), pp. 191–206;

Thomas Hodgkin, *African Political Parties,* (London: Penguin, 1961), pp. 171–78; and William John Hanna and Judith Lynne Hanna, *Politics in Black Africa: A Selective Bibliography of Relevant Periodical Literature* (East Lansing, Michigan: African Studies Center, Michigan State University, 1964).

A. BOOKS, PAMPHLETS AND DISSERTATIONS

Aaronovitch, S., and K. *Crisis in Kenya.* London: Lawrence and Wishart, 1947.

Adelphoi (an anonymous group of Christian believers). *His Kingdom in Kenya.* London: Hodder and Stoughton, 1953.

Altrincham, Lord. See Gregg, E. M. W.

Andrews, C. F. *The Indian Question in Kenya.* (Nairobi: The Swift Press, 1921. For private circulation only).

Arkell-Hardwick, A. *An Ivory Trader in North Kenia.* London: Longmans, Green, 1903.

Askwith, Tom. *The Story of Kenya's Progress.* Nairobi: Eagle Press, 1953.

Barker, Eric E. *A Short History of Nyanza.* Nairobi: East African Literature Bureau, 1958.

Barnett, Donald. "Mau Mau: The Structural Integration and Disintegration of Aderdare Guerilla Forces." Unpublished Ph.D. Dissertation, University of California, Los Angeles, 1963.

Bennett, George. *Kenya: A Political History; The Colonial Period.* London: Oxford University Press, 1963.

Bennett, George, and Carl G. Rosberg. *The Kenyatta Election: Kenya 1960–1961.* London: Oxford University Press, 1961.

Bewes, T. F. C. *Kikuyu Conflict.* London: Highway Press, 1953.

Blixen, Karen. *Out of Africa.* London: Penguin Books, 1954. First published 1937.

Blundell, Sir Michael. *So Rough a Wind.* London: Weidenfeld and Nicolson, 1964.

Boyes, J. *The Company of Adventurers.* London: East Africa, Ltd., 1928.

Brockway, Fenner. *African Journeys.* London: Victor Gollancz, 1955.

Buchanan, Sir George. *British East Africa (Kenya Colony) Wanted a Policy.* London: Rhodes House Library, n.d.

Buell, Raymond L. *The Native Problem in Africa.* 2 vols. New York: Macmillan, 1928.

Bulpett, C. W. L., ed. *John Boyes, King of the Wa-Kikuyu.* London: Methuen, 1911.

Buxton, Clarence. *The Kenya Question.* Nairobi: East African Standard, 1948.

Cagnolo, Father C. *The Akikuyu: Their Customs, Traditions and Folklore.* Trans. by V. M. Pick. Nyeri: The Mission Printing School, 1933.

Capon, Rev. M. G. *Towards Unity in Kenya.* Nairobi: Christian Council of Kenya, 1962.

Carey, Walter J. *Crisis in Kenya: Christian Common Sense on Mau Mau and the Colour Bar.* London: A. R. Mowbray, 1953.

Cavendish-Bentinck, F. *Indians and the Kenya Highlands.* Nairobi: East African Standard, 1939.

Churchill, W. S., *My African Journey.* London: Hodder and Stoughton, 1908.

Cloete, Stuart. *Storm Over Africa: A Study of the Mau Mau Rebellion, Its Causes, Effects, and Implications in Africa South of the Sahara.* Cape Town: Culemborg Publishers, 1956.

Coupland, R. *East Africa and its Invaders: From the Earliest Times to the Death of Seyyid Said in 1856.* Oxford: Clarendon Press, 1938.

———. *The Exploitation of East Africa, 1856–1890: The Slave Trade and the Scramble.* London: Faber and Faber, 1939.

Cox, Richard. *Pan Africanism in Practice: PAFMECSA 1958–1964.* London: Oxford University Press for the Institute of Race Relations, 1964.

Cranworth, Lord. *A Colony in the Making, Or Sport and Profit in British East Africa.* London: Macmillan, 1912.

———. *Kenya Chronicles,* London: Macmillan, 1939.

Creech Jones, Arthur, ed. *New Fabian Colonial Essays.* London: Hogarth Press, 1959.

Delf, George, *Jomo Kenyatta: Towards Truth about "The Light of Kenya."* New York: Doubleday, 1961.

Dilley, Ruth. *British Policy in Kenya Colony.* New York: Thomas Nelson and Sons, 1937.

Dougall, J. W. C. *Building Kenya's Future*. Edinburgh: Church of Scotland Foreign Missions Committee, 1955.

Driberg, J. H. *The East African Problem*. London: Williams and Norgate, 1930.

Dundas, C. *African Crossroads*. London: Macmillan, 1955.

Economist Intelligence Unit. *The Economy of East Africa: A Study of Trends*. Nairobi: for the East African Railways and Harbours Administration, 1955.

Eliot, Sir Charles, *The East Africa Protectorate*, London: Edward Arnold, 1905.

Elphinstone, Howard. *Africans and the Law*. Nairobi: Eagle Press, 1951.

Evans, Peter, *Law and Disorder*. London: Secker and Warburg, 1956.

Farson, Negley. *Behind God's Back*. London: Victor Gollancz, 1940.

———. *Last Chance in Africa*. London: Victor Gollancz, 1951.

Fearn, Hugh, *An African Economy: A Study of the Economic Development of the Nyanza Province of Kenya, 1903–53*. London: Oxford University Press for East African Institute of Social Research, 1961.

Foran, W. R. *A Cuckoo in Kenya: The Reminiscences of a Pioneer Police Officer in British East Africa*. London: Hutchinson, 1936.

———. *The Kenya Police, 1887–1960*. London: R. Hale, 1962.

Forrester, Marion W. *Kenya To-day: Social Prerequisites for Economic Development*. 's-Gravenhage: Mouton, 1962.

Gatheru, Jugo. *Child of Two Worlds*. New York: Vintage Books, 1965.

Gecaga, B. M. *Home Life in Kikuyu-Land, Or Kariuki and Muthoni*. Nairobi: The Eagle Press, 1949.

Ghai, Dharam, P. ed. *Portrait of a Minority: Asians in East Africa*. Nairobi: Oxford University Press, 1965.

Gicaru, Muga. *Land of Sunshine: Scenes of Life in Kenya before Mau Mau*. London: Lawrence and Wishart, 1958.

Goldsmith, F. H. *John Ainsworth: Pioneer Kenya Administrator, 1864–1946*. London: Macmillan, 1955.

Goldthorpe, J. E. *An African Elite: Makerere College Students*

1922–1960. Nairobi: Oxford University Press for the East Africa Institute of Social Research, 1965.

———. *Outlines of East Africa Society.* Kampala: Department of Sociology, Makerere College, 1958.

Gregory, J. W. *The Foundation of British East Africa.* London: H. Marshall, 1901.

Gregory, Robert G. *Sidney Webb and East Africa: Labour's Experiment with the Doctrine of Native Paramountcy.* Berkeley and Los Angeles: University of California Press, 1962.

Grigg, E. M. W. (later Lord Altrincham). *The Constitutional Problem in Kenya.* Nottingham: Cust Foundation Lecture, University College, 1933.

———. *Kenya's Opportunity: Memories, Hopes and Ideas.* London, Faber and Faber, 1955.

———. *Speeches by Sir E. M. W. Grigg, 1925–1930, as Governor of Kenya Colony and High Commisioner for Transport in Kenya and Uganda.* (Nairobi: n.d.) .

Groves, C. P., *The Planting of Christianity in Africa.* Vol. IV, 1914–1954. London: Zubberworth Press, 1958.

Gulliver, Pamela, and P. H. Gulliver, *The Central Nilo-Hamites.* Ethnographic Survey of Africa: East Central Africa, Part VII. London: International African Institute, 1953.

Gulliver, P. H. *The Family Herds: A Study of Two Pastoral Tribes in East Africa, the Jie and Turkana.* London: Routledge and Kegan Paul, 1955.

Hailey, Lord. *Native Administration and Political Development in British Tropical Africa, 1940–42.* London: Colonial Office, 1942.

———. *Native Administration in the British African Territories.* Part I: East Africa. London: H.M.S.O., 1950.

Hancock, W. K. *Survey of British Commonwealth Affairs,* Vol. I, *Problems of Nationality 1918–1936.* London, Oxford University Press, 1937.

Harlow, Vincent, and E. M. Chilver., ed. *History of East Africa.* Vol. II. Oxford: Clarendon Press, 1965.

Harries, Lyndon P. *Islam in East Africa.* London: Parrett and Neves, 1954.

Henderson, Ian, with Philip Goodhart. *The Hunt for Kimathi.* London: Hamish Hamilton, 1958.

Hill, M. F. *The Dual Policy in Kenya.* Nakuru: Kenya Weekly News, 1944.

——. *Permanent Way: The Story of the Kenya and Uganda Railway.* Nairobi: East African Railways and Harbours, 1950.

Hindlip, Lord. *British East Africa: Past, Present and Future.* London: T. F. Unwin, 1905.

Hobley, C. W. *Bantu Beliefs and Magic: With Particular Reference to the Kikuyu and Kamba Tribes of Kenya Colony.* London: Witherby, 1938. First published, 1922.

——. *Kenya, From Chartered Company to Crown Colony.* London: Witherby, 1929.

Hollis, A. C. *The Masai: Their Language and Folklore.* Oxford: Clarendon Press, 1905.

——. *The Nandi: Their Language and Folklore.* Oxford: Clarendon Press, 1909.

Hooper, H. D. *Africa in the Making.* London, 1924.

Hordern, Charles, compiler. *Military Operations, East Africa.* Vol. I, August 1914–September 1916. London: H.M.S.O., 1941.

Hotchkiss, W. R. *Then and Now in Kenya Colony: Forty Adventurous Years in East Africa.* London and New York: Fleming H. Revell, 1937.

Huntingford, G. W. B. *The Eastern Tribes of the Bantu Kavirondo.* The Peoples of Kenya, No. 14. Nairobi: C.M.S., 1944.

——. *The Nandi of Kenya: Tribal Control in a Pastoral Society.* London: Routledge and Kegan Paul, 1953.

——. *The Southern Nilo-Hamites.* Ethnographic Survey of Africa: East Central Africa, Part VIII. London: The International African Institute, 1953.

Huntingford, G. W. B., and C. R. V. Bell. *East African Background.* 2d. ed. London: Longmans, Green, 1950.

Huxley, Elspeth. *The Flame Trees of Thika: Memories of an African Childhood.* New York: W. Morrow, 1959.

——. *A New Earth: An Experiment in Colonialism.* London: Chatto and Windus, 1960.

——. *No Easy Way: A History of the Kenya Farmers' Association and the UNGA Limited.* Nairobi: East Africa Standard, n.d.

————. *Red Strangers*. London: Chatto and Windus, 1939.

————. *Settlers of Kenya*. Nairobi: Highway Press, 1948.

————. *The Sorcerer's Apprentice*. London: Chatto and Windus, 1948.

————. *White Man's Country: Lord Delamere and the Making of Kenya*. 2 vols. London: Chatto and Windus, 1935.

Huxley, Elspeth, and Margery Perham. *Race and Politics in Kenya*. Revised ed., London: Faber and Faber, 1955.

Huxley, J. S. *African View*. London: Chatto and Windus, 1931.

The Indian Problem in Kenya: Being a Selection from Speeches, Articles and Correspondence Appearing in the East African Press, April to October, 1921. Nairobi: 1922.

Ingham, Kenneth, *A History of East Africa*, London: Longmans, Green, 1962.

Jackson, F. *Early Days in East Africa*. London: Edward Arnold, 1930.

Johnston, H. H. *The Uganda Protectorate*, 2 vols. New York: Dodd, Mead, 1904.

Jones, Thomas Jesse, *Education in East Africa*. New York: Phelps-Stokes Fund, 1925.

Kabutu, P. Kibaara, *Mbaara Ya Wiyathi Wa Kenya Kuuma 1890–1963*. Nairobi: Published by P. K. Kabutu, 1963.

————, compiler, *Jinsi Kenya Ilivyookolewa*. Nairobi: Published by P. K. Kabutu, 1964.

Kariuki, Josiah Mwangi. *Mau Mau Detainee: The Account by a Kenya African of his Experiences in Detention Camps, 1953–1960*. London: Oxford University Press, 1963.

Kenya: A Story of Progress. Prepared by the Kenya Government and the Central Office of Information. Text by Alastair Matheson. London, 1955.

The Kenya Settlement Handbook 1949. Nairobi: Kenya Information Office, 1949.

Kenyatta, Jomo. *Facing Mount Kenya: The Tribal Life of the Gikuyu*. London: Secker and Warburg, 1953.

————. *Harambee! The Prime Minister of Kenya's Speeches 1963–64*. Nairobi: Oxford University Press, 1964.

————. *Kenya: The Land of Conflict*. London: Panaf Service, 1944.

————. *My People of Kikuyu and the Life of Chief Wangombe.* London: United Society for Christian Literature, 1944.

Kitson, Frank. *Gangs and Counter-Gangs.* London: Barrie and Rockliff, 1960.

Koinange, Mbiyu. *The People of Kenya Speak for Themselves.* Detroit: Kenya Publication Fund, 1955.

Krapf, Rev. Dr. J. Lewis. *Travels, Researches and Missionary Labours, During an Eighteen Years' Residence in Eastern Africa.* London: Trübner, 1860.

La Fontaine, S. H. and J. H. Mower. *Local Government in Kenya: Its Origins and Development.* Nairobi: The Eagle Press, 1955.

Lambert, H. E. *Kikuyu Social and Political Institutions.* London: Oxford Press for the International African Institute, 1956.

————. *The Systems of Land Tenure in the Kikuyu Land Unit.* Communications, School of African Studies, No. 22. Capetown: 1950.

Larby, Norman. *The Kamba.* The Peoples of Kenya, No. 8. Nairobi: Highway Press, 1944.

Lavers, Anthony. *The Kikuyu Who Fight Mau Mau—Wakikuyu wanaopigana na Mau Mau.* [In English and Swahili.]. Nairobi: Eagle Press, 1955.

Leakey, L. S. B. *Defeating Mau Mau.* London: Methuen, 1954.

————. *Kenya: Contrasts and Problems.* London: Methuen, 1936.

————. *Mau Mau and the Kikuyu.* London: Methuen, 1952.

————. *White African.* London: Hodder and Stoughton, 1937.

Leigh, Ione. *In the Shadow of the Mau Mau.* London: W. H. Allen, 1954.

Leys, Norman M. *Kenya.* London: Hogarth Press, 1924.

————. *A Last Chance in Kenya.* London: Hogarth Press, 1931.

The Life-Story of a Kenya Chief. The life of Chief Kasina Ndoo as told to J. B. Carson. London: Evans Brothers, 1958.

Lindblom, G. *The Akamba in British East Africa.* 2d. ed. Uppsala: Appelbergs boktryckeri aktiebolag, 1920.

Lipscomb, J. F. *We Built a Country.* London: Faber and Faber, 1955.

————. *White Africans.* London: Faber and Faber, 1956.

Lloyd-Jones, W. *K.A.R.: Being an Unofficial Account of the*

Origin and Activities of the King's African Rifles. London: Arrowsmith, 1926.

Loftus, E. A. *Thomson: Through Masai Land.* London: Nelson, 1951.

Lonsdale, J. M. "European Penetration into the Nyanza Province of Kenya, 1890–1914." Unpublished Phd. Dissertation. Cambridge University, 1964.

Lugard. *Rise of Our East African Empire,* 2 vols. Edinburgh: W. Blackwood, 1893.

Noel, Anthony Scawen, The Earl of Lytton. *The Desert and the Green.* London: Macdonald, 1957.

MacDermott, P. L. compiler. *British East Africa; Or I.B.E.A.* London: Chapman and Hall, 1893.

MacDonald, J. R. L. *Soldiering and Surveying in British East Africa,* 1891–1894. London: E. Arnold, 1897.

Macmillan, Mona, *Introducing East Africa.* London: Faber and Faber, 1952.

Maher, Colin. *Peasantry or Prosperity.* East Africa Problems. No. 3. Nairobi: East African Standard, n.d.

Maina, Daudi Wa Kiragu. *Kiria Giatumira Independent Igie* [in Kikuyu]. Nairobi, n.d.

Mair, L. P. *Native Policies in Africa.* London: Routledge and Sons, 1936.

———. *Primitive Government.* Harmondsworth: Penguin Books, 1962.

Majdalany, Fred. *State of Emergency: The Full Story of Mau Mau.* Boston: Houghton Mifflin, 1963. First American edition.

Mason, Philip. *A New Deal in East Africa.* London: Royal Institute of International Affairs, 1935.

The Mau Mau in Kenya. Foreword by Granville Roberts, Kenya Public Relations Officer. London: Hutchinson, 1954.

Mayer, Philip, *The Lineage Principle in Gusii Society.* Memorandum No. 2. London: Oxford University Press for the International African Institute, 1949.

———. *Two Studies in Applied Anthropology in Kenya.* With an Introduction by Arthur Phillips. London: H.M.S.O. for the Colonial Office, 1951.

Mboya, Paul. *Utawala na Maendeleo ya. Local Government*

South Nyanza, 1926–1957. Nairobi: The Eagle Press, 1959.

Mboya, Tom. *Freedom and After.* London: André Deutsch, 1963.

———. *The Kenya Question: An African Answer.* London: Fabian Colonial Bureau, 1956.

———. *Kenya Faces the Future.* New York: American Committee on Africa, 1959.

Meek, C. K. *Land, Law and Custom in the Colonies.* London: Oxford University Press, 2d ed., 1949.

Meinertzhagen. Colonel R., *Kenya Diary: 1902–1906.* London: Oliver and Boyd, 1957.

Michuki, D. N. *Bururi wa Embu.* Nairobi: 1962.

Middleton, John. *The Kikuyu and Kamba of Kenya.* Ethnographic Survey of Africa: East Central Africa, Part V. London: The International African Institute, 1953.

Mitchell, Philip E. *African Afterthoughts.* London: Hutchinson, 1954.

Mockerie, Parmenas Githendu. *An African Speaks for his People.* London: Leonard and Virginia Woolf, 1934.

Moyse-Bartlett, Lt. Col. H. *The King's African Rifles: A Study in the Military History of East and Central Africa, 1890–1945.* Aldershot: Gale and Polden, 1956.

Ngugi, James. *The River Between.* London: Heinemann, 1965.

———. *Weep Not, Child.* London: Heinemann, 1964.

Ogot, B. A. "Migration and Settlement Among the Southern Luo Peoples." Unpublished Ph.D. Dissertation, University of London, 1965.

Oliver, Roland. *The Missionary Factor in East Africa.* London: Longmans, Green, 1952.

Oliver, Roland and Gervase Mathew, eds. *History of East Africa.* Vol. I. Oxford: Clarendon Press, 1963.

Ominde, Simon H. *The Luo Girl: From Infancy to Marriage.* London: Macmillan, 1952.

Pan Africa—Kenya Uhuru Souvenir. Nairobi: Pan African Press, Dec. 12, 1963.

Pankhurst, Richard K. P. *Kenya: The History of Two Nations.* London: Independent Publishing, 1955.

Parker, Mary. *How Kenya is Governed.* Nairobi: Eagle Press, 1951.

————. *Political and Social Aspects of the Development of Municipal Government in Kenya with Special Reference to Nairobi*. London: Colonial Office, n.d. [1949?] mimeo.

Parker, Mary, and George Noyle. *British East Africa*. London: Macmillan, 1954.

Patel, Ambu H. ed. *Jomo the Great: A Short Pictorial Story of the Great Patriot of Africa*. Nairobi: New Kenya Publishers, 1961.

Patterson, J. H. *The Man-Eaters of Tsavo and Other East Africa Adventures*. London: Macmillan, 1934. First published in 1904.

Penwill, D. J. *Kamba Customary Law: Notes Taken in the Machakos District of Kenya Colony*. London: Macmillan, 1951.

Perham, Margery. *Lugard: The Years of Adventure, 1858–1898*. London: Collins, 1956.

Peristiany, J. G. *The Social Institutions of the Kipsigis*. London: Routledge, 1939.

Philp, H. R. A. *New Day in Kenya*. London: World Dominion Press, 1936.

Pickering, Else. *When the Windows Were Opened: Life on a Kenya Farm*. London: Godfrey Bles, 1957.

Pio Gama Pinto: Independent Kenya's First Martyr. Nairobi: Pan African Press, Ltd., 1966.

Portal, Sir Gerald. *The British Mission to Uganda in 1893*. London: Arnold, 1894.

Preston, R. O. *The Genesis of Kenya Colony*. Nairobi: Colonial Printing Works, 1947?

————. *Oriental Nairobi*. Nairobi: Colonial Printing Works, 1938.

Prins, A. H. J. *The Coastal Tribes of the North-Eastern Bantu*. (Pokomo, Nyika, Teita.) Ethnographic Survey of Africa: East Central Africa, Part III. London: The International African Institute, 1952.

————. *East African Age-Class Systems*. Djakarta: J. B. Wolters, 1953.

————. *The Swahili-Speaking Peoples of Zanzibar and the East African Coast*. (Arabs, Shirazi and Swahili.) Ethnographical Survey of Africa, Part XII. London: The International Africa Institute, 1961.

Rake, Alan. *Tom Mboya: Young Man of New Africa.* New York: Doubleday, 1962.

Rawcliffe, D. H. *The Struggle for Kenya.* London: Victor Gollancz, 1954.

Registration of Persons: National Registration. Nairobi: East African Standard, n.d.

Richards, C. G. *Archdeacon Owen of Kavirondo.* Nairobi: Highway Press, 1947.

Richards, Elizabeth. *Fifty Years in Nyanza 1906–1956: The History of the C.M.S. and the Anglican Church in Nyanza Province, Kenya.* Maseno: published for the Nyanza Jubilee Committee, 1956.

Robinson, Kenneth. *The Dilemmas of Trusteeship: Aspects of British Colonial Policy Between the Wars.* London: Oxford University Press, 1965.

Ross, W. McGregor. *Kenya From Within: A Short Political History.* London: Allen and Unwin, 1927.

Routledge, Willam Scoresby, and Katherine Routledge. *With A Prehistoric People: The Akikuyu of British East Africa.* London: Edward Arnold, 1910.

Salvadori, Max. *La Colonisation Européenne au Kenya.* Paris: Larose Editeurs, 1938.

Schapera, I. *Some Problems of Anthropological Research in Kenya Colony.* International African Institute, Memo. No. 23. London: Oxford University Press, 1949.

Seaton, Henry. *Lion in the Morning.* London: Murray, 1963.

Shepperson, George, and Thomas Price. *Independent African: John Chilembwe and the Origins, Setting and Significance of the Nyasaland Native Rising of 1915.* Edinburgh: The University Press, 1958.

Slater, Montagu. *The Trial of Jomo Kenyatta.* London: Secker and Warburg, 1955.

Smart, J. *A Jubilee History of Nairobi, 1900–1950.* Nairobi, East African Standard, 1950.

Sorrenson, M. P. K. "Land Policy, Legislation and Settlement in the East African Protectorate." Unpublished D. Phil. Dissertation. Oxford University, 1962.

Southall, Aidan. *Lineage Formation Among The Luo.* International African Institute, Memo. No. 26. London: Oxford University Press, 1952.

Spencer, Paul. *The Samburu: A Study of Gerontocracy in a Nomadic Tribe.* Berkeley and Los Angeles: University of California Press, 1965.

Sandford, G. R. *An Administrative and Political History of the Masai Reserve.* London, 1919.

Stoneham, C. T. *Mau Mau.* London: Museum Press, 1953.

———. *Out of Barbarism.* London: Museum Press, 1955.

Ternan, Brigadier-General Trevor. *Some Experiences of an Old Bromsgrovian.* Birmingham: Cornish Brothers, 1930.

Thomson, Joseph. *Through Masailand.* London: Low, Marston, Searle and Rivington, 1885.

Thurnwald, Richard C. *Black and White in East Africa.* London: Routledge, 1935.

Totty, L. H., and G. H. Chaudy. *The People and Districk of West Suk.* The Peoples of Kenya, No. 17. Nairobi: Highway Press, 1952. Reprint. First published, 1944.

Trimingham, J. Spencer. *Islam in East Africa.* Oxford: Clarendon Press, 1964.

Tyson, George A. *The African Housing Problem.* Nairobi: English Press, 1953.

Vandeleur, C. F. S. *Campaigning on the Upper Nile and Niger.* London: Methuen, 1898.

Vere-Hodge, E. R. *Imperial British East Africa Company.* London: Macmillan, 1960.

Vere-Hodge, E. R., and P. Collister. *Pioneers of East Africa.* Nairobi, Eagle Press, 1956.

Wagner, Gunther. *The Bantu of North Kavirondo.* London: Oxford University Press for the International African Institute. Vol. I, 1949. Vol. II, 1956.

———. *The Changing Family Among the Bantu Kavirondo.* Supplement to *Africa,* Vol. XII, No. 1. London: Oxford University Press for the International Institute of African Languages and Cultures, 1939.

Walmsley, R. W. *Nairobi: The Geography of a New City.* East Africa Local Studies, No. 1. Nairobi: Eagle Press, 1957.

Wanjau, Gakaara. *Wikumie na Muhiriga Waku.* Nairobi and Karatina: M/s. Gakaara Publishing Service, n.d.

Ward, H. F., and J. W. Milligan, compilers. *A Handbook of British East Africa 1912–13.* London: Sifton Praed, 1912.

Were, C. S. "The Abaluyia of Western Kenya and Their Neighbors: History Down to 1930." Unpublished Phd. Dissertation, University of Wales, 1966.

Welbourn, F. B. *East African Rebels: A Study of Some Independent Churches.* London: S.C.M. Press, 1961.

Who's Who in East Africa, 1963–1964. Nairobi: Marco Surveys, 1964.

Williams, Howard. *Paradise Precarious.* Nairobi, Welcome Press, n.d.

Wills, Colin. *Who Killed Kenya?* London: Dennis Dobson, 1953.

Wilson, Christopher J. *Before the White Man in Kenya.* London: McCorquodale, 1952.

————. *Kenya's Warning: The Challenge to White Supremacy in Our British Colony.* Nairobi: Printed by the English Press, 1954.

Wiseman, E. M. *Kikuyu Martyrs.* London: Highway Press, 1958.

Wood, Susan. *Kenya: The Tensions of Progress.* London: Oxford University Press for Institute of Race Relations, 1960.

B. ARTICLES AND PAPERS

Abrahams, Peter. "The Conflict of Culture," *International Affairs,* XXX:3 (July, 1954).

"African Writer Views Politics of Post Mau Mau Kenya, Sees Stepped-Up Struggle for Power," *Africa Special Report* (June 27, 1957), p. 3.

Alport, C. J. M. "Kenya's Answer to the Mau Mau Challenge," *African Affairs,* LIII:212 (July, 1954), pp. 241–47.

Armstrong, Robert G. "East Africa," *Phylon,* XVI:4 (1955), pp. 435–47.

Askwith, Tom. "Tribalism in Nairobi," *Corona,* II:8 (August, 1950), pp. 292–96.

Banow, H. "Status Reversal and Political Reaction: A Case Study of the Masai of Kenya and Tanzania," *Proceedings of the*

Conference at the East African Institute of Social Research,
January, 1965. (Mimeo.)

Beattie, J. H. M. "Ethnographic and Sociological Research in
East Africa: A Review," *Africa,* XXVI:3 (July, 1956), pp.
265–75.

Beckley, V. A. and Violet E. Notley, "Drying of Vegetables," *The
East African Agricultural Journal* (July, 1941).

Beech, M. W. H. "Kikuyu System of Land Tenure," *Journal of
the African Society,* XVII (1917), pp. 46–59, 136–44.

Beecher, Leonard J. "Au Kenya: Nationalisme et Eglises separa-
tistes africaines," *Monde non Chrétien* (Paris), No. 23
(July–September, 1952), pp. 324–36.

———. "Rehabilitation in Kenya: The Churches' Part in Establishing a New Way of Life," *Times British Colonies Review,*
14 (Summer, 1954), p. 12.

——— (Bishop of Mombasa). "After Mau Mau—What?" *International Review of Missions,* XLIV:174 (1955), pp. 205–11.

——— (Archbishop of East Africa). "Hope in Place of Hopelessness," in *Which Road for Kenya?.* A "Guardian Symposium"
(Nairobi: East African Printers, 1961), p. 7.

Bennett, George. "The Development of Political Organizations
in Kenya," *Political Studies,* V:2 (June, 1957), pp. 113–30.

———. "Early Procedural Developments in the Kenya Legislative Council" (in two parts), *Parliamentary Affairs,* X:3,4
(Summer, Autumn, 1957), pp. 296–307, 469–79.

———. "The Eastern Boundary of Uganda in 1902," *Uganda
Journal,* XXIII:1 (1959), pp. 69–72.

———. "Kenyatta and the Kikuyu," *International Affairs,*
XXXVII:4 (October, 1961), pp. 477–82.

———. "Paramountcy to Partnership: J. H. Odham and Africa,"
Africa (October, 1960), pp. 356–61.

———. "Imperial Paternalism: The Representation of African
Interests in the Kenya Legislative Council," *Essays in Imperial
Government,* edited by Kenneth Robinson and Frederick Mad-
den, Oxford: Basil Blackwell, 1963.

Bewes, T. F. C. "The Work of the Christian Church among the
Kikuyu," *International Affairs,* XXIX:3 (July, 1952), pp. 316–
25.

Brett, E. "Economic Policy in Kenya Colony: A Study in the Politics of Resource Allocation," *Proceedings of the Conference of the East African Institute of Social Research,* January, 1965. (Mimeo.)

Bunche, Ralph J. "The Land Equation in Kenya Colony. (As Seen by a Kikuyu Chief)," *Journal of Negro History,* XXIV:1 (January, 1939), pp. 33–43.

Cauche, Vickie. "Les Origines de la Crise du Kenya," *Cahiers Internationaux* (September, 1952), pp. 82–90.

Cliffe, L. "Nationalism and the Reaction to Enforced Agricultural Improvement in Tanganyika during the Colonial Period," *Proceedings of the Conference of the East African Institute of Social Research,* January, 1965. (Mimeo.)

Cowley, K. "The Native Authority System in Kenya," *Proceedings of the Conference of the East African Institute of Social Research,* June, 1952. (Mimeo.)

Deverell, N. M. "The African Child in an Urban Environment (Nairobi)," *East African Medical Journal,* XXXI:4 (April, 1954), pp. 175–79.

Drake, St. Clair. "Some Observations on Interethnic Conflict as One Type of Intergroup Conflict," *Conflict Resolution,* I:2 (June, 1957), pp. 155–78.

East African Statistical Department. "East African Population Census 1948: Analysis of Civil Population by District and Race, Main Tribes, Population Density," *East African Economic and Statistical Bulletin,* No. 29 (September, 1955), pp. 6–14.

"Education in Kenya Colony" (by an African in Kenya), *Pan-Africa* (August, 1947), pp. 32–34.

Engholm, O. F. "African Elections in Kenya, March 1957," in *Five Elections in Africa,* W. J. M. Mackenzie and Kenneth E. Robinson, eds. (Oxford: Clarendon Press, 1960), pp. 391–461.

———. "Kenya's First Direct Elections for Africans, March 1957," *Parliamentary Affairs,* X:4 (Autumn, 1957), pp. 424–33.

Evans, M. N. "Local Government in the African Areas of Kenya," *Journal of African Administration,* VII:3 (July, 1955), pp. 123–27.

Evans-Pritchard, E. E. "Luo Tribes and Clans," *Human Problems in British Central Africa*, No. 7 (1949), pp. 24–40.

————. "Marriage Customs of the Luo of Kenya," *Africa*, XX:2 (April, 1950), p. 132.

Fearn, Hugh. "Cotton Production in the Nyanza Province of Kenya Colony, 1908–1954," *The Empire Cotton Growing Review*, XXXIII:2 (1956), pp. 1–14.

————. "Population as a Factor in Land Usage in the Nyanza Province of Kenya Colony," *East African Agricultural Journal* (Amani) XX:3 (January, 1955), pp. 198–201.

Foran, Robert W. "The Kipsigis Laibons," *Kenya Weekly News* (May 12, 1961), p. 26.

Fosbrooke, H. A. "An Administrative Survey of the Masai Social System," *Tanganyika Notes and Records*, XXVI (1948), pp. 1–50.

Francis, E. Carey. "Kenya's Problems as Seen by a Schoolmaster in Kikuyu Country," *African Affairs*, LIV:216 (July, 1955), pp. 186–95.

————. "Mau Mau is Really a Resistance Movement," *East Africa and Rhodesia* (April 14, 1955), pp. 1086–89.

Hall, B. E. F. "How Peace Came to Kikuyu," *Journal of the African Society*, XXXVII (1938), pp. 423–48.

Harris, Grace. "The Position of Lower Chiefs in Taita," *Proceedings of the Conference of the East African Institute of Social Research*, June, 1952. (Mimeo.)

————. "Possession Hysteria in a Kenya Tribe," *American Anthropologist*, LIX:6 (December, 1957), pp. 1046–66.

Hennings, K. D. "Some Trends and Problems of African Land Tenure in Kenya," *Journal of African Administration*, IV:4 (October, 1952), pp. 122–34.

Holland, D. C. "Law and Order in Kenya," *Anti-Slavery Reporter* (London), series VI, X:1 (January, 1955), pp. 8–16. (Reprint from *Current Legal Problems*, 1954.)

Hughes, O. B. E. "Villages in the Kijuyu Country," *Journal of African Administration*, VII:4 (October, 1955), p. 170.

Huxley, Elspeth. "The Cause and Cure of Mau Mau," *New Commonwealth* (January 18, 1954), pp. 62–66.

Ingham, K. "Uganda's Old Eastern Province: The Transfer to East Africa Protectorate in 1902," *Uganda Journal,* XXI:1 (1957), pp. 41–46.

"Kenya After Mau Mau," *Manchester Guardian Weekly.* (September 8, 1955, p. 3; September 15, 1955, p. 3; September 22, 1955, p. 7; September 29, 1955, p. 7).

"Kenya Speaks for Itself," *Pan-Africa* (January, 1947), pp. 19–23.

"Kenya, The Settlers' Case," *The Round Table,* No. 101 (1935). pp. 82–97.

Kenyatta, Jomo. Letters to the *Manchester Guardian* (May–October, 1938).

Kiano, Gikonyo. "The Mau Mau in Africa: An African's View," *Saturday Review of Literature* (May 3, 1953), pp. 17–19, 41–42.

———. "The Pan-African Freedom Movement of East and Central Africa," *Africa Today* (September, 1959), pp. 11–14.

"A Kikuyu Testament," *New Commonwealth* (April 15, 1954), pp. 378 f.

Kilson, Martin L., Jr. "Land and the Kikuyu: A Study of the Relationship Between Land and Kikuyu Political Movements," *Journal of Negro History,* XL:2 (April, 1955), pp. 103–53.

———. "Land and Politics in Kenya: An Analysis of African Politics in a Plural Society," *Western Political Quarterly,* X:3 (September, 1957), pp. 559–81.

Knowles, E. J. F. "Foundations of Government in Kenya," *Journal of African Administration,* VI:3 (July, 1954), pp. 137–39.

"Labor Compulsion in Kenya," *International Labor Review,* XLV (June, 1942), pp. 680–82.

Lambert, H. E. "The Background to Mau Mau: Widespread Use of Secret Oaths in Kenya," *Times British Colonies Review,* 8 (Winter, 1952), p. 21.

Leakey, L. S. B. "The Economics of Kikuyu Tribal Life," *East African Economics Review,* III:1 (July, 1956), pp. 165–80.

———. "The Kikuyu Problem of the Initiation of Girls," *Journal of the Royal Anthropological Institute,* LXI (1931), pp. 277–85.

————. "Mau Mau as a Religion," *Manchester Guardian* (June 24–25, 1954).

————. "Some Aspects of Black and White in Kenya," *The Bulletin of the John Rylands Library,* XV:2 (July, 1931).

LeVine, Robert A. "The Internalization of Political Values in Stateless Societies," *Human Organization,* XIX:2 (Summer, 1960), pp. 51–58.

LeVine, Robert A., and Walter Sangree. "The Diffusion of Age-Group Organization in East Africa: A Controlled Comparison," *Africa,* XXXII:2 (April, 1962), pp. 97–110.

Lonsdale, J. M. "Archdeacon Owen and the Kavirondo Taxpayers Welfare Association," *Proceedings of the Conference of the East African Institute of Social Research,* January, 1963. (Mimeo.)

————. "Rural Resistance and Mass Political Mobilization Amongst the Luo of Western Kenya," *East African History Conference, Dar es Salaam,* 1965. (Mimeo.)

Maher, Colin. "A Note on Economic and Social Problems in Kenya and their Relationship to Soil Erosion," *C.R. INCIDI* 25 Annexe (2) 28–30 (November, 1949), pp. 63–72.

Manners, Robert A. "The Kipsigis—Change with Alacrity," in *Markets in Africa: Eight Subsistence Economies in Transition,* Paul Bohannan and George Dalton, eds. (New York: Doubleday, 1965), pp. 214–49.

Martin, C. J. "An Estimate of the General Age Distribution, Fertility and Rate of Natural Increase of the African Population of British East Africa," *Population Studies,* VII:2 (November, 1953), pp. 181–99.

Mason, Philip. "The Plural Society of Kenya," *INCIDI:* Ethnic and Cultural Pluralism in Intertropical Communities. Report of the 30th Meeting Held in Lisbon, April, 1957, pp. 325–37.

Matson, A. T. "Asian Settlement in Kenya," *Kenya Weekly News,* Part I, (January 25, 1963), p. 22 f; Part II (February 1, 1963), p. 22.

————. "Francis George Hall: The Story of a District Officer," *Kenya Weekly News,* Part I (October 18, 1963), p. 24 ff; Part II (October 25, 1963); Part III (November 1, 1963), p. 27.

————. "The Coming of the White Man," *Kenya Weekly News* (April 27, 1962), p. 24 f.

————. "Early Newspapers of East Africa," *Kenya Weekly News*, Part I (July 14, 1961), p. 32 ff; Part II (July 21, 1961), p. 32 ff.

————. "Mumia: The Man and the Myth," *Kenya Weekly News* (October 27, 1961), p. 32 f.

————. "Uganda's Old Eastern Province and East Africa's Federal Capital," *Uganda Journal*, XXII:1 (March, 1958), pp. 43–53.

————. "The Pacification of Kenya," *Kenya Weekly News* (September 14, 1962), p. 24 f.

Mazrui, Ali. "On Heroes and Uhuru-Worship," *Transition*, III:11 (November, 1963), pp. 23–28.

Mboya, Tom. "Trade Unionism in Kenya," *Africa South*, I (January–March, 1957), pp. 77–86.

McWilliam, M. D. "Economic Problems during the Transfer of Power in Kenya," *The World Today*, XVIII:4 (April, 1962), pp. 164–75.

————. "Economic Viability and the Race Factor in Kenya," *Economic Development and Cultural Change*, XII:1 (October, 1963), pp. 55–69.

Mitchell, Sir Philip. "Mau Mau," in *Africa Today*, C. Grove Haines, ed. (Baltimore: Johns Hopkins Press, 1955), pp. 485–93.

Monkhouse, Patrick. "The Mau Mau in Kenya." *Manchester Guardian* (November 12, 17, 18, 24, 1952).

Murra, John V. "Kenya and the Emergency," *Current History*, XXX:177 (May, 1956), pp. 279–84.

Noon, John A. "Political Developments in East Africa," in *Africa in the Modern World*, Calvin W. Stillman, ed. (Chicago: University of Chicago Press, 1955), pp. 182–203.

Nottingham, J. C. "Sorcery Among the Akamba in Kenya," *Journal of African Administration*, XI:1 (January, 1959), pp. 2–14.

Ogot, Bethwell A. "British Administration in the Central Nyanza District of Kenya, 1900–1960," *Journal of African History*, IV:2 (1963), pp. 249–74.

O'Hagan, Desmond. "Africans' Part in Nairobi Local Government," *Journal of African Administration,* I:4 (October, 1949), p. 156.

"Overstocking in Kenya," *The East African Agricultural Journal,* I (July, 1935).

Padmore, George. "Behind the Mau Mau," *Phylon,* XIV:4 (1953), pp. 355–72.

Parker, Mary. "Municipal Government and the Growth of African Political Institutions in the Urban Areas of Kenya," *Zaire,* III (June, 1949), pp. 649–62.

———. "Race Relations and Political Development in Kenya," *African Affairs,* L:198 (January, 1951), pp. 41–52.

Pedraza, G. J. W. "Land Consolidation in the Kikuyu Areas of Kenya," *Journal of African Administration,* VIII:2 (April, 1956), pp. 82–87.

Phillips, Arthur. "The African Court System in Kenya," *Journal of African Administration,* IV:4 (October, 1952), pp. 135–38.

Philp, H. R. A. "Artificial Atresia in Kikuyu Women," *Kenya Medical Journal,* II:3 (June, 1925), pp. 86–87.

———. "Native Gynaecology," *Journal of the Kenya Medical Service,* I:8 (January, 1924), pp. 3–4.

Pratt, Cranford. " 'Multi-Racialism' and Local Government in Tanganyika," *Race* II (November, 1960), pp. 33–49.

Rau, Santha Rama. "The Trial of Jomo Kenyatta," *The Reporter* (March 16, 1954), pp. 10 ff.

Raw, Joyce. "Some Memories of Legislative Council," *Kenya Weekly News,* Part I, April 12, 1963, pp. 24 ff; Part II, April 19, 1963, p. 20.

Rayner, J. "The Economic Problem and Colonial Policy in an East African Reserve," *Economica,* I:4 (1952), pp. 145–9.

"Reconstruction in Kenya," *Round Table,* No. 175 (June, 1954), pp. 251–58.

Richards, Audrey I. "Tribal Groups in Kenya," *Times British Colonies Review,* No. 29 (1958) pp. 21–22.

Rosberg, Carl G., Jr. "Political Conflict and Change in Kenya," in *Transition in Africa,* Gwendolyn Carter and Robert Brown, eds. (Boston: Boston University Press, 1958), pp. 90–120.

———. "Independent Kenya: Problems and Prospects," *Africa Report,* VIII:11 (December, 1963), pp. 3–7.

Rosenstiel, Annette, "An Anthropological Approach to the Mau Mau Problem," *Political Science Quarterly*, LXVIII (September, 1953), pp. 419–32.

Rotberg, Robert. "The Rise of African Nationalism: The Case of East and Central Africa," *World Politics* XV:4 (October, 1962), pp. 75–90.

Sanger, Clyde, and John Nottingham. "The Kenya General Election of 1963." *Journal of Modern African Studies*, II:1 (1964), pp. 1–40.

Sangree, Walter H. "The Bantu Tiriki of Western Kenya," in *Peoples of Africa*, James L. Gibbs, Jr., ed. (New York: Holt, Rinehart and Winston, 1965), pp. 41–80.

Savage, Donald C. "Labour Protest in Kenya, The Early Phase: 1914–1939," *Proceedings of the Conference at the East African Institute of Social Research*, June, 1963. (Mimeo.)

Schapera, I. "Anthropology and the Administration," *Journal of African Administration*, III:3 (July, 1951), p. 128.

Schneider, Harold K. "Pakot Resistance to Change," in *Continuity and Change in African Cultures*, William R. Bascom and Melville J. Herskovits, eds. (Chicago: University of Chicago Press, 1959), pp. 144–67.

Scott, H. S. "European Settlement and Native Development in Kenya," *Journal of the Royal African Society (African Affairs)*, XXXV (1936), pp. 178–90.

Shannon, Mary I. "Land Consolidation in Kenya: Helping Africans to Make the Best Use of Their Land," *African World* (June, 1957), pp. 11–12.

————. "Rehabilitating the Kikuyu," *African Affairs*, LIV:215 (April, 1955), pp. 129–37.

————. "Social Revolution in Kikuyuland: Rehabilitation and Welfare Work in Kenya's New Village Communities," *African World* (September–October, 1955), pp. 7–9, 11–12.

————. "Women's Place in Kikuyu Society: Impact of Modern Ideas on Tribal Life—a Long-term Plan for Female Education," *African World* (September, 1954), pp. 7–10.

Silberman, Leo. "The Social Survey of the Old Town of Mombasa," *Journal of African Administration*, I:1 (January, 1950), p. 14.

Sillitoe, K. K. "Land Use and Community in Nyeri, Kenya," *Proceedings of the Conference at the East African Institute of Social Research,* January, 1963. (Mimeo.)

Sofer, S., and R. Ross. "Some Characteristics of an European Population," *The British Journal of Sociology,* II:4 (December, 1951), pp. 315–27.

Sorrenson, M. "The Official Mind and Kikuyu Land Tenure, 1895–1939," *Proceedings of the Conference at the East African Institute of Social Research,* January, 1963. (Mimeo.)

———. "Counter Revolution to Mau Mau: Land Consolidation in Kikuyuland, 1952–1960," *Proceedings of the Conference at the East African Institute of Social Research,* June, 1963. (Mimeo.)

"Two Studies in Applied Anthropology in Kenya," *Journal of African Administration,* III:3 (July, 1951), p. 135.

Usher-Wilson, L. C. "Bishop's Study of 'Dina ya Misambwa': First published account of a dangerous African movement." *East Africa and Rhodesia,* 1414 and 1416 (November, 1951), pp. 282–83, 345–46.

Vasey, E. A. "Economic and Political Trends in Kenya," *African Affairs,* LV:219 (April, 1956), pp. 101–8.

Wagner, Gunter. "The Political Organization of the Bantu of Kavirondo," in *African Political Systems,* M. Fortes and E. E. Evans-Pritchard, eds. (London: Oxford University Press for the International African Institute, 1940), pp. 197–236.

Wallbank, T. W. "American Reflections on Kenya," *Journal of the Royal African Society (African Affairs),* Vol. 37, suppl.

Ward, Kendall, "Kenya," *United Empire,* XLV:6 (November–December, 1954), pp. 222–26.

Welbourn, F. B. "Comment on Corfield," *Race,* II:2 (May, 1961), pp. 7–27.

Whisson, M. G. "The Rise of Asembo and the Curse of Kakia," *Proceedings of the Conference of the East African Institute of Social Research,* 1961. (Mimeo.)

Whiteley, W. H. "The Changing Position of Swahili in East Africa," *Africa,* XXVI:4 (October, 1956), pp. 343–53.

———. "Language and Politics in East Africa," *Tanganyika Notes,* XLVII/XLVIII (June–September, 1957), pp. 159–73.

Wilkinson, John. "The Mau Mau Movement: Some General and Medical Aspects," *East African Medical Journal,* XXXI:7 (July, 1954), pp. 295–314.

Willis, J. J. "Christianity or Mohammedism in the Uganda Diocese," *Church Missionary Intelligencer,* XXIX (1904).

Wilson, Fergus. "Kenya: A District Team at Work (North Nyanza District)" (in two parts), *Corona,* III:8,9 (August, September, 1951), pp. 295–300, 337–39.

Wilson, Gordon. "Mombasa—A Modern Colonial Municipality," in *Social Change in Modern Africa,* Aidan Southall, ed. (London: Oxford University Press, 1961), pp. 98–112.

Wilson, R. G. "Land Consolidation in the Fort Hall District of Kenya," *Journal of African Administration,* VIII:3 (July, 1956), p. 144.

C. DOCUMENTS AND PUBLICATIONS OF ORGANIZATIONS

Africa Bureau. *Future of East Africa.* A summary of the report of the Royal Commission with an index to the report. London, 1955.

African Unofficial Members Organization. *Method of Electing African Members of Kenya Legislative Council.* Nairobi, 1955.

The British Survey. *Kenya: Mau Mau and the Kikuyu Problem.* London: British Society for International Understanding, May, 1954.

Brockway, Fenner, M. P. *Why Mau Mau? An Analysis and a Remedy.* London: Congress of Peoples Against Imperialism, March, 1953.

Church of Scotland. *Memorandum Prepared by the Kikuyu Mission Council on Female Circumcision.* Kikuyu, 1931. Confidential. (Mimeo.)

Church of Scotland Foreign Mission Committee. *Kenya 1898–1948.*

———. *Mau Mau and the Church.* Edinburgh, 1953.

Commonwealth Parliamentary Association. *Report of the Parliamentary Delegation to Kenya, January–February 1957.* London: Executive Committee of the United Kingdom Branch of the Commonwealth Parliamentary Association, 1957.

Convention of Associations. *Constitution and Rules.* Nairobi, 1931.

Electors' Union of Kenya. *Constitution.* Nairobi, 1944.

———. *An Outline of Policy for the Colony and Protectorate of Kenya.* Nairobi, 1946.

———. *Kenya Plan.* Nairobi, 1949.

———. *The Kenya Land Problem: A History of African and European Land Settlement.* Nairobi, 1952.

Fabian Colonial Bureau. *Kenya, White Man's Country?* Research Series No. 7. London, 1944.

———. *Kenya Controversy.* Controversy Series No. 4. London, 1947.

———. *East African Future.* Controversy Series No. 9. London, 1952.

———. *Opportunity in Kenya.* Research Series No. 162. London, 1953.

Gathani, Bachulal. *Presidential Address to the Thirteenth Session of the Federation of Indian Chambers of Commerce and Industry of East Africa,* held in Nairobi on February 21 and 22, 1953. Nairobi, 1953.

Kavirondo Taxpayers Welfare Association. *Memorandum to the Parliamentary Commission, 1924.* (Typescript)

Kenya Association. *Kenya, Britain's Most Attractive Colony.* Nairobi: East African Standard, n.d.

Kenya Indian Congress. *The Presidential Address* by N. S. Mangat, delivered at the twenty-third session at Nairobi on July 31, August 1 and 2, 1954, with the resolutions adopted thereat. Nairobi: D. L. Patel Press, 1954.

———. *A Spotlight on the Asians of Kenya.* Kenya Independence-Day Souvenir, December 12, 1963. Nairobi: Times Press, 1963.

Kikuyu Central Association. *Correspondence between the K.C.A. and the Colonial Office, 1929–1930.* Published as a pamphlet.

———. *Memorandum of the Kikuyu Central Association, Fort Hall, to be Presented to the Hilton Young Commission.* n.d.

Kikuyu Independent Schools Association (established 1929) and Connected with the African Independent Pentecostal Church, *Report and Constitution, 1938.* Nyeri: The Executive Committee of the Kikuyu Independent Schools Association.

Kikuyu Provincial Association. *Rules and Regulations.* Nairobi, 1939.

Koinange, Mbiyu, with Achieng Oneko. *Land Hunger in Kenya*. London: Union of Democratic Control, 1952.

Makerere Kikuyu Embu and Meru Students Association. *Comment on Corfield*. Kampala, 1960. (The mimeographed booklet was prepared under the guidance of F. B. Welbourn, who published a summary of it in *Race*, Vol. II, No. 2 [May, 1961].)

Native Landowners of Tigoni (Limuru). *Memorandum on Native Land of Tigoni*. Presented by Marius N. Karatu. Nairobi, 1936.

Settlement Board. *Accepted Schemes for European Settlement*. Nairobi; East African Standard, n.d.

――――. *To Farm in Kenya?* Nairobi, n.d.

Student Christian Movement. *East Africa in Transition*. London, 1929.

Taxpayers' Protection League. *The "Compromise."* Full text of Correspondence between the Elected Members' Organisation and the Government, September–December, 1936. Nairobi: East African Standard, n.d.

The Voice of Kenya. *A General Survey*. Nairobi, 1953.

――――. *Historical Background*. Nairobi, 1953.

――――. *The Kikuyu Tribe and Mau Mau*. Nairobi, n.d.

D. GOVERNMENT DOCUMENTS: GREAT BRITAIN
(ARRANGED CHRONOLOGICALLY)

Correspondence Relating to the Tenure of Land in the East Africa Protectorate. Cd. 4117. 1908.

Papers Relating to Native Disturbances in Kenya. Cmd. 1961. 1922.

Indians in Kenya: A Memorandum. Cmd. 1922. 1923.

Report of the East Africa Commission, 1924. Cmd. 2387. 1925.

Tours in the Native Reserves and Native Development in Kenya. Cmd. 2573. 1926.

Future Policy in Regard to Eastern Africa. Cmd. 2904. 1927.

Report of the Commission on Closer Union for the Dependencies in East and Central Africa. (Sir E. Hilton Young, chairman.) Cmd. 3234. 1929.

Report of Sir Samuel Wilson on his Visit to East Africa. Cmd. 3378. 1929.

Memorandum on Native Policy in East Africa. Cmd. 3573. 1930.

Statement of the Conclusion of His Majesty's Government in the United Kingdom as Regards Closer Union in East Africa. Cmd. 3574. 1930.

Report of the Joint Select Committee on Closer Union in East Africa. 3 vols. H.C. Paper No. 156. 1931.

Papers Relating to the Question of Closer Union of Kenya, Uganda and Tanganyika Territory. Col. 57. 1931.

Certain Questions in Kenya: Report by the Financial Commissioner. Cmd. 4093. 1932.

Correspondence Arising from the Report of the Joint Select Committee on Closer Union in East Africa, 1931–32. Cmd. 4141. 1932.

Kenya Land Commission: Evidence and Memoranda. 3 vols. Col. 91. 1933.

Report of Kenya Land Commission. Cmd. 4556. 1934.

Kenya Land Commission Report: Summary of Conclusions Reached by H. M. Government. Cmd. 4580. 1934.

Report of the Commission of Enquiry into the Administration of Justice in Kenya, Uganda, and the Tanganyika Territory in Criminal Matters, May 1933, and Correspondence Arising out of the Report. Col. 96. 1934.

Report of the Commission Appointed to Enquire into and Report on the Financial Position and System of Taxation in Kenya. Col. 116. 1936.

Report of the Commission on Higher Education in East Africa. Col. 142. 1937.

Inter-Territorial Organization in East Africa. Col. 191. 1945.

Labour Conditions in East Africa: A Report by Major G. Orde Brown. Col. 193. 1946.

C. H. Northcott, ed. *African Labour Efficiency Survey, 1947.* Colonial Research Publication No. 3. 1947.

Inter-Territorial Organization in East Africa: Revised Proposals. Col. 210. 1947.

Land and Population in East Africa: An Exchange of Correspondence Between the Secretary of State for the Colonies and the Government of Kenya on the Appointment of the Royal Commission. Col. 290. 1952.

Baring, Sir Evelyn. *The Kenya Emergency and the Future.* (Address to the Kenya Legislative Council on 20th, October, 1953.) Central Office of Information, 1953.

Report to the Secretary of State for the Colonies by the Parliamentary Delegation to Kenya, January, 1954. (Walter Elliott, Chairman.) Cmd. 9081. 1954.

Kenya: Proposals for a Reconstruction of the Government. Cmd. 9103. 1954.

East Africa Royal Commission 1953–1955: Report. (Sir Hugh Dow, Chairman.) Cmd. 9475. 1955.

Despatches from the Governors of Kenya, Uganda and Tanganyika and from the Administrator, East Africa High Commission, Commenting on the East Africa Royal Commission, 1953–55 Report. Cmd. 9801. 1956.

Kenya: Proposals for New Constitutional Arrangements. Cmnd. 309. 1957.

Kenya: Despatch on the New Constitutional Arrangements. Cmnd. 369. 1958.

Record of Proceedings and Evidence in the Inquiry into the Deaths of Eleven Mau Mau Detainees at Hola Camp in Kenya 1959.

Documents relating to the deaths of eleven Mau mau detainees at Hola Camp in Kenya. Cmnd. 778. 1959.

Further Documents Relating to the Deaths of Eleven Mau Mau Detainees at Hola Camp in Kenya. Cmnd. 816. 1959.

Report of the Kenya Constitutional Conference Held in London in January and February, 1960. Cmnd. 960. 1960.

Historical Survey of the Origins and Growth of Mau Mau. Cmnd. 1030. 1960.

E. GOVERNMENT DOCUMENTS: KENYA
(ARRANGED CHRONOLOGICALLY)

Report of the Land Committee, 1905. 1905.

Native Labour Commission, 1912–13: Evidence and Report. 1913.

Nairobi Sanitary Commission 1913 Report and Evidence. n.d.

Report of the Land Settlement Commission. 1919.

Final Report of the Economic Commission of the East Africa Protectorate, 1919. Part I. Nairobi: Swift Press, 1919.

Evidence of the Education Commission of the East Africa Protectorate, 1919. Nairobi: Swift Press, 1919.

Report of the Labour Bureau Commission, 1921.

Report of the Committee on the Working of the Resident Native Labourers Ordinance 1925.

Interim Report of Economic and Finance Committee on Native Labour. 1925.

Conference of Governors of the Eastern Dependencies, 1926: Summary of Proceedings.

Report of the Feetham Commission on Local Government. 2 vols. London: Crown Agents, for the Gov. of Kenya, 1927.

District Councils Legislation 1928. 1928.

Native Land Tenure in Kikuyu Province: Report of Committee. Nairobi: East Africa Standard, 1929.

Report of the Agricultural (Hall) Commission. 1929.

Cost of Living Commission Report of Enquiry. 1929.

Report of the Committee on Government Housing Policy. 1930.

Report of Inquiry into Organization of Administrative Offices. 1930.

Report of Committee on Native Land Tenure in the North Kavirondo. 1931.

Report of Select Committee of Legislative Council Appointed to Consider the Establishment of a Native Betterment Fund. 1933.

Report of the Alternative Revenue Proposals Committee. 1933.

Report of the Expenditure Advisory Committee. 1933.

Report of the Economic Development Committee. 1935.

Report of the Select Committee on Economy. 1935.

Report of the Commission Appointed to Inquire into and Report upon Allegations of Abuse and Hardships in the Collection of Non-Native Graduated Poll Tax and of Native Hut and Poll Tax. 1936.

Walsh, G., and H. R. Montgomery. *Report on Native Taxation.* 1936.

Mather, Colin. *Soil Erosion and Land Utilization in the Ukamba Reserve* (Machakos). 1937. (Mimeo.)

Report on Provincial and District Reorganization. 1937.

Pole-Evans, I. B. *Report on a Visit to Kenya.* 1939.

Report of the Commission of Inquiry Appointed to Examine the Labour Conditions in Mombasa. 1939.

Report by a Committee Appointed to Consider Local Native Council Finance in Relationship to Government Finance. 1941.

Post-War Employment Committee Report and Report of the Sub-Committee on Post-War Employment of Africans. 1943.

Report of Settlement Schemes Committee to the Chairman, Agricultural Production and Settlement Board. 1944.

Interim Report on Development. 1945.

Humphrey, N., *et al. The Kikuyu Lands.* 1945.

Land Utilization and Settlement: A Statement of Government Policy. Sessional Paper No. 8 of 1945.

Phillips, Arthur. *Report on Native Tribunals.* 1945.

Proposals for the Reorganization of the Administration of Kenya. Sessional Paper No. 3 of 1945.

Report and Recommendations Regarding Industrial Development. East African Industrial Council. 1945.

Bassett, R. H. *Report and Recommendations on the Development of Agricultural Marketing in Kenya.* 1946.

Man Power, Demobilization and Reabsorption Report, 1945. 1946.

Mitchell, Sir Philip. "General Aspects of the Agrarian Situation in Kenya as it Affects the African Population," *Despatch No. 44, 7 April, 1946.* 1946.

Ogilvie, G. C. W. compiler. *The Housing of Africans in the Urban Areas of Kenya.* Kenya Information Office, 1946.

Report of the Development Committee. 2 vols. 1946.

Special Labour Census, 1945. Labour Department. 1946.

Woods, Sir Wilfred. *Report on a Fiscal Survey of Kenya, Uganda and Tanganyika.* 1946.

Humphrey, Norman. *The Liguru and the Land: Sociological Aspects of Some Agricultural Problems of North Kavirondo.* 1947.

Mitchell, Sir Philip. *The Agrarian Problem in Kenya.* 1947.

Report of the Taxation Enquiry Committee. 1947.

Report on African Labour Census, 1947. East African Statistical Department, 1948.

Report of the Committee on Educational Expenditure. (European and Asian.) 1948.

A Ten Year Plan for the Development of African Education. 1948.

African Education in Kenya: Report of the Committee Appointed to Inquire into the Scope, Content and Methods of African Education, Its Administration and Finance and to Make Recommendations. 1949.

Report on African Labour Census, 1948. East Africa Statistical Department, 1949.

Report of the Select Committee on Indian Education. 1949.

Cost of Living Commission Report. 1950.

Report of the Commission of Inquiry into the Affray at Kolloa, Baringo. 1950.

Report of the Committee on Agricultural Credit for Africans. 1950.

Vasey, E. A. *Report on African Housing in Townships and Trading Centres.* 1950.

African Education: A Statement of Policy. 1951.

Report of the Planning Committee. 1951.

Report of the Board under the Chairmanship of Sir William Ibbotson on the Marketing of Maize and Other Produce. 1952.

Kenya, Report on the Enumeration of Non-Native Employees, November 1952. East African Statistical Department, 1953.

African Development in Kenya, 1946–1955: Land, Livestock and Water. 1953.

Inquiry into the General Economy of Farming in the Highlands. Report by L. G. Troup. 1953.

Notes on Commerce and Industry in Kenya. Office of the Member for Commerce and Industry, 1953.

Potter, H. S. *Some Aspects of the Development of Kenya Government Services for the Benefit of Africans from 1946 Onwards.* 1953.

Carothers, Dr. J. C. *The Psychology of Mau Mau.* 1954.

A Plan to Intensify the Development of African Agriculture in Kenya. 1954.

Purvis, A. W., compiler. *Legislative Council: Standing Orders and Letters Patent, Royal Instructions and Ordinances Under Which the Council Functions.* 1954.

Report of the Commission on the Civil Services of the East African Territories and the East Africa High Commission 1953–1954. (Sir David Lidbury, Chairman.) Report to the Chairman, East Africa High Commission, the Governors of Kenya, Uganda, and Tanganyika, and the British Resident, Zanzibar. 1954.

Report of the Committee on African Wages. In three parts. 1954.

The Implementation of the Recommendations of the Report of the Committee on African Wages. Sessional Paper No. 217 of 1954.

Report of the Cost of Living Committee. 1954.

The Development Programme 1954–1957. Sessional Paper No. 51 of 1955. 1955.

Progress Report on the Three-and-a-half-year Development Plan. Sessional Paper No. 97 of 1955. 1955.

Report of the Commissioner Appointed to Enquire into Methods for the Selection of African Representatives to the Legislative Council. (W. F. Coutts, Commissioner.) 1955.

African Development in Kenya, 1946–1955: Land, Livestock and Water. Ministry of Agriculture. 1956.

Report of the Commission of Inquiry into Alleged Corruption or Other Malpractices in Relation to the Affairs of the Nairobi City Council. 1956.

Report of the Commissioner Appointed to Enquire into Methods for the Selection of African Representatives to the Legislative Council. Statement of Government policy on Coutts report. 1956.

Agricultural Census 1955 (Highlands and Asian settled area). 1957.

The Development Programme 1957/60. Sessional Paper No. 77 of 1956/57. 1957.

Report on the Government's Eighteen-Point Statement of Policy: Achievements and Future Policy. 1957.

Report on Asian and European Education in Kenya, 1958. 1958.

Report of Working Party on African Land Tenure 1957–1958. 1958.

Sessional Paper No. 1 of 1958/59. Statement of Government Policy. 1958.

White Paper No. 1, 1957/58: Financial Relationships Between the Kenya Government and African District Councils. 1958.

Administrative Enquiry into Allegations of Ill-treatment and Irregular Practices Against Detainees at Manyani Detention Camp and Fort Hall District Works Camp. 1959.

Commerce and Industry in Kenya, 1959. 1959.

Consideration of the Recommendations of the Report on Asian and European Education in Kenya. 1959.

Contractor Finance Proposals for Nairobi African Housing. Sessional Paper No. 3 of 1959. 1959.

Kolbe, L. H., and S. F. Fouche. *Land Consolidation and Farm Planning in the Central Province.* Department of Agriculture. 1959.

Land Tenure and Control Outside the Native Lands. Sessional Paper No. 10 of 1958/59. 1959.

The Patterns of Income, Expenditure and Consumption of Africans in Nairobi 1957/58. 1959.

Report of a Board of Inquiry Appointed to Inquire into Employment in the Port of Mombasa. 1959.

Report of the Committee on Emergency Detention Camps, With an Exchange of Despatches Between the Secretary of State for the Colonies and the Governor of Kenya. Special Supplement to Kenya *Gazette*, 1.9.1959.

Reported Employment and Wages in Kenya 1958. 1959.

★

Colonial Reports, Annual, British East Africa Protectorate. London, 1905–20.

Colonial Reports, Annual, Colony and Protectorate of Kenya. London, 1921–28, 1946–60.

Annual Reports of the following Departments and Agencies:
Agriculture Department
African Land Development Board
Board of the Land and Agricultural Bank
Community Development and Rehabilitation Department
Commissioner for Local Government
Education Department

Labour Department
Medical Department
Native Affairs Reports, 1923–38; Report on Native Affairs, 1939–45, 1946–1947; African Affairs, Annual Report, 1948 *et seq.*
Registrar of Co-operative Societies
Registrar-General
Trade Report

★

Censuses:

Spencer, C. E. *Report on the Census of Non-Natives, 24 April, 1921* (1921).

Baker, A. G. *Report on the Non-Native Census, Enumeration Made in the Colony and Protectorate of Kenya on the Night of 21 February, 1926* (1927).

Walter, A. *Report of the Non-Native Census Enumeration in the Colony and Protectorate of Kenya on the Night of 6th March, 1931* (1932).

Martin, C. J. *Report on the Census of the Non-Native Population of Kenya Colony and Protectorate Taken on the Night of the 25th February, 1948* (1953).

African Population Census, 1948: Geographical and Tribal Studies (1953).

Kenya Population Census, 1962. Advance report of Volumes I and II (1964).

★

Kenya Legislative Council:

Summary of the Proceedings of the Legislative Council of the East Africa Protectorate, 1911–15.

Minutes of the Proceedings of the Legislative Council of East Africa, 1915–20.

Minutes of the Proceedings of the Legislative Council of Kenya Colony, 1920–24.

Debates, 1925–60.

F. KENYA NEWSPAPERS AND PERIODICALS

In the postwar period but prior to the Emergency in 1952, a large number of vernacular papers were published at different times. Among these were *Mumenyereri, Sauti ya Mwafrika, Mwaraniria, Mucemanio, Nyanzia Times, Radio Posta, Ramogi, Gikuyu Times, Muthamaki* and *Mwalimu*. Few copies of these papers remain, though a summary in English of some of their contents was available in Nairobi Secretariat Records in 1957.

A discussion of the Press and Broadcasting at the time of the 1961 General Election appears in George Bennett and Carl Rosberg, *The Kenyatta Election, 1960–1961* (1961), pp. 218–20.

The following newspapers and periodicals of Kenya were directly relevant to this study:

East African Chronicle, 1922
East African Standard, daily and weekly, 1918–63
Kenya Weekly News, 1940–63
Leader of British East Africa, 1918–21
Muigwithania, 1928 and May, 1931
Mumenyereri, October, 1947, and September and October, 1952
Mwalimu Annual, 1945–46
Baraza, 1940–52

G. JOURNALS

Africa, International African Institute, London.
African Affairs, Royal African Society, London.
Africa Digest, Africa Bureau, London.
Africa Report, The African-American Institute, Washington, D. C.
African World, African Publications, Ltd., London.
Comment, East African News Review, Ltd., Nairobi, 1951–1953.
East Africa, London, 1928–1935, thereafter *East Africa and Rhodesia,* London.
Journal of African Administration, H.M.S.O., London, 1949–1961, thereafter *Journal of Local Administration Overseas,* H.M.S.O., London.

Pan-Africa, A Monthly Journal of African Life, History and Thought, London, 1947.

Politica, A Monthly Journal of the Makerere Political Society, Kampala, 1953; *New Politica,* A Monthly Journal of the Makerere Political Society, Kampala, 1957–1958.

The New Kenya, Kenya Office, Cairo, 1959.

The East African Economics Review, Journal of the Economic Club of Kenya and the Uganda Economic Society, Nairobi.

The Voice of Kenya, London, 1953–1955.

Uganda Journal, The Journal of the Uganda Society, Kampala.

Venture, Fabian Colonial Bureau, London.

Index

Abaluhyia Central Assoc., *see* North Kavirondo Central Assoc.

Aberdares Range, 297f

Adala, John, 162

Administration, colonial, in Kenya, 12, 18–20, 59–60, 71, 323–24; relations with settlers, 21–22, 33–34, 60–61, 64–70, 161, 196–97, 200–201, 203, 226–33 *passim*, 278, 311; labor and land policies, 18–22, 45–46, 61, 153–54, 164–74, 178, 205–10 *passim*, 237–39, 303–8, 323; and local chiefs, 35, 80–84, 90, 162–63, 280, 285, 295, 357; supports moderate politics, 42, 44, 84–85, 90, 106, 115–16, 140; and Thuku, 49–50, 54, 138–40; and transtribal politics, 55–56; and nationalism, 87, 216, 311, 316f, 354; rel. with KCA, 98–99, 116–17, 137–38, 174, 186–87, 189, 218–20; and circumcision crisis, 113–14, 119, 123, 135; and the Taita, 175–77; the emergency, 277, 279, 294–303 *passim*; and KAU, 214f, 220–21, 224–25, 279f, 308–10; view of "Mau Mau," 280–81, 282, 291–92, 294–95, 320–21, 331–32; and loyalists, 295–96, 305–6, 310–11, 317. *See also* Legislative Council *and governors by name.*

Administration, local, 71–72. *See also* Local Native Councils.

Africa Inland Mission (AIM), 17, 31, 110, 325; sphere of influence, 106–7, 108; and circumcision, 112, 121, 123ff

African Brotherhood Church, 325

African Independent Pentecostal Church (AIPC), 125, 130, 135

African Orthodox Church, 125, 129–30, 135, 326

African Workers Federation, 209f. *See also* Trade unions.

Age-grade system, 147–52 *passim*

Age-group (*riika*), 9, 150, 180–81, 220 259; All-Kikuyu Age Groups, 193, 332; "Forty Group," 240

Agikuyu, The, 132

Agricultural Production & Settlement boards, 195

Agriculture, 2, 4, 7, 9, 78–79; cash crops, 18, 22, 74–75, 84, 98, 161, 205–6, 303; gov't. policy and African resistance, 164–73, 174, 205–7, 236–38, 255, 273, 328; expansion, 195–96; reforms, 303–8, 324

Ahoi (tenants), 152, 249, 289, 305

AIM, *see* Africa Inland Mission

Ainsworth, John, 19, 28, 61, 80, 156, 323

Alexander, Archbishop Daniel, 129–30

All-Kikuyu Age Groups, 193, 332

Alliance of Protestant Missions, 110–11, 124, 127–29

Alliance High School, 75–76, 124, 208, 212, 214

Anake a 40 ("Forty Group"), 240

Andrews, Rev. C. F., 48, 103

Apindi, Rev. Ezekiel, 60n, 62, 140

Apostolic Faith Mission, 17

Arabs in Kenya, 5, 9, 222, 230f; represented, 32, 230f; in Mombasa, 183

Arathi (prophets), 133, 327

Army, British, 190, 191–95. *See also* Carrier Corps.

Arwings-Kodhek, C. M. G., 308, 314, 316

Arthur, Dr. John S. (CSM), 31, 49, 88, 108, 268; his leadership, 110–12; and circumcision, 117–19, 120–21

Asians, 157, 160f, 236, 312, 355; in